BLOODY MONDAY

VOLUME 1

Story by Ryou Ryumon
Art by Kouji Megumi

Translated by Mari Morimoto
Lettered by North Market Street Graphics

KC
KODANSHA
COMICS

A Kodansha Comics Trade Paperback Original

Published in the United States by Kodansha Comics, an imprint of Kodansha USA Publishing, LLC, New York.

Publication rights for this English edition arranged through Kodansha Ltd, Tokyo.

First published in Japan in 2007 by Kodansha Ltd., Tokyo.

ISBN 978-1-935-42922-7

Original cover design by Takashi Shimoyama (Red Rooster)

Printed in the United States of America.

www.kodanshacomics.com

9 8 7 6 5 4 3 2 1

Translator: Mari Morimoto
Lettering: North Market Street Graphics

BLOODY MONDAY

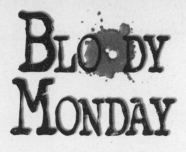

CONTENTS

AUTHOR'S NOTES

When the hackers who broke into the supposedly impenetrable U.S. Department of Defense (a.k.a. Pentagon) computer systems were arrested, they turned out to be teenage high school students—I remember shivering simultaneously with excitement and dread at the frightening times we were now living in, upon seeing that news report some years ago. What if those high school students were heroes who possess a strong sense of justice despite also enjoying pranks…? That idea was the inspiration for the genius hacker 'Falcon'. Incidentally, it's rumored that those same high school students who hacked into the Pentagon were later scouted by the Department of Defense, but could it be true?
—Ryou Ryumon

This is a suspense thriller, with such-and-such a main character and enemies like so on and so forth, leading to all sorts of incidents. Every day, I stare at my materials. The more I draw, the more I become irritated at the inadequacy of my own abilities. I worked hard to make this a splendid piece. I am a naïve oaf, but I humbly ask for your support.
—Kouji Megumi

HONORIFICS EXPLAINED

Throughout the Kodansha Comics books, you will find Japanese honorifics left intact in the translations. For those not familiar with how the Japanese use honorifics and, more important, how they differ from American honorifics, we present this brief overview.

Politeness has always been a critical facet of Japanese culture. Ever since the feudal era, when Japan was a highly stratified society, use of honorifics—which can be defined as polite speech that indicates relationship or status—has played an essential role in the Japanese language. When addressing someone in Japanese, an honorific usually takes the form of a suffix attached to one's name (example: "Asuna-san"), is used as a title at the end of one's name, or appears in place of the name itself (example: "Negi-sensei," or simply "Sensei!").

Honorifics can be expressions of respect or endearment. In the context of manga and anime, honorifics give insight into the nature of the relationship between characters. Many English translations leave out these important honorifics and therefore distort the feel of the original Japanese. Because Japanese honorifics contain nuances that English honorifics lack, it is our policy at Kodansha Comics not to translate them. Here, instead, is a guide to some of the honorifics you may encounter in Kodansha Comics.

-san: This is the most common honorific and is equivalent to Mr., Miss, Ms., or Mrs. It is the all-purpose honorific and can be used in any situation where politeness is required.

-sama: This is one level higher than "-san" and is used to confer great respect.

-dono: This comes from the word "tono," which means "lord." It is an even higher level than "-sama" and confers utmost respect.

-kun: This suffix is used at the end of boys' names to express familiarity or endearment. It is also sometimes used by men among friends, or when addressing someone younger or of a lower station.

-chan: This is used to express endearment, mostly toward girls. It is also used for little boys, pets, and even among lovers. It gives a sense of childish cuteness.

Bozu: This is an informal way to refer to a boy, similar to the English terms "kid" and "squirt."

Sempai/
Senpai: This title suggests that the addressee is one's senior in a group or organization. It is most often used in a school setting, where underclassmen refer to their upperclassmen as "sempai." It can also be used in the workplace, such as when a newer employee addresses an employee who has seniority in the company.

Kohai: This is the opposite of "sempai" and is used toward under-classmen in school or newcomers in the workplace. It connotes that the addressee is of a lower station.

Sensei: Literally meaning "one who has come before," this title is used for teachers, doctors, or masters of any profession or art.

-[blank]: This is usually forgotten in these lists, but it is perhaps the most significant difference between Japanese and English. The lack of honorific means that the speaker has permission to address the person in a very intimate way. Usually, only family, spouses, or very close friends have this kind of permission. Known as *yobisute*, it can be gratifying when someone who has earned the intimacy starts to call one by one's name without an honor-ific. But when that intimacy hasn't been earned, it can be very insulting.

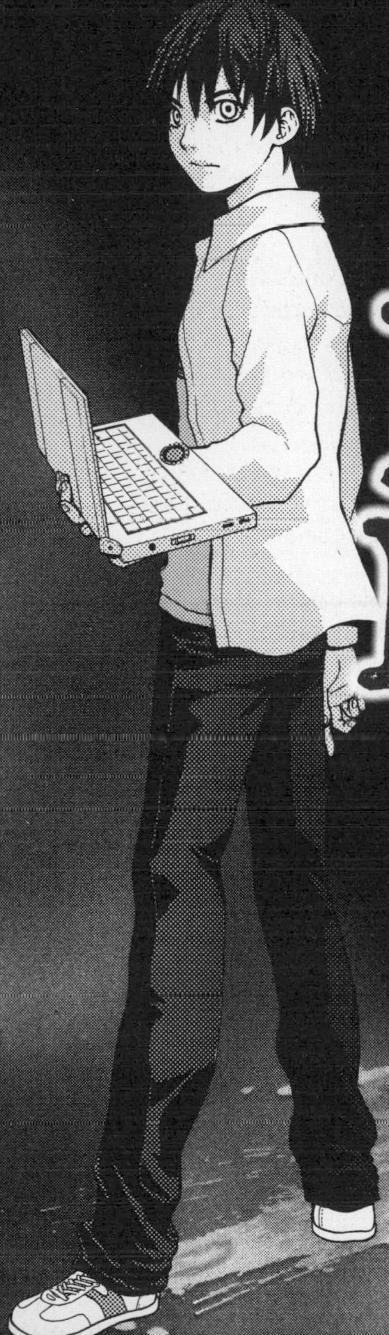

BLOODY MONDAY

VOLUME 1

Story by Ryou Ryumon

Art by Kouji Megumi

CONTENTS

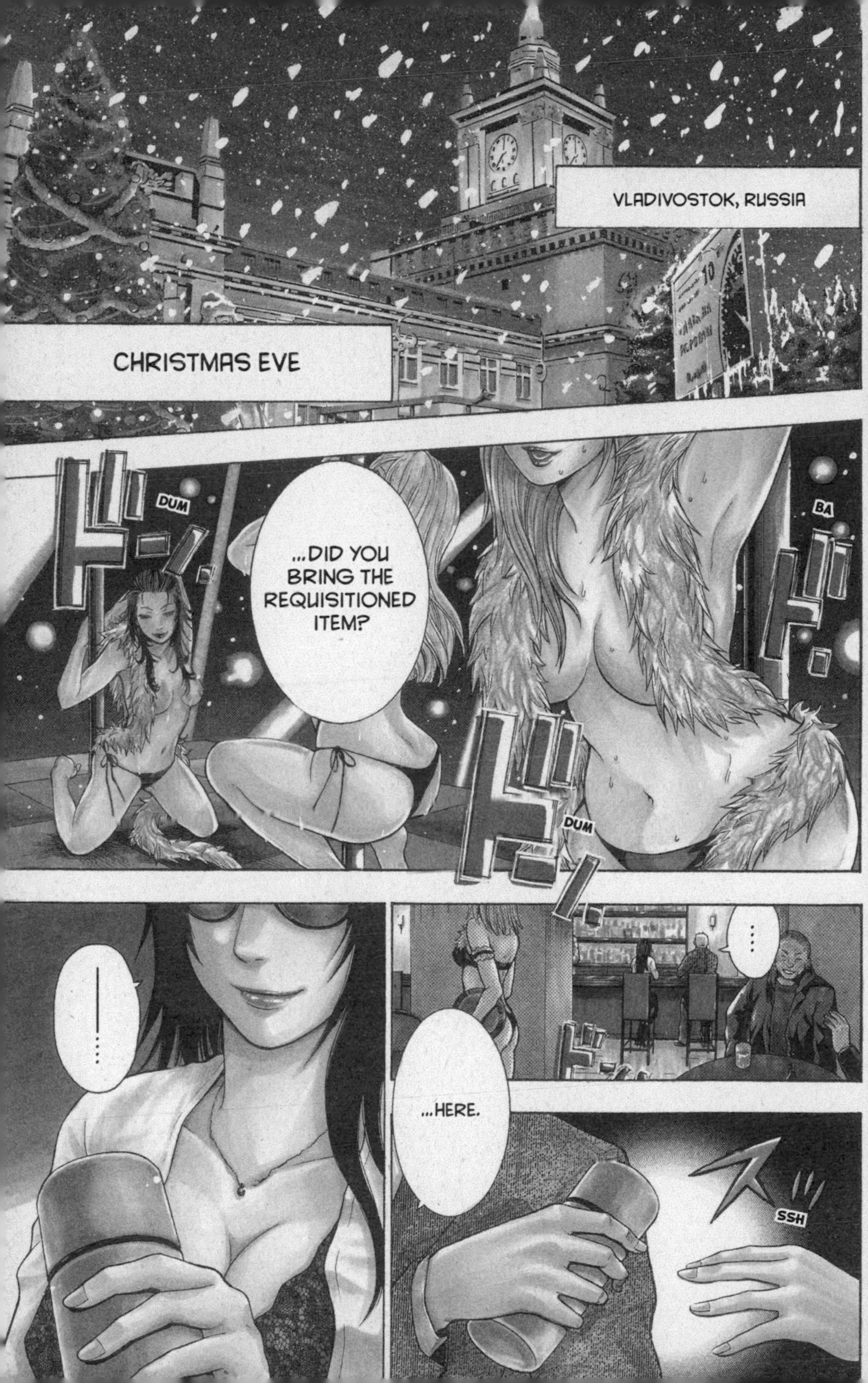

VLADIVOSTOK, RUSSIA
CHRISTMAS EVE
BA
...DID YOU BRING THE REQUISITIONED ITEM?
DUM
DUM
....
...HERE.
SSH
—....

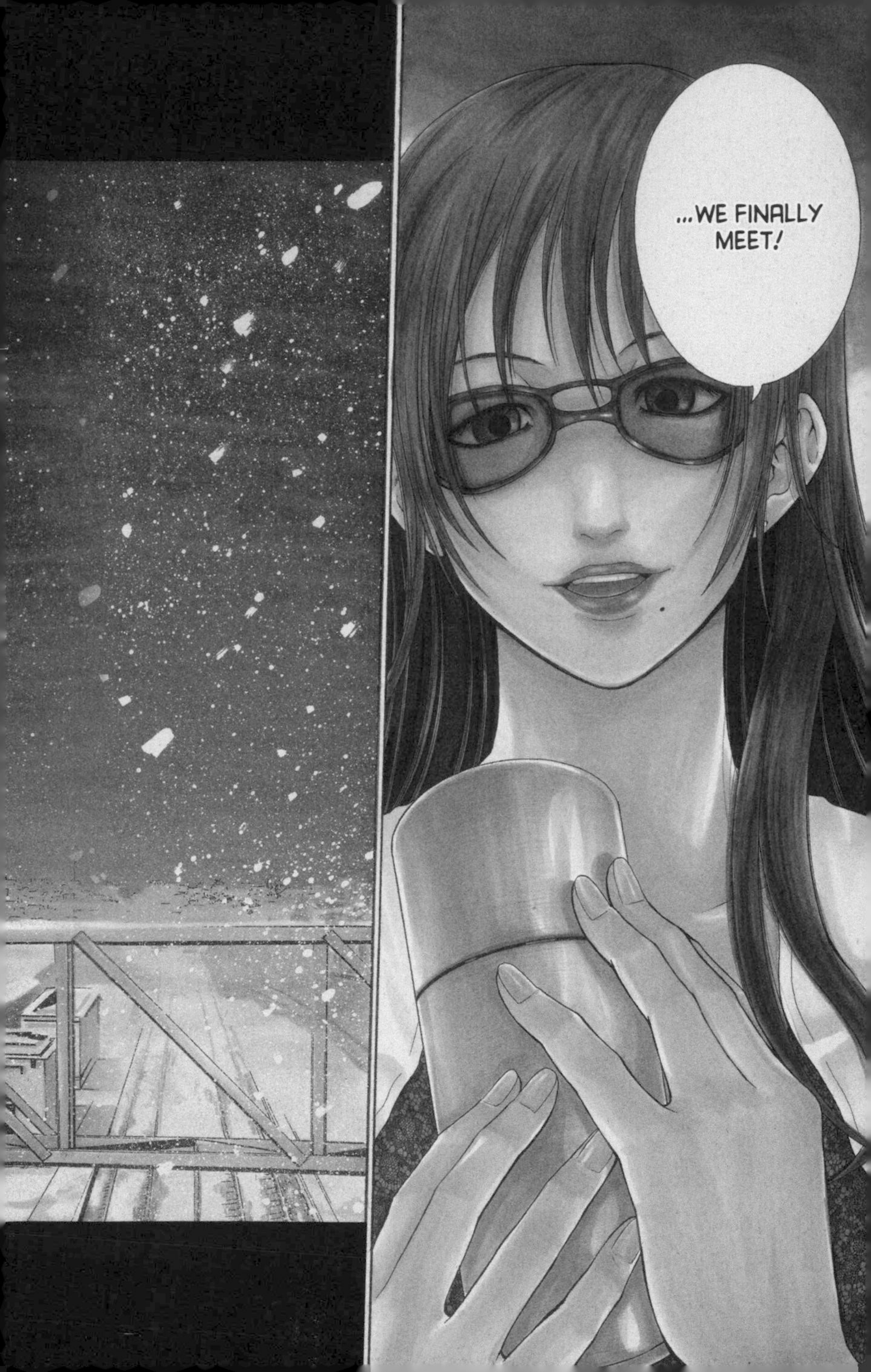
...WE FINALLY MEET!

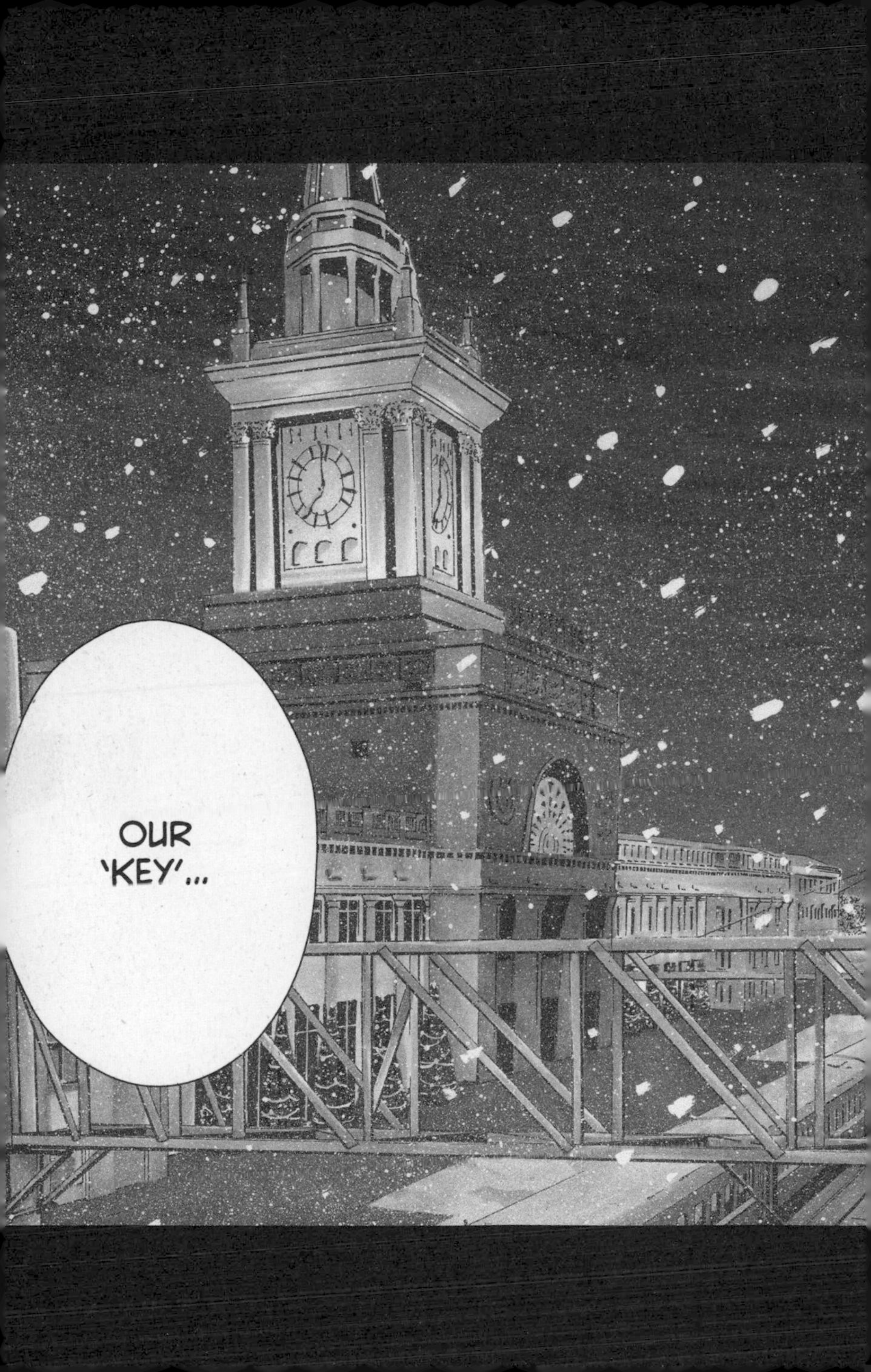
OUR 'KEY'...

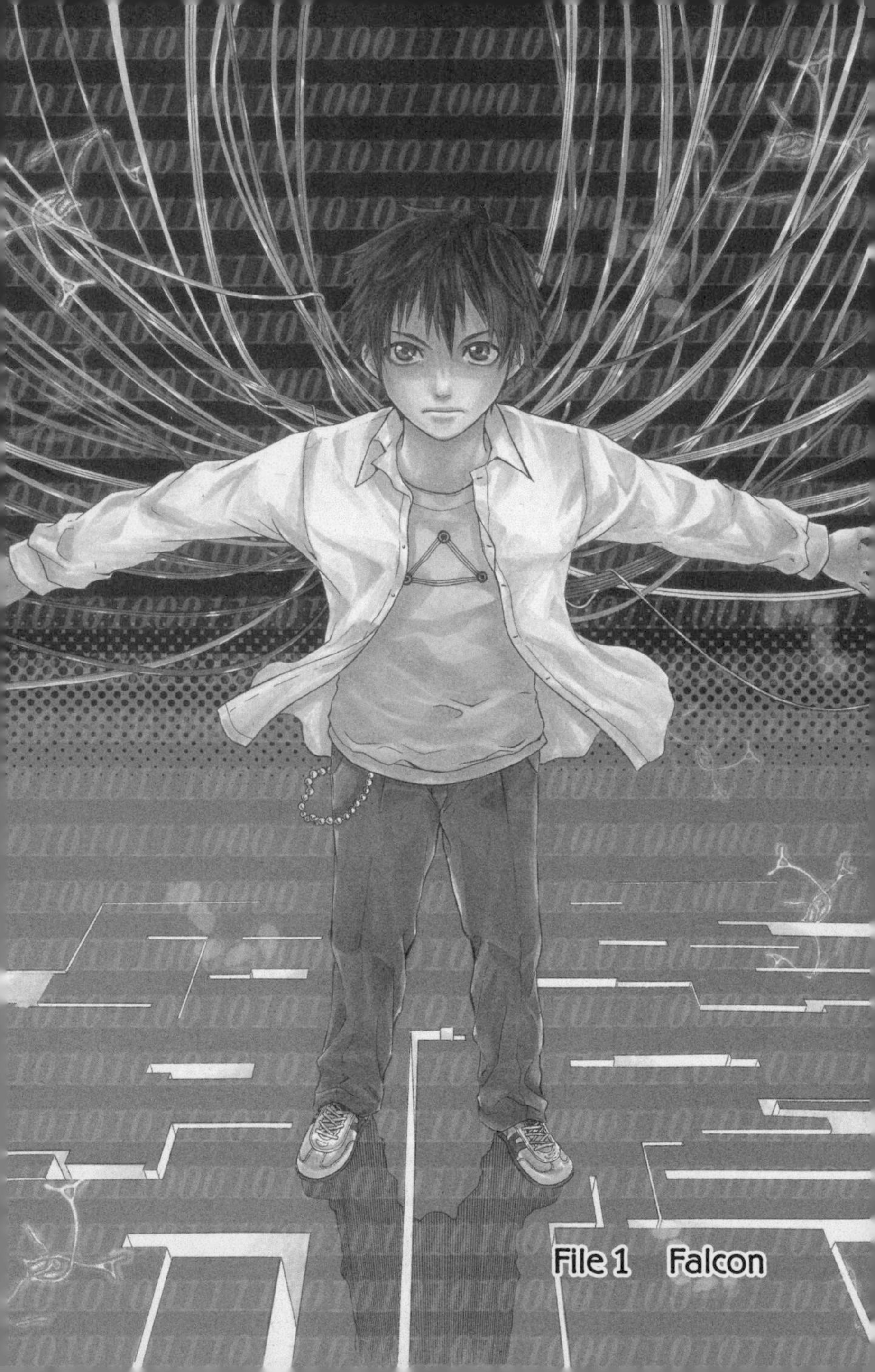
File 1 Falcon

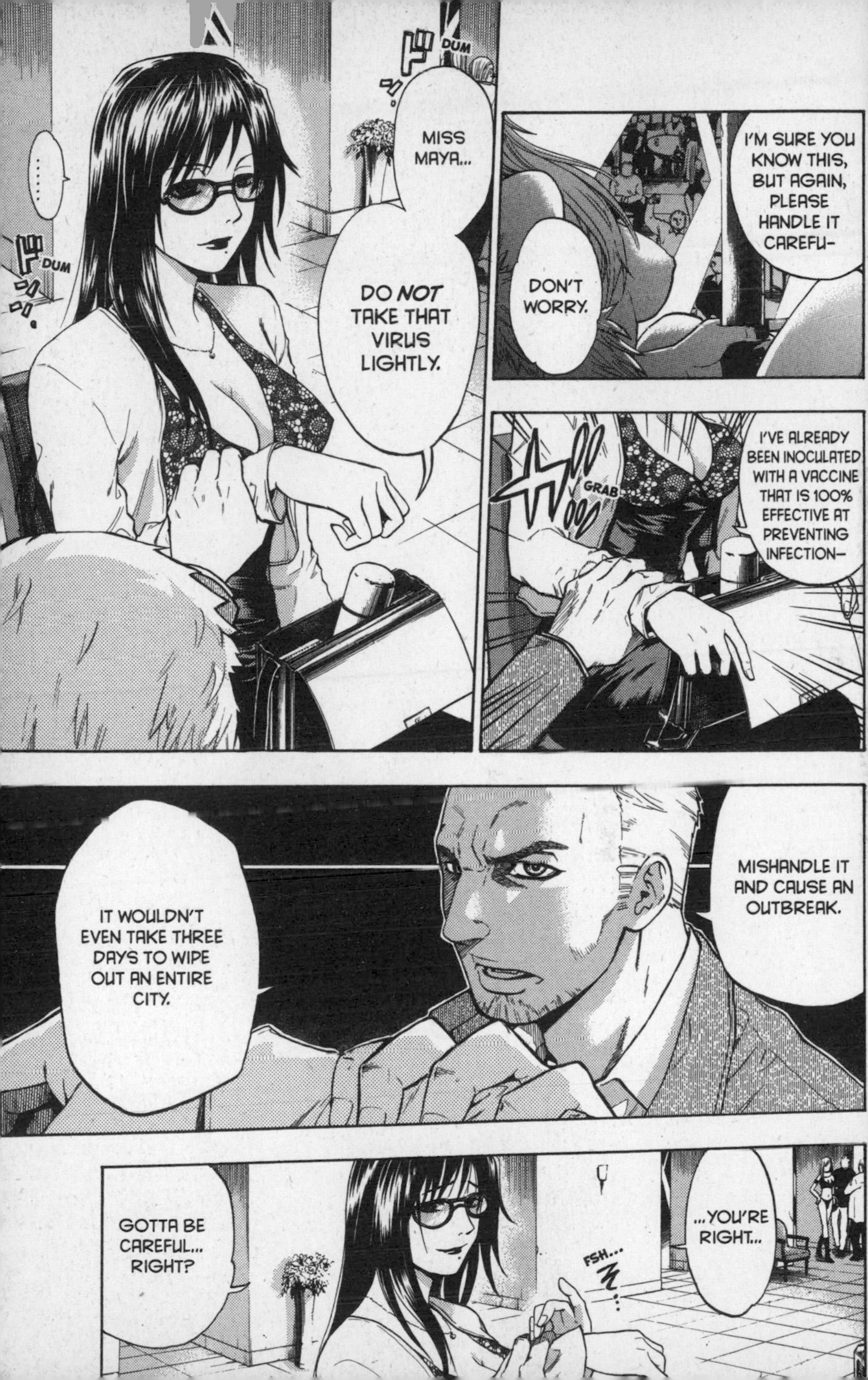
I'M SURE YOU KNOW THIS, BUT AGAIN, PLEASE HANDLE IT CAREFU–
DON'T WORRY.
I'VE ALREADY BEEN INOCULATED WITH A VACCINE THAT IS 100% EFFECTIVE AT PREVENTING INFECTION–
GRAB
DUM
MISS MAYA...
DO *NOT* TAKE THAT VIRUS LIGHTLY.
DUM
......
MISHANDLE IT AND CAUSE AN OUTBREAK.
IT WOULDN'T EVEN TAKE THREE DAYS TO WIPE OUT AN ENTIRE CITY.
...YOU'RE RIGHT...
FSH...
GOTTA BE CAREFUL... RIGHT?

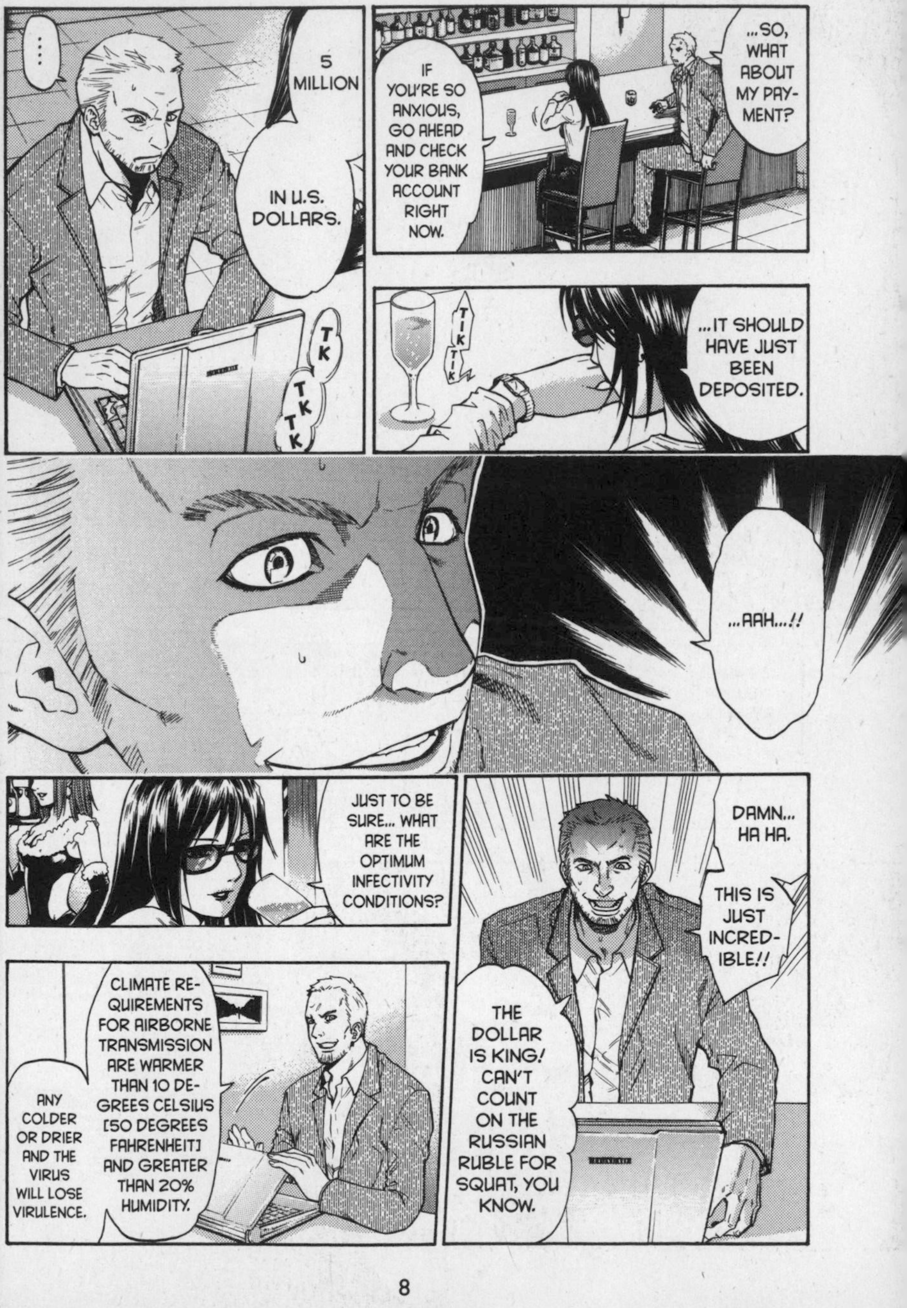
...SO, WHAT ABOUT MY PAY-MENT?
IF YOU'RE SO ANXIOUS, GO AHEAD AND CHECK YOUR BANK ACCOUNT RIGHT NOW.
TIK TIK
...IT SHOULD HAVE JUST BEEN DEPOSITED.
5 MILLION
IN U.S. DOLLARS.
....
TK TK TK TK
...AAH...!!
DAMN... HA HA.
THIS IS JUST INCRED-IBLE!!
THE DOLLAR IS KING! CAN'T COUNT ON THE RUSSIAN RUBLE FOR SQUAT, YOU KNOW.
JUST TO BE SURE... WHAT ARE THE OPTIMUM INFECTIVITY CONDITIONS?
CLIMATE RE-QUIREMENTS FOR AIRBORNE TRANSMISSION ARE WARMER THAN 10 DE-GREES CELSIUS [50 DEGREES FAHRENHEIT] AND GREATER THAN 20% HUMIDITY.
ANY COLDER OR DRIER AND THE VIRUS WILL LOSE VIRULENCE.

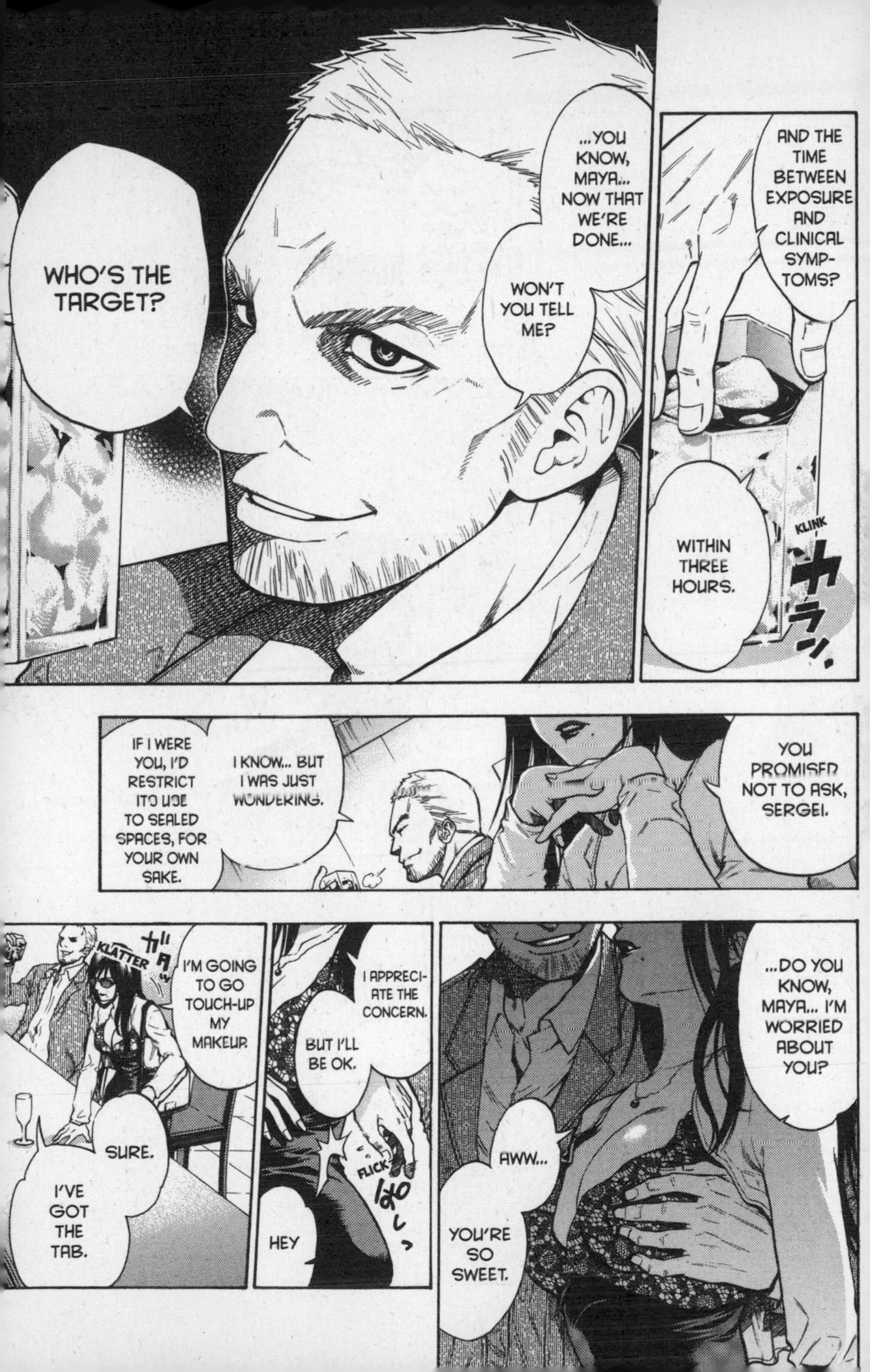
AND THE TIME BETWEEN EXPOSURE AND CLINICAL SYMP-TOMS?
WITHIN THREE HOURS.
KLINK
...YOU KNOW, MAYA... NOW THAT WE'RE DONE...
WON'T YOU TELL ME?
WHO'S THE TARGET?
YOU PROMISED NOT TO ASK, SERGEI.
I KNOW... BUT I WAS JUST WONDERING.
IF I WERE YOU, I'D RESTRICT ITS USE TO SEALED SPACES, FOR YOUR OWN SAKE.
...DO YOU KNOW, MAYA... I'M WORRIED ABOUT YOU?
AWW...
YOU'RE SO SWEET.
I APPRECI-ATE THE CONCERN.
BUT I'LL BE OK.
FLICK
HEY
KLATTER
I'M GOING TO GO TOUCH-UP MY MAKEUP.
SURE.
I'VE GOT THE TAB.

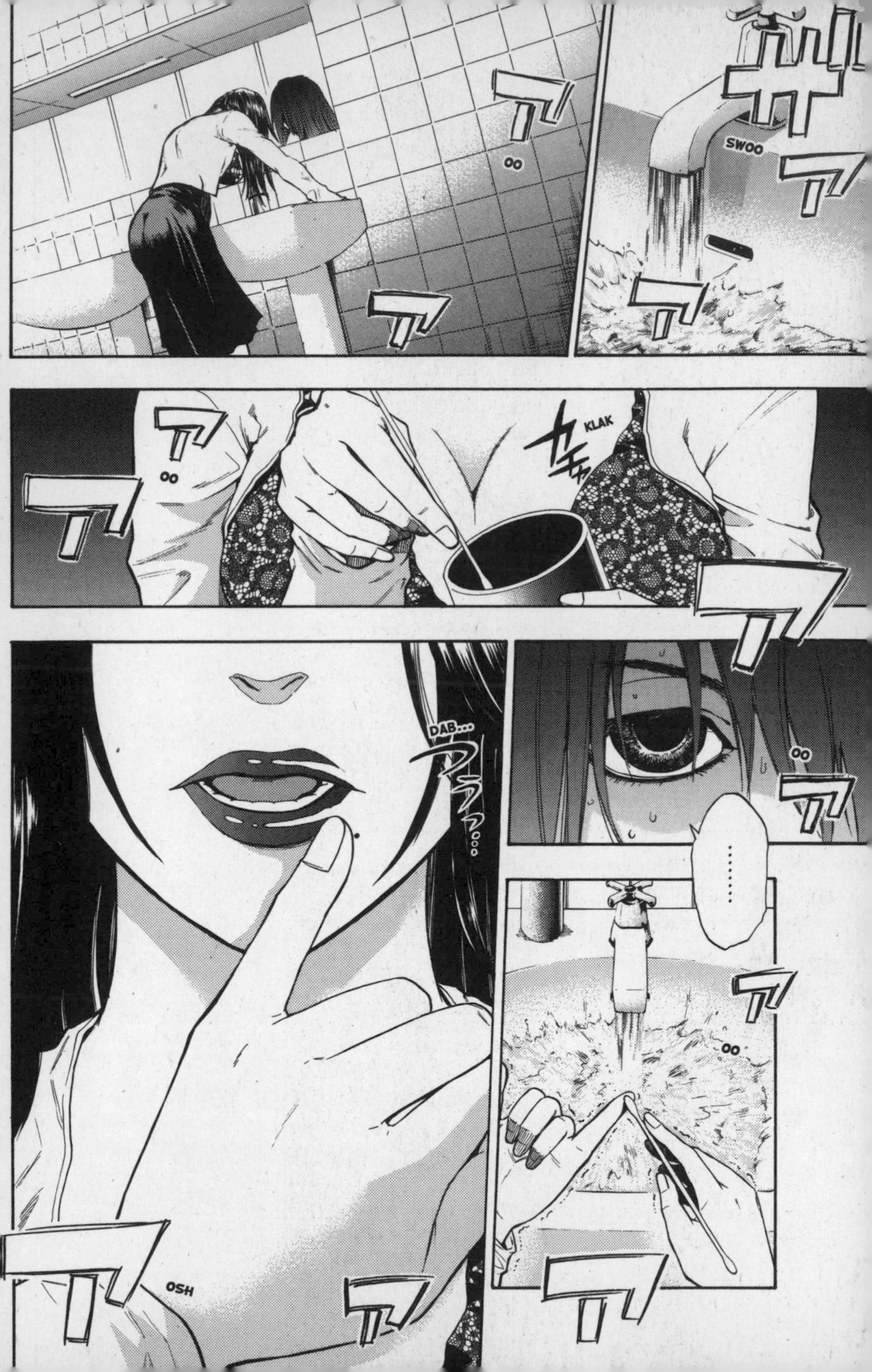
SWOO
oo
KLAK
oo
oo
......
oo
DAB...
OSH

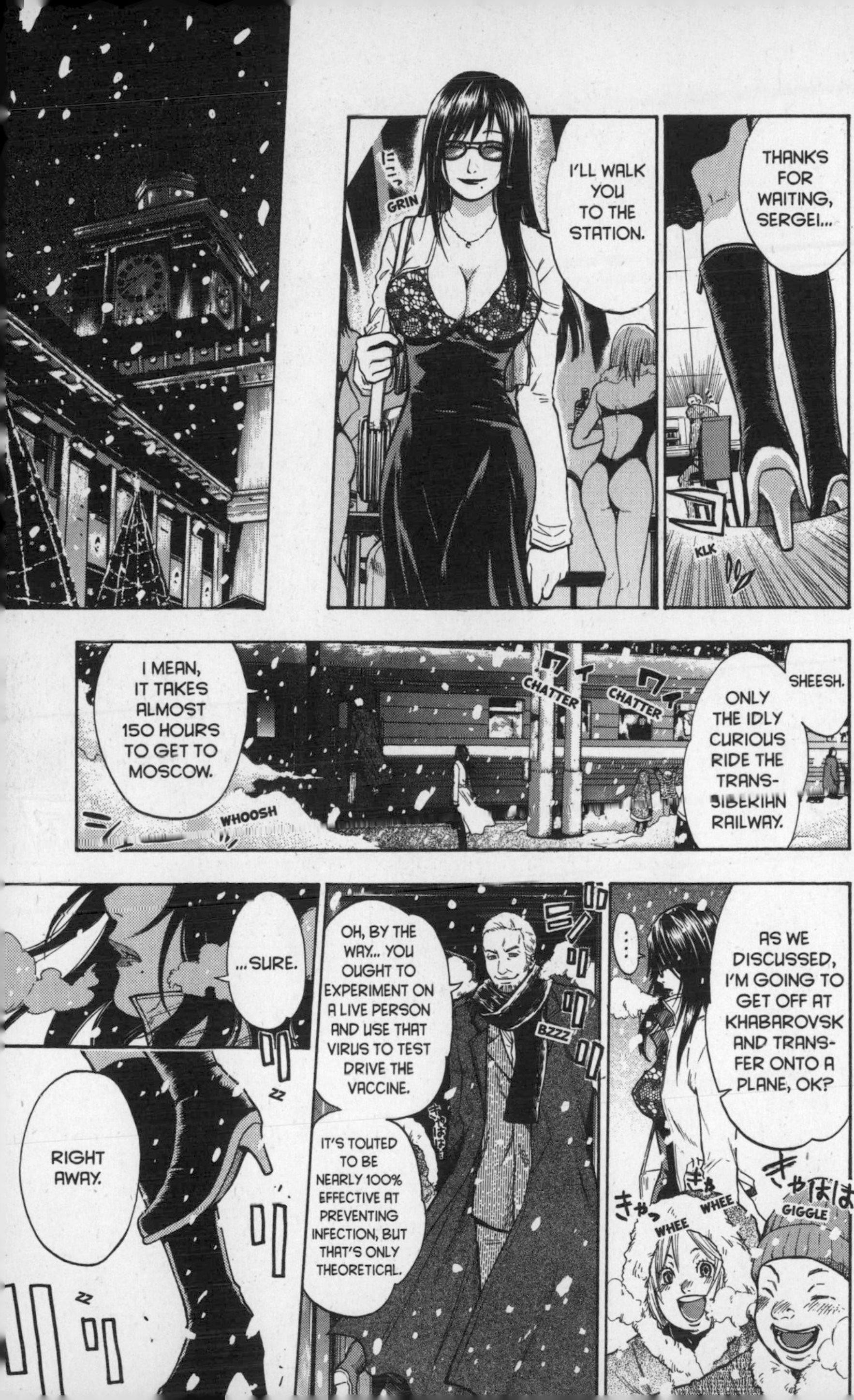
THANKS FOR WAITING, SERGEI...
KLK
I'LL WALK YOU TO THE STATION.
GRIN
SHEESH.
ONLY THE IDLY CURIOUS RIDE THE TRANS-SIBERIAN RAILWAY.
CHATTER
CHATTER
I MEAN, IT TAKES ALMOST 150 HOURS TO GET TO MOSCOW.
WHOOSH
AS WE DISCUSSED, I'M GOING TO GET OFF AT KHABAROVSK AND TRANSFER ONTO A PLANE, OK?
....
WHEE
WHEE
GIGGLE
OH, BY THE WAY... YOU OUGHT TO EXPERIMENT ON A LIVE PERSON AND USE THAT VIRUS TO TEST DRIVE THE VACCINE.
BZZZ
IT'S TOUTED TO BE NEARLY 100% EFFECTIVE AT PREVENTING INFECTION, BUT THAT'S ONLY THEORETICAL.
...SURE.
RIGHT AWAY.
ZZ
ZZ

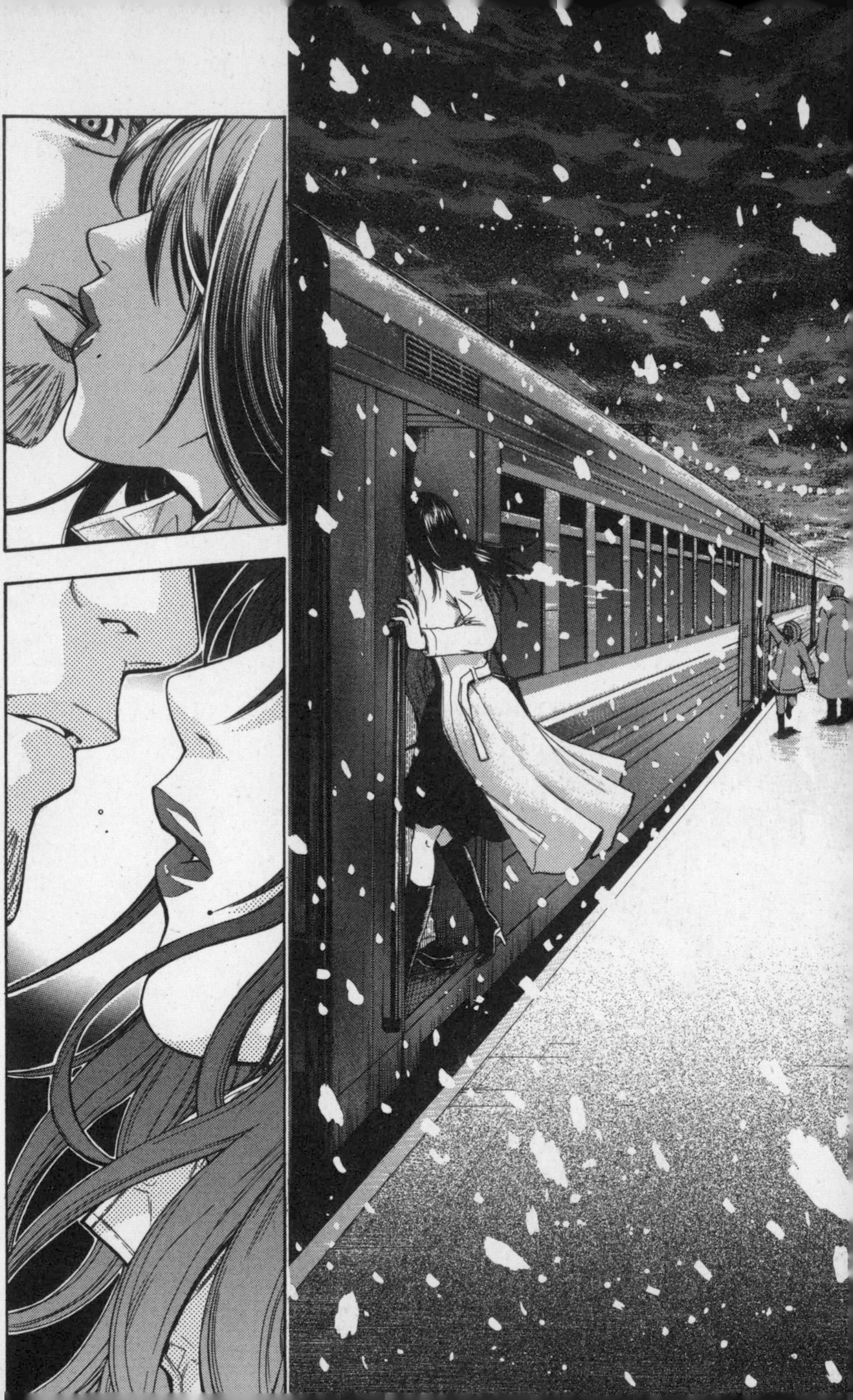

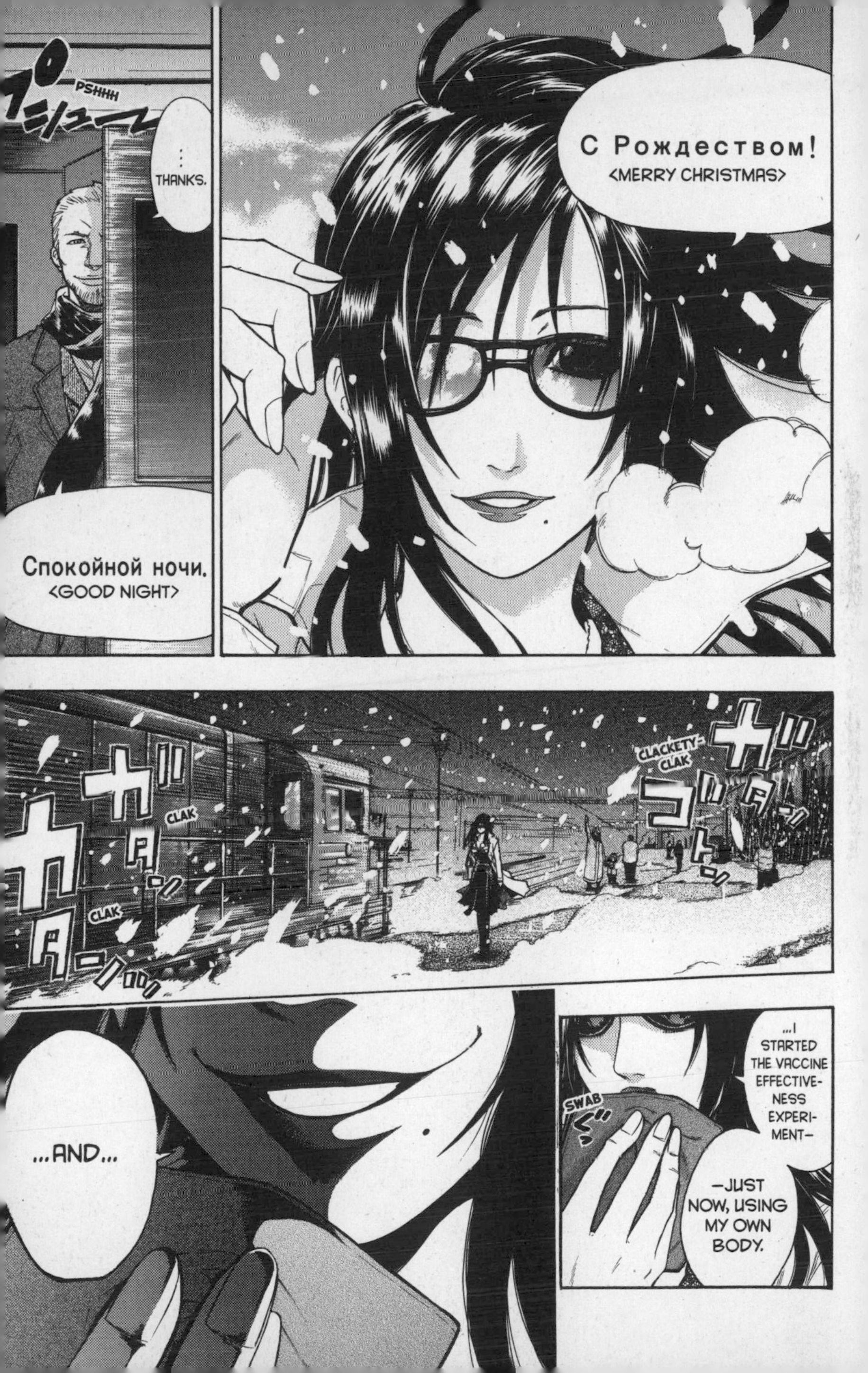
С Рождеством!
<MERRY CHRISTMAS>
PSHHH
...THANKS.
Спокойной ночи.
<GOOD NIGHT>
CLACKETY-CLAK
CLAK
CLAK
...I STARTED THE VACCINE EFFECTIVENESS EXPERIMENT—
SWAB
—JUST NOW, USING MY OWN BODY.
...AND...

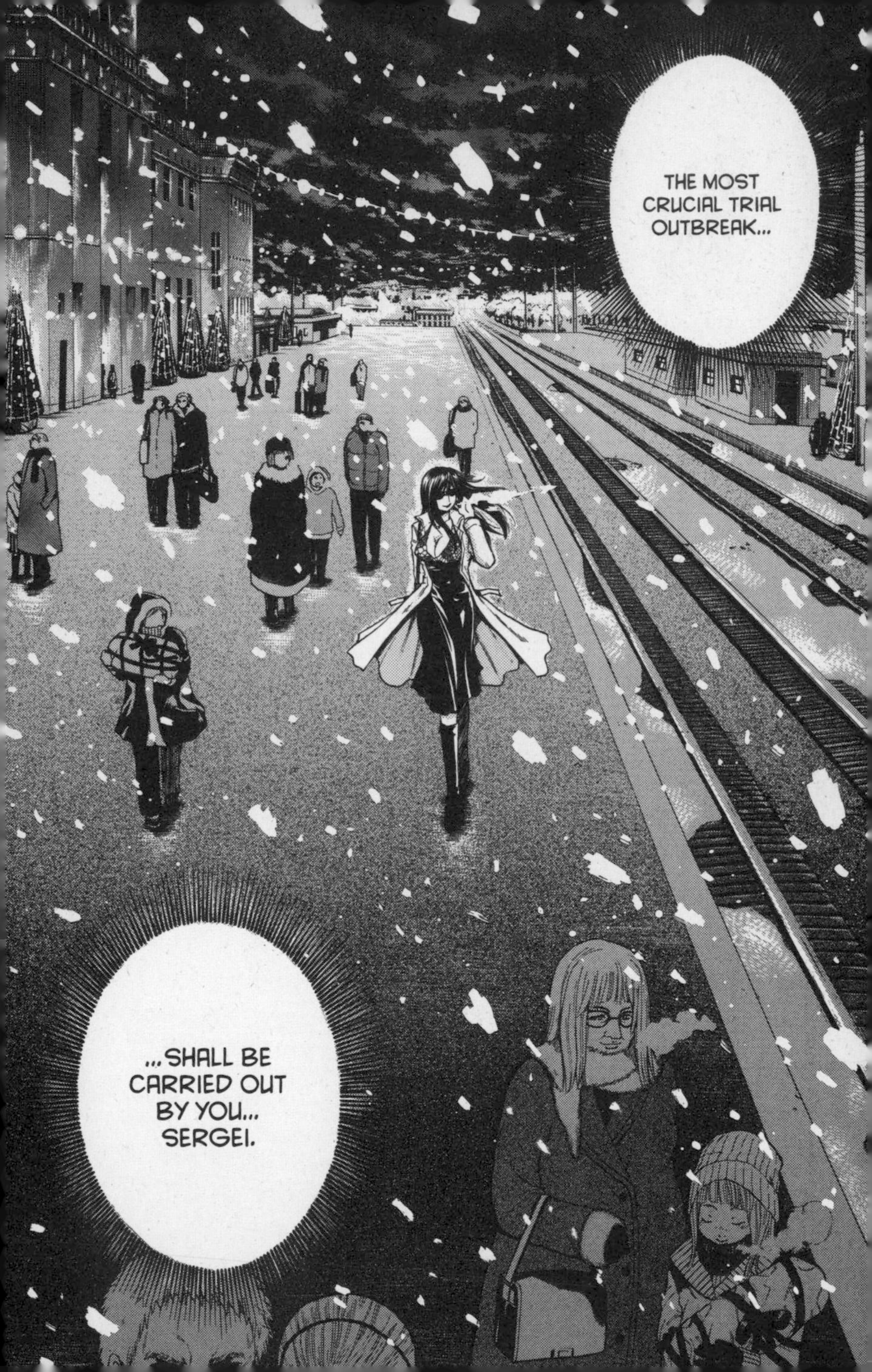
THE MOST CRUCIAL TRIAL OUTBREAK...
...SHALL BE CARRIED OUT BY YOU... SERGEI.

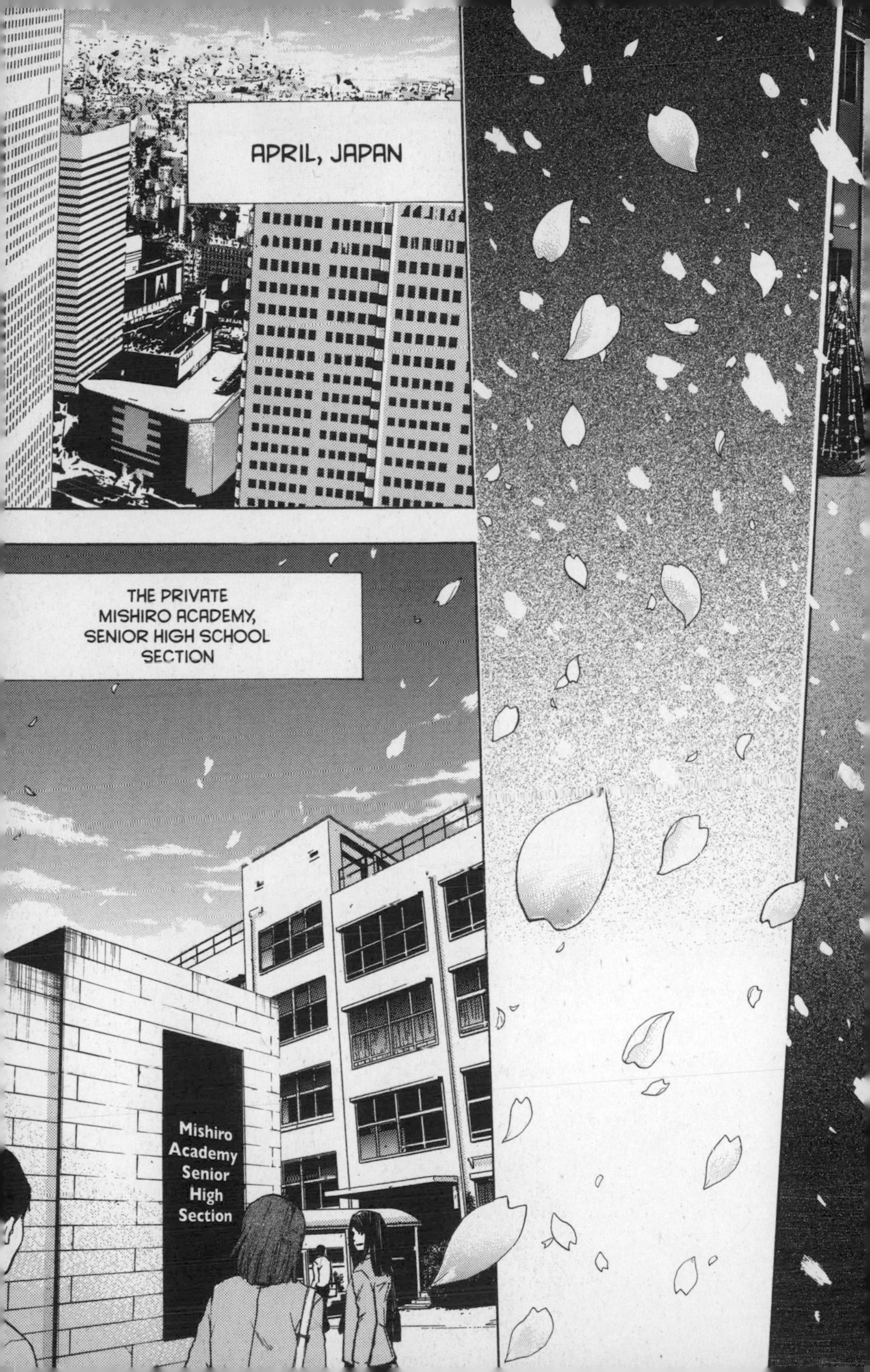
APRIL, JAPAN
THE PRIVATE MISHIRO ACADEMY, SENIOR HIGH SCHOOL SECTION
Mishiro Academy Senior High Section

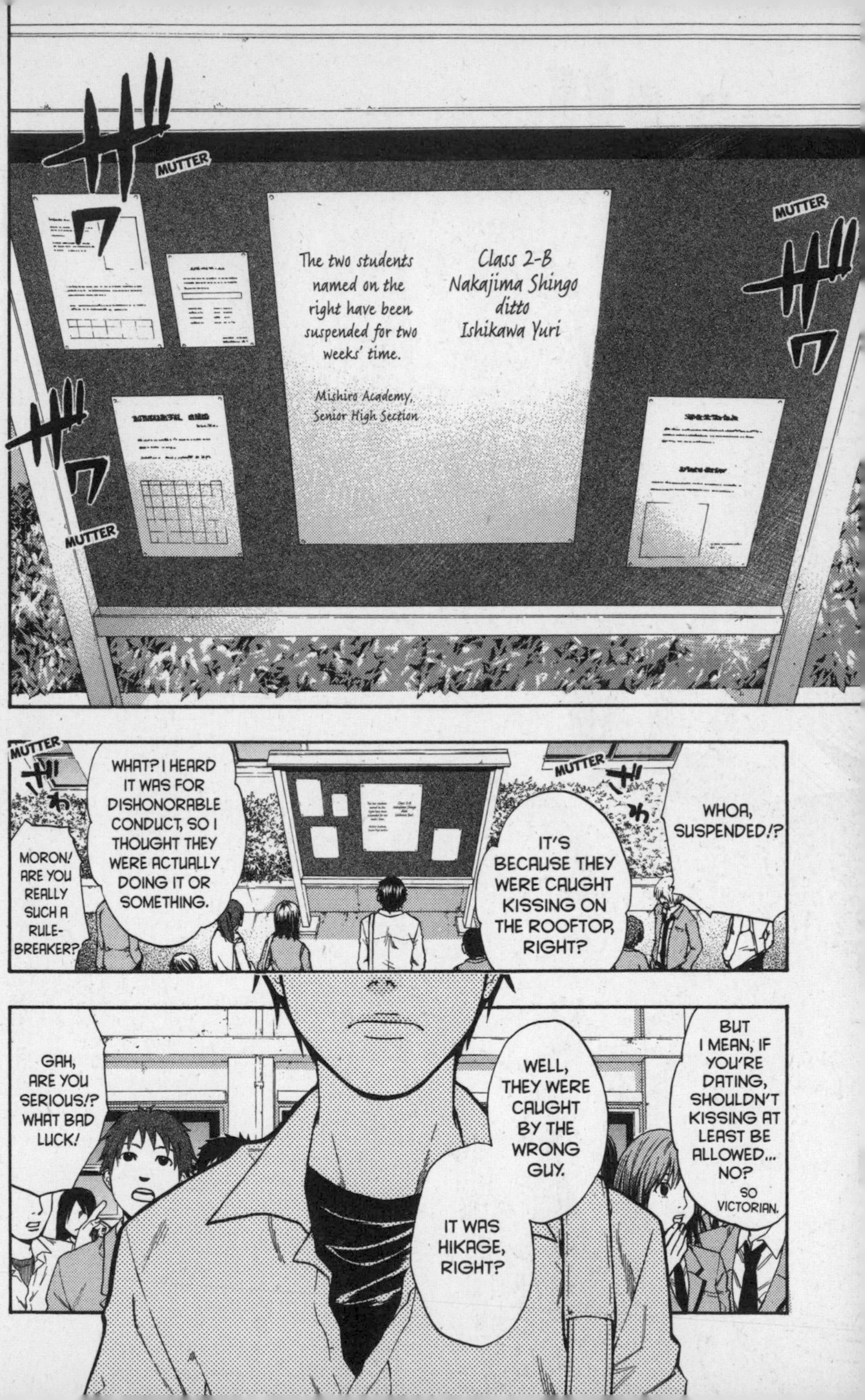
MUTTER
MUTTER
MUTTER
The two students named on the right have been suspended for two weeks' time.
Mishiro Academy, Senior High Section
Class 2-B Nakajima Shingo
ditto Ishikawa Yuri
MUTTER
WHOA, SUSPENDED!?
IT'S BECAUSE THEY WERE CAUGHT KISSING ON THE ROOFTOP, RIGHT?
WHAT? I HEARD IT WAS FOR DISHONORABLE CONDUCT, SO I THOUGHT THEY WERE ACTUALLY DOING IT OR SOMETHING.
MORON! ARE YOU REALLY SUCH A RULE-BREAKER?
MUTTER
BUT I MEAN, IF YOU'RE DATING, SHOULDN'T KISSING AT LEAST BE ALLOWED... NO?
SO VICTORIAN.
WELL, THEY WERE CAUGHT BY THE WRONG GUY.
IT WAS HIKAGE, RIGHT?
GAH, ARE YOU SERIOUS!? WHAT BAD LUCK!

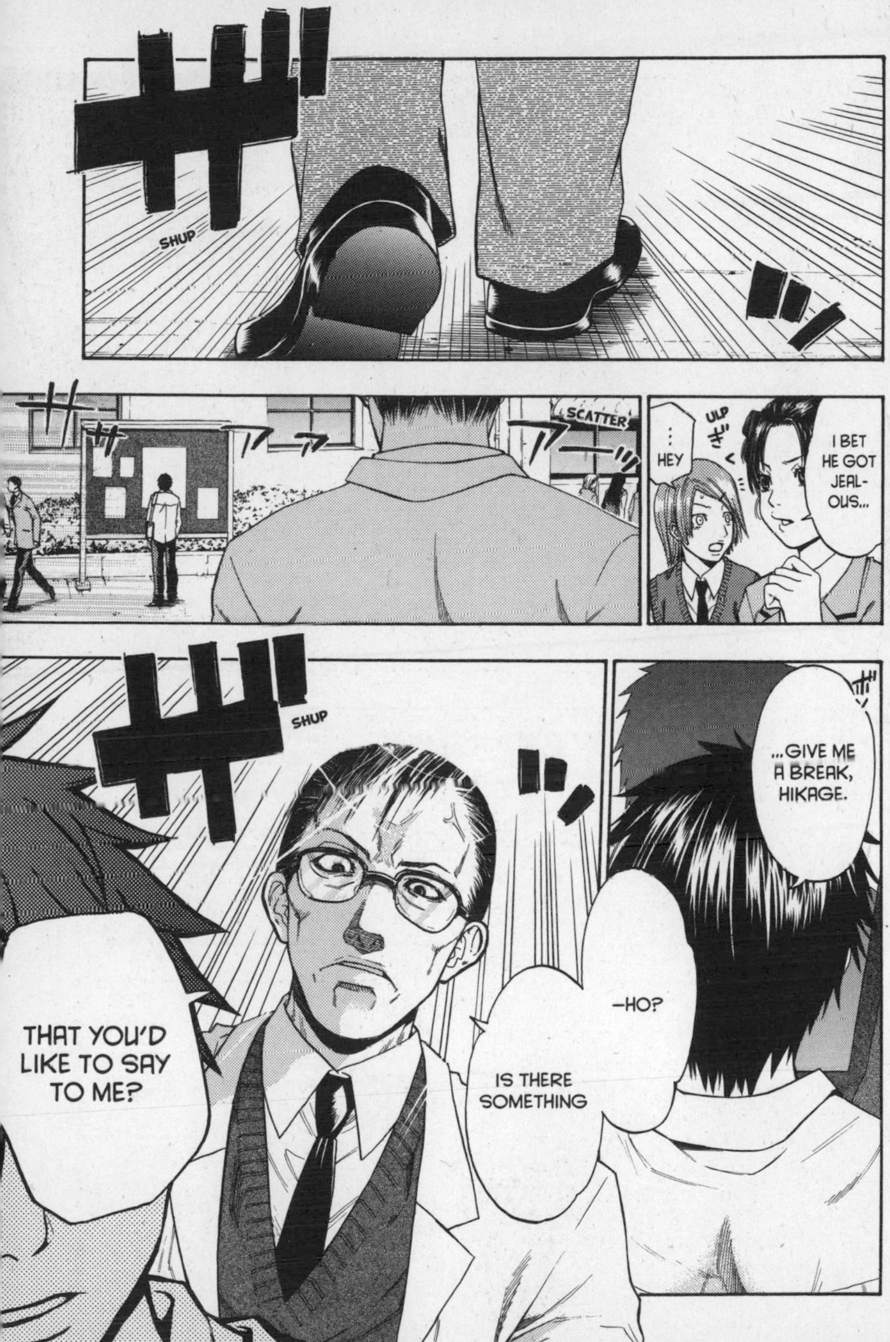
SHUP
I BET HE GOT JEAL-OUS...
ULP
... HEY
SCATTER
...GIVE ME A BREAK, HIKAGE.
SHUP
—HO?
IS THERE SOMETHING
THAT YOU'D LIKE TO SAY TO ME?

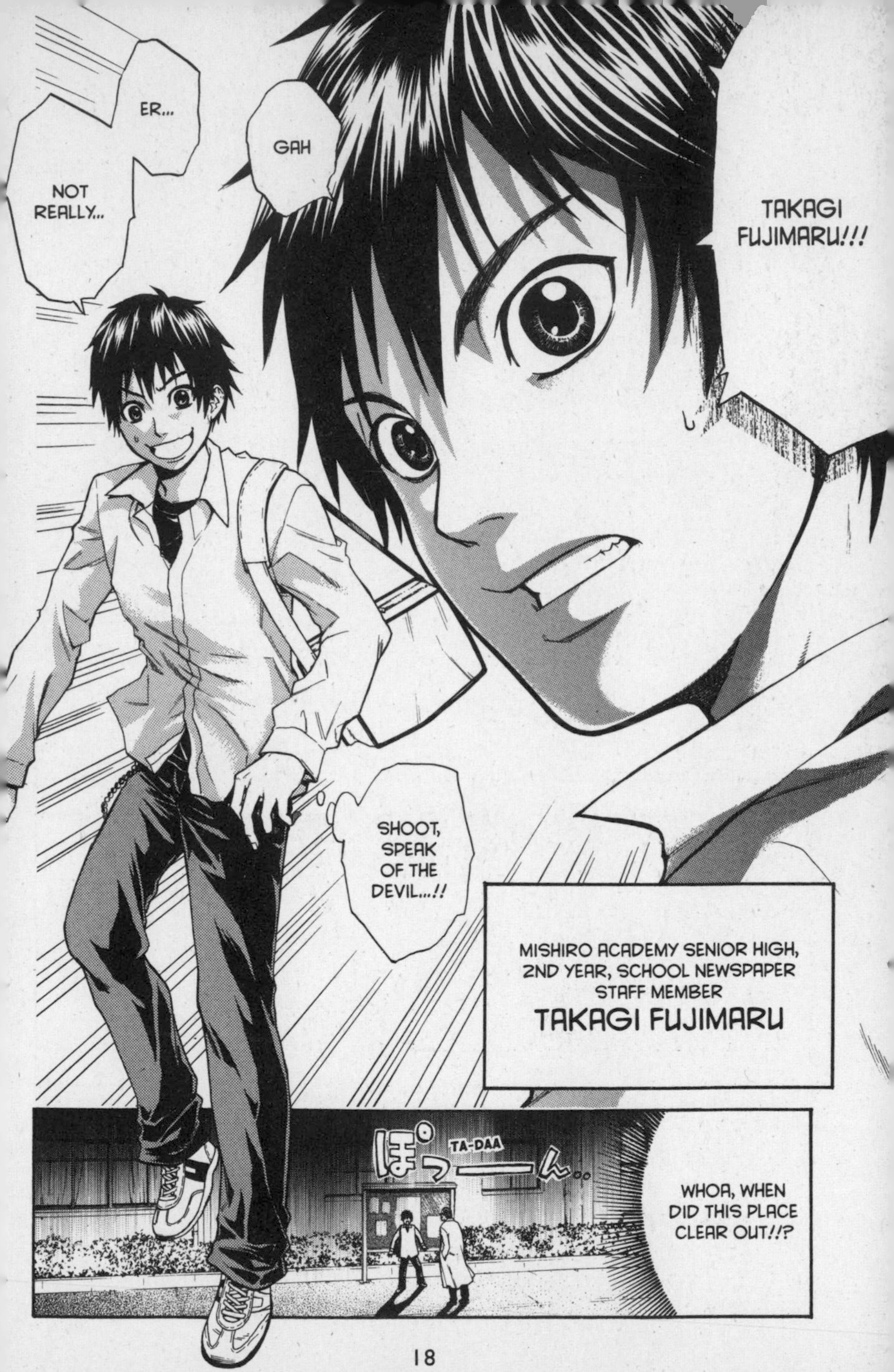
TAKAGI FUJIMARU!!!
GAH
ER...
NOT REALLY...
SHOOT, SPEAK OF THE DEVIL...!!
MISHIRO ACADEMY SENIOR HIGH, 2ND YEAR, SCHOOL NEWSPAPER STAFF MEMBER
TAKAGI FUJIMARU
ぽっーーん。。
TA-DAA
WHOA, WHEN DID THIS PLACE CLEAR OUT!!?

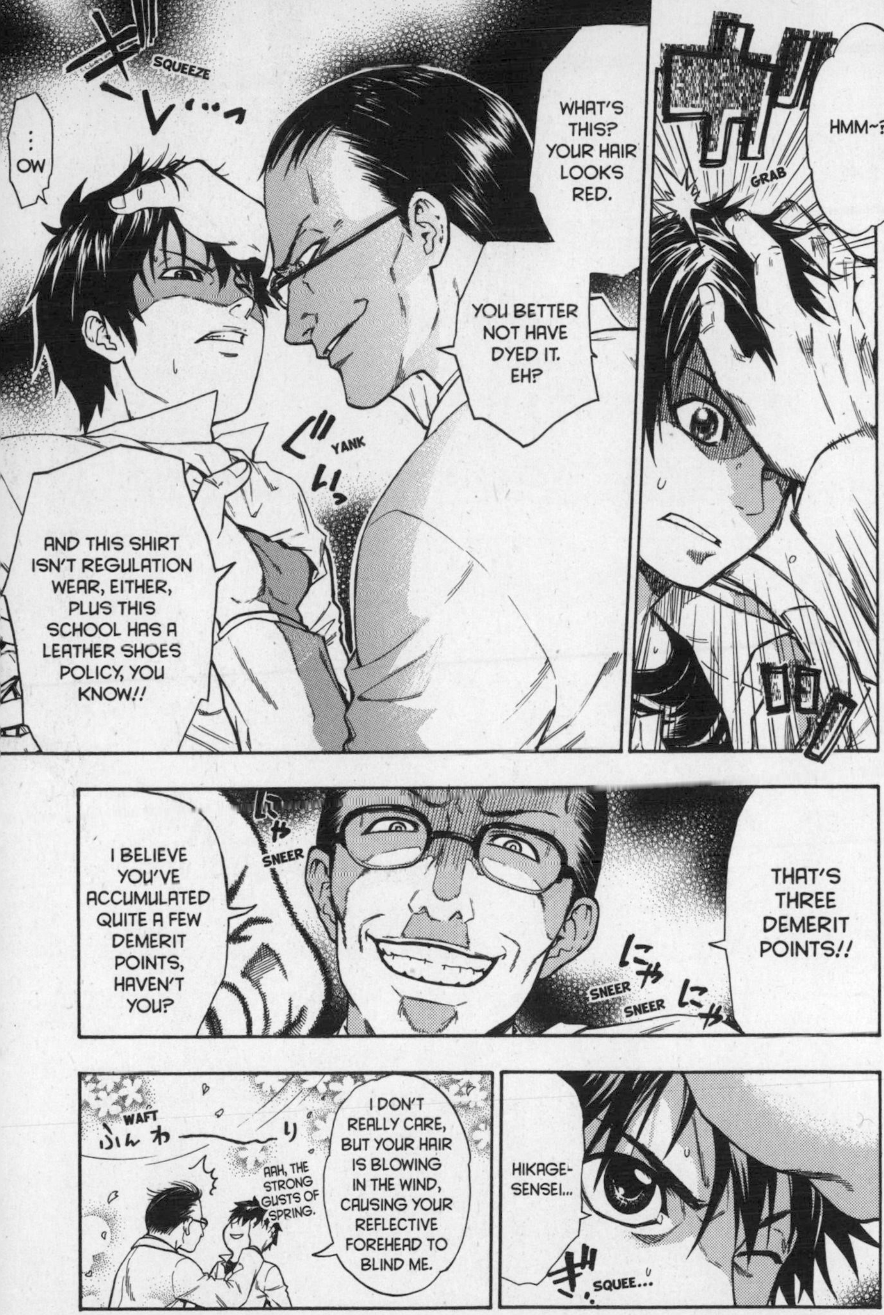
HMM~?
GRAB
WHAT'S THIS? YOUR HAIR LOOKS RED.
YOU BETTER NOT HAVE DYED IT. EH?
SQUEEZE
... OW
YANK
AND THIS SHIRT ISN'T REGULATION WEAR, EITHER, PLUS THIS SCHOOL HAS A LEATHER SHOES POLICY, YOU KNOW!!
THAT'S THREE DEMERIT POINTS!!
SNEER
SNEER
SNEER
I BELIEVE YOU'VE ACCUMULATED QUITE A FEW DEMERIT POINTS, HAVEN'T YOU?
HIKAGE-SENSEI...
SQUEE...
I DON'T REALLY CARE, BUT YOUR HAIR IS BLOWING IN THE WIND, CAUSING YOUR REFLECTIVE FOREHEAD TO BLIND ME.
AAH, THE STRONG GUSTS OF SPRING.
WAFT

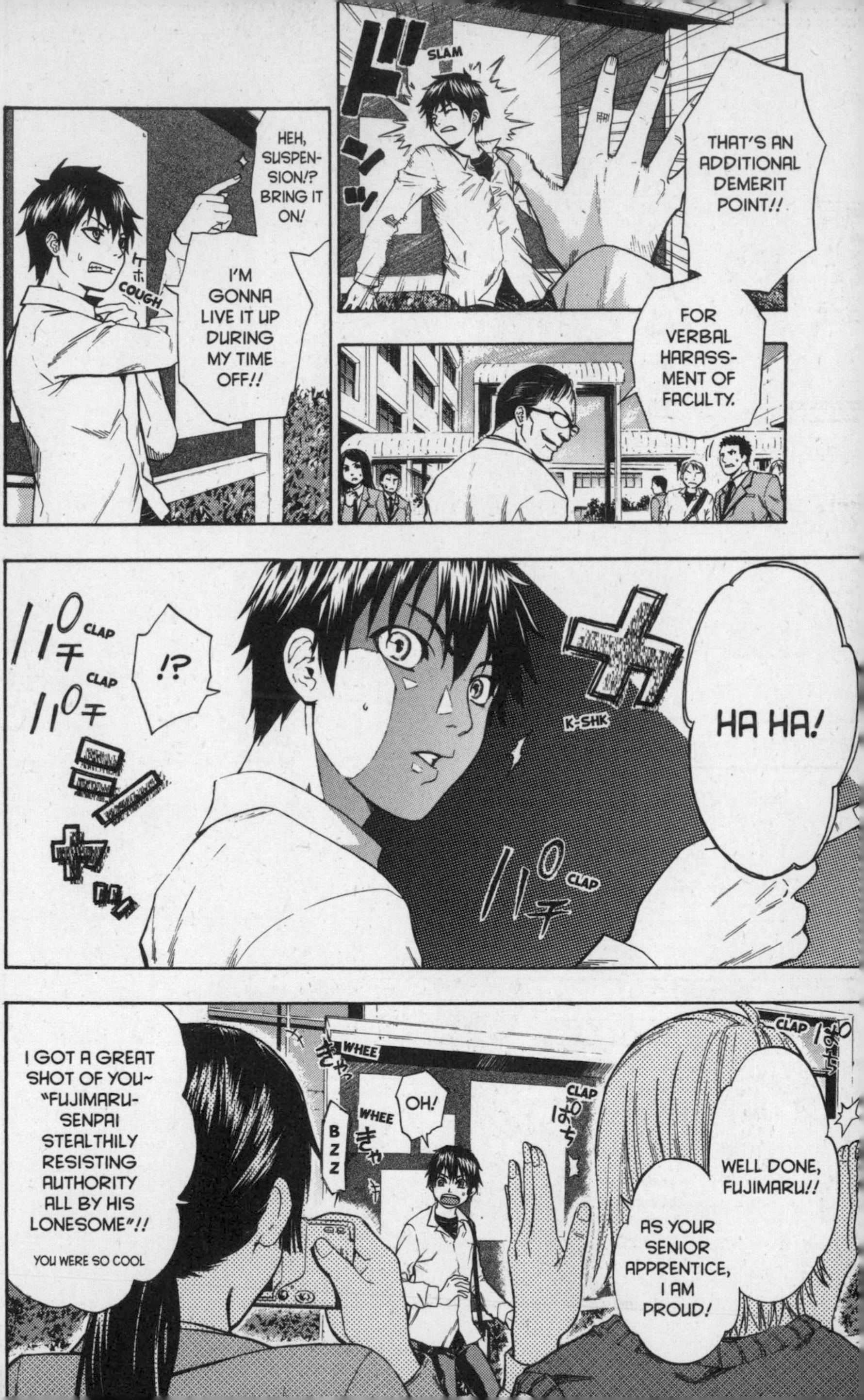
SLAM
THAT'S AN ADDITIONAL DEMERIT POINT!!
FOR VERBAL HARASSMENT OF FACULTY.
HEH, SUSPENSION!? BRING IT ON!
COUGH
I'M GONNA LIVE IT UP DURING MY TIME OFF!!
HA HA!
K-SHK
CLAP
!?
CLAP
CLAP
CLAP
WELL DONE, FUJIMARU!!
AS YOUR SENIOR APPRENTICE, I AM PROUD!
CLAP
OH!
WHEE
WHEE
BZZ
I GOT A GREAT SHOT OF YOU~ "FUJIMARU-SENPAI STEALTHILY RESISTING AUTHORITY ALL BY HIS LONESOME"!!
YOU WERE SO COOL

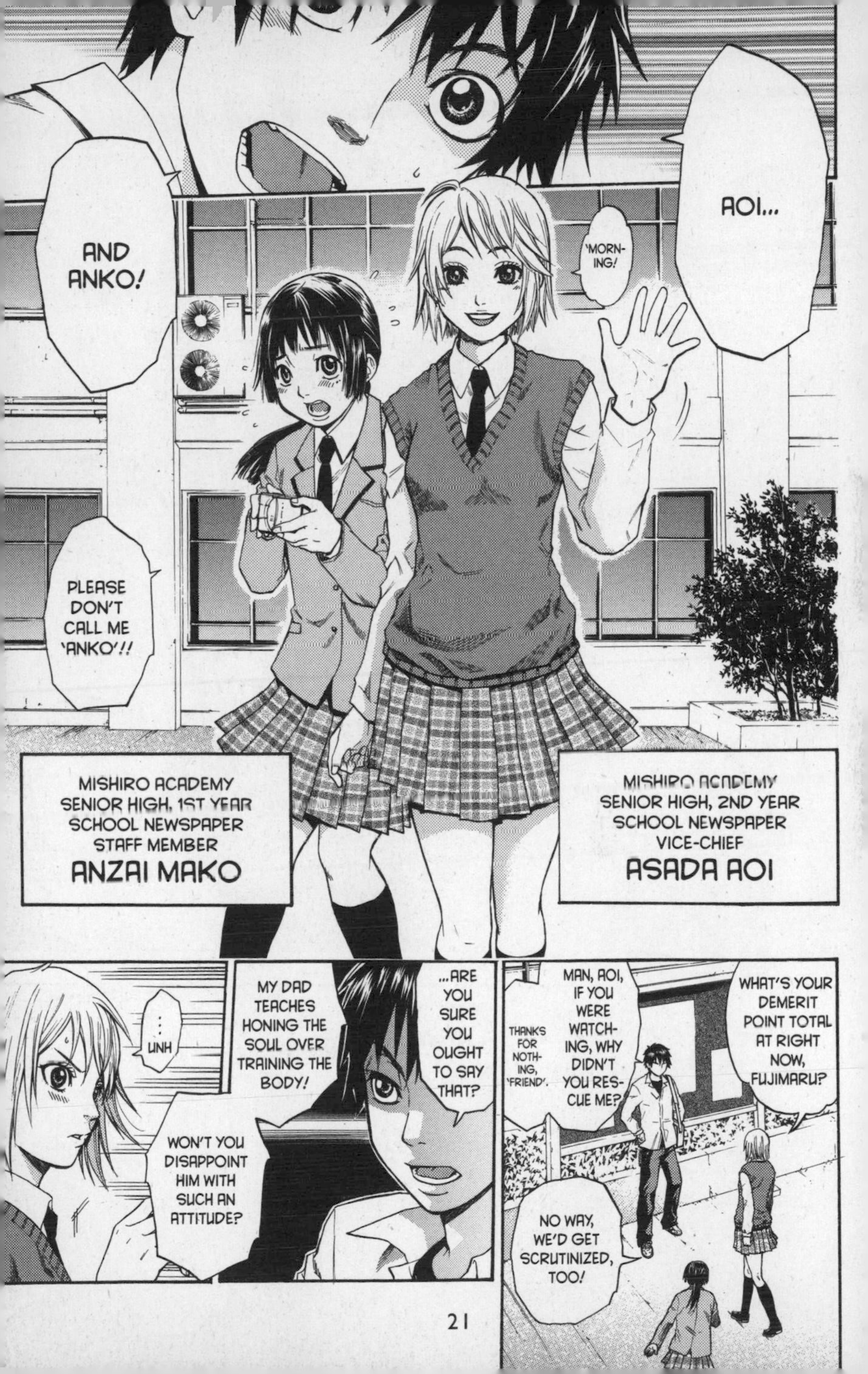
AOI...
'MORNING!
AND ANKO!
PLEASE DON'T CALL ME 'ANKO'!!
MISHIRO ACADEMY SENIOR HIGH, 2ND YEAR SCHOOL NEWSPAPER VICE-CHIEF
ASADA AOI
MISHIRO ACADEMY SENIOR HIGH, 1ST YEAR SCHOOL NEWSPAPER STAFF MEMBER
ANZAI MAKO
WHAT'S YOUR DEMERIT POINT TOTAL AT RIGHT NOW, FUJIMARU?
MAN, AOI, IF YOU WERE WATCHING, WHY DIDN'T YOU RESCUE ME?
THANKS FOR NOTHING, 'FRIEND'.
NO WAY, WE'D GET SCRUTINIZED, TOO!
...ARE YOU SURE YOU OUGHT TO SAY THAT?
MY DAD TEACHES HONING THE SOUL OVER TRAINING THE BODY!
... UNH
WON'T YOU DISAPPOINT HIM WITH SUCH AN ATTITUDE?

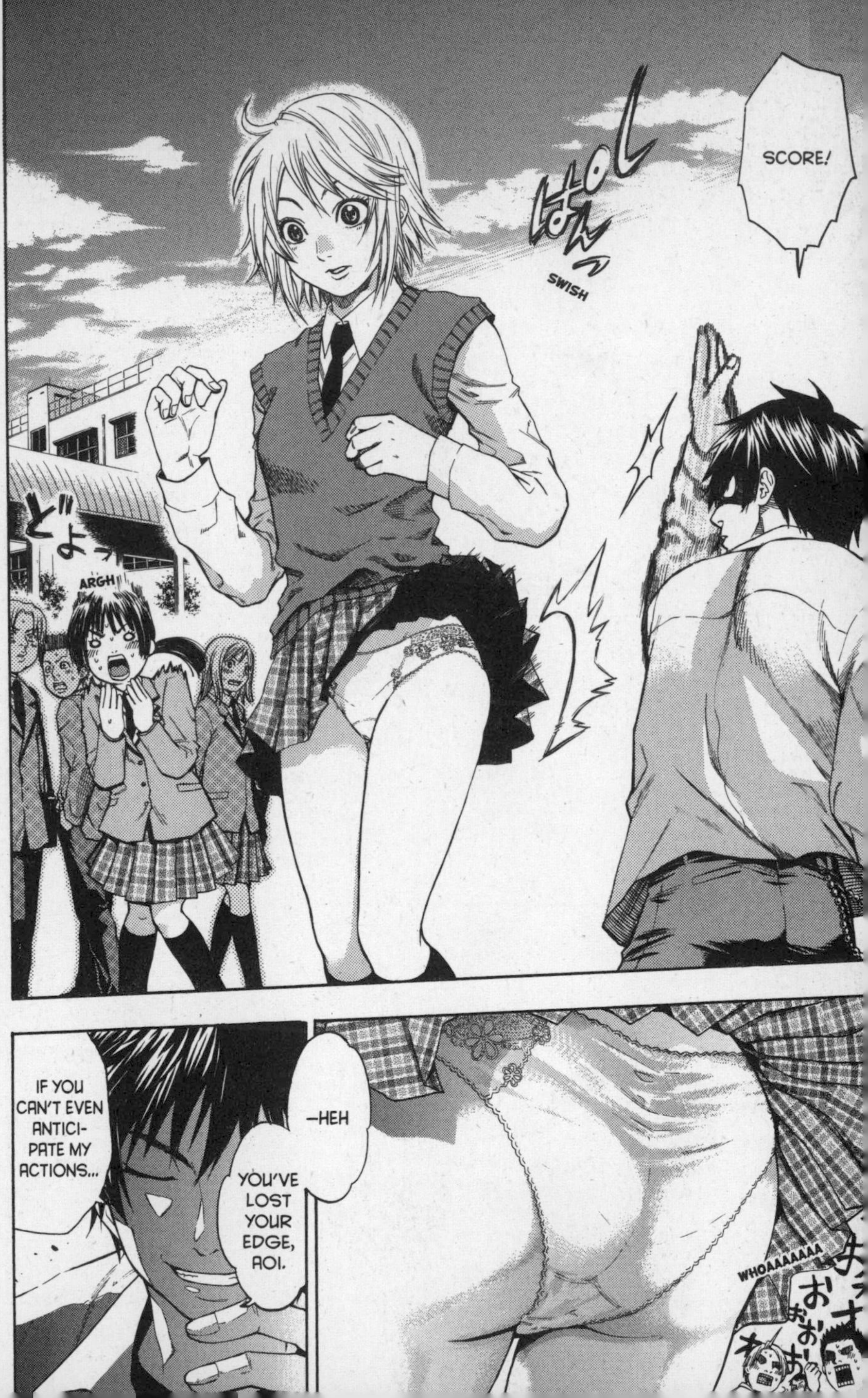
SCORE!
SWISH
どよっ
ARGH
—HEH
YOU'VE LOST YOUR EDGE, AOI.
WHOAAAAAA
IF YOU CAN'T EVEN ANTICI-PATE MY ACTIONS...

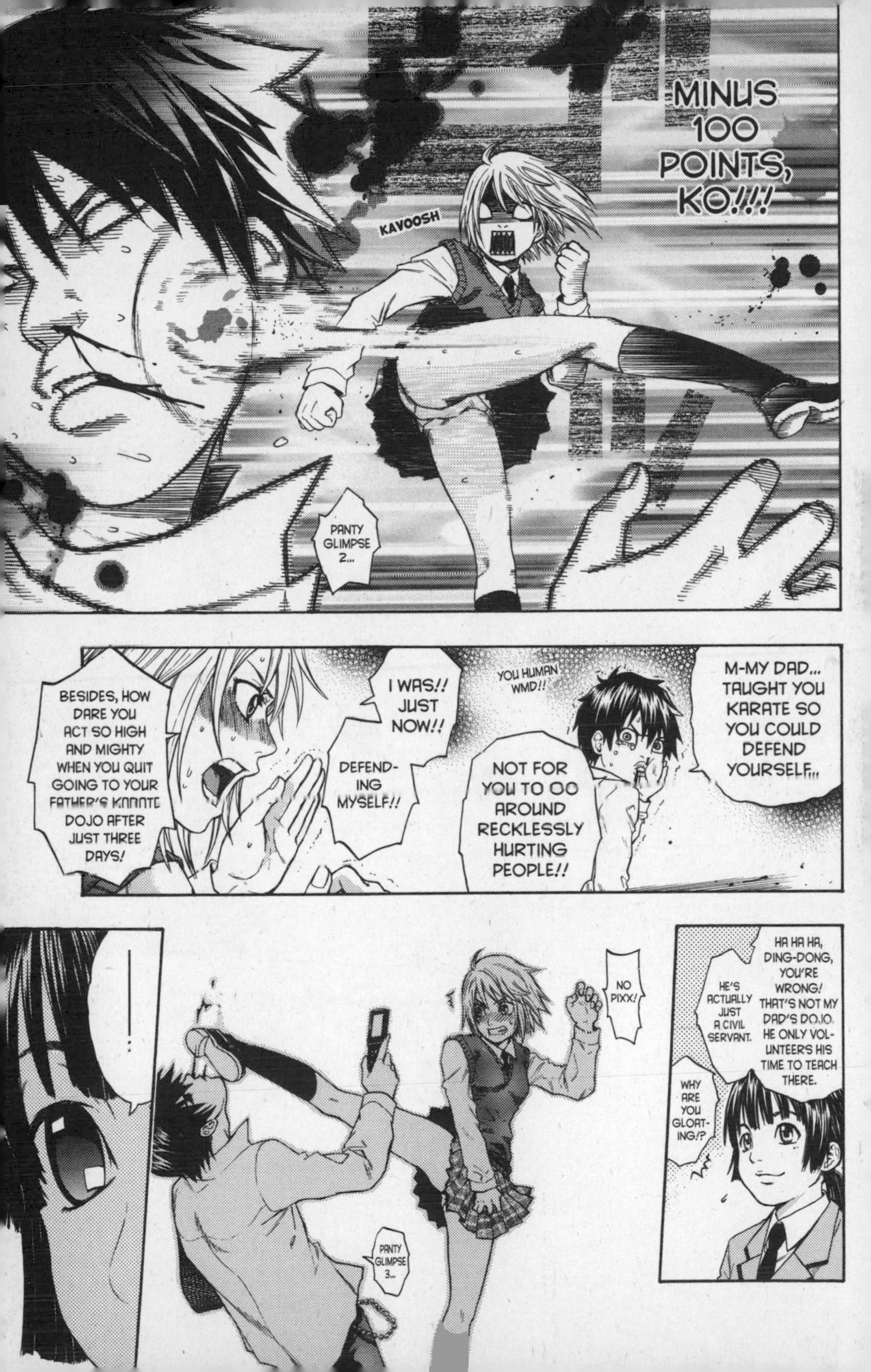
MINUS 100 POINTS, KO!!!!
KAVOOSH
PANTY GLIMPSE 2...
M-MY DAD... TAUGHT YOU KARATE SO YOU COULD DEFEND YOURSELF...
YOU HUMAN WMD!!
NOT FOR YOU TO GO AROUND RECKLESSLY HURTING PEOPLE!!
I WAS!! JUST NOW!!
DEFENDING MYSELF!!
BESIDES, HOW DARE YOU ACT SO HIGH AND MIGHTY WHEN YOU QUIT GOING TO YOUR FATHER'S KARATE DOJO AFTER JUST THREE DAYS!
HA HA HA, DING-DONG, YOU'RE WRONG! THAT'S NOT MY DAD'S DOJO. HE ONLY VOLUNTEERS HIS TIME TO TEACH THERE.
HE'S ACTUALLY JUST A CIVIL SERVANT.
WHY ARE YOU GLOATING!?
NO PIXX!
PANTY GLIMPSE 3...

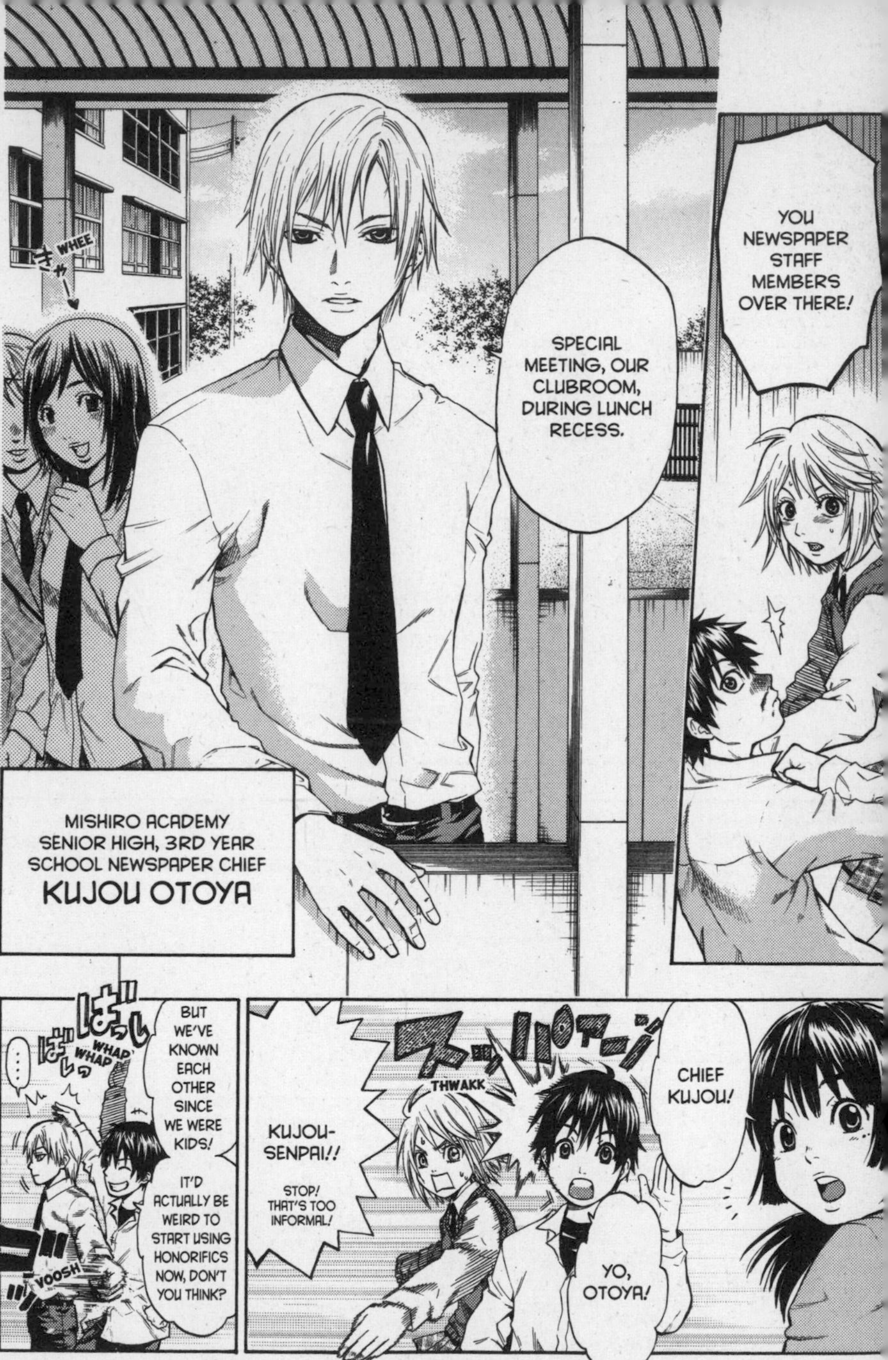
YOU NEWSPAPER STAFF MEMBERS OVER THERE!
WHEE
SPECIAL MEETING, OUR CLUBROOM, DURING LUNCH RECESS.
MISHIRO ACADEMY SENIOR HIGH, 3RD YEAR SCHOOL NEWSPAPER CHIEF
KUJOU OTOYA
CHIEF KUJOU!
YO, OTOYA!
THWAKK
KUJOU-SENPAI!!
STOP! THAT'S TOO INFORMAL!
BUT WE'VE KNOWN EACH OTHER SINCE WE WERE KIDS!
WHAP
...
IT'D ACTUALLY BE WEIRD TO START USING HONORIFICS NOW, DON'T YOU THINK?
VOOSH

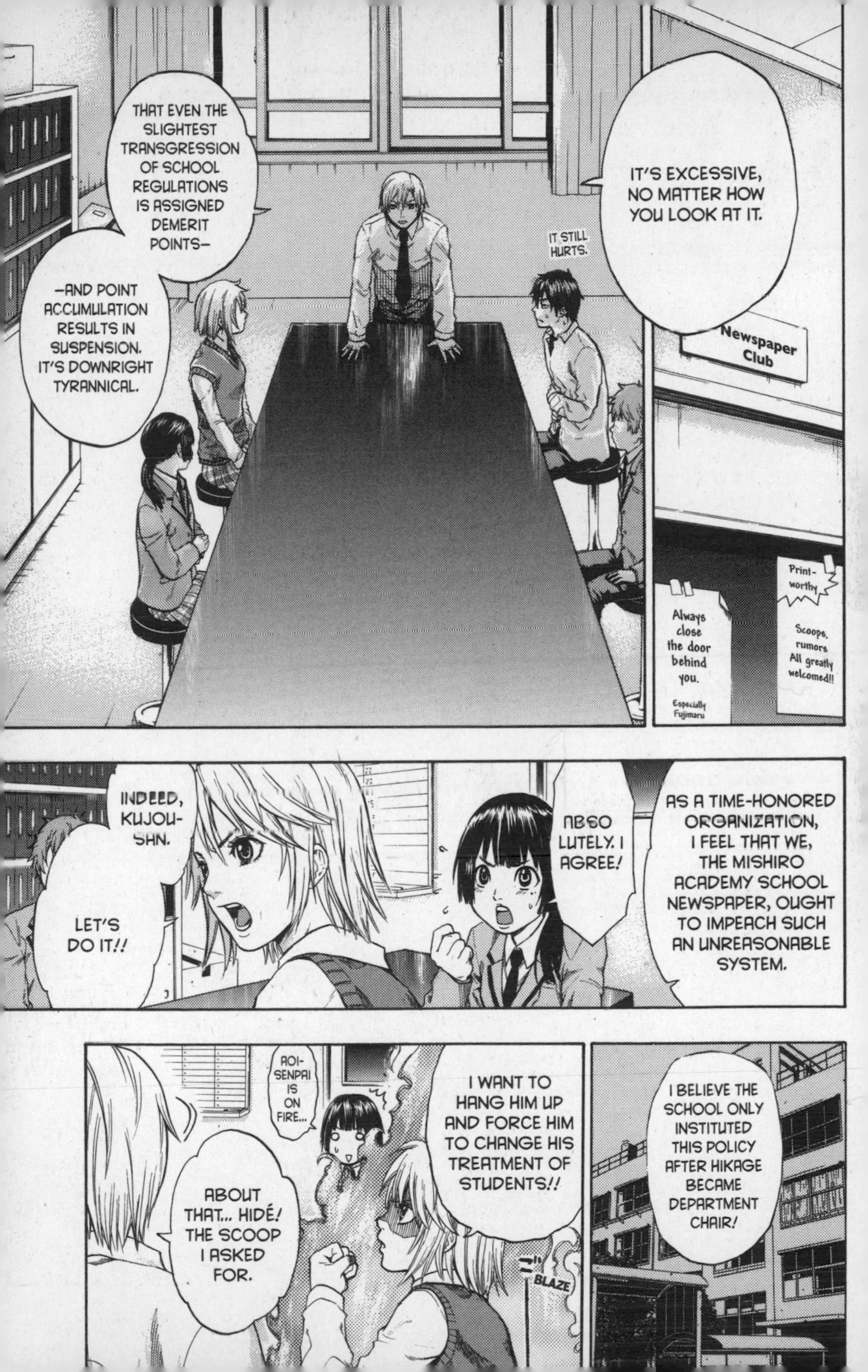
Newspaper Club
Print-worthy
Scoops, rumors All greatly welcomed!!
Always close the door behind you.
Especially Fujimaru
IT'S EXCESSIVE, NO MATTER HOW YOU LOOK AT IT.
IT STILL HURTS.
THAT EVEN THE SLIGHTEST TRANSGRESSION OF SCHOOL REGULATIONS IS ASSIGNED DEMERIT POINTS—
—AND POINT ACCUMULATION RESULTS IN SUSPENSION. IT'S DOWNRIGHT TYRANNICAL.
AS A TIME-HONORED ORGANIZATION, I FEEL THAT WE, THE MISHIRO ACADEMY SCHOOL NEWSPAPER, OUGHT TO IMPEACH SUCH AN UNREASONABLE SYSTEM.
ABSO LUTELY. I AGREE!
INDEED, KUJOU-SAN.
LET'S DO IT!!
I BELIEVE THE SCHOOL ONLY INSTITUTED THIS POLICY AFTER HIKAGE BECAME DEPARTMENT CHAIR!
I WANT TO HANG HIM UP AND FORCE HIM TO CHANGE HIS TREATMENT OF STUDENTS!!
AOI-SENPAI IS ON FIRE...
BLAZE
ABOUT THAT... HIDÉ! THE SCOOP I ASKED FOR.

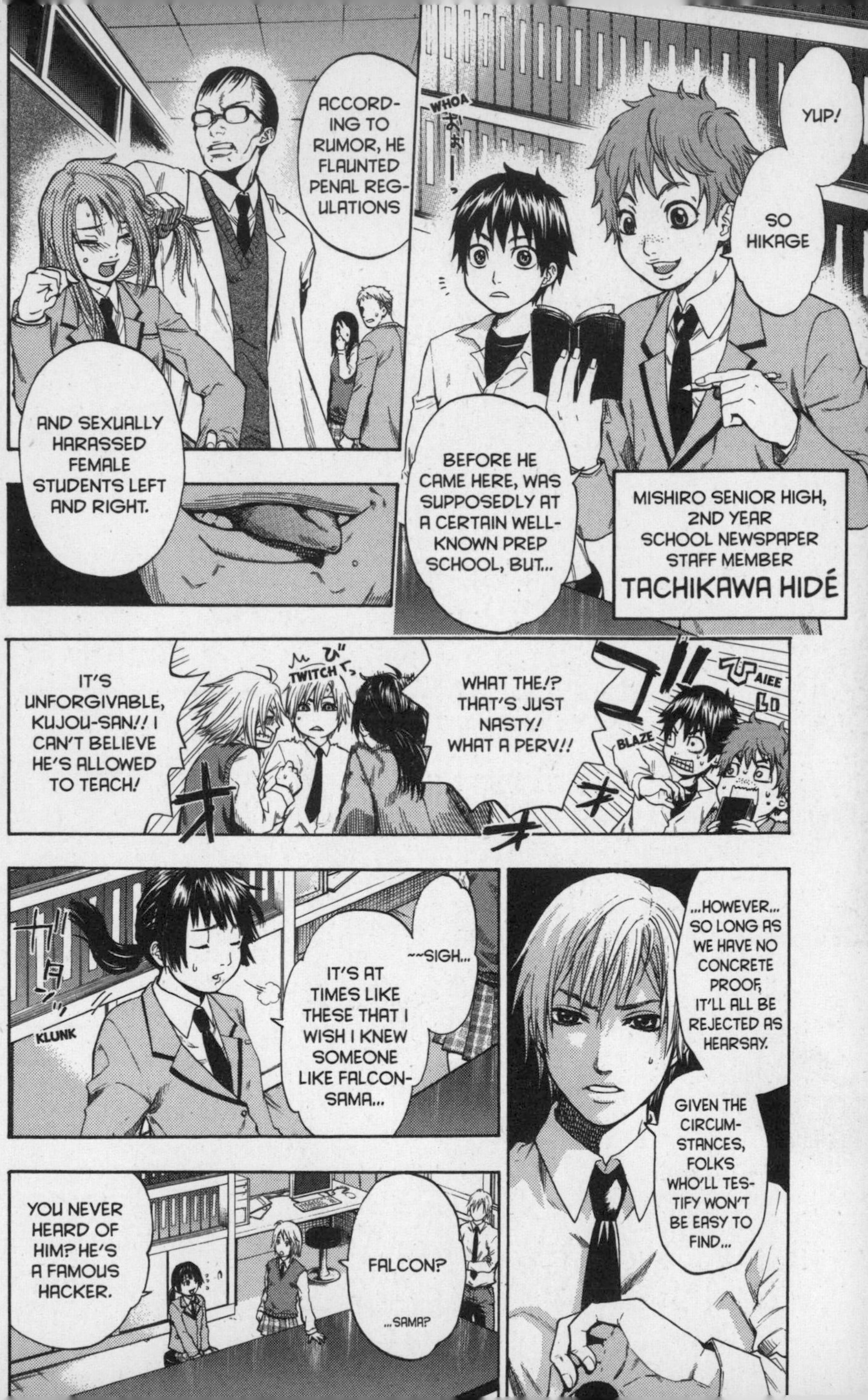
YUP!
SO HIKAGE
WHOA
BEFORE HE CAME HERE, WAS SUPPOSEDLY AT A CERTAIN WELL-KNOWN PREP SCHOOL, BUT...
MISHIRO SENIOR HIGH, 2ND YEAR SCHOOL NEWSPAPER STAFF MEMBER TACHIKAWA HIDÉ
ACCORDING TO RUMOR, HE FLAUNTED PENAL REGULATIONS
AND SEXUALLY HARASSED FEMALE STUDENTS LEFT AND RIGHT.
AIEE
BLAZE
WHAT THE!? THAT'S JUST NASTY! WHAT A PERV!!
TWITCH
IT'S UNFORGIVABLE, KUJOU-SAN!! I CAN'T BELIEVE HE'S ALLOWED TO TEACH!
...HOWEVER... SO LONG AS WE HAVE NO CONCRETE PROOF, IT'LL ALL BE REJECTED AS HEARSAY.
GIVEN THE CIRCUMSTANCES, FOLKS WHO'LL TESTIFY WON'T BE EASY TO FIND...
~~SIGH...
IT'S AT TIMES LIKE THESE THAT I WISH I KNEW SOMEONE LIKE FALCON-SAMA...
KLUNK
FALCON?
...SAMA?
YOU NEVER HEARD OF HIM? HE'S A FAMOUS HACKER.

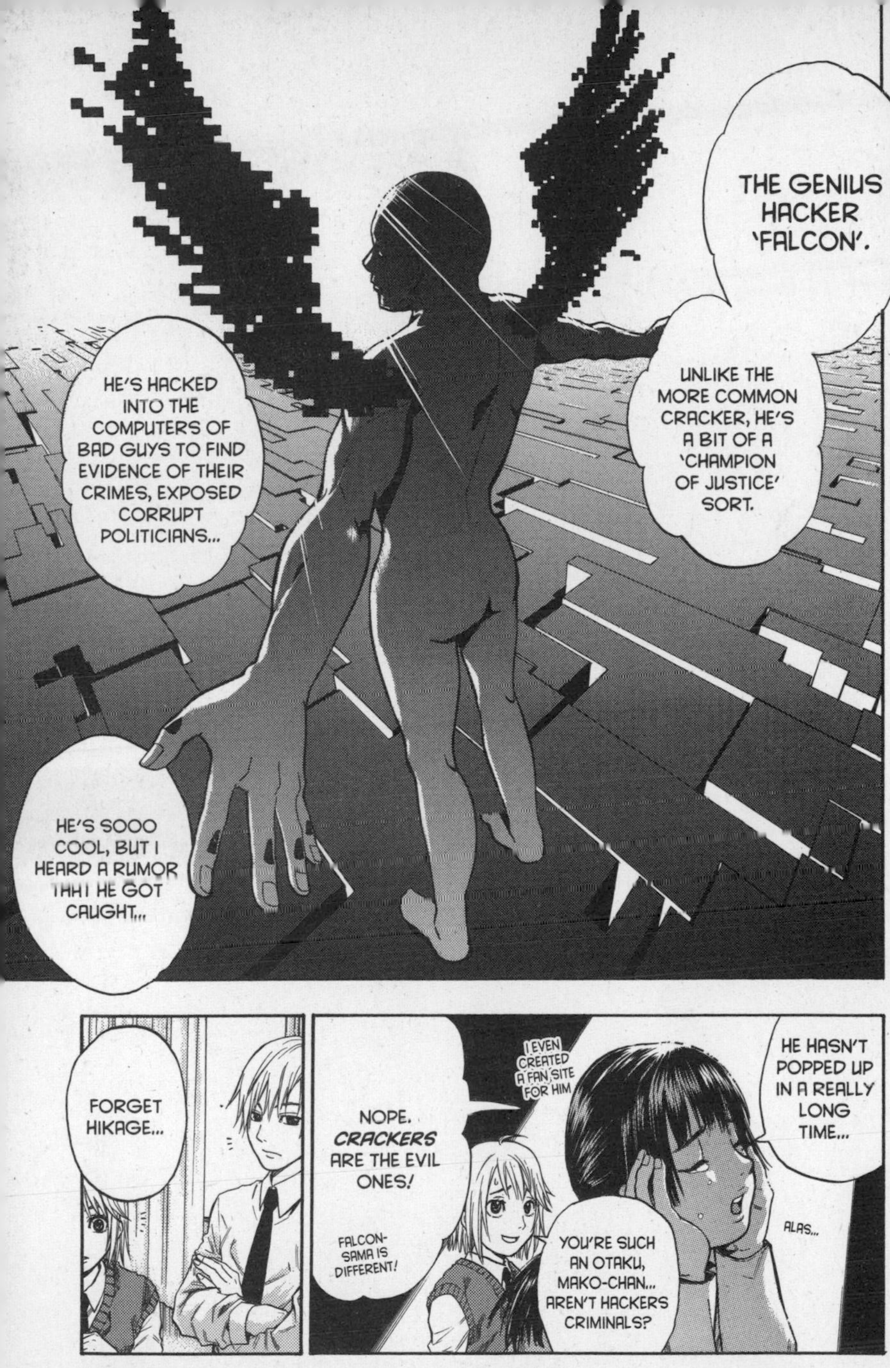
THE GENIUS HACKER 'FALCON'.
UNLIKE THE MORE COMMON CRACKER, HE'S A BIT OF A 'CHAMPION OF JUSTICE' SORT.
HE'S HACKED INTO THE COMPUTERS OF BAD GUYS TO FIND EVIDENCE OF THEIR CRIMES, EXPOSED CORRUPT POLITICIANS...
HE'S SOOO COOL, BUT I HEARD A RUMOR THAT HE GOT CAUGHT...
HE HASN'T POPPED UP IN A REALLY LONG TIME...
ALAS...
I EVEN CREATED A FAN SITE FOR HIM
YOU'RE SUCH AN OTAKU, MAKO-CHAN... AREN'T HACKERS CRIMINALS?
NOPE. *CRACKERS* ARE THE EVIL ONES!
FALCON-SAMA IS DIFFERENT!
FORGET HIKAGE...

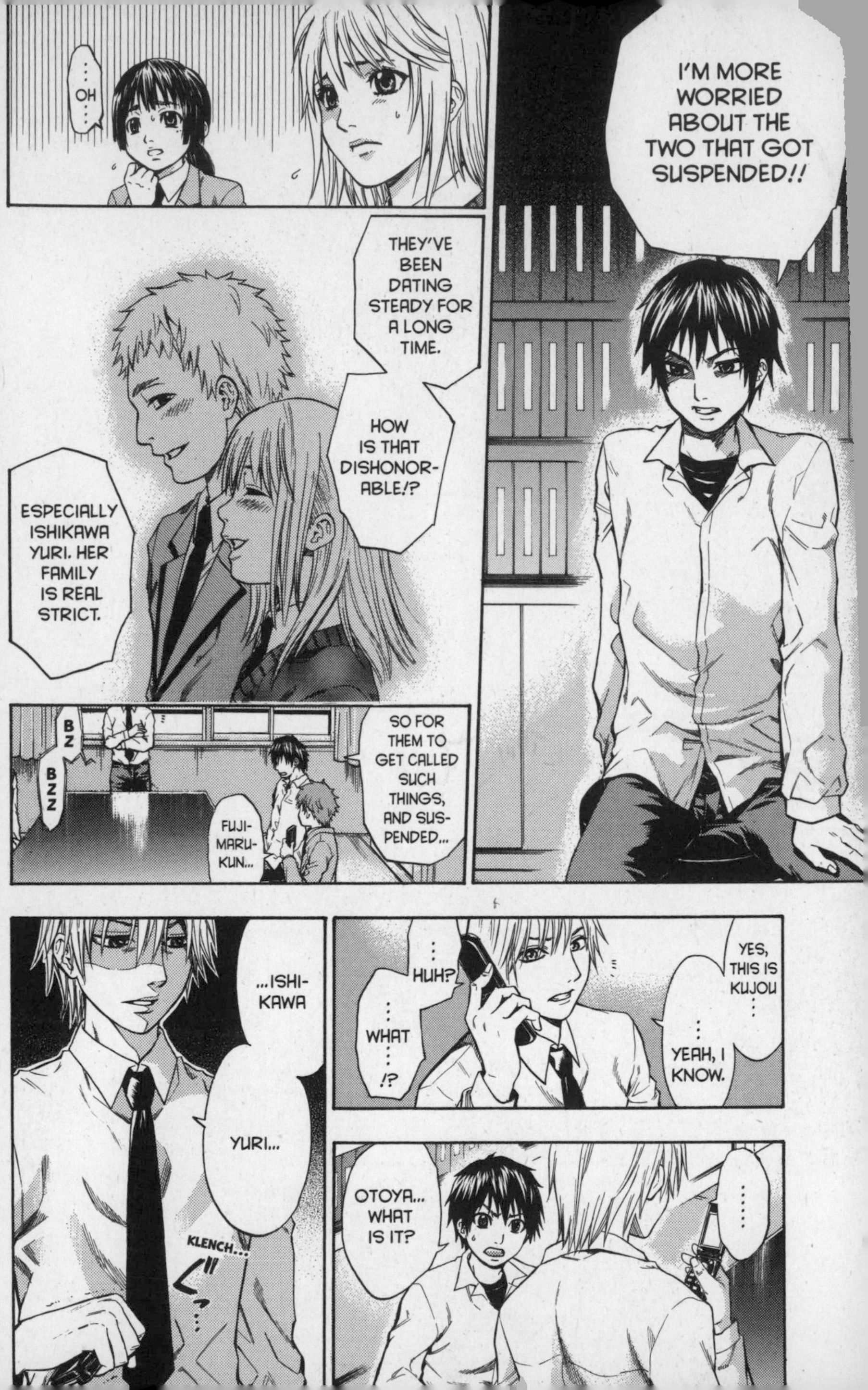
I'M MORE WORRIED ABOUT THE TWO THAT GOT SUSPENDED!!
...OH...
THEY'VE BEEN DATING STEADY FOR A LONG TIME.
HOW IS THAT DISHONOR-ABLE!?
ESPECIALLY ISHIKAWA YURI. HER FAMILY IS REAL STRICT.
SO FOR THEM TO GET CALLED SUCH THINGS, AND SUS-PENDED...
BZ
BZZ
FUJI-MARU-KUN...
YES, THIS IS KUJOU...
...YEAH, I KNOW.
...HUH?
...WHAT...!?
......
OTOYA... WHAT IS IT?
...ISHI-KAWA
YURI...
KLENCH...

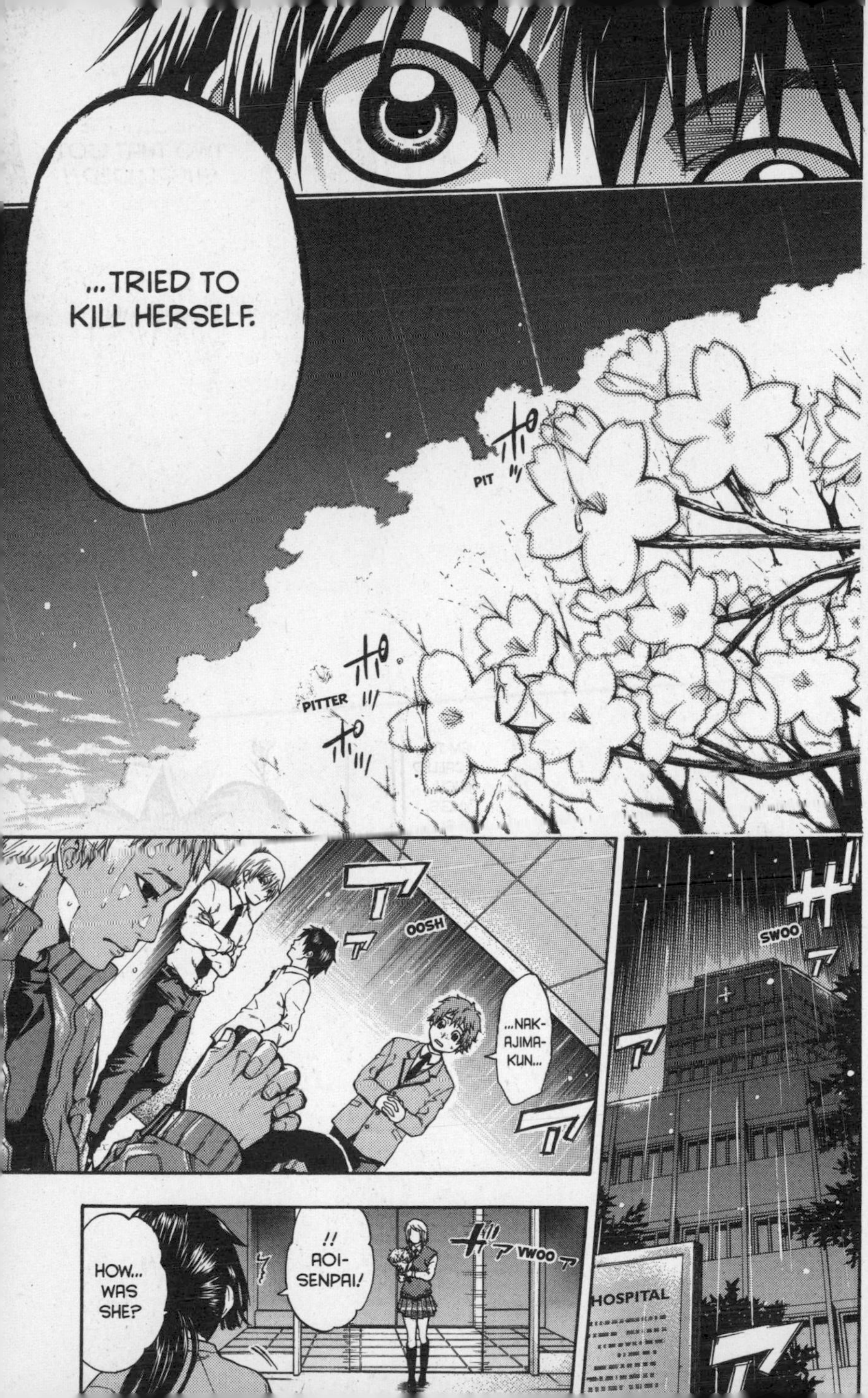
...TRIED TO KILL HERSELF.
PIT
PITTER
SWOO
HOSPITAL
OOSH
...NAKAJIMA-KUN...
VWOO
!! AOI-SENPAI!
HOW... WAS SHE?

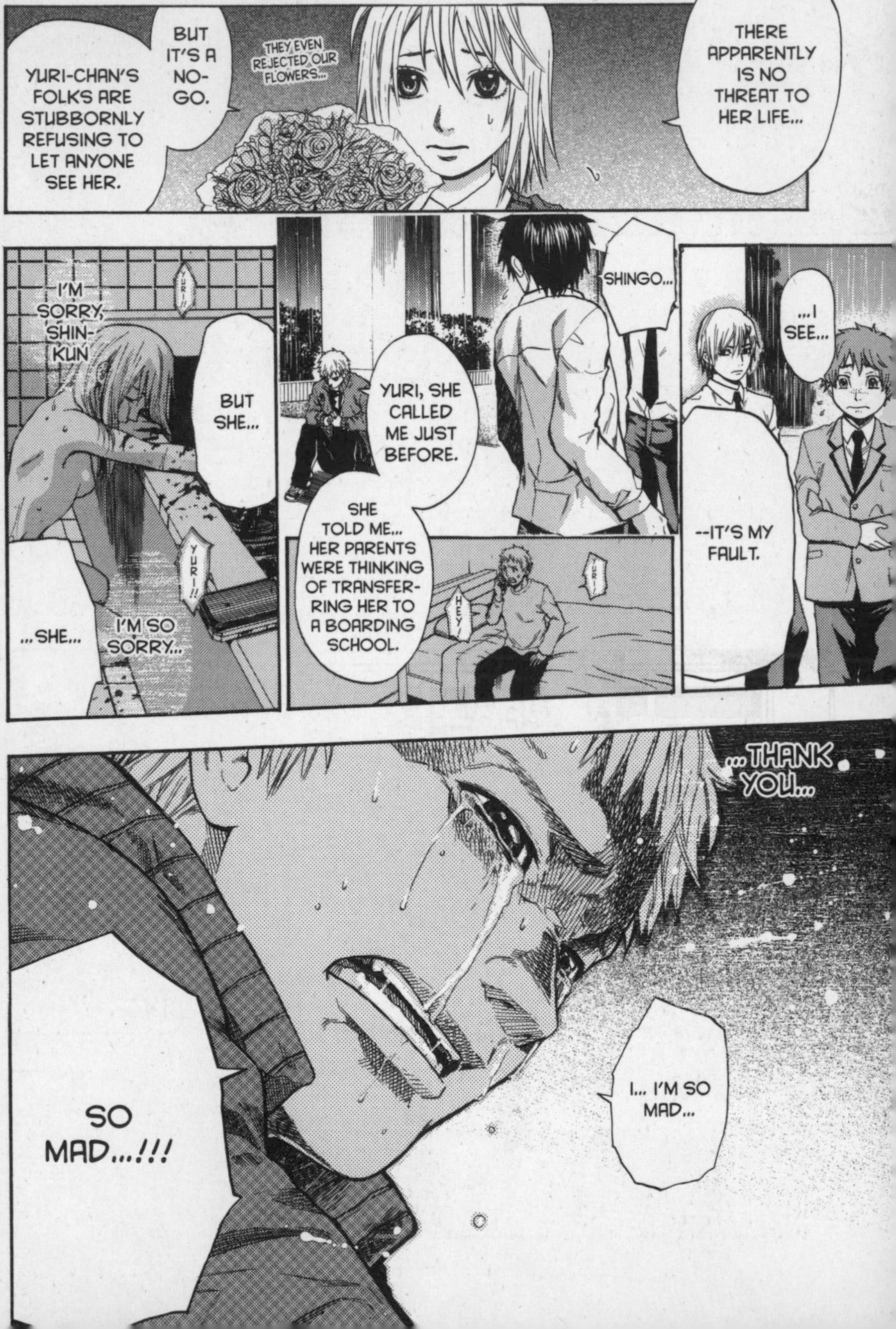
THERE APPARENTLY IS NO THREAT TO HER LIFE...
THEY EVEN REJECTED OUR FLOWERS...
BUT IT'S A NO-GO.
YURI-CHAN'S FOLKS ARE STUBBORNLY REFUSING TO LET ANYONE SEE HER.
...I SEE...
--IT'S MY FAULT.
SHINGO...
YURI, SHE CALLED ME JUST BEFORE.
SHE TOLD ME... HER PARENTS WERE THINKING OF TRANSFER-RING HER TO A BOARDING SCHOOL.
YURI!
HEY!
YURI!!
I'M SORRY, SHIN-KUN
BUT SHE...
YURI!!
I'M SO SORRY...
...SHE...
...THANK YOU...
I... I'M SO MAD...
SO MAD...!!!

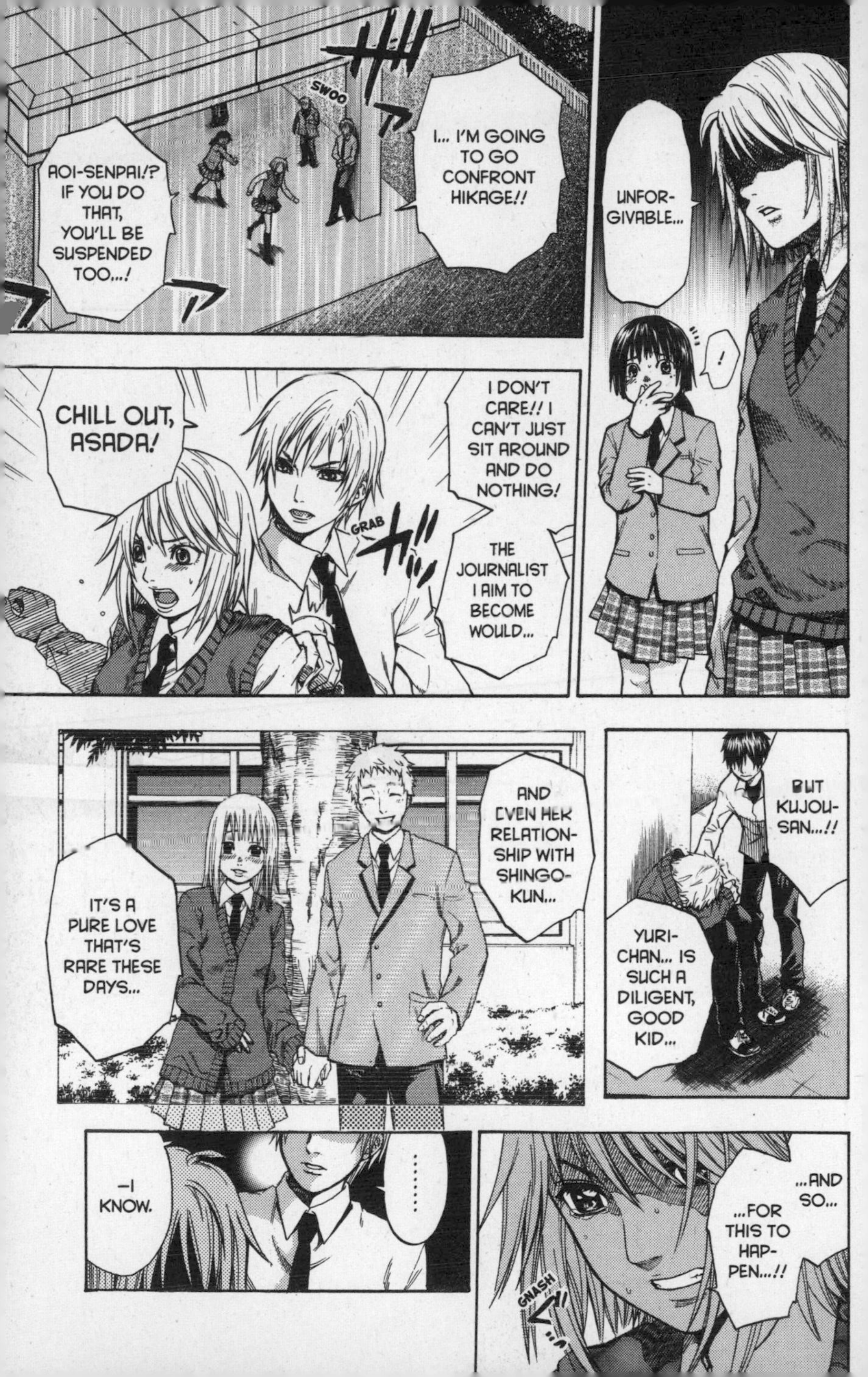
UNFORGIVABLE...
!
I... I'M GOING TO GO CONFRONT HIKAGE!!
SWOO
AOI-SENPAI!? IF YOU DO THAT, YOU'LL BE SUSPENDED TOO...!
I DON'T CARE!! I CAN'T JUST SIT AROUND AND DO NOTHING!
GRAB
THE JOURNALIST I AIM TO BECOME WOULD...
CHILL OUT, ASADA!
BUT KUJOU-SAN...!!
YURI-CHAN... IS SUCH A DILIGENT, GOOD KID...
AND EVEN HER RELATIONSHIP WITH SHINGO-KUN...
IT'S A PURE LOVE THAT'S RARE THESE DAYS...
...AND SO...
...FOR THIS TO HAPPEN...!!
GNASH
......
—I KNOW.

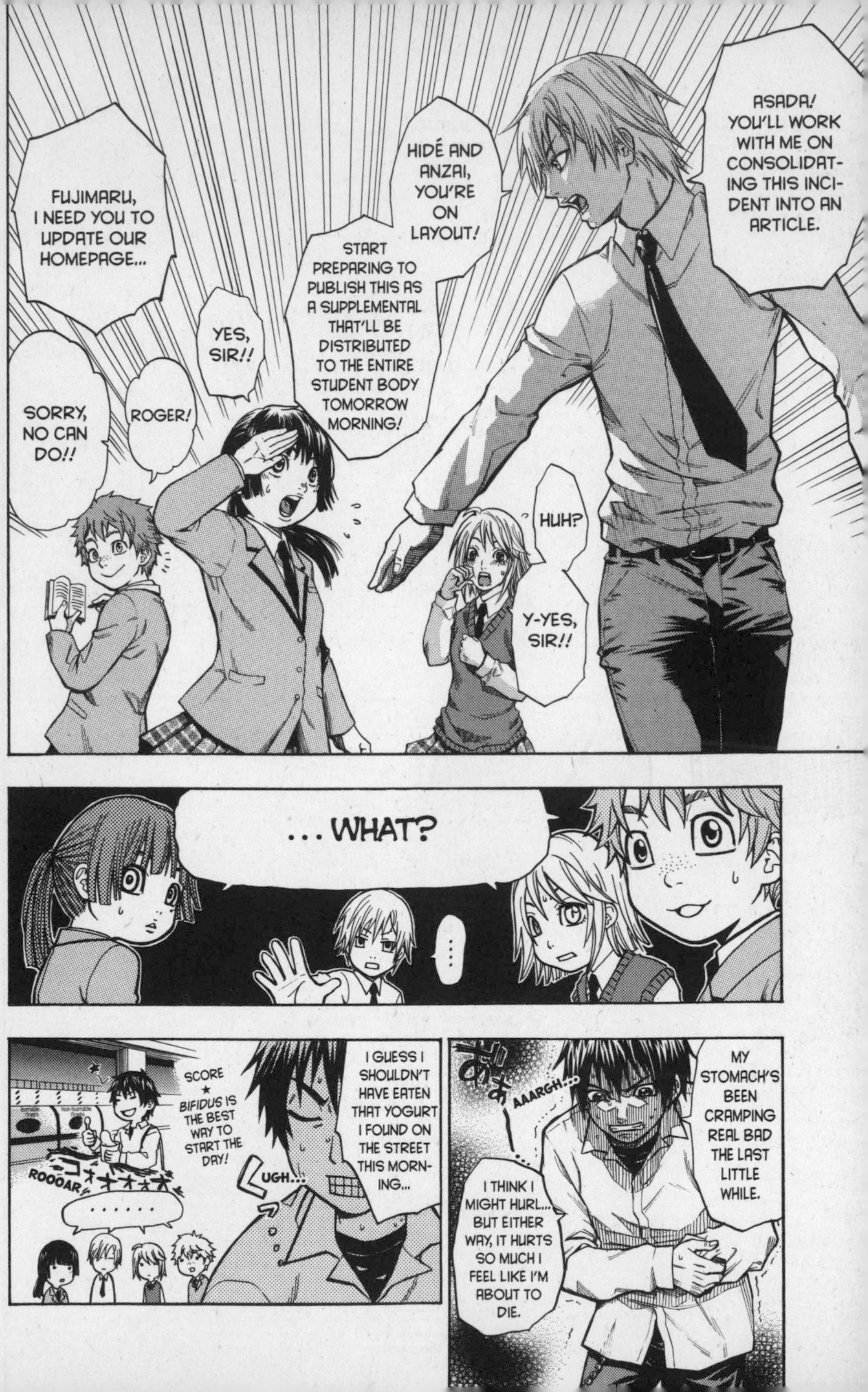
ASADA! YOU'LL WORK WITH ME ON CONSOLIDATING THIS INCIDENT INTO AN ARTICLE.
HIDÉ AND ANZAI, YOU'RE ON LAYOUT!
START PREPARING TO PUBLISH THIS AS A SUPPLEMENTAL THAT'LL BE DISTRIBUTED TO THE ENTIRE STUDENT BODY TOMORROW MORNING!
FUJIMARU, I NEED YOU TO UPDATE OUR HOMEPAGE...
HUH?
Y-YES, SIR!!
YES, SIR!!
ROGER!
SORRY, NO CAN DO!!
... WHAT?
....
MY STOMACH'S BEEN CRAMPING REAL BAD THE LAST LITTLE WHILE.
AAARGH...
I THINK I MIGHT HURL... BUT EITHER WAY, IT HURTS SO MUCH I FEEL LIKE I'M ABOUT TO DIE.
I GUESS I SHOULDN'T HAVE EATEN THAT YOGURT I FOUND ON THE STREET THIS MORNING...
UGH...
SCORE ★ BIFIDUS IS THE BEST WAY TO START THE DAY!
ROOOAR
......

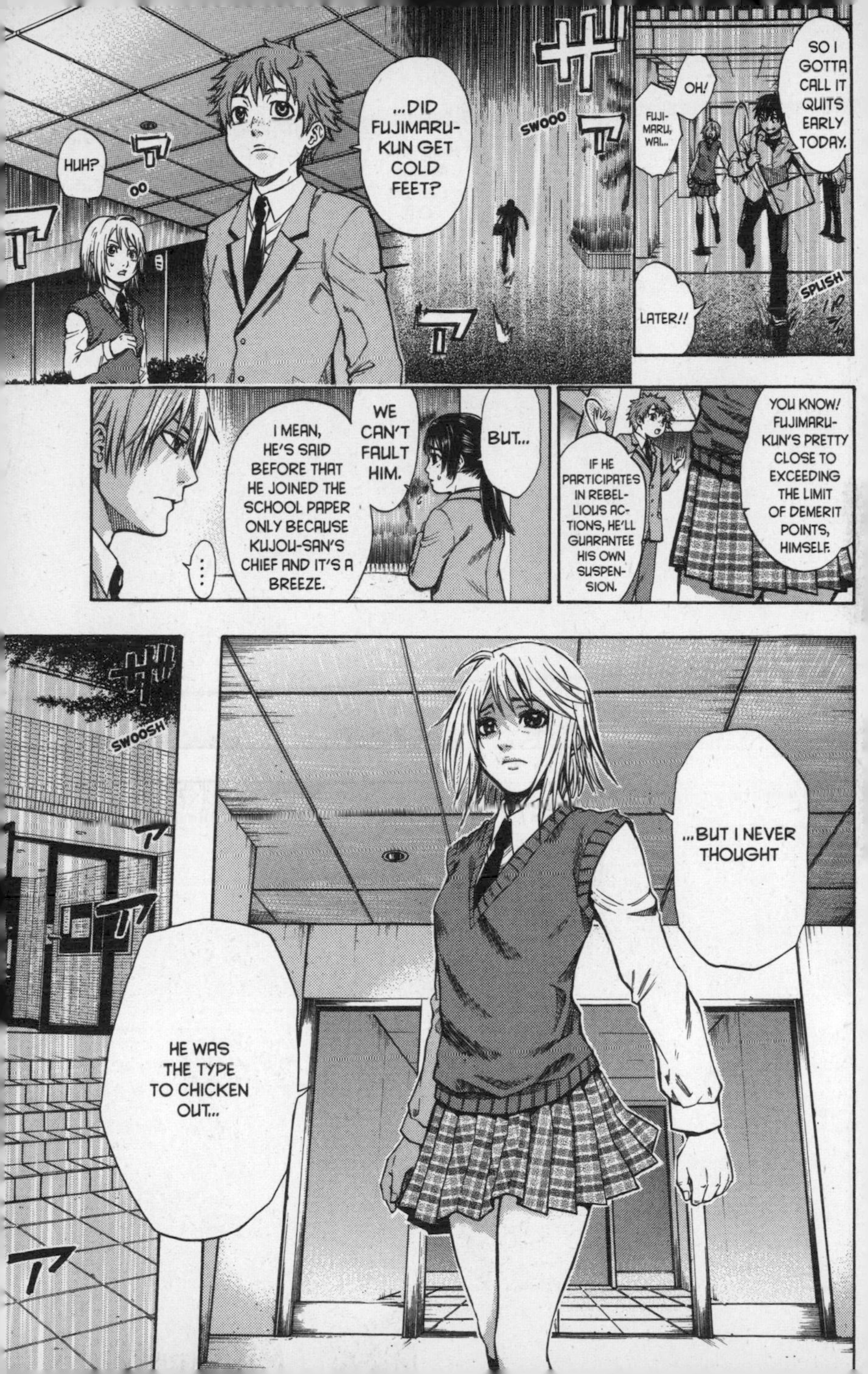
SO I GOTTA CALL IT QUITS EARLY TODAY.
OH!
FUJI-MARU, WAI...
LATER!!
SPLISH
SWOOO
...DID FUJIMARU-KUN GET COLD FEET?
HUH?
YOU KNOW! FUJIMARU-KUN'S PRETTY CLOSE TO EXCEEDING THE LIMIT OF DEMERIT POINTS, HIMSELF.
IF HE PARTICIPATES IN REBEL-LIOUS AC-TIONS, HE'LL GUARANTEE HIS OWN SUSPEN-SION.
BUT...
WE CAN'T FAULT HIM.
I MEAN, HE'S SAID BEFORE THAT HE JOINED THE SCHOOL PAPER ONLY BECAUSE KUJOU-SAN'S CHIEF AND IT'S A BREEZE.
....
...BUT I NEVER THOUGHT
HE WAS THE TYPE TO CHICKEN OUT...
SWOOSH

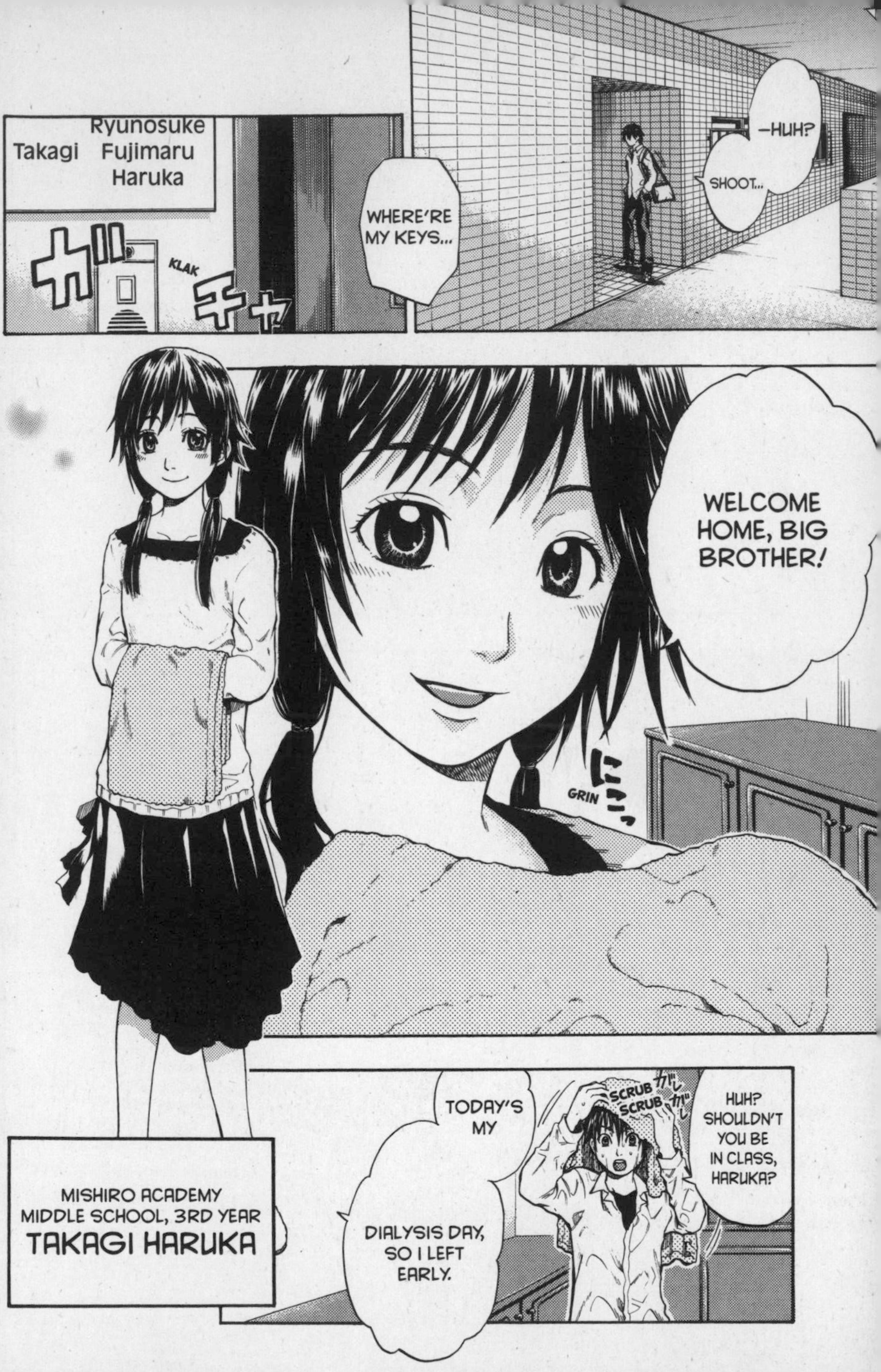
—HUH?
SHOOT...
WHERE'RE MY KEYS...
Ryunosuke
Takagi Fujimaru
Haruka
カチャ
KLAK
WELCOME HOME, BIG BROTHER!
にこっ
GRIN
MISHIRO ACADEMY
MIDDLE SCHOOL, 3RD YEAR
TAKAGI HARUKA
SCRUB SCRUB
HUH? SHOULDN'T YOU BE IN CLASS, HARUKA?
TODAY'S MY
DIALYSIS DAY, SO I LEFT EARLY.

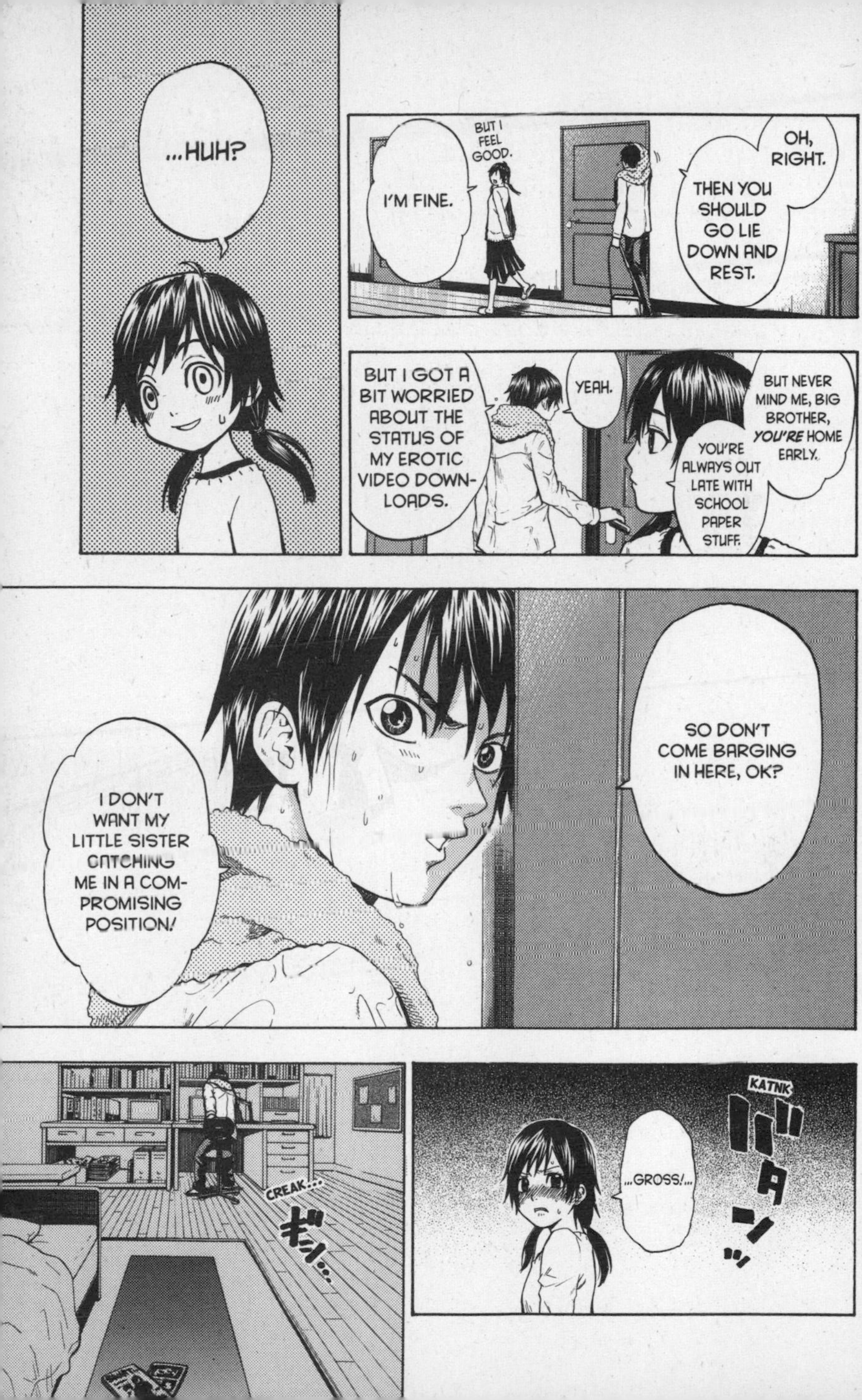
OH, RIGHT. THEN YOU SHOULD GO LIE DOWN AND REST.
BUT I FEEL GOOD.
I'M FINE.
BUT NEVER MIND ME, BIG BROTHER, *YOU'RE* HOME EARLY.
YOU'RE ALWAYS OUT LATE WITH SCHOOL PAPER STUFF.
YEAH.
BUT I GOT A BIT WORRIED ABOUT THE STATUS OF MY EROTIC VIDEO DOWN-LOADS.
...HUH?
SO DON'T COME BARGING IN HERE, OK?
I DON'T WANT MY LITTLE SISTER CATCHING ME IN A COM-PROMISING POSITION!
KATNK
...GROSS!...
CREAK...

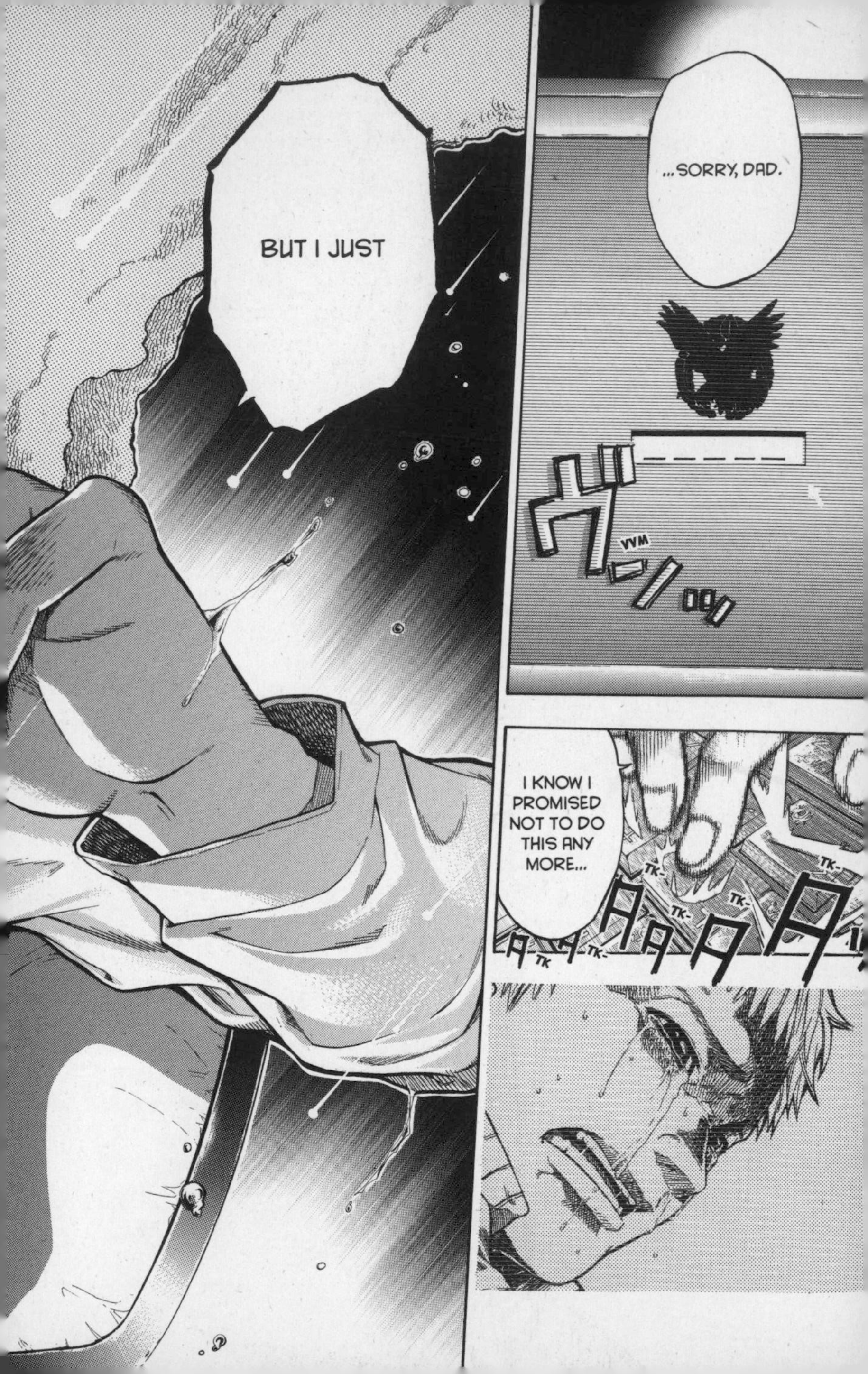
...SORRY, DAD.
VVM
I KNOW I PROMISED NOT TO DO THIS ANY MORE...
TK-
TK-
TK-
TK-
TK-
TK
BUT I JUST

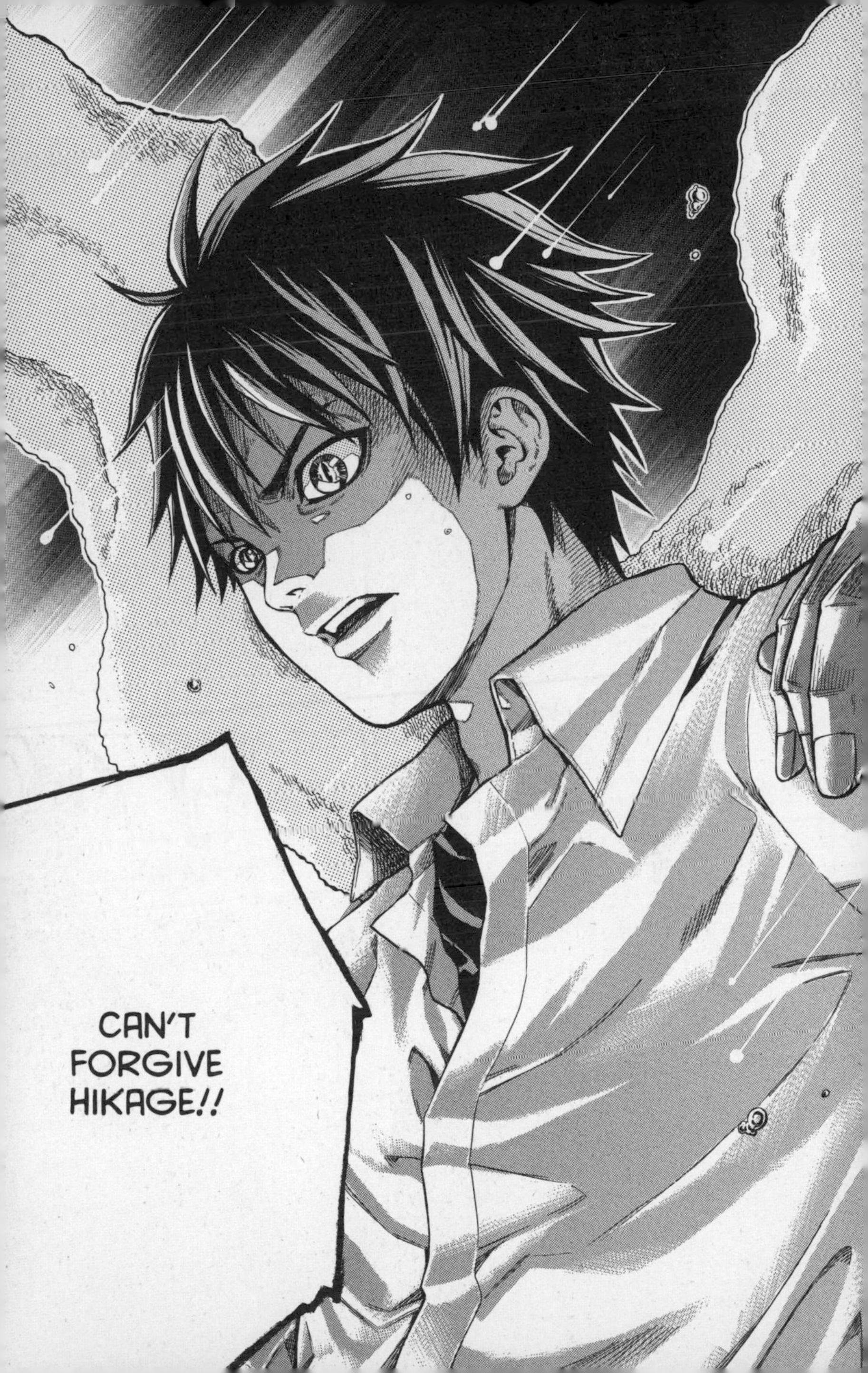
CAN'T FORGIVE HIKAGE!!

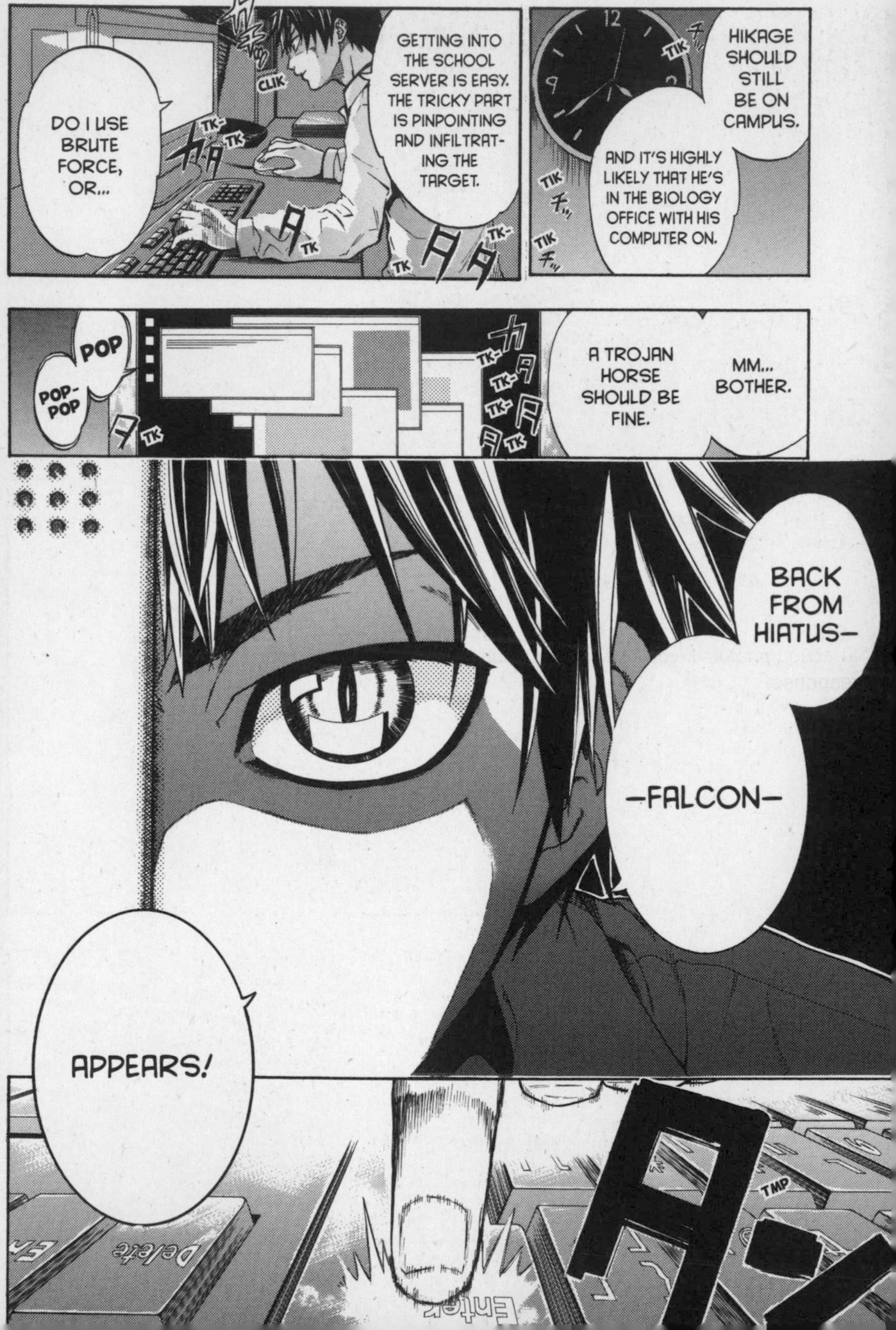
TIK
HIKAGE SHOULD STILL BE ON CAMPUS.
AND IT'S HIGHLY LIKELY THAT HE'S IN THE BIOLOGY OFFICE WITH HIS COMPUTER ON.
TIK
TIK
GETTING INTO THE SCHOOL SERVER IS EASY. THE TRICKY PART IS PINPOINTING AND INFILTRATING THE TARGET.
CLIK
TK-TK
TK
TK
TK-
DO I USE BRUTE FORCE, OR...
MM... BOTHER.
A TROJAN HORSE SHOULD BE FINE.
TK-TK-TK-TK
TK
POP
POP-POP
BACK FROM HIATUS—
—FALCON—
APPEARS!
TMP
Delete

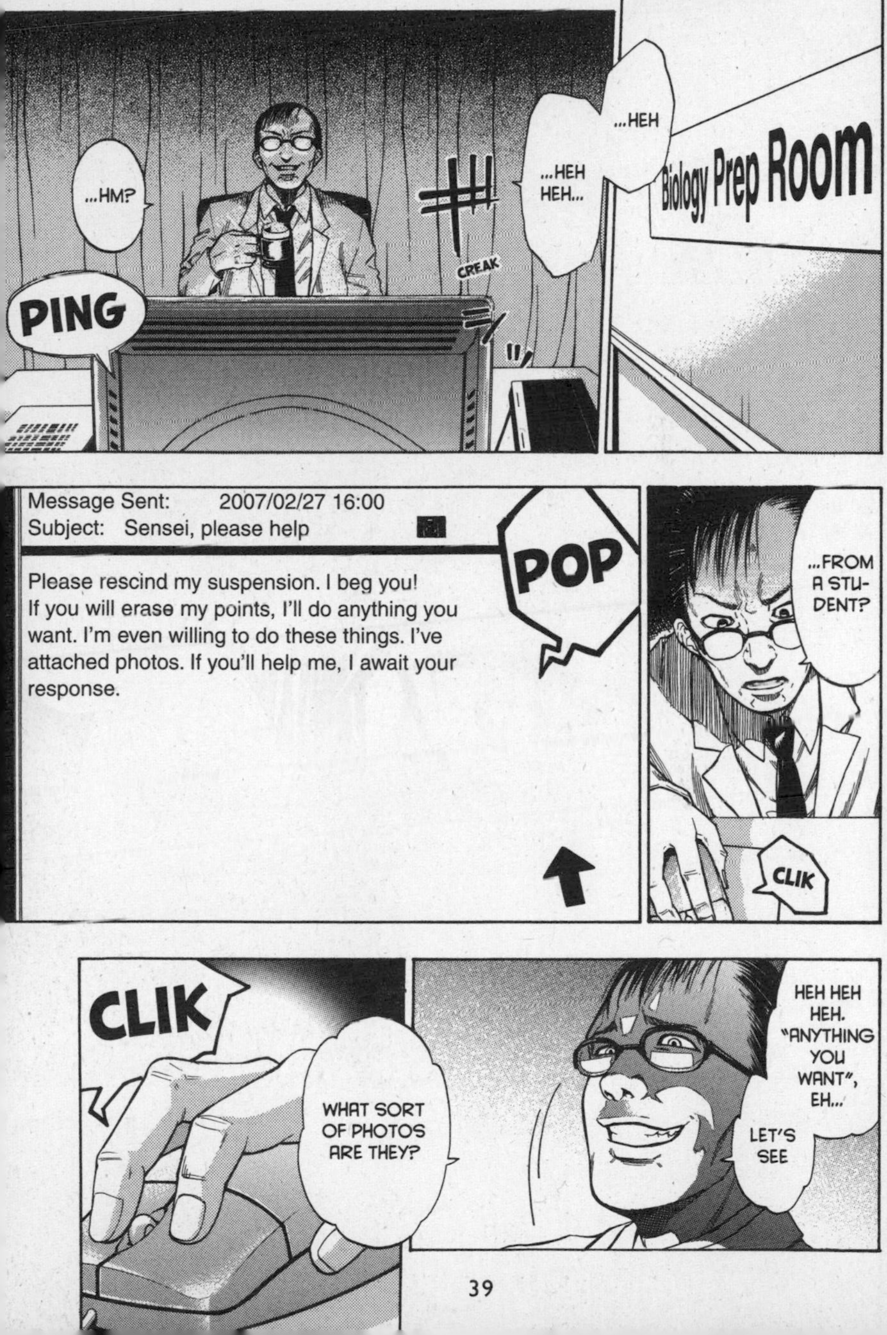
Biology Prep Room
...HEH
...HEH HEH...
CREAK
...HM?
PING
...FROM A STU-DENT?
CLIK
Message Sent: 2007/02/27 16:00
Subject: Sensei, please help
Please rescind my suspension. I beg you! If you will erase my points, I'll do anything you want. I'm even willing to do these things. I've attached photos. If you'll help me, I await your response.
POP
HEH HEH HEH. "ANYTHING YOU WANT", EH...
LET'S SEE
WHAT SORT OF PHOTOS ARE THEY?
CLIK

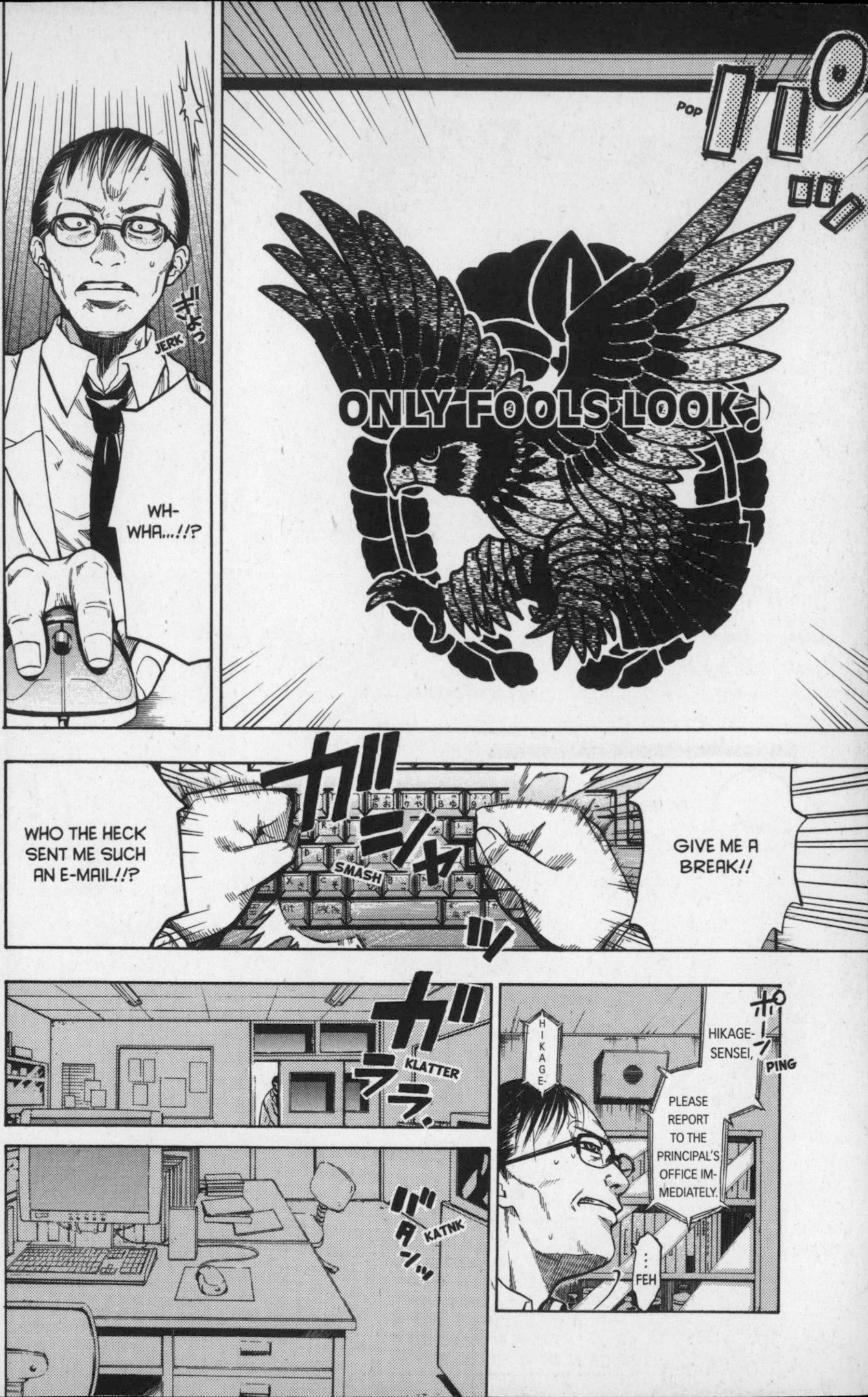
POP
ONLY FOOLS LOOK♪
JERK
WH-
WHA...!!?
GIVE ME A BREAK!!
SMASH
WHO THE HECK SENT ME SUCH AN E-MAIL!!?
HIKAGE-
HIKAGE-SENSEI,
PING
PLEASE REPORT TO THE PRINCIPAL'S OFFICE IM-MEDIATELY.
...FEH
KLATTER
KATNK

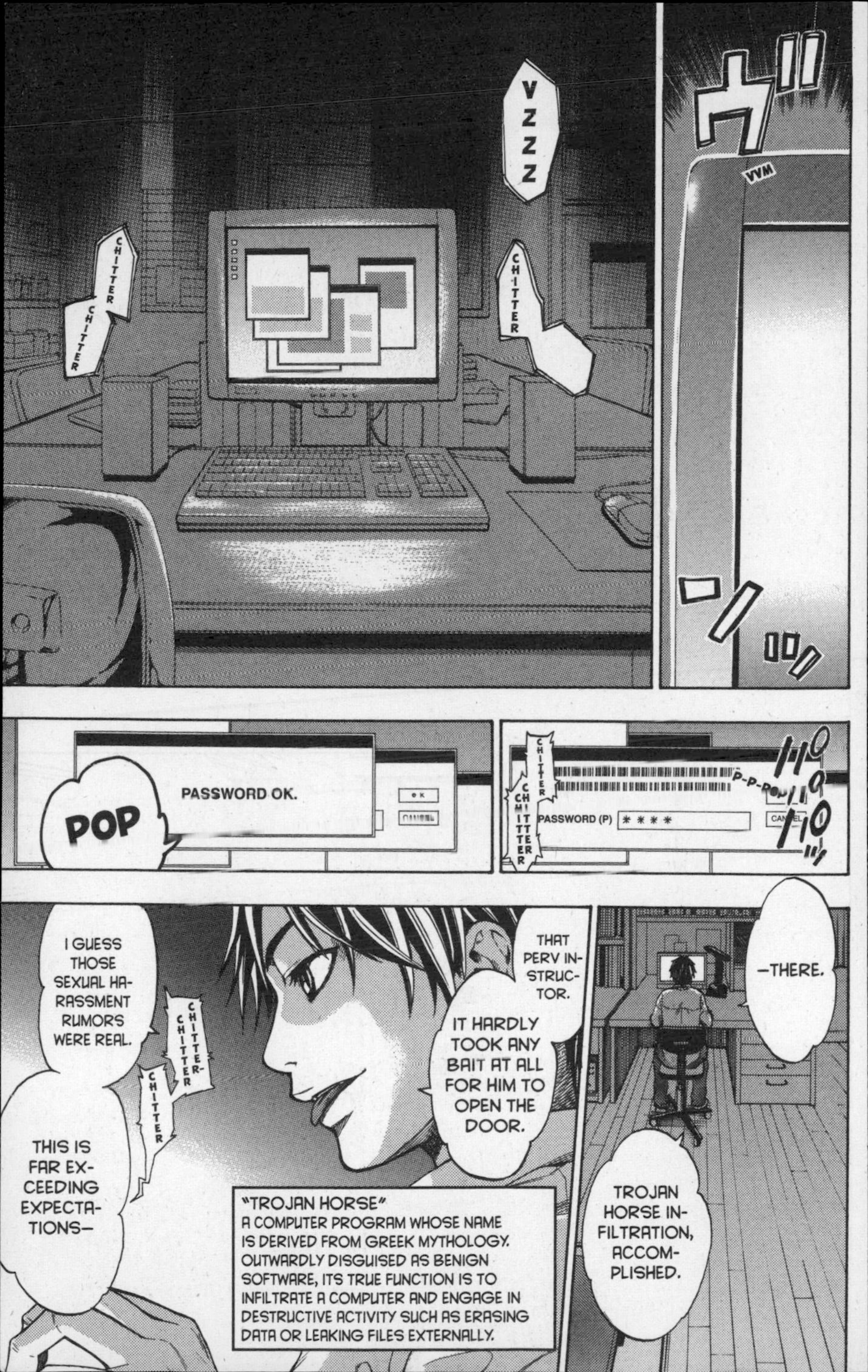
VVM
VZZZ
CHITTER
CHITTER
CHITTER
P-P-POP
CHITTER
CHITTER
PASSWORD (P) ****
POP
PASSWORD OK.
—THERE.
TROJAN HORSE INFILTRATION, ACCOMPLISHED.
THAT PERV INSTRUCTOR.
IT HARDLY TOOK ANY BAIT AT ALL FOR HIM TO OPEN THE DOOR.
I GUESS THOSE SEXUAL HARASSMENT RUMORS WERE REAL.
CHITTER-CHITTER
CHITTER
THIS IS FAR EXCEEDING EXPECTATIONS—
"TROJAN HORSE"
A COMPUTER PROGRAM WHOSE NAME IS DERIVED FROM GREEK MYTHOLOGY. OUTWARDLY DISGUISED AS BENIGN SOFTWARE, ITS TRUE FUNCTION IS TO INFILTRATE A COMPUTER AND ENGAGE IN DESTRUCTIVE ACTIVITY SUCH AS ERASING DATA OR LEAKING FILES EXTERNALLY.

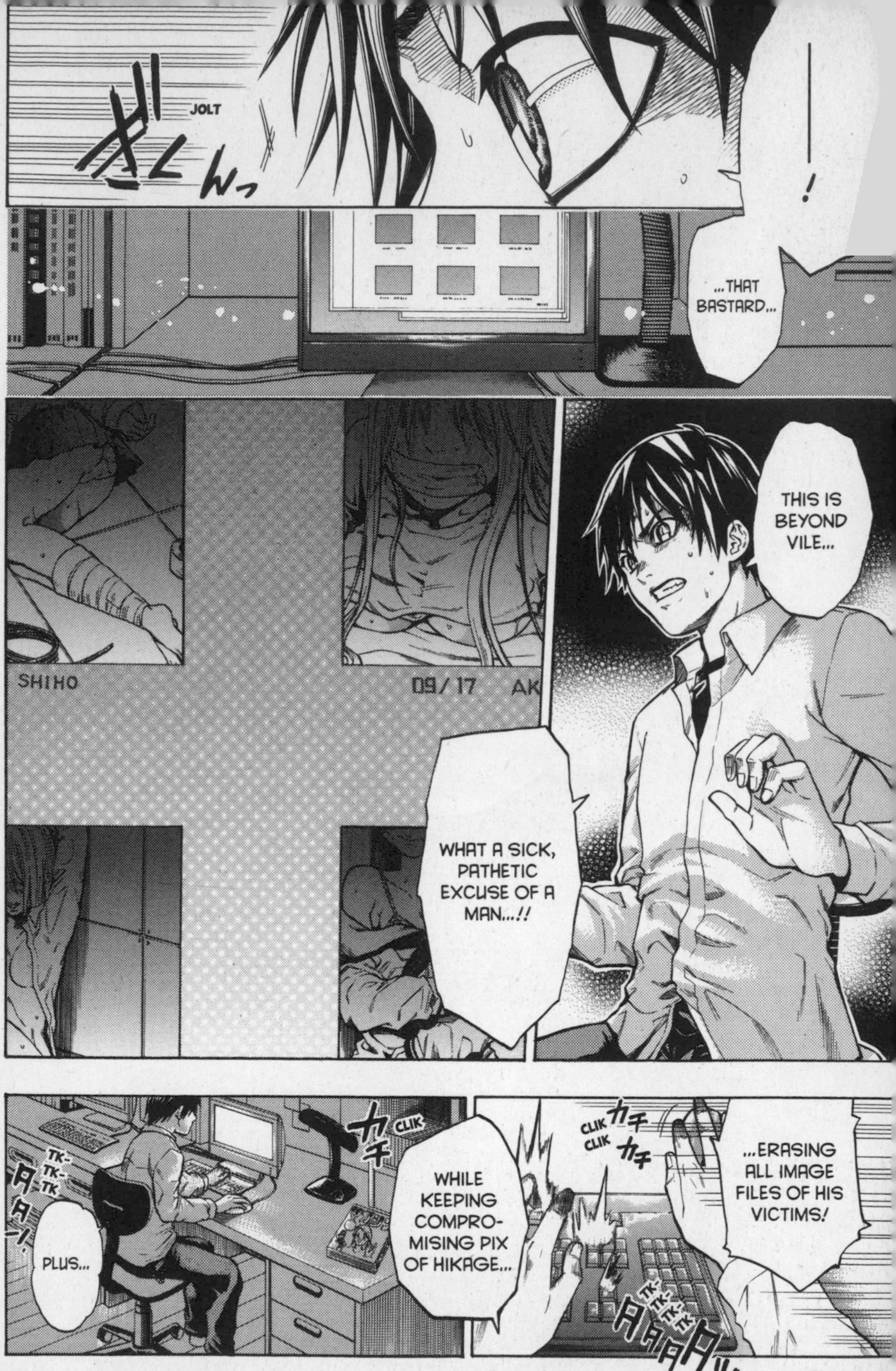
JOLT
—!
...THAT BASTARD...
THIS IS BEYOND VILE...
WHAT A SICK, PATHETIC EXCUSE OF A MAN...!!
SHIHO
09/17 AK
CLIK CLIK
...ERASING ALL IMAGE FILES OF HIS VICTIMS!
TK-TK-TK-TK
WHILE KEEPING COMPRO-MISING PIX OF HIKAGE...
CLIK
TK-TK-TK
PLUS...

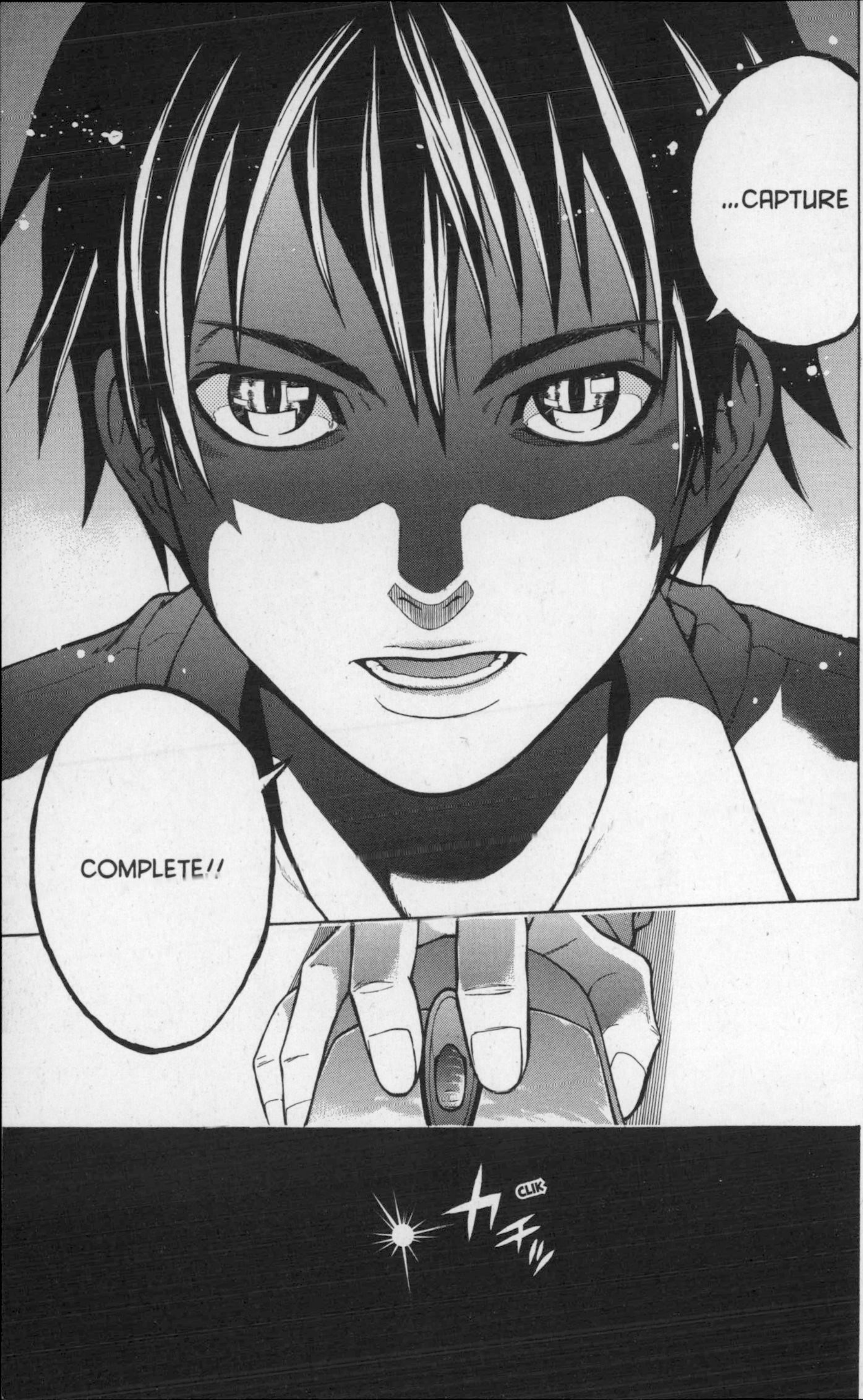
...CAPTURE
COMPLETE!!
CLIK
カチッ

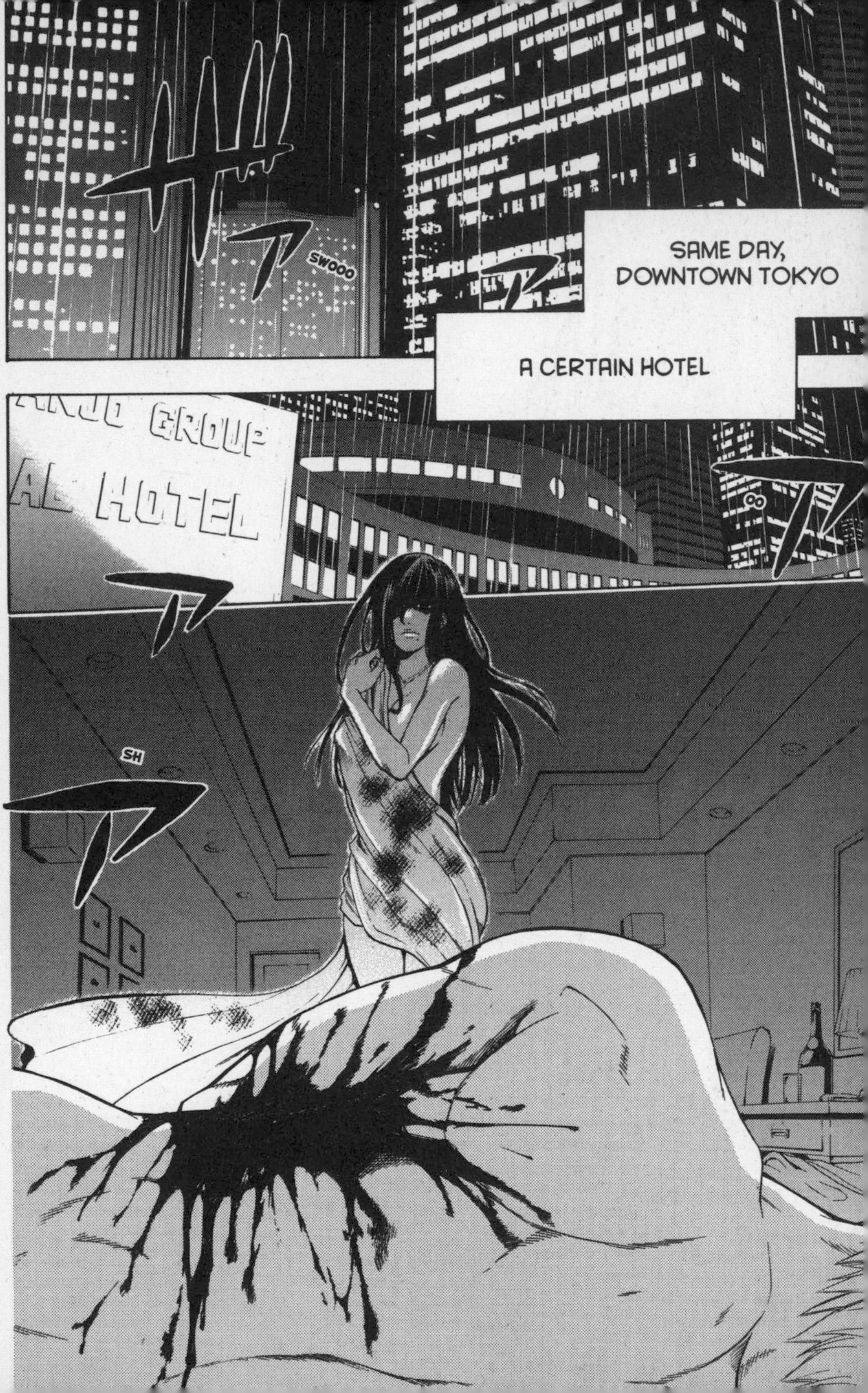
SAME DAY,
DOWNTOWN TOKYO
SWOOO
A CERTAIN HOTEL
GROUP
HOTEL
SH

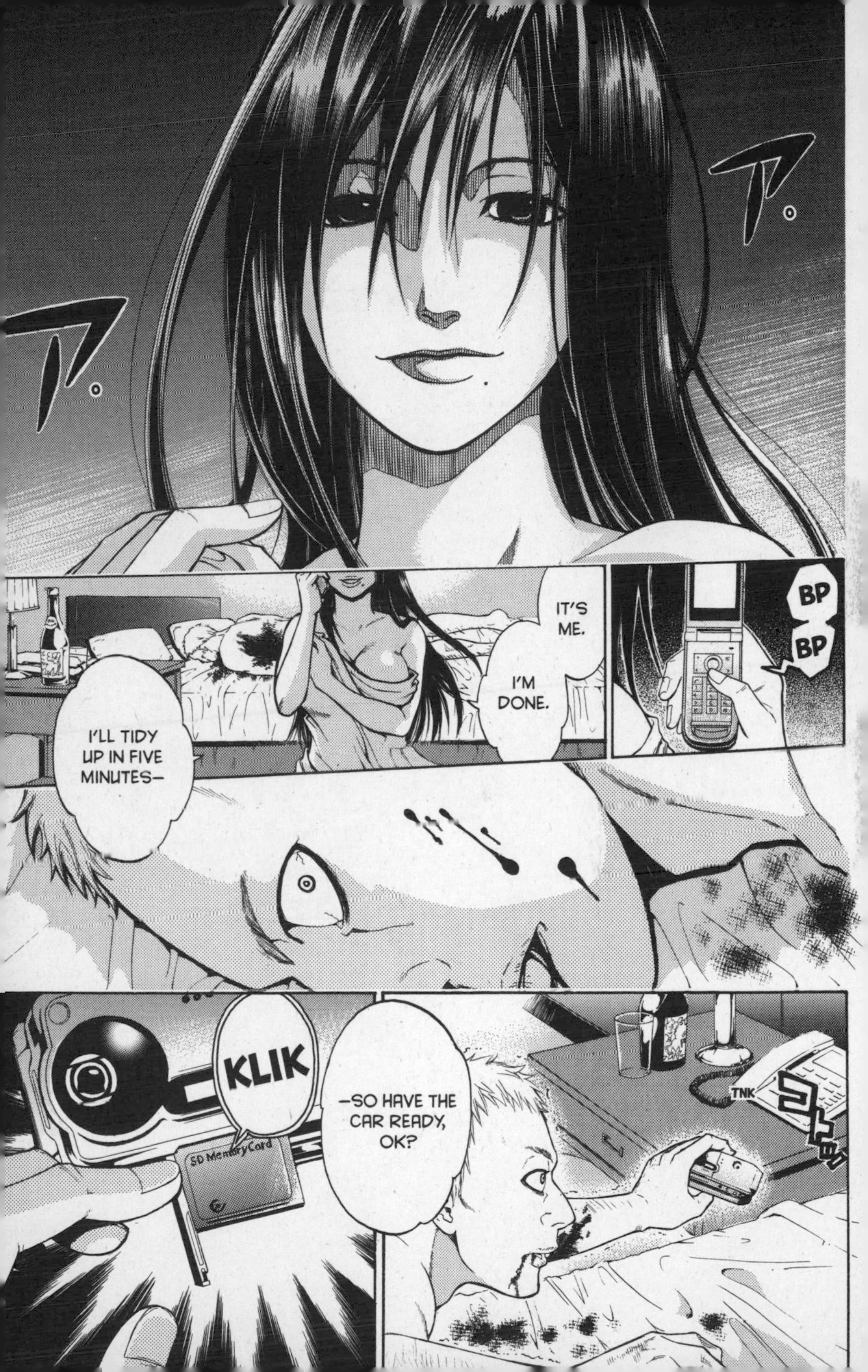
ア.
ア.
BP
BP
IT'S ME.
I'M DONE.
I'LL TIDY UP IN FIVE MINUTES—
—SO HAVE THE CAR READY, OK?
TNK
KLIK
SD MemoryCard

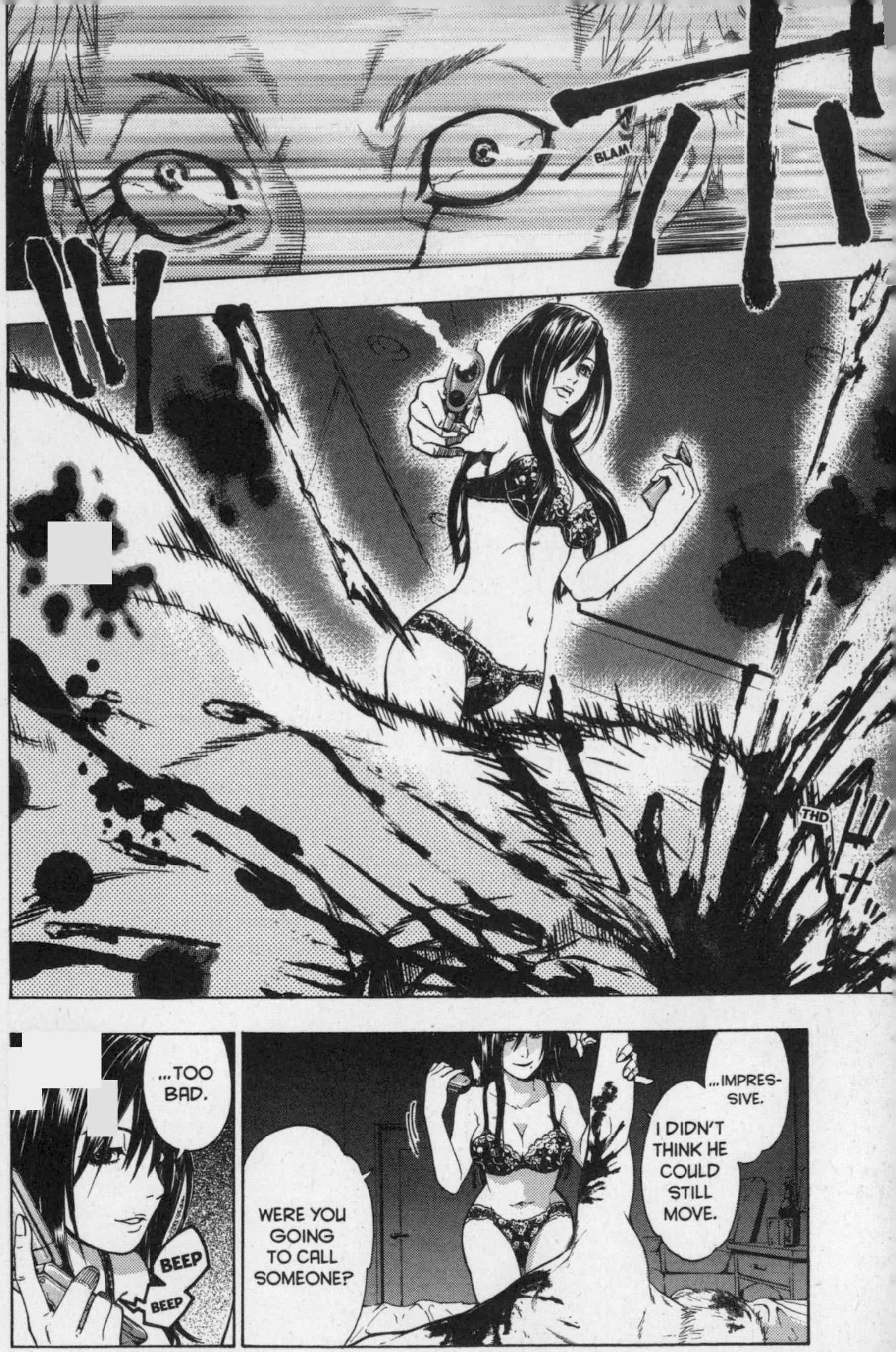
BLAM
THD
...IMPRES-SIVE.
I DIDN'T THINK HE COULD STILL MOVE.
WERE YOU GOING TO CALL SOMEONE?
...TOO BAD.
BEEP
BEEP

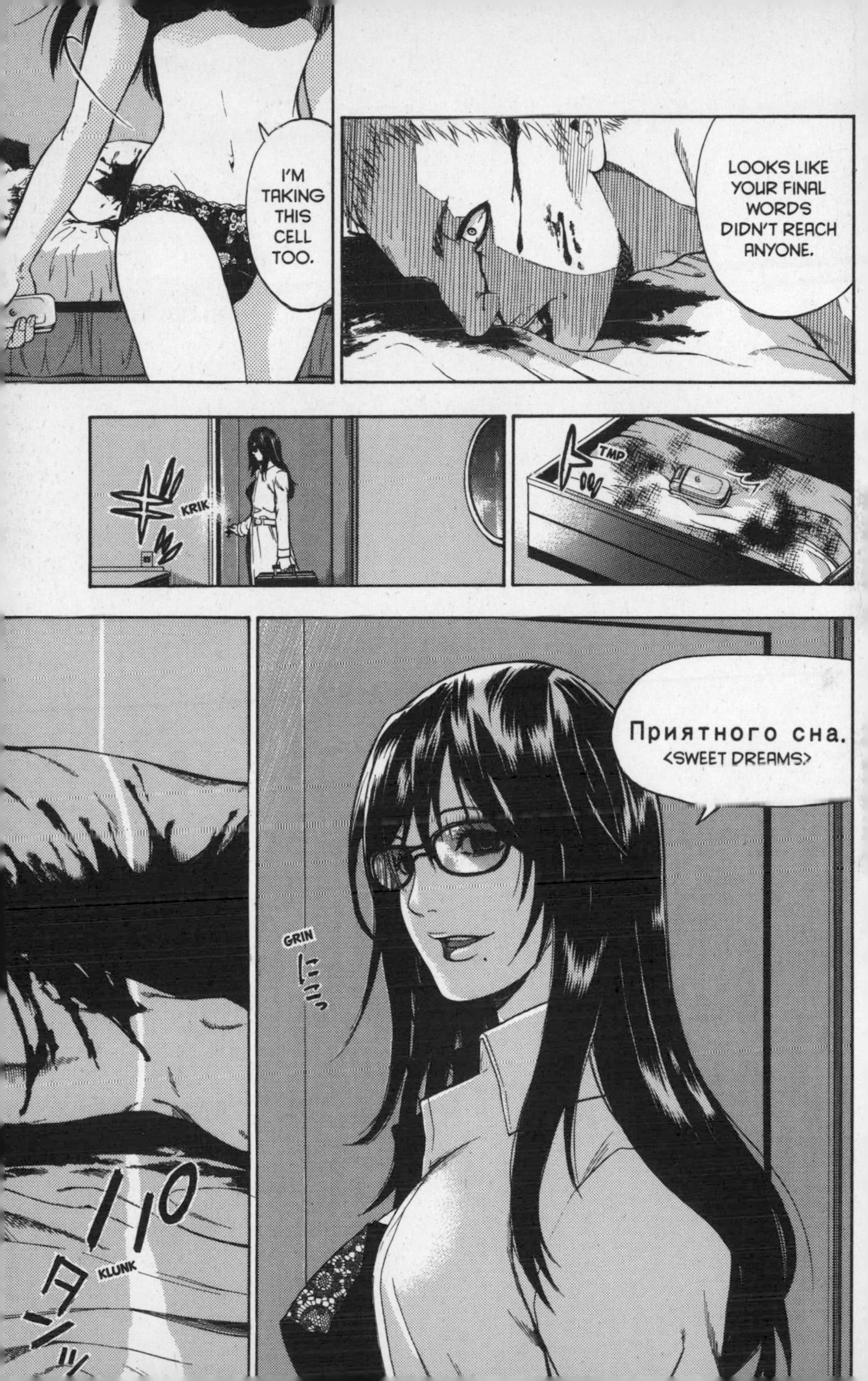
LOOKS LIKE YOUR FINAL WORDS DIDN'T REACH ANYONE.
I'M TAKING THIS CELL TOO.
TMP
KRIK
Приятного сна.
<SWEET DREAMS>
GRIN
KLUNK

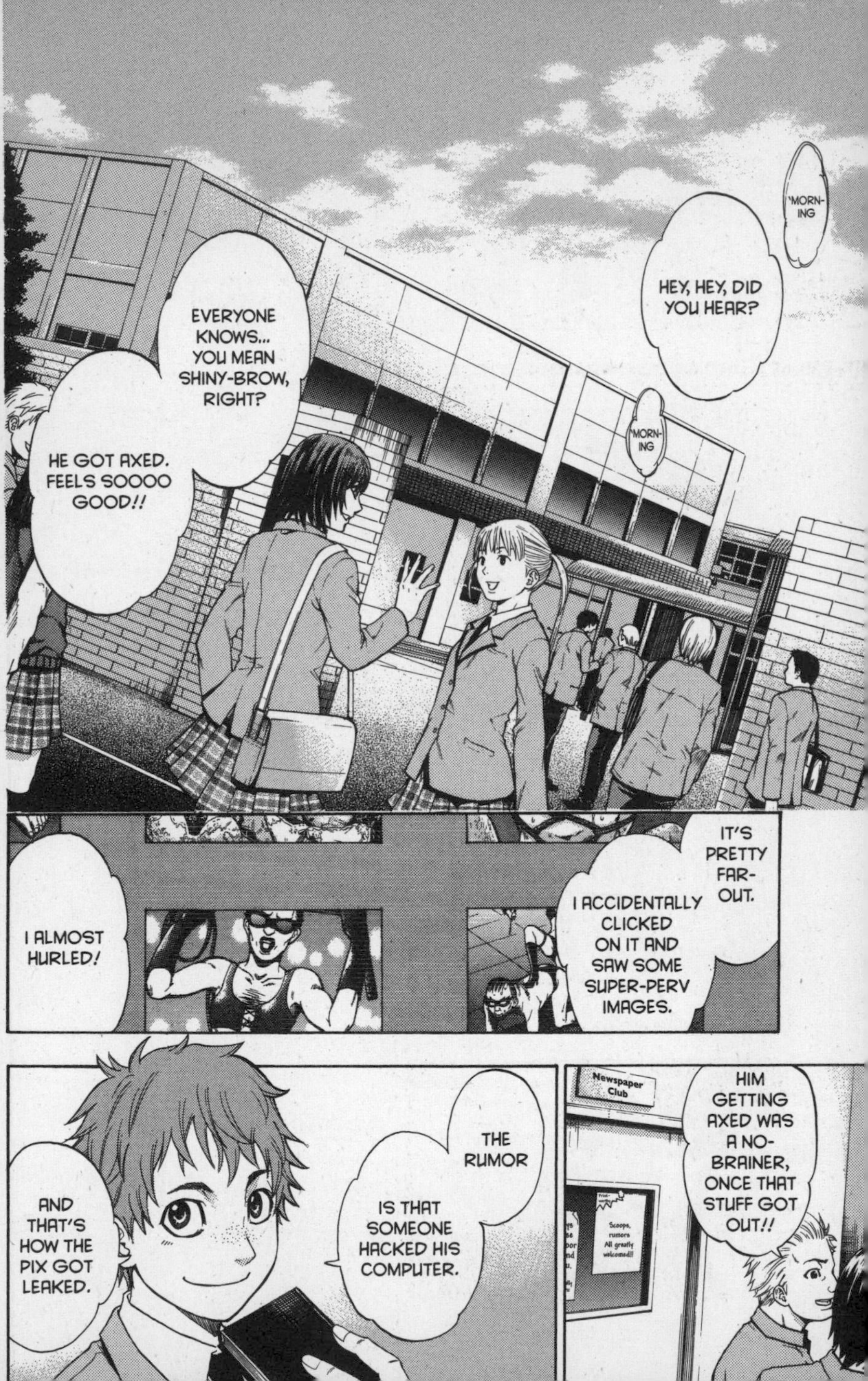
'MORNING
HEY, HEY, DID YOU HEAR?
'MORNING
EVERYONE KNOWS... YOU MEAN SHINY-BROW, RIGHT?
HE GOT AXED. FEELS SOOOO GOOD!!
IT'S PRETTY FAR-OUT.
I ACCIDENTALLY CLICKED ON IT AND SAW SOME SUPER-PERV IMAGES.
I ALMOST HURLED!
Newspaper Club
HIM GETTING AXED WAS A NO-BRAINER, ONCE THAT STUFF GOT OUT!!
Scoops, rumors All greatly welcomed!!
THE RUMOR
IS THAT SOMEONE HACKED HIS COMPUTER.
AND THAT'S HOW THE PIX GOT LEAKED.

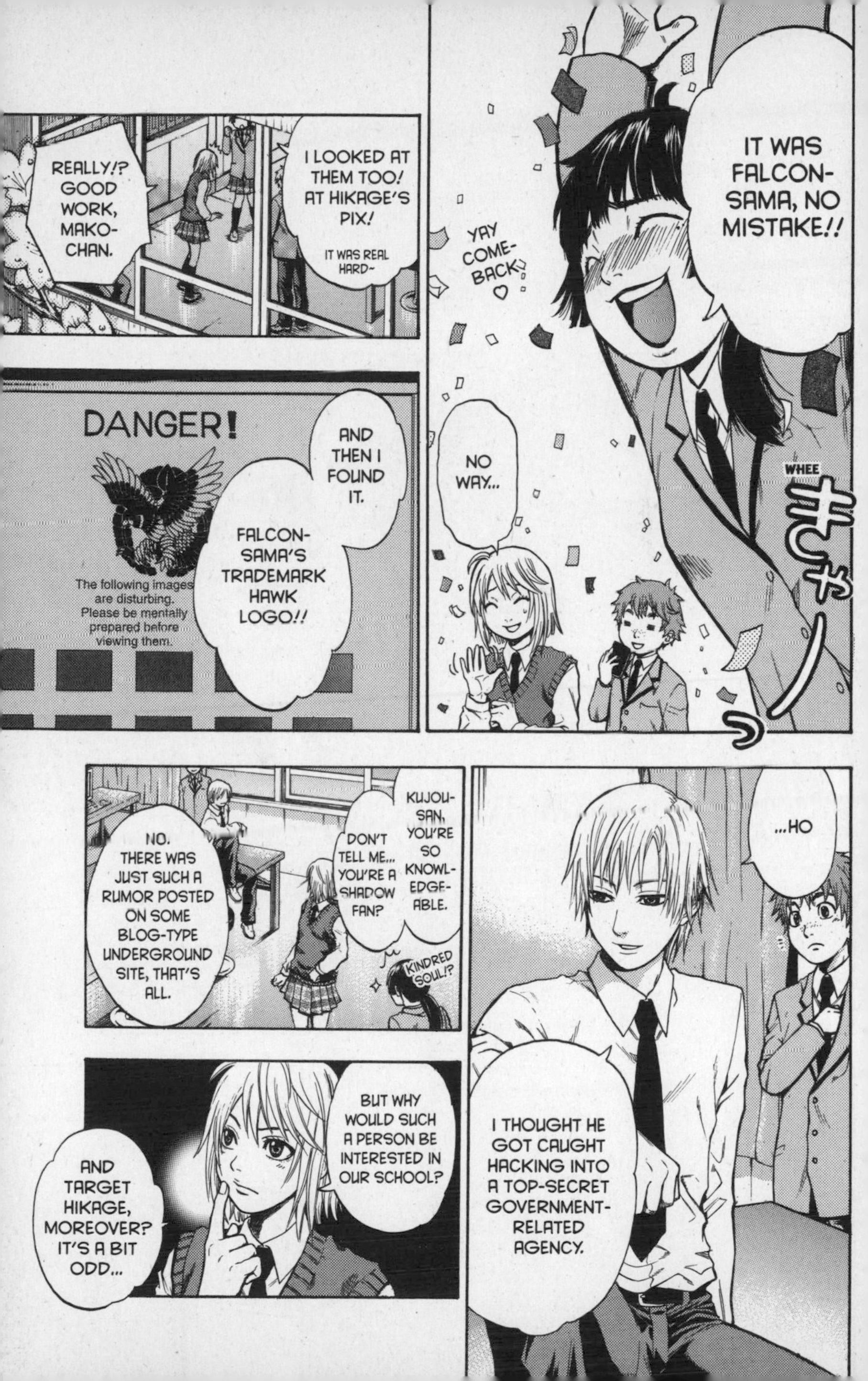
IT WAS FALCON-SAMA, NO MISTAKE!!
WHEE
YAY COMEBACK ♡
NO WAY...
I LOOKED AT THEM TOO! AT HIKAGE'S PIX!
IT WAS REAL HARD~
REALLY!? GOOD WORK, MAKO-CHAN.
AND THEN I FOUND IT.
FALCON-SAMA'S TRADEMARK HAWK LOGO!!
DANGER!
The following images are disturbing. Please be mentally prepared before viewing them.
...HO
I THOUGHT HE GOT CAUGHT HACKING INTO A TOP-SECRET GOVERNMENT-RELATED AGENCY.
KUJOU-SAN, YOU'RE SO KNOWLEDGEABLE.
DON'T TELL ME... YOU'RE A SHADOW FAN?
KINDRED SOUL!?
NO. THERE WAS JUST SUCH A RUMOR POSTED ON SOME BLOG-TYPE UNDERGROUND SITE, THAT'S ALL.
BUT WHY WOULD SUCH A PERSON BE INTERESTED IN OUR SCHOOL?
AND TARGET HIKAGE, MOREOVER? IT'S A BIT ODD...

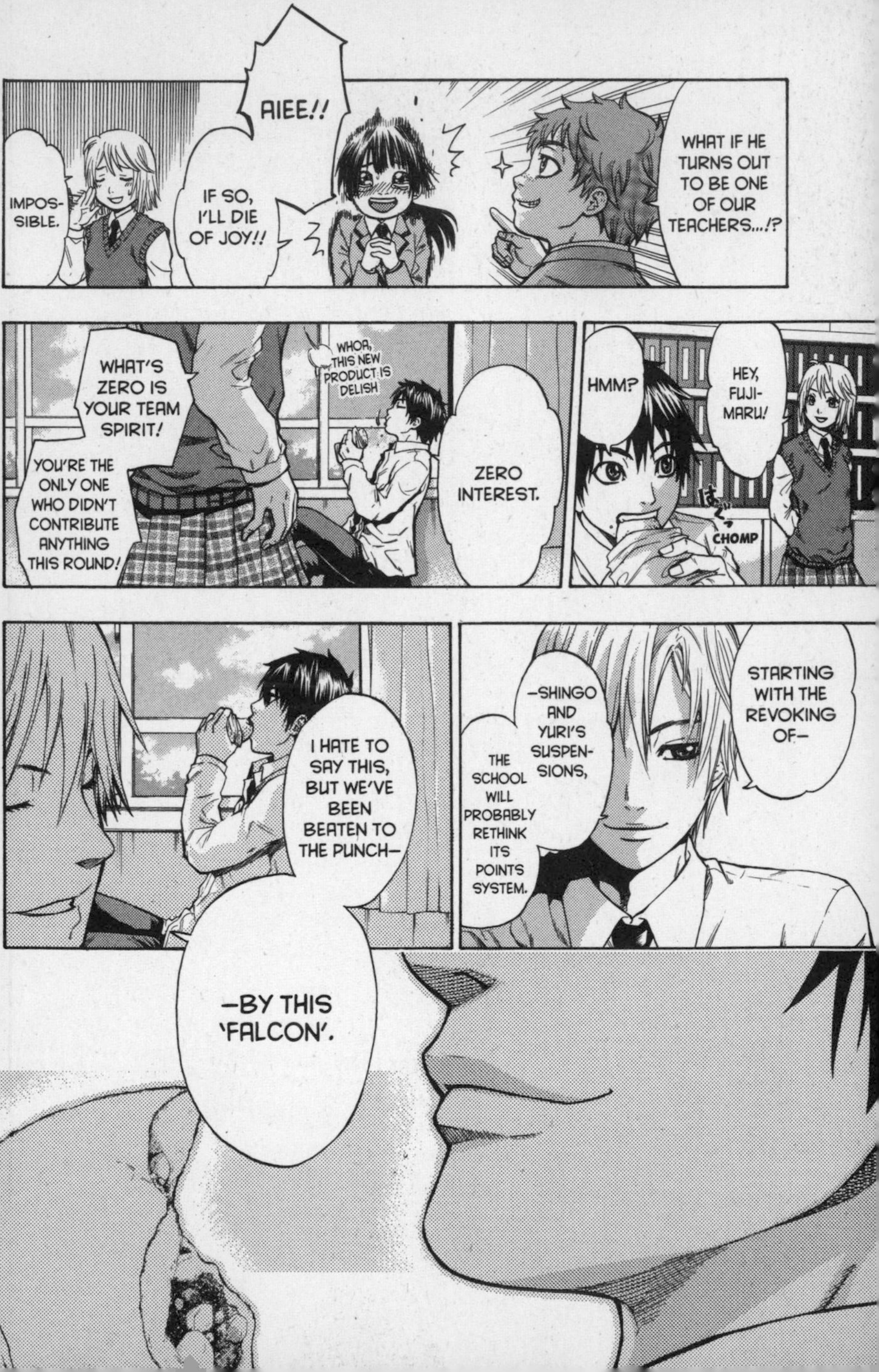
WHAT IF HE TURNS OUT TO BE ONE OF OUR TEACHERS...!?
AIEE!!
IF SO, I'LL DIE OF JOY!!
IMPOS-SIBLE.
HEY, FUJI-MARU!
HMM?
はぐっ
CHOMP
ZERO INTEREST.
WHOA, THIS NEW PRODUCT IS DELISH
WHAT'S ZERO IS YOUR TEAM SPIRIT!
YOU'RE THE ONLY ONE WHO DIDN'T CONTRIBUTE ANYTHING THIS ROUND!
STARTING WITH THE REVOKING OF—
—SHINGO AND YURI'S SUSPEN-SIONS,
THE SCHOOL WILL PROBABLY RETHINK ITS POINTS SYSTEM.
I HATE TO SAY THIS, BUT WE'VE BEEN BEATEN TO THE PUNCH—
—BY THIS 'FALCON'.

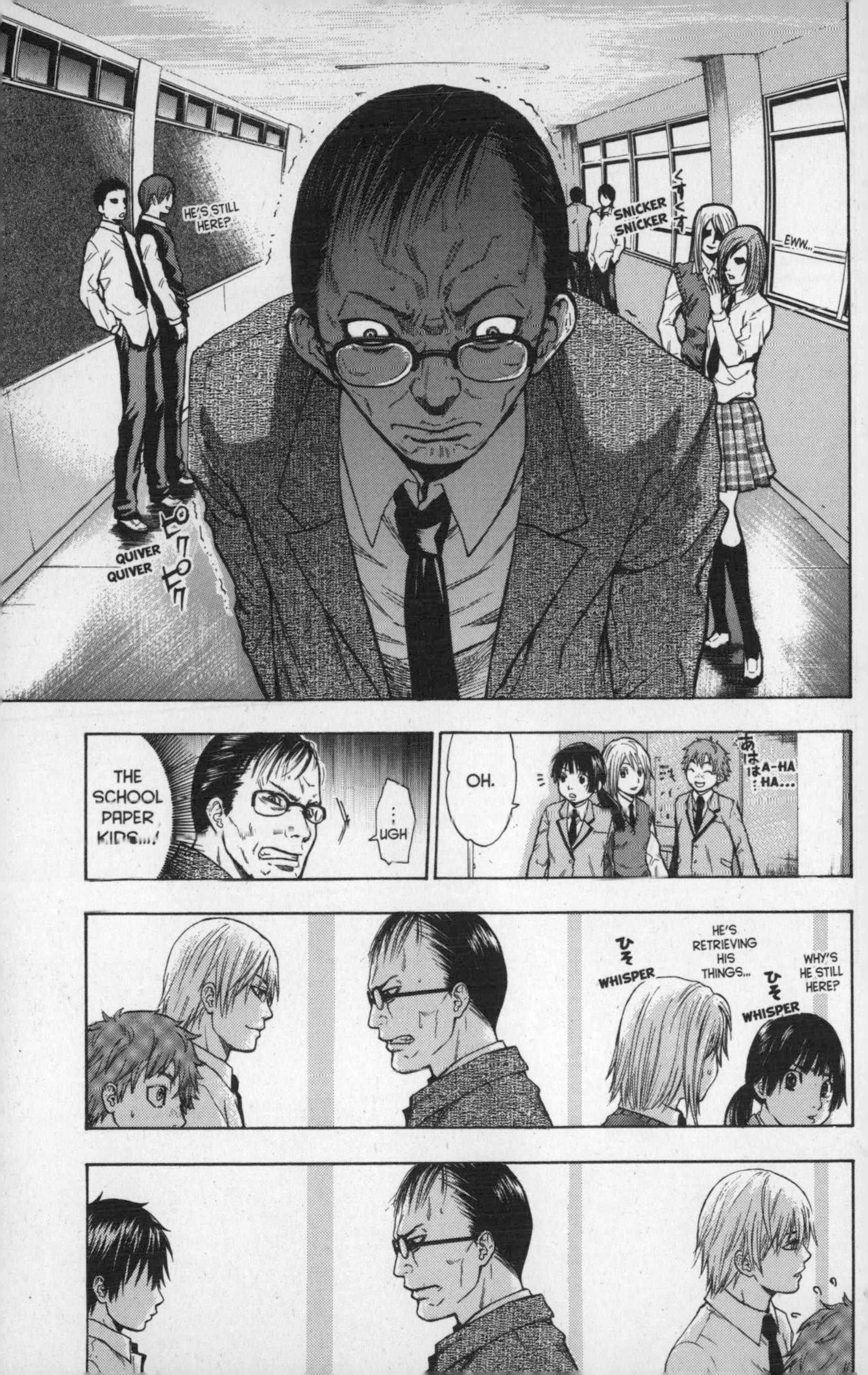
EWW...
くすくす
SNICKER SNICKER
HE'S STILL HERE?
ヒクヒク
QUIVER QUIVER
あはは…
A-HA HA...
OH.
...UGH
THE SCHOOL PAPER KIDS...!
WHY'S HE STILL HERE?
ひそ
WHISPER
HE'S RETRIEVING HIS THINGS...
ひそ
WHISPER

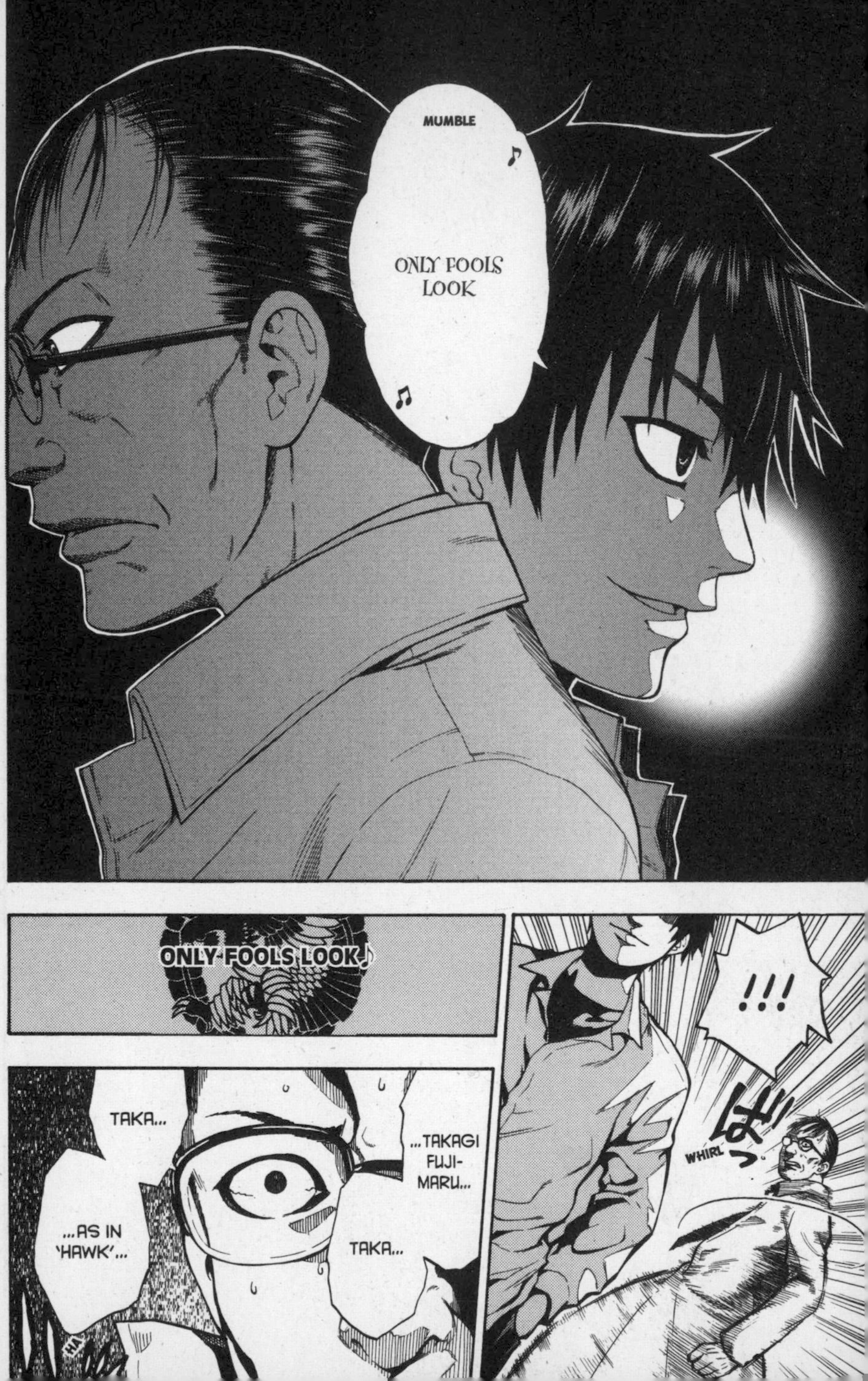
MUMBLE
ONLY FOOLS LOOK ♪ ♪
!!!
ぱっ
WHIRL
ONLY FOOLS LOOK♪
...TAKAGI FUJI-MARU...
TAKA...
TAKA...
...AS IN 'HAWK'...
HA

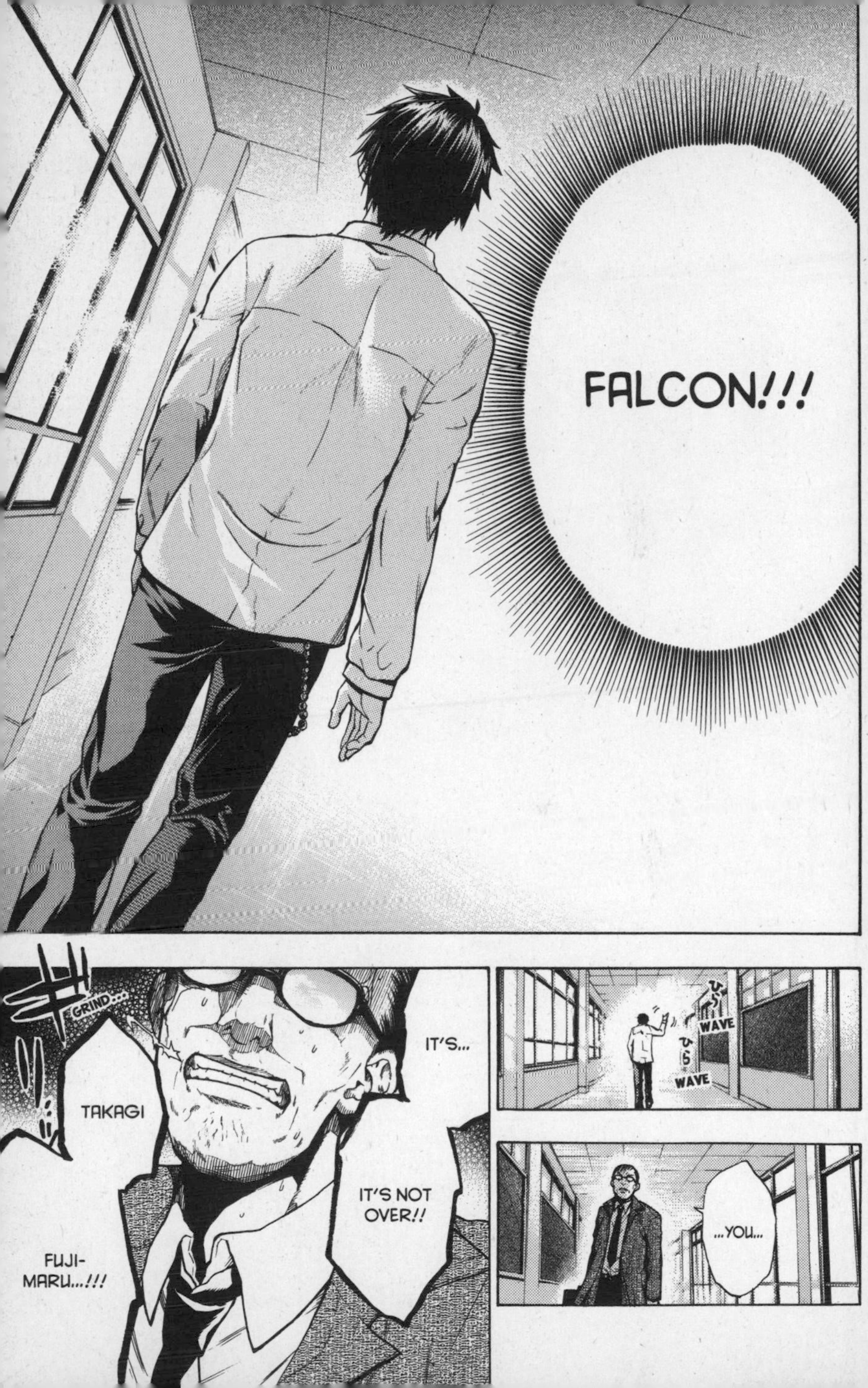
FALCON!!!
ひら
WAVE
ひら
WAVE
...YOU...
IT'S...
GRIND...
TAKAGI
IT'S NOT OVER!!
FUJI-MARU...!!!

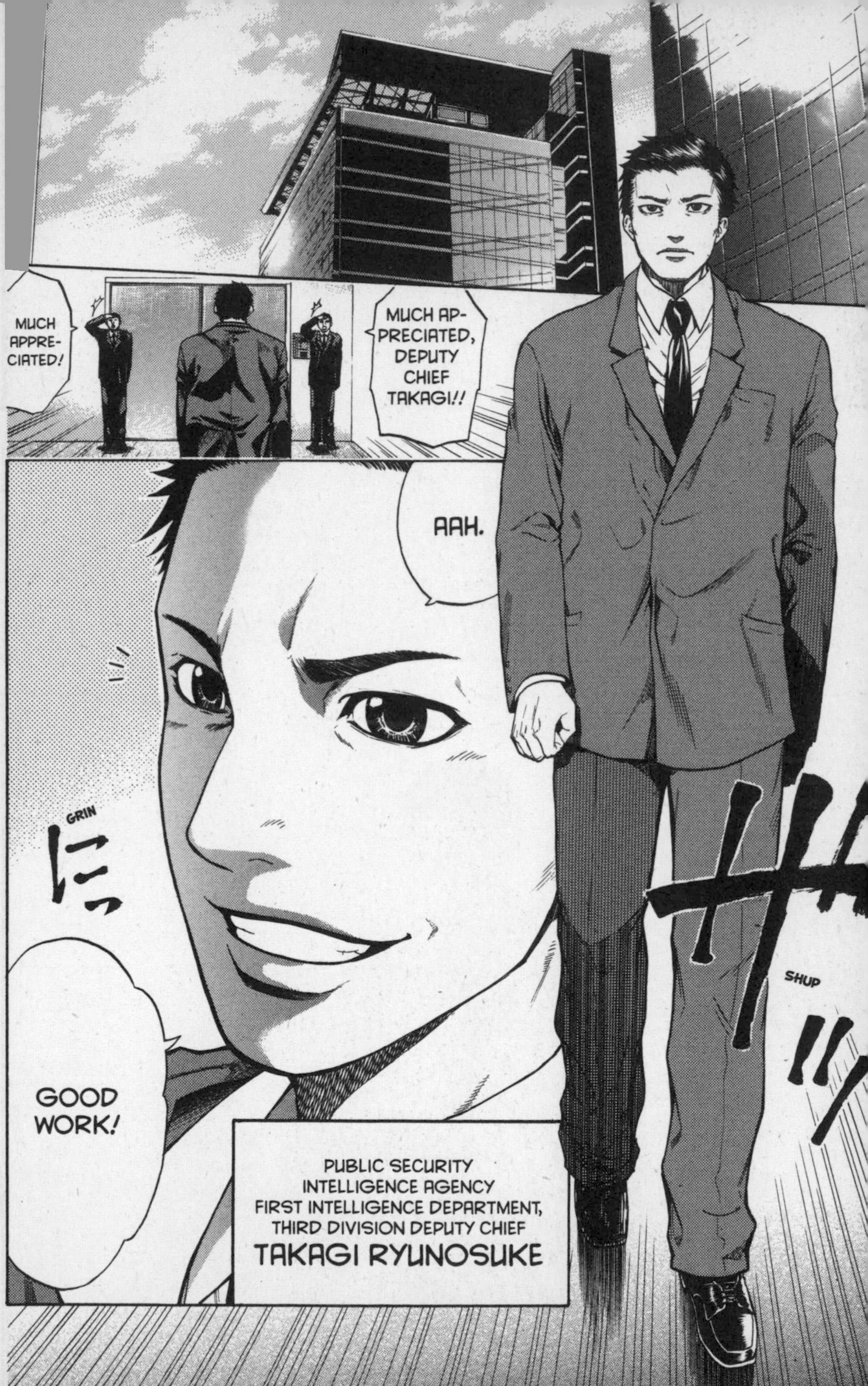
SHUP
MUCH APPRECIATED, DEPUTY CHIEF TAKAGI!!
MUCH APPRECIATED!
AAH.
GRIN
GOOD WORK!
PUBLIC SECURITY INTELLIGENCE AGENCY FIRST INTELLIGENCE DEPARTMENT, THIRD DIVISION DEPUTY CHIEF
TAKAGI RYUNOSUKE

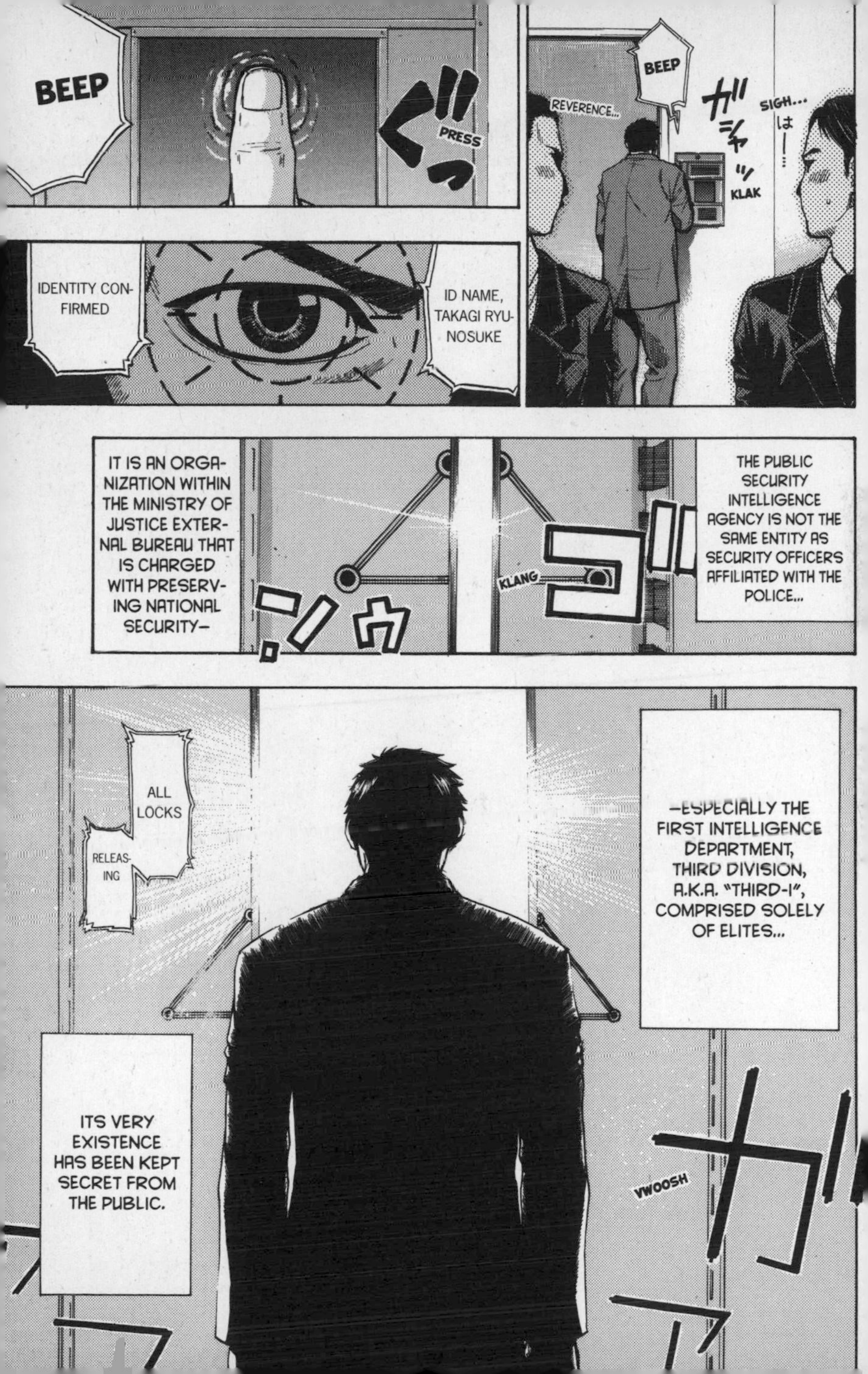
BEEP
REVERENCE...
ガチャッ
KLAK
SIGH...
は—…
ぐっ
PRESS
BEEP
ID NAME, TAKAGI RYU-NOSUKE
IDENTITY CON-FIRMED
THE PUBLIC SECURITY INTELLIGENCE AGENCY IS NOT THE SAME ENTITY AS SECURITY OFFICERS AFFILIATED WITH THE POLICE...
KLANG
IT IS AN ORGA-NIZATION WITHIN THE MINISTRY OF JUSTICE EXTER-NAL BUREAU THAT IS CHARGED WITH PRESERV-ING NATIONAL SECURITY—
—ESPECIALLY THE FIRST INTELLIGENCE DEPARTMENT, THIRD DIVISION, A.K.A. "THIRD-I", COMPRISED SOLELY OF ELITES...
ALL LOCKS
RELEAS-ING
VWOOSH
ITS VERY EXISTENCE HAS BEEN KEPT SECRET FROM THE PUBLIC.

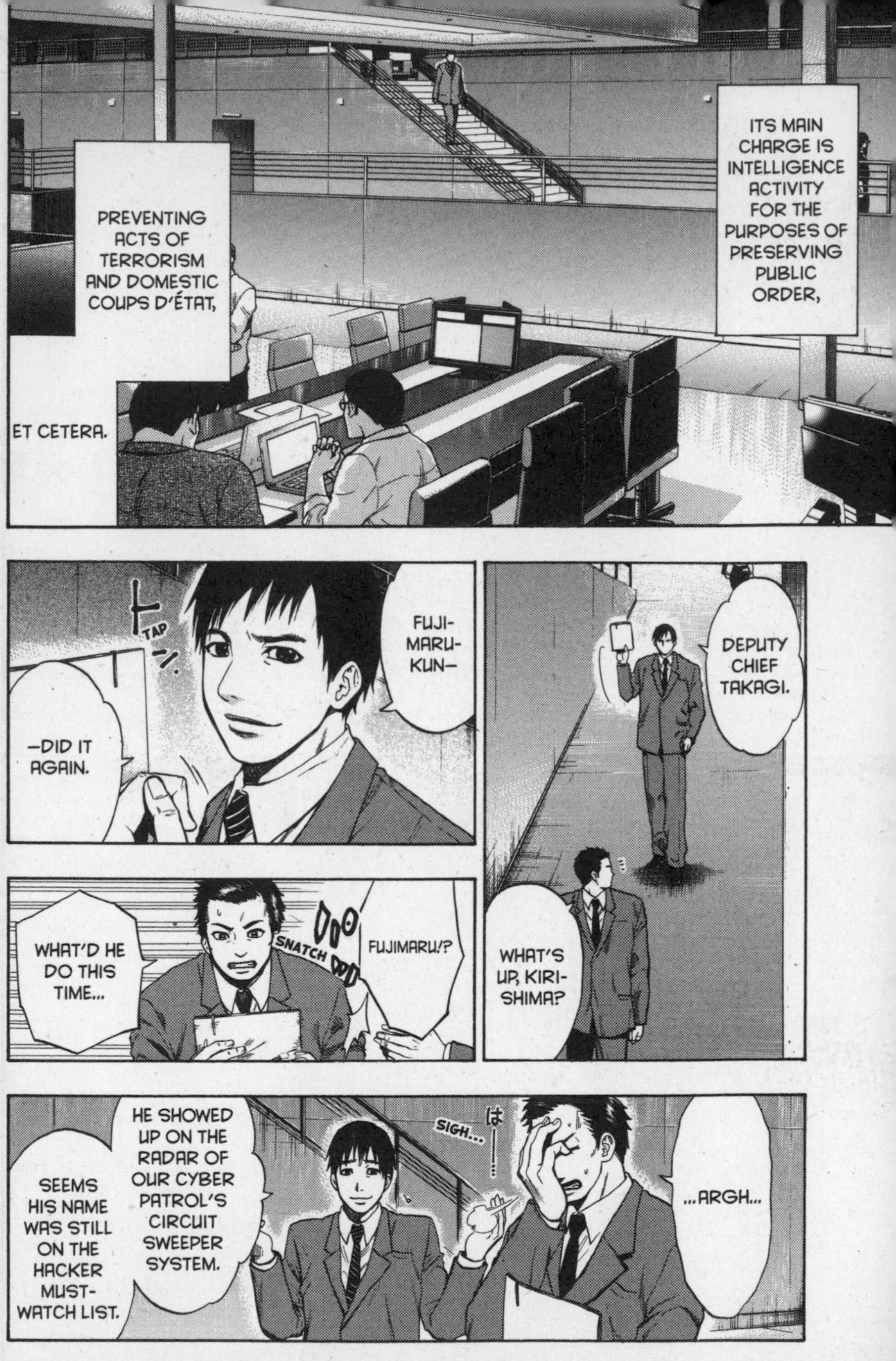
ITS MAIN CHARGE IS INTELLIGENCE ACTIVITY FOR THE PURPOSES OF PRESERVING PUBLIC ORDER,
PREVENTING ACTS OF TERRORISM AND DOMESTIC COUPS D'ÉTAT,
ET CETERA.
DEPUTY CHIEF TAKAGI.
WHAT'S UP, KIRI-SHIMA?
FUJI-MARU-KUN—
TAP
—DID IT AGAIN.
FUJIMARU!?
SNATCH
WHAT'D HE DO THIS TIME...
...ARGH...
SIGH...
は一…
HE SHOWED UP ON THE RADAR OF OUR CYBER PATROL'S CIRCUIT SWEEPER SYSTEM.
SEEMS HIS NAME WAS STILL ON THE HACKER MUST-WATCH LIST.

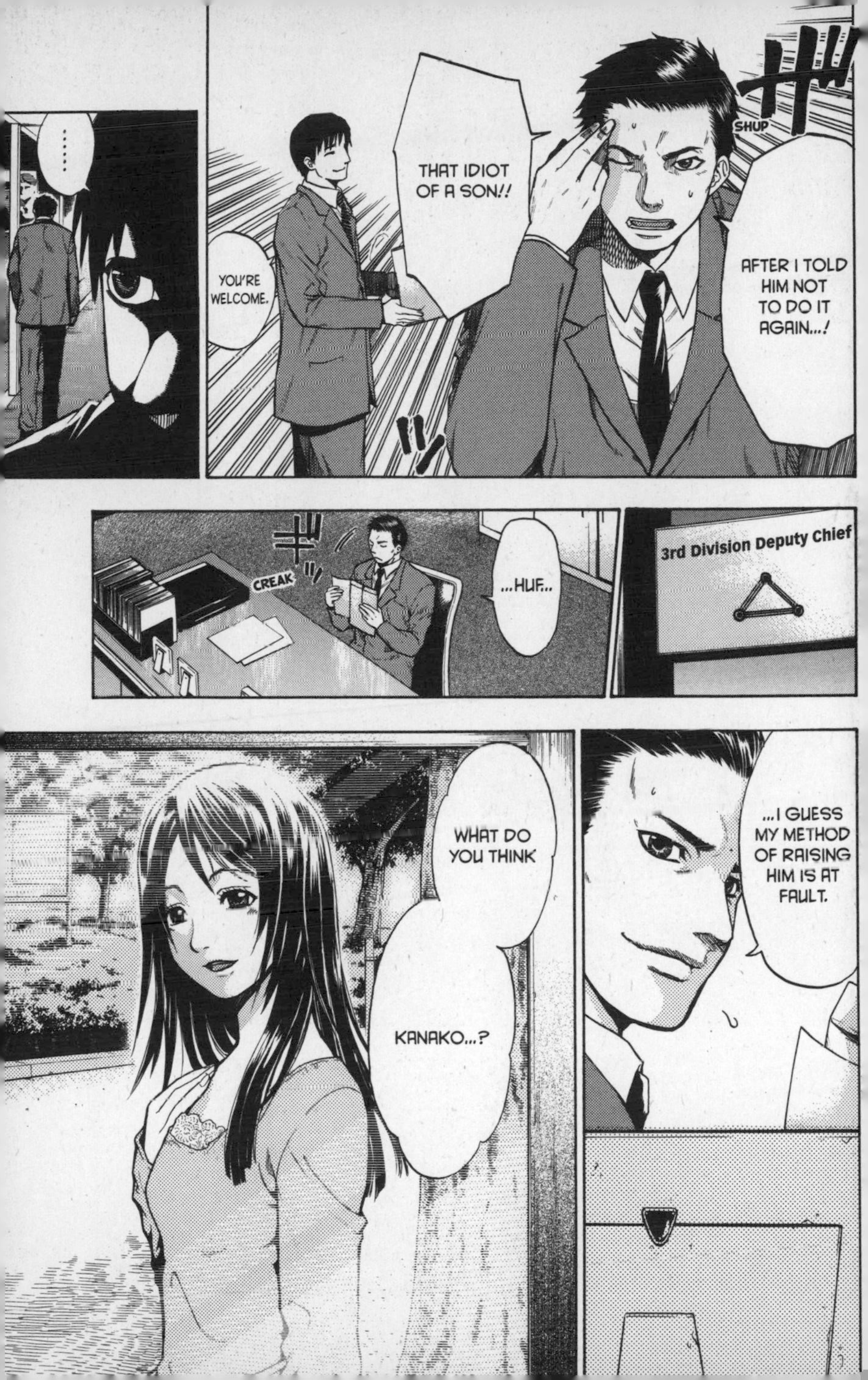
SHUP
AFTER I TOLD HIM NOT TO DO IT AGAIN...!
THAT IDIOT OF A SON!!
YOU'RE WELCOME.
......
3rd Division Deputy Chief
...HUF...
CREAK
...I GUESS MY METHOD OF RAISING HIM IS AT FAULT.
WHAT DO YOU THINK
KANAKO...?

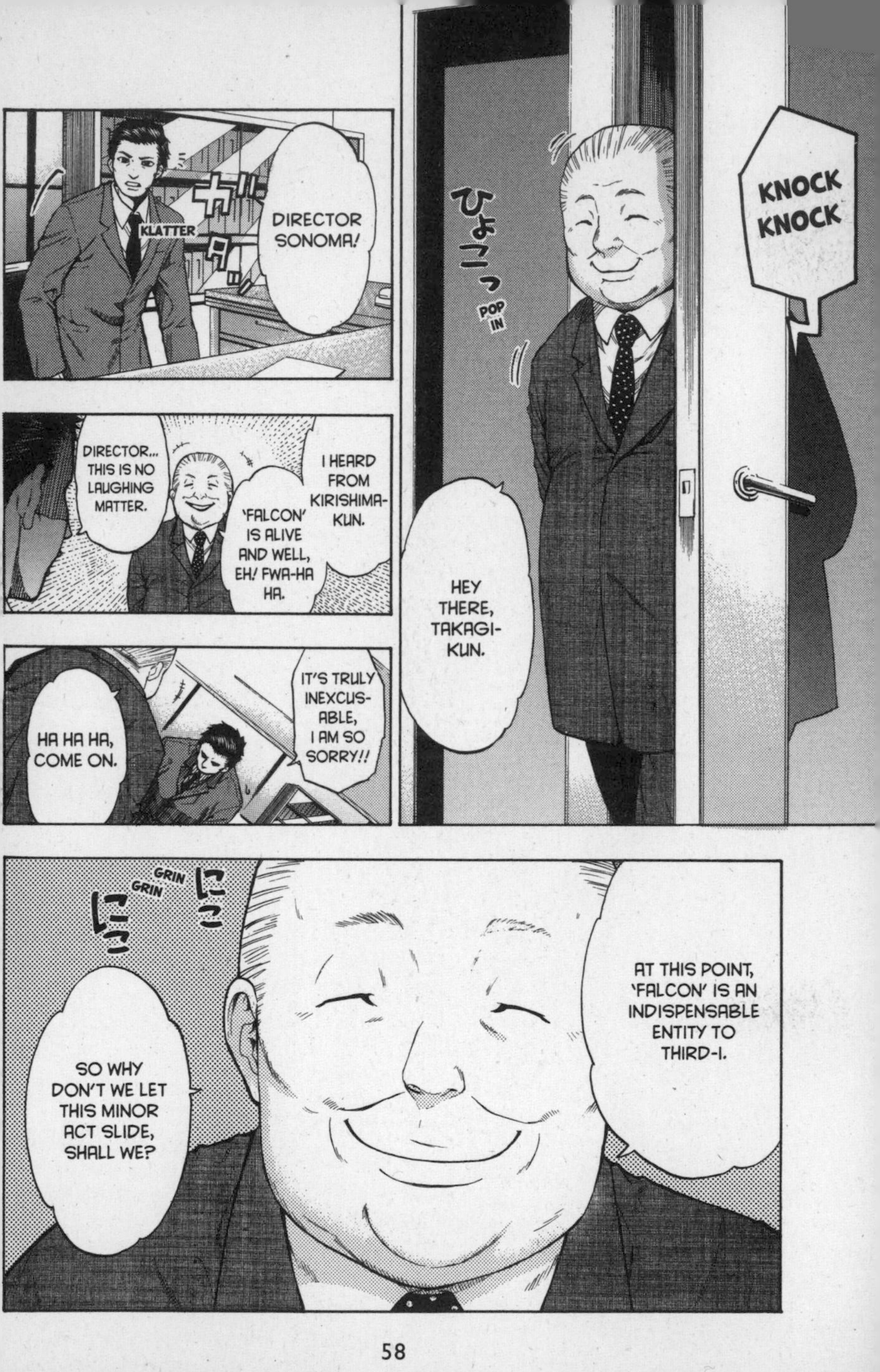
KNOCK KNOCK
ひょこっ
POP IN
HEY THERE, TAKAGI-KUN.
DIRECTOR SONOMA!
カタッ
KLATTER
I HEARD FROM KIRISHIMA-KUN.
'FALCON' IS ALIVE AND WELL, EH! FWA-HA HA.
DIRECTOR... THIS IS NO LAUGHING MATTER.
IT'S TRULY INEXCUSABLE, I AM SO SORRY!!
HA HA HA, COME ON.
AT THIS POINT, 'FALCON' IS AN INDISPENSABLE ENTITY TO THIRD-I.
にこ
GRIN
にこ
GRIN
SO WHY DON'T WE LET THIS MINOR ACT SLIDE, SHALL WE?

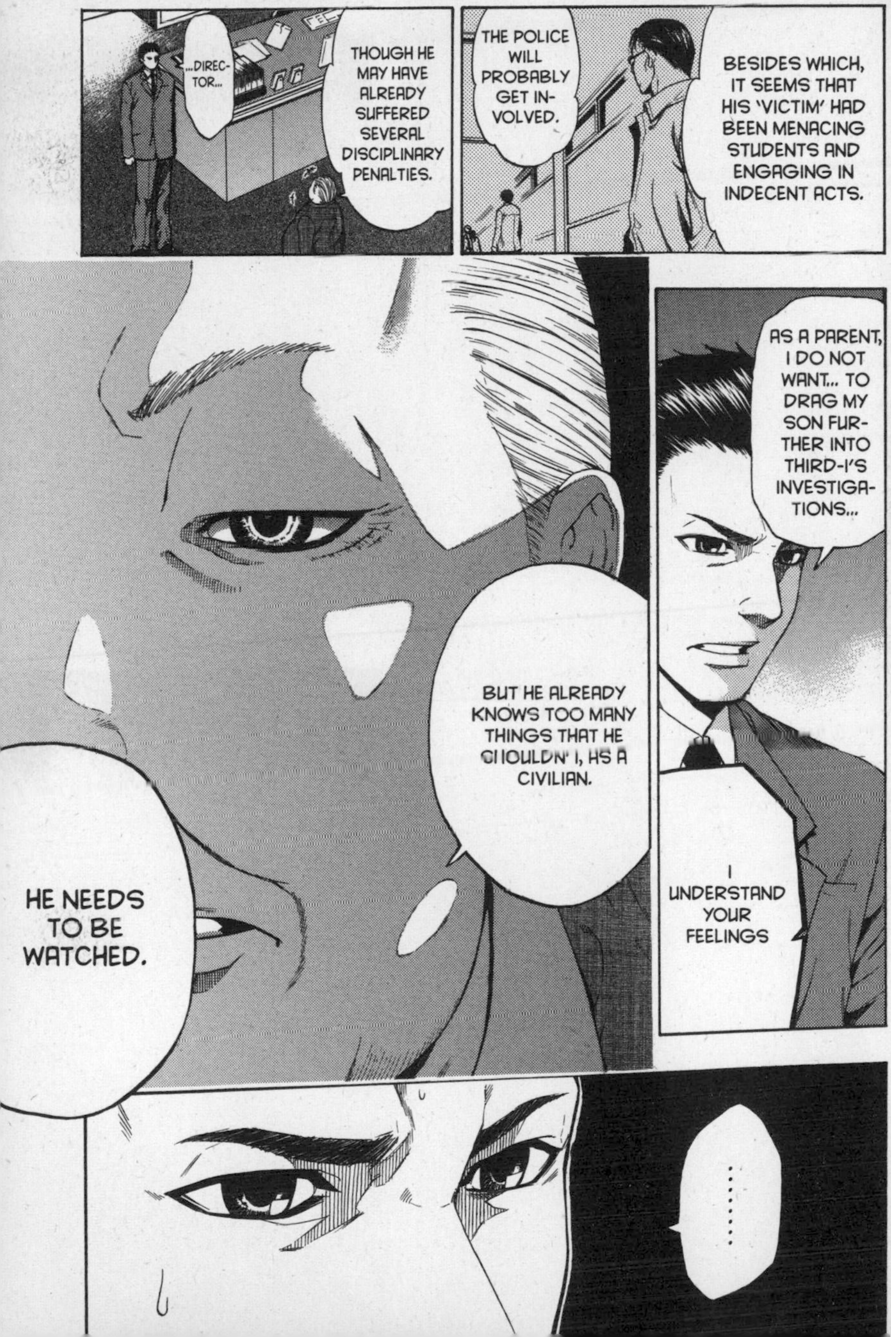
BESIDES WHICH, IT SEEMS THAT HIS 'VICTIM' HAD BEEN MENACING STUDENTS AND ENGAGING IN INDECENT ACTS.
THE POLICE WILL PROBABLY GET IN-VOLVED.
THOUGH HE MAY HAVE ALREADY SUFFERED SEVERAL DISCIPLINARY PENALTIES.
...DIREC-TOR...
AS A PARENT, I DO NOT WANT... TO DRAG MY SON FUR-THER INTO THIRD-I'S INVESTIGA-TIONS...
I UNDERSTAND YOUR FEELINGS
BUT HE ALREADY KNOWS TOO MANY THINGS THAT HE SHOULDN'T, AS A CIVILIAN.
HE NEEDS TO BE WATCHED.
....

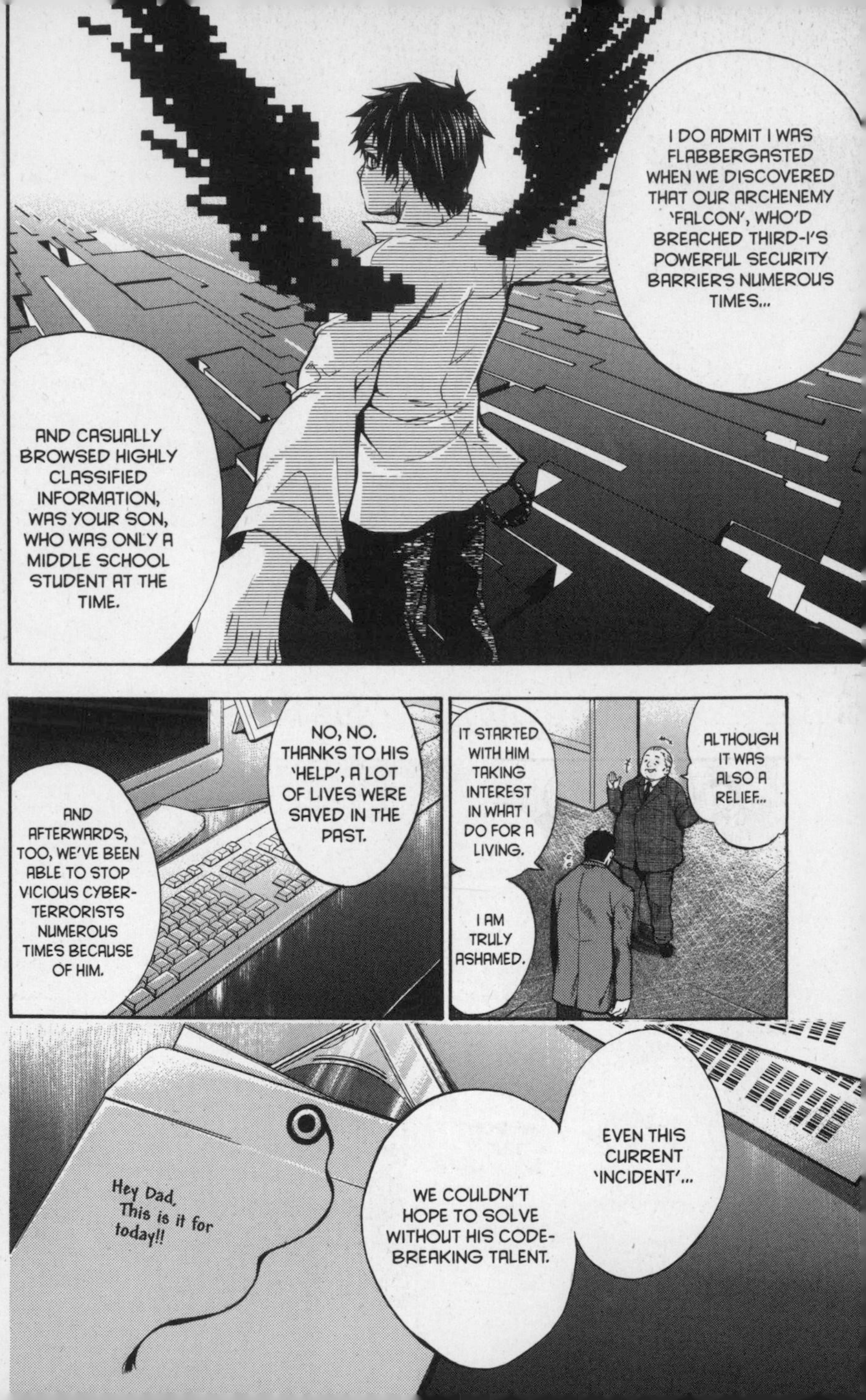
I DO ADMIT I WAS FLABBERGASTED WHEN WE DISCOVERED THAT OUR ARCHENEMY 'FALCON', WHO'D BREACHED THIRD-I'S POWERFUL SECURITY BARRIERS NUMEROUS TIMES...
AND CASUALLY BROWSED HIGHLY CLASSIFIED INFORMATION, WAS YOUR SON, WHO WAS ONLY A MIDDLE SCHOOL STUDENT AT THE TIME.
ALTHOUGH IT WAS ALSO A RELIEF...
IT STARTED WITH HIM TAKING INTEREST IN WHAT I DO FOR A LIVING.
I AM TRULY ASHAMED.
NO, NO. THANKS TO HIS 'HELP', A LOT OF LIVES WERE SAVED IN THE PAST.
AND AFTERWARDS, TOO, WE'VE BEEN ABLE TO STOP VICIOUS CYBER-TERRORISTS NUMEROUS TIMES BECAUSE OF HIM.
EVEN THIS CURRENT 'INCIDENT'...
WE COULDN'T HOPE TO SOLVE WITHOUT HIS CODE-BREAKING TALENT.
Hey Dad, This is it for today!!

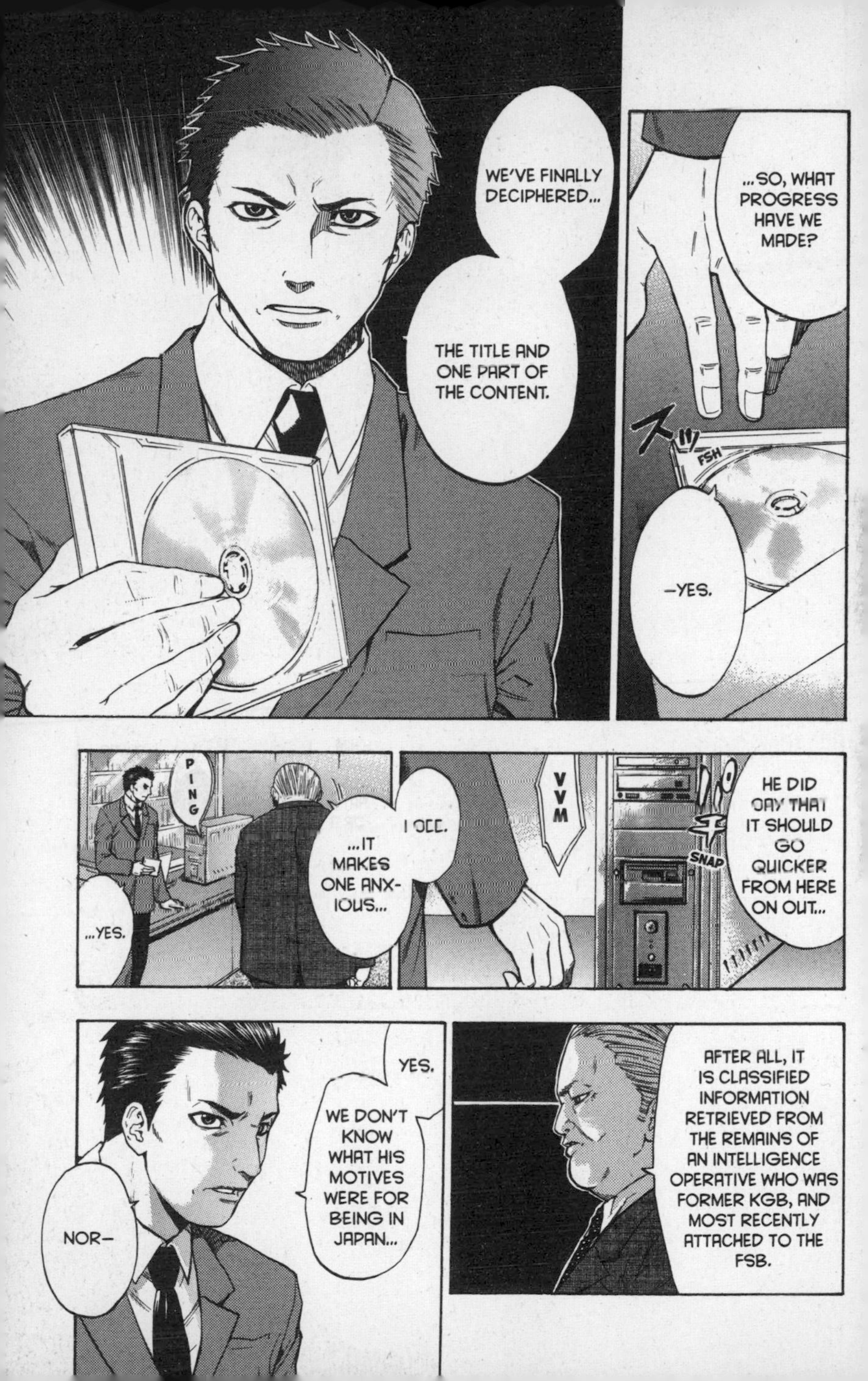
...SO, WHAT PROGRESS HAVE WE MADE?
FSH
—YES.
WE'VE FINALLY DECIPHERED...
THE TITLE AND ONE PART OF THE CONTENT.
HE DID SAY THAT IT SHOULD GO QUICKER FROM HERE ON OUT...
SNAP
VVM
I SEE.
...IT MAKES ONE ANX-IOUS...
PING
...YES.
AFTER ALL, IT IS CLASSIFIED INFORMATION RETRIEVED FROM THE REMAINS OF AN INTELLIGENCE OPERATIVE WHO WAS FORMER KGB, AND MOST RECENTLY ATTACHED TO THE FSB.
YES.
WE DON'T KNOW WHAT HIS MOTIVES WERE FOR BEING IN JAPAN...
NOR—

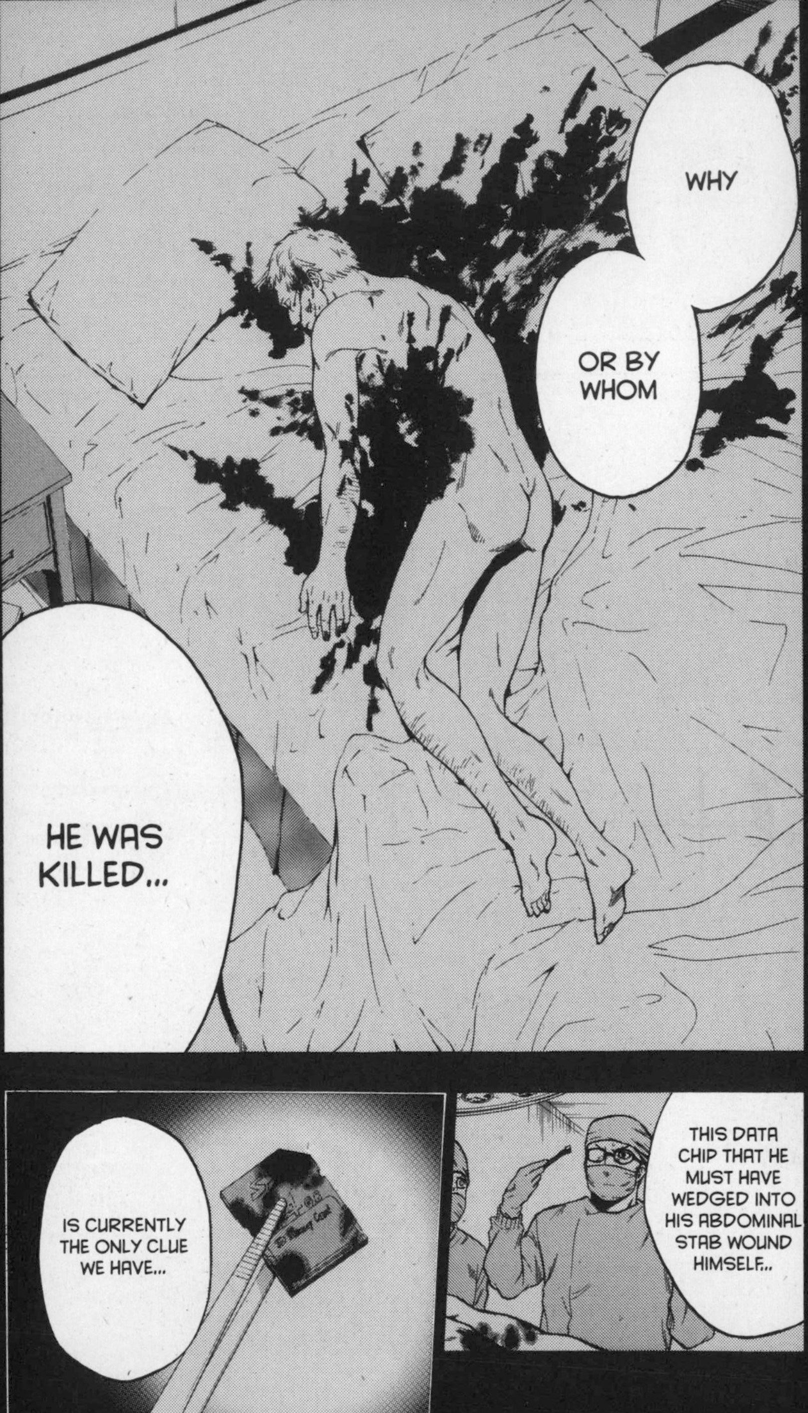
WHY
OR BY WHOM
HE WAS KILLED...
THIS DATA CHIP THAT HE MUST HAVE WEDGED INTO HIS ABDOMINAL STAB WOUND HIMSELF...
IS CURRENTLY THE ONLY CLUE WE HAVE...

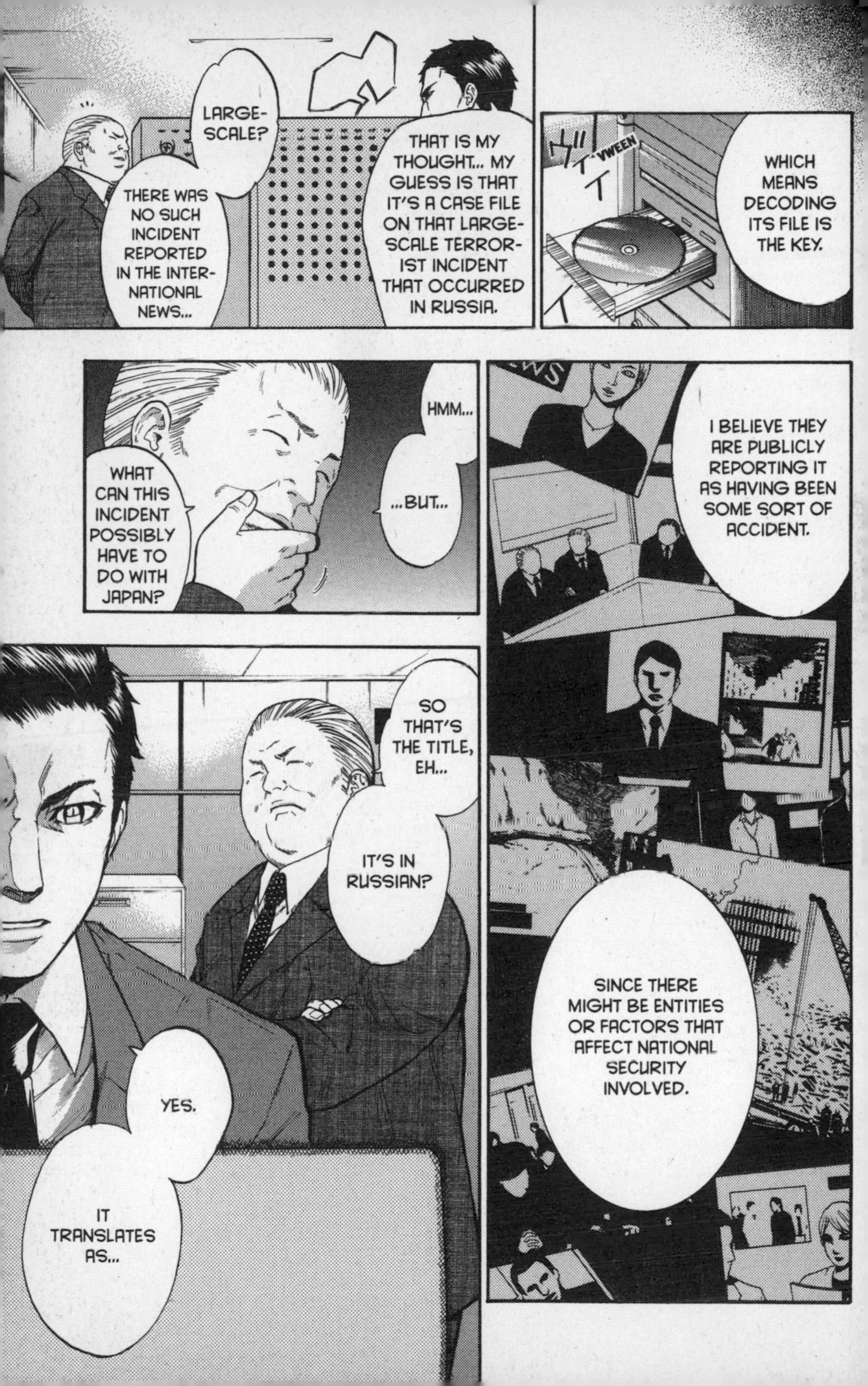
VWEEN
WHICH MEANS DECODING ITS FILE IS THE KEY.
LARGE-SCALE?
THAT IS MY THOUGHT... MY GUESS IS THAT IT'S A CASE FILE ON THAT LARGE-SCALE TERROR-IST INCIDENT THAT OCCURRED IN RUSSIA.
THERE WAS NO SUCH INCIDENT REPORTED IN THE INTER-NATIONAL NEWS...
I BELIEVE THEY ARE PUBLICLY REPORTING IT AS HAVING BEEN SOME SORT OF ACCIDENT.
SINCE THERE MIGHT BE ENTITIES OR FACTORS THAT AFFECT NATIONAL SECURITY INVOLVED.
HMM...
...BUT...
WHAT CAN THIS INCIDENT POSSIBLY HAVE TO DO WITH JAPAN?
SO THAT'S THE TITLE, EH...
IT'S IN RUSSIAN?
YES.
IT TRANSLATES AS...

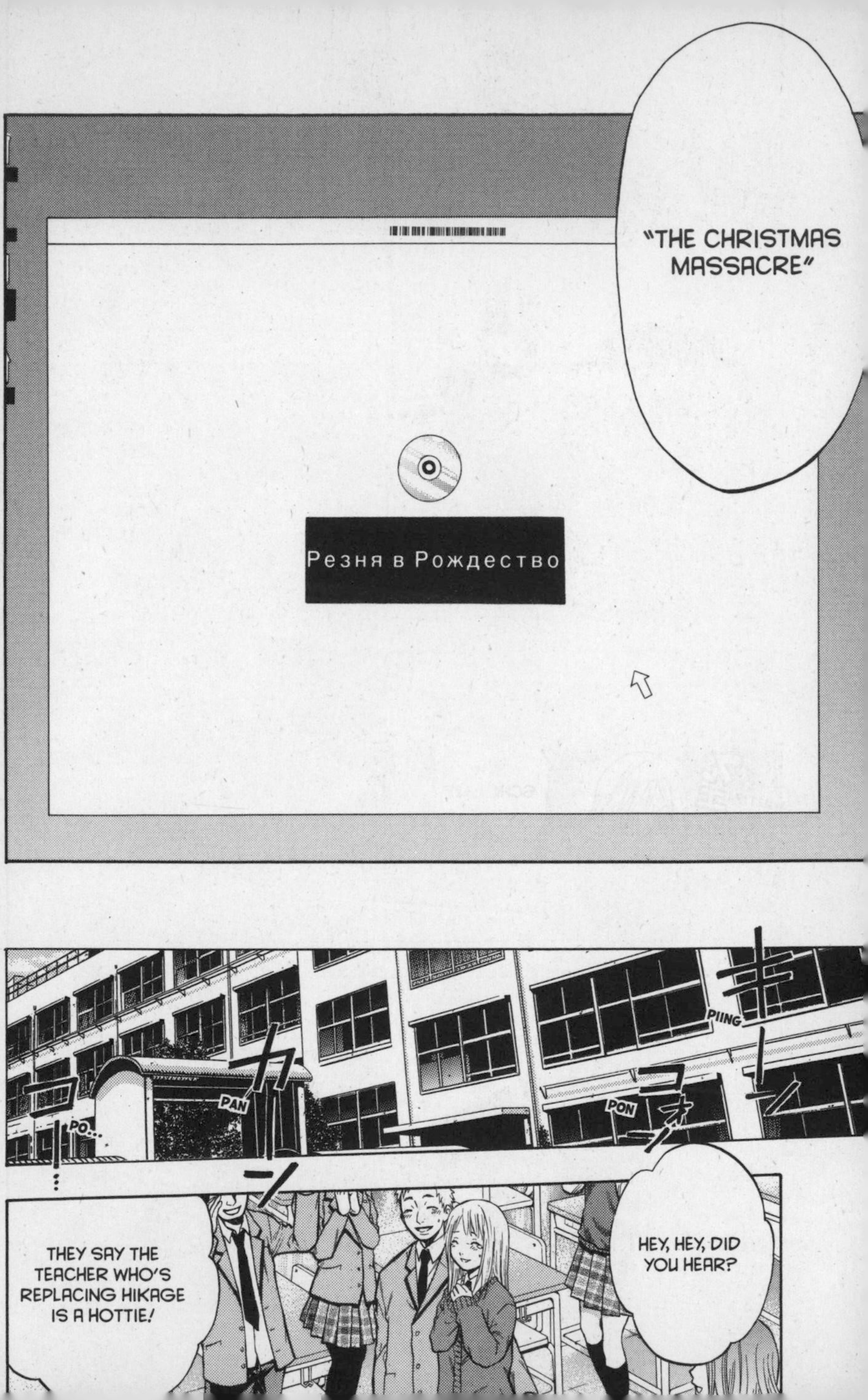
"THE CHRISTMAS MASSACRE"
Резня в Рождество
PIING
PON
PAN
PO...
HEY, HEY, DID YOU HEAR?
THEY SAY THE TEACHER WHO'S REPLACING HIKAGE IS A HOTTIE!

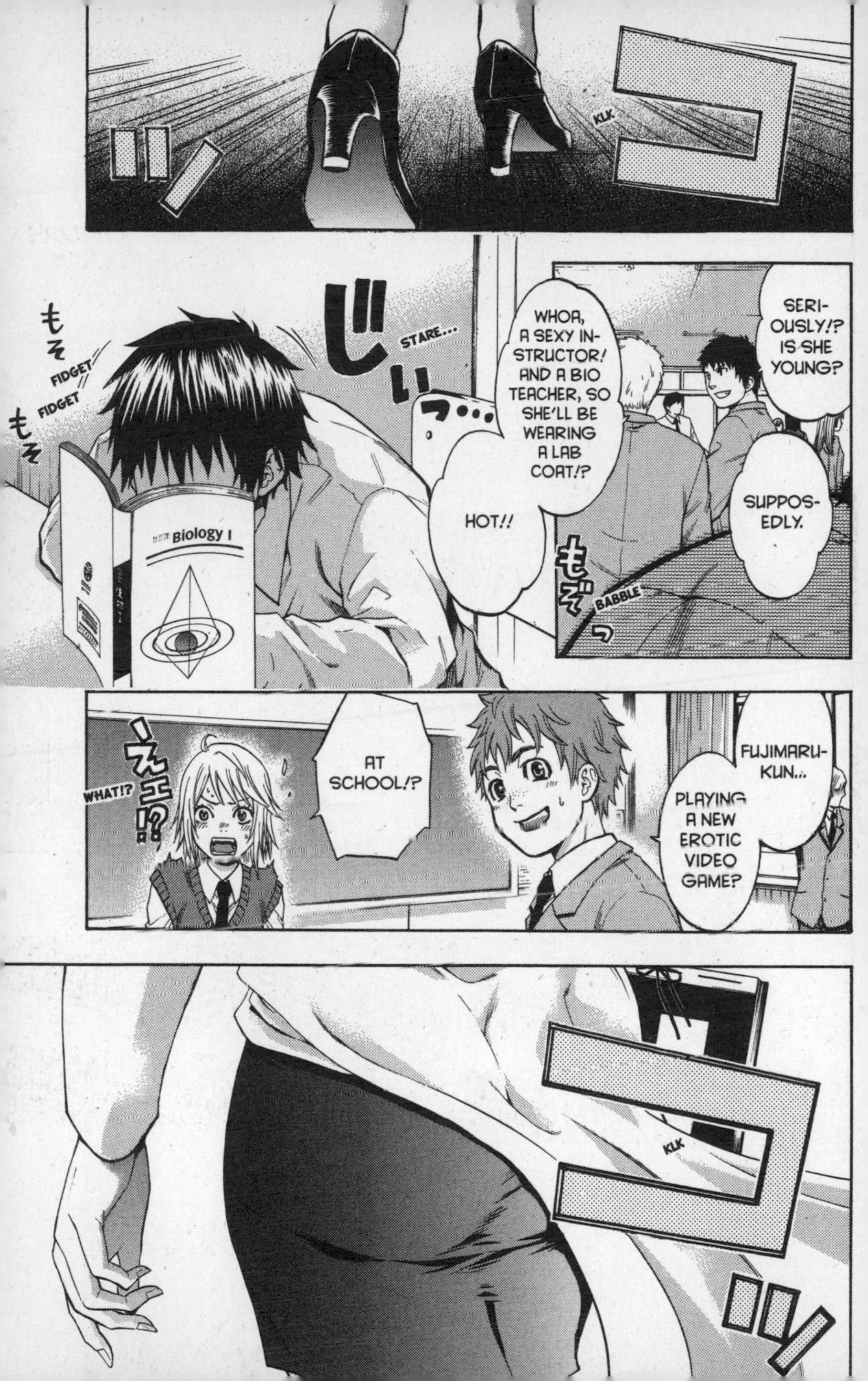
KLK
SERI-OUSLY!? IS SHE YOUNG?
SUPPOS-EDLY.
WHOA, A SEXY IN-STRUCTOR! AND A BIO TEACHER, SO SHE'LL BE WEARING A LAB COAT!?
HOT!!
もぞ
BABBLE
じぃっ…
STARE...
もぞ
FIDGET FIDGET
もぞ
Biology I
FUJIMARU-KUN...
PLAYING A NEW EROTIC VIDEO GAME?
AT SCHOOL!?
ええ!?
WHAT!?
KLK

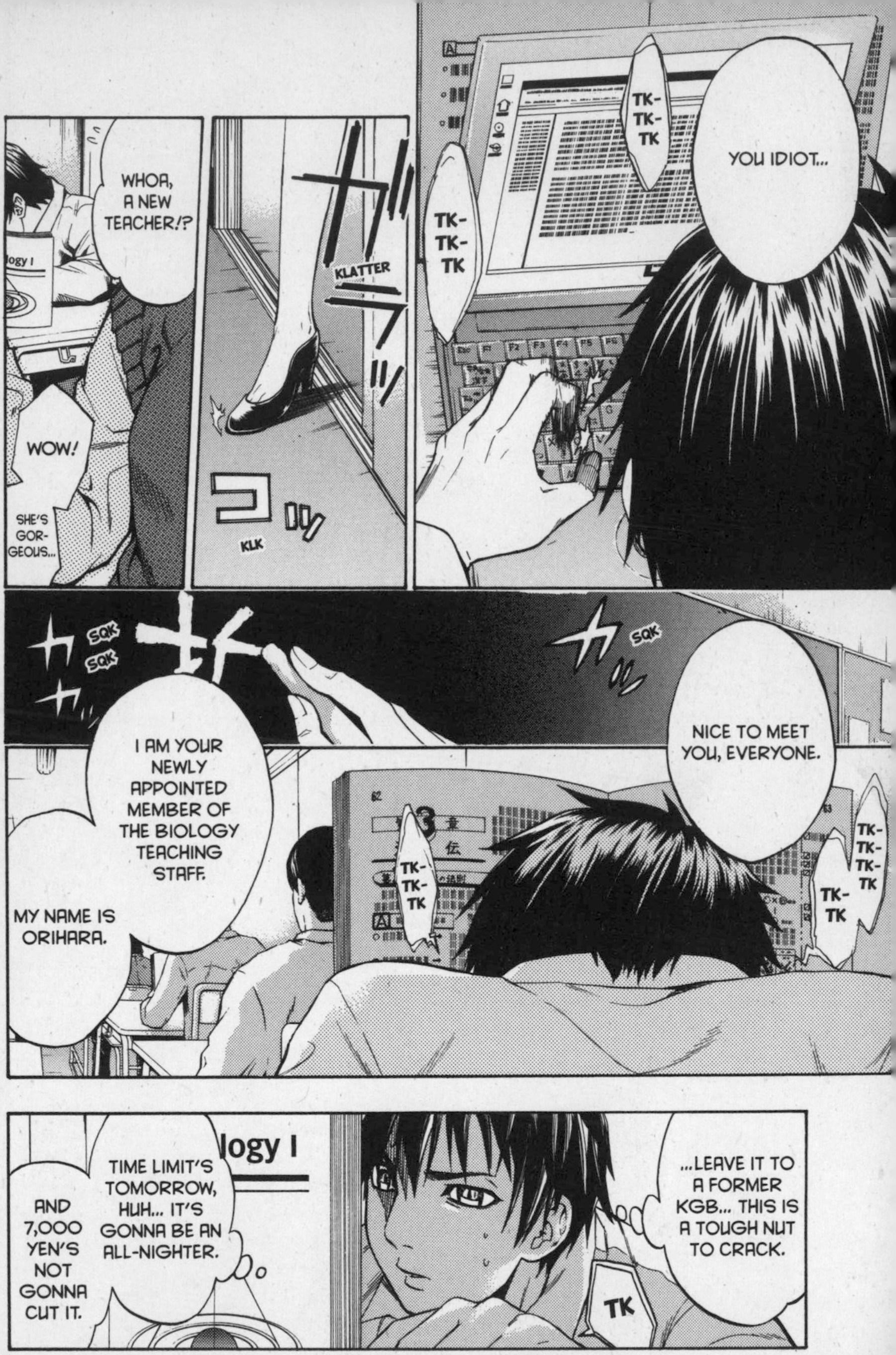
YOU IDIOT...
TK-TK-TK
TK-TK-TK
KLATTER
KLK
WHOA, A NEW TEACHER!?
WOW!
SHE'S GORGEOUS...
SQK
SQK SQK
NICE TO MEET YOU, EVERYONE.
TK-TK-TK-TK
TK-TK
TK-TK-TK
I AM YOUR NEWLY APPOINTED MEMBER OF THE BIOLOGY TEACHING STAFF.
MY NAME IS ORIHARA.
...LEAVE IT TO A FORMER KGB... THIS IS A TOUGH NUT TO CRACK.
TK
TIME LIMIT'S TOMORROW, HUH... IT'S GONNA BE AN ALL-NIGHTER.
AND 7,000 YEN'S NOT GONNA CUT IT.

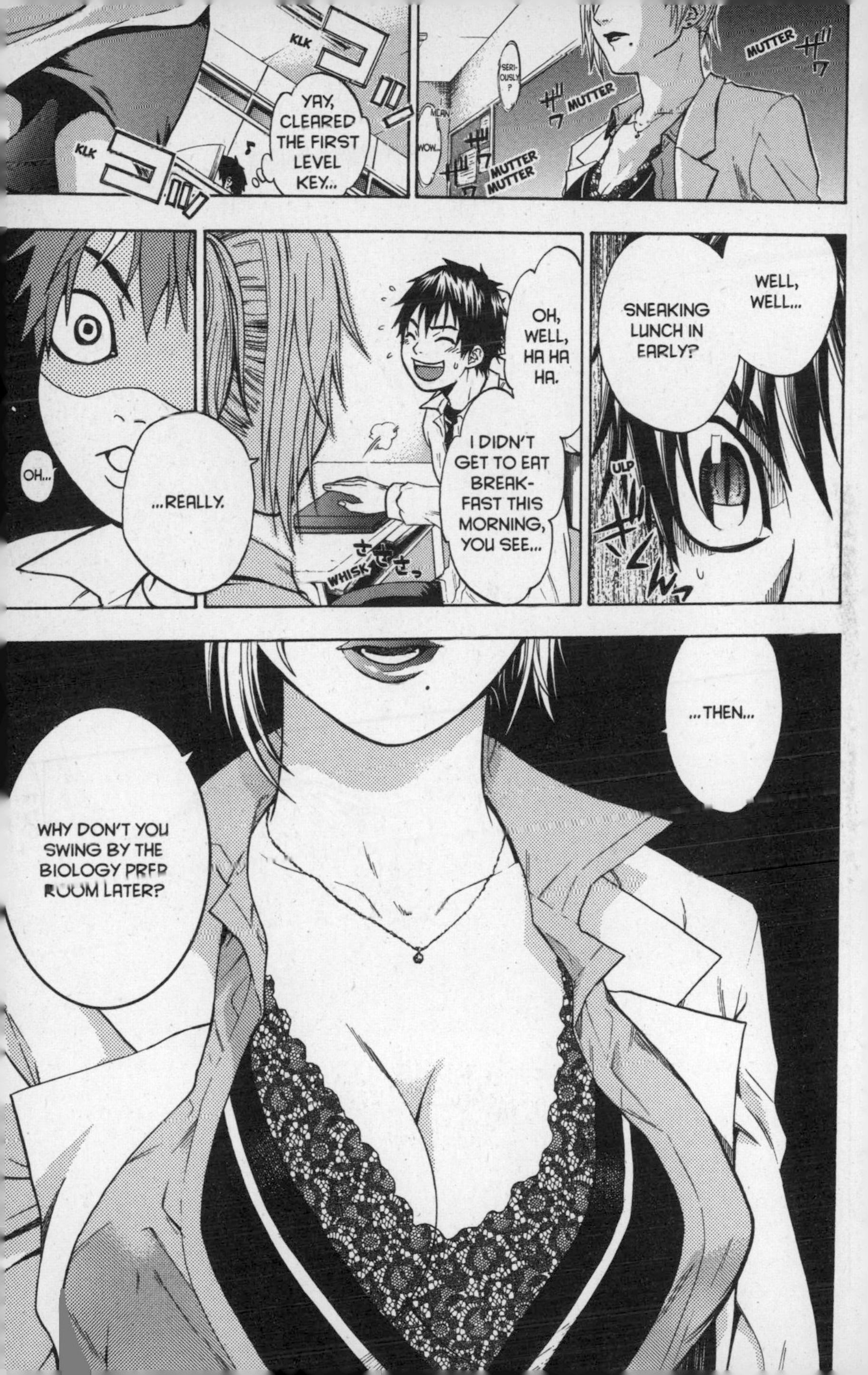
MUTTER
MUTTER
MUTTER MUTTER
SERI-OUSLY?
I MEAN
WOW...
KLK
YAY, CLEARED THE FIRST LEVEL KEY...
KLK
WELL, WELL...
SNEAKING LUNCH IN EARLY?
ULP
OH, WELL, HA HA HA.
I DIDN'T GET TO EAT BREAK-FAST THIS MORNING, YOU SEE...
WHISK
...REALLY.
OH...
...THEN...
WHY DON'T YOU SWING BY THE BIOLOGY PREP ROOM LATER?

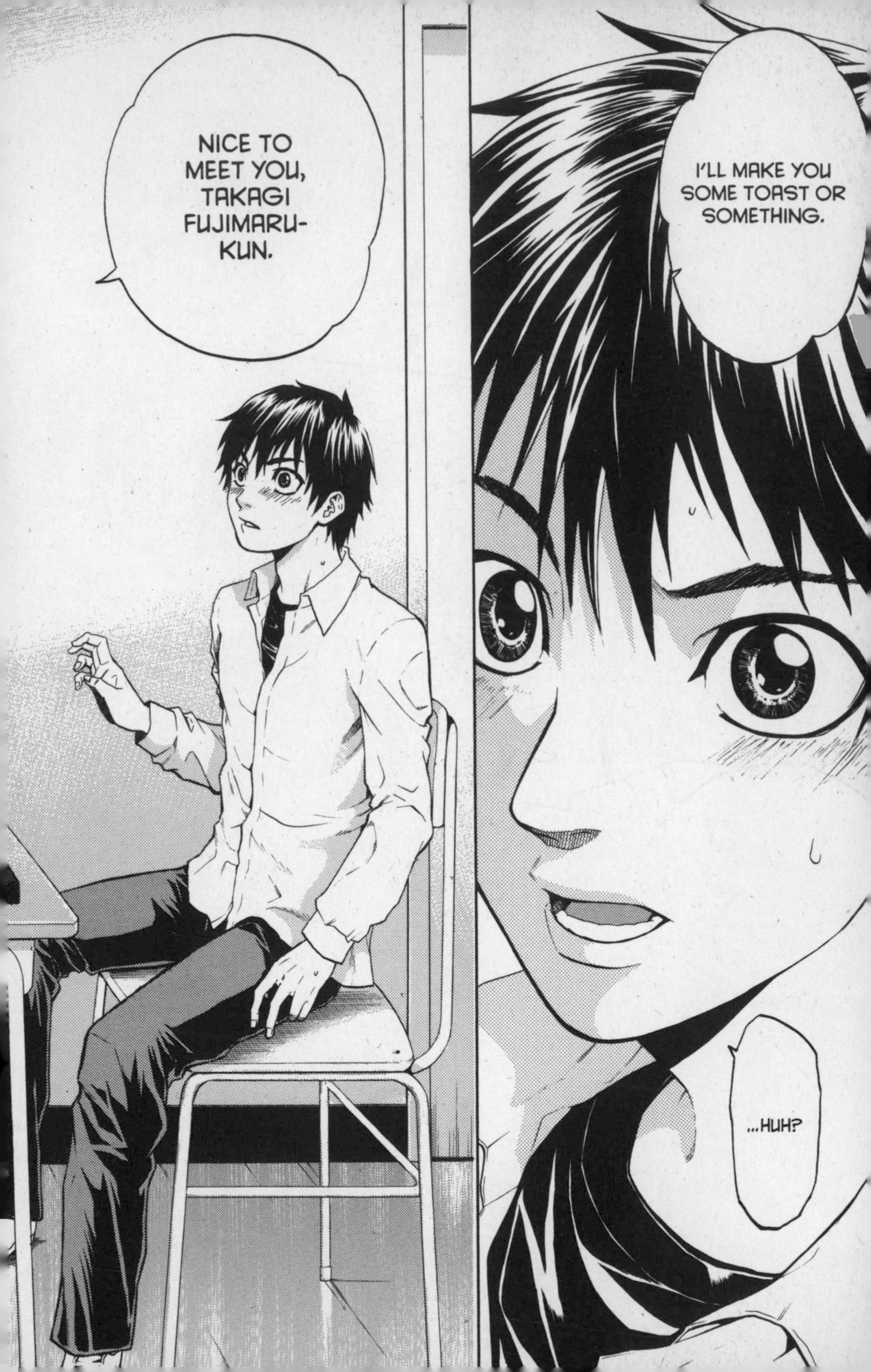
I'LL MAKE YOU SOME TOAST OR SOMETHING.
...HUH?
NICE TO MEET YOU, TAKAGI FUJIMARU-KUN.

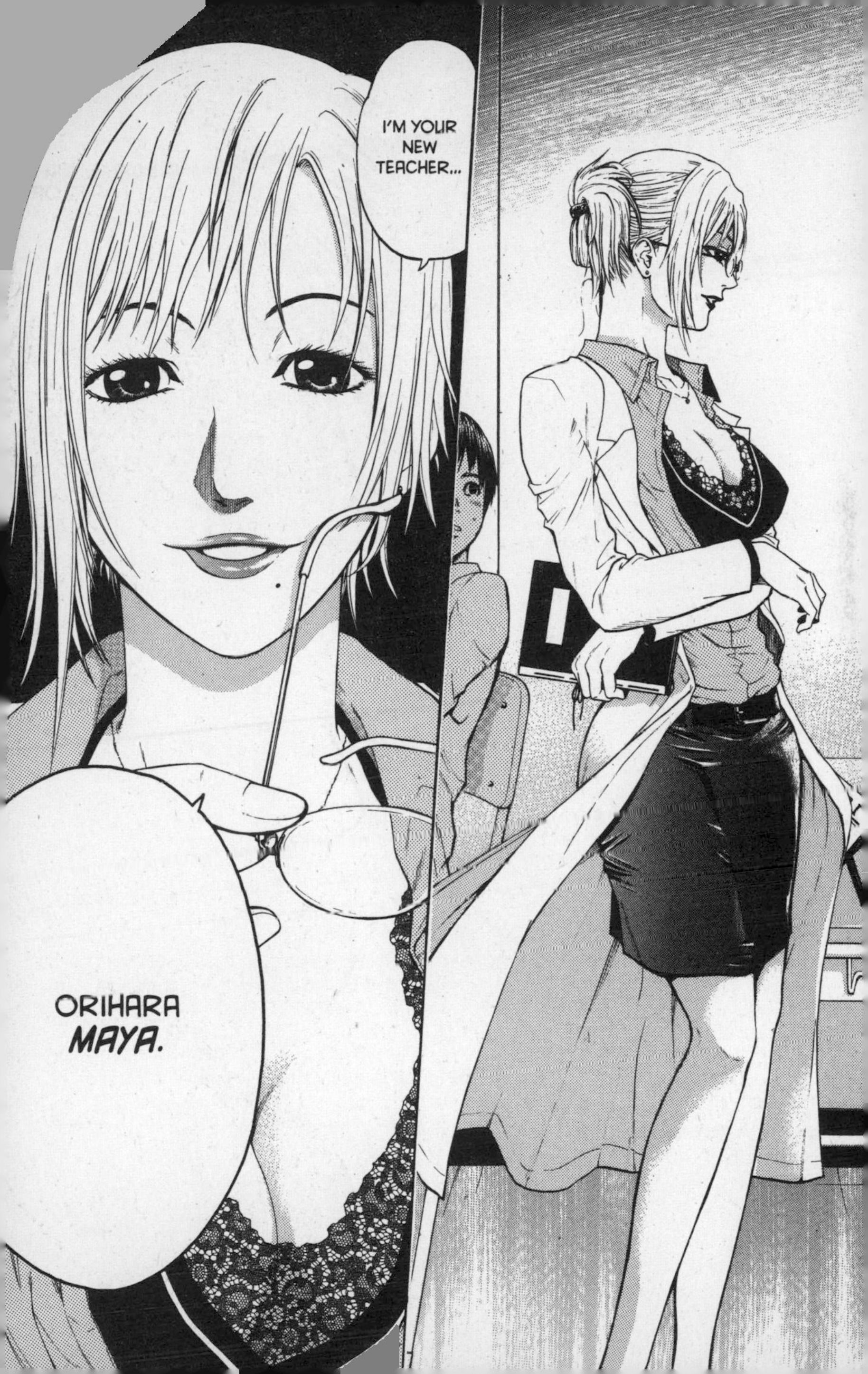
I'M YOUR NEW TEACHER...
ORIHARA MAYA.

BLOODY MONDAY

~ GLOSSARY OF TERMS • LIST 1 ~

VIRUS P7

A MICROORGANISM THAT CAN BE A CAUSE OF INFECTIOUS DISEASE. ONE OF THE MOST SIMPLE TYPES OF MICROORGANISMS, THEY ARE ENVELOPED IN A PROTEIN COAT. BECAUSE THEY CANNOT PERFORM FUNCTIONS NECESSARY FOR LIFE ON THEIR OWN, THEY MUST PARASITIZE ANIMALS, PLANTS, OR BACTERIA IN ORDER TO SURVIVE AND PROPAGATE.

VACCINE P7

A SUBSTANCE THAT IS USED TO STIMULATE AN ORGANISM'S IMMUNE SYSTEM IN ORDER TO PROTECT IT AGAINST INFECTION. VACCINES ARE DEVELOPED FROM PATHOGENS THAT CAUSE INFECTIOUS DISEASE, WHERE THE PATHOGEN'S VIRULENCE HAS BEEN WEAKENED OR DESTROYED.

OUTBREAK P7

A SITUATION WHERE AN EXTREMELY HIGH INCIDENCE OF A DISEASE OCCURS, ESPECIALLY ON A GLOBAL SCALE.

EXAMPLES OF OUTBREAKS INCLUDE THE SPANISH FLU OF 1918, THE ASIAN FLU OF 1957, THE SARS VIRUS IN 2003, AND BIRD FLU.

THE 1918 SPANISH FLU WAS A PARTICULARLY SEVERE PANDEMIC, INFECTING OVER A FOURTH OF THE WORLD'S POPULATION AND LEADING TO MORE THAN 20 MILLION DEATHS.

PUBLIC SECURITY INTELLIGENCE AGENCY P7

AN ADMINISTRATIVE BODY ESTABLISHED AS AN EXTERNAL BUREAU OF THE MINISTRY OF JUSTICE. IT INVESTIGATES GROUPS SUCH AS TERRORIST ORGANIZATIONS THAT HOLD POTENTIAL FOR VIOLENT AND SUBVERSIVE ACTS, AND IF POLICING IS DEEMED NECESSARY, IT ACTS TO RESTRICT SUCH A GROUP'S ACTIVITIES OR EVEN ENGINEERS ITS DISSOLUTION.

IN ADDITION, IT ALSO AIDS THE DAY-TO-DAY GOVERNING OF THE NATION BY FORWARDING ANY INTELLIGENCE GLEANED FROM ITS INVESTIGATIONS TO OTHER GOVERNMENTAL AGENCIES, SUCH AS THE OFFICE OF THE PRIME MINISTER, AS NECESSARY.

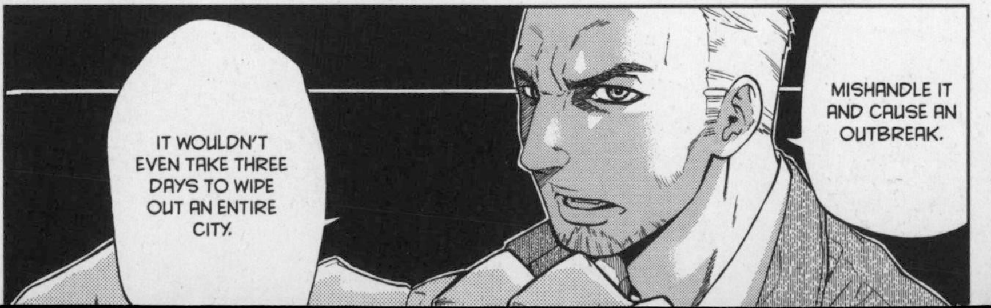
MISHANDLE IT AND CAUSE AN OUTBREAK.
IT WOULDN'T EVEN TAKE THREE DAYS TO WIPE OUT AN ENTIRE CITY.

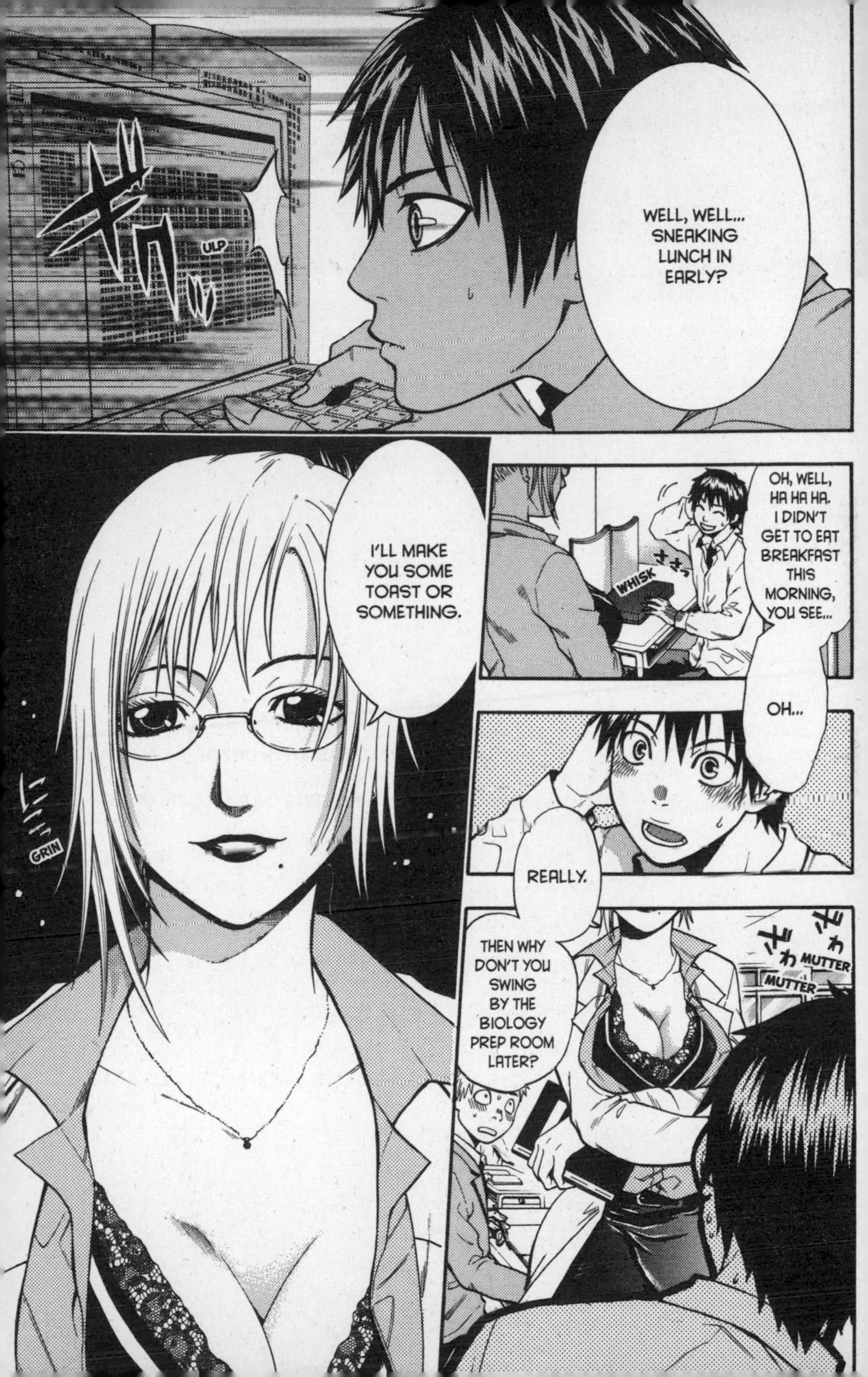
ULP
WELL, WELL... SNEAKING LUNCH IN EARLY?
OH, WELL, HA HA HA. I DIDN'T GET TO EAT BREAKFAST THIS MORNING, YOU SEE...
WHISK
OH...
REALLY.
THEN WHY DON'T YOU SWING BY THE BIOLOGY PREP ROOM LATER?
MUTTER
MUTTER
I'LL MAKE YOU SOME TOAST OR SOMETHING.
GRIN

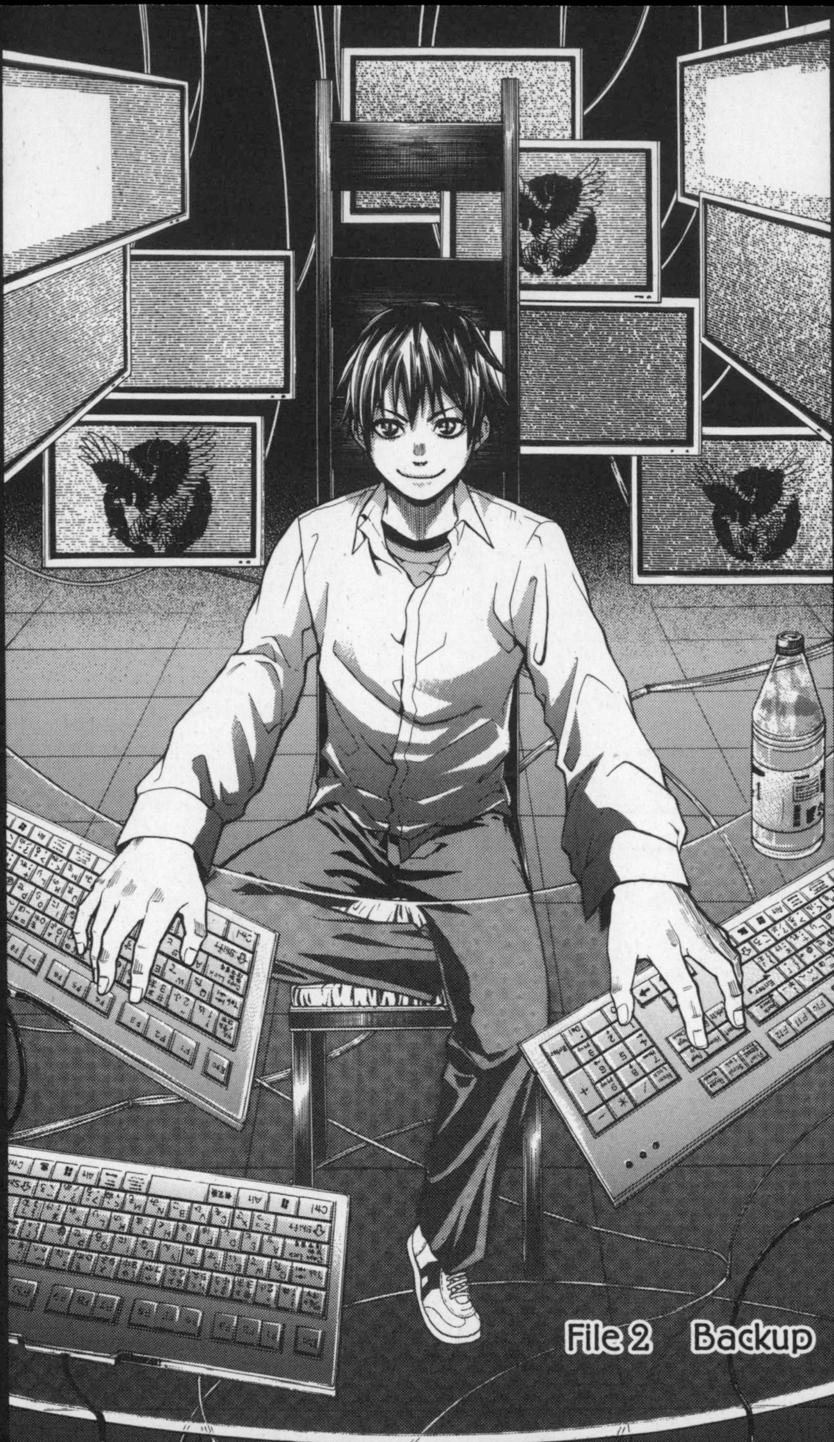

File 2 Backup

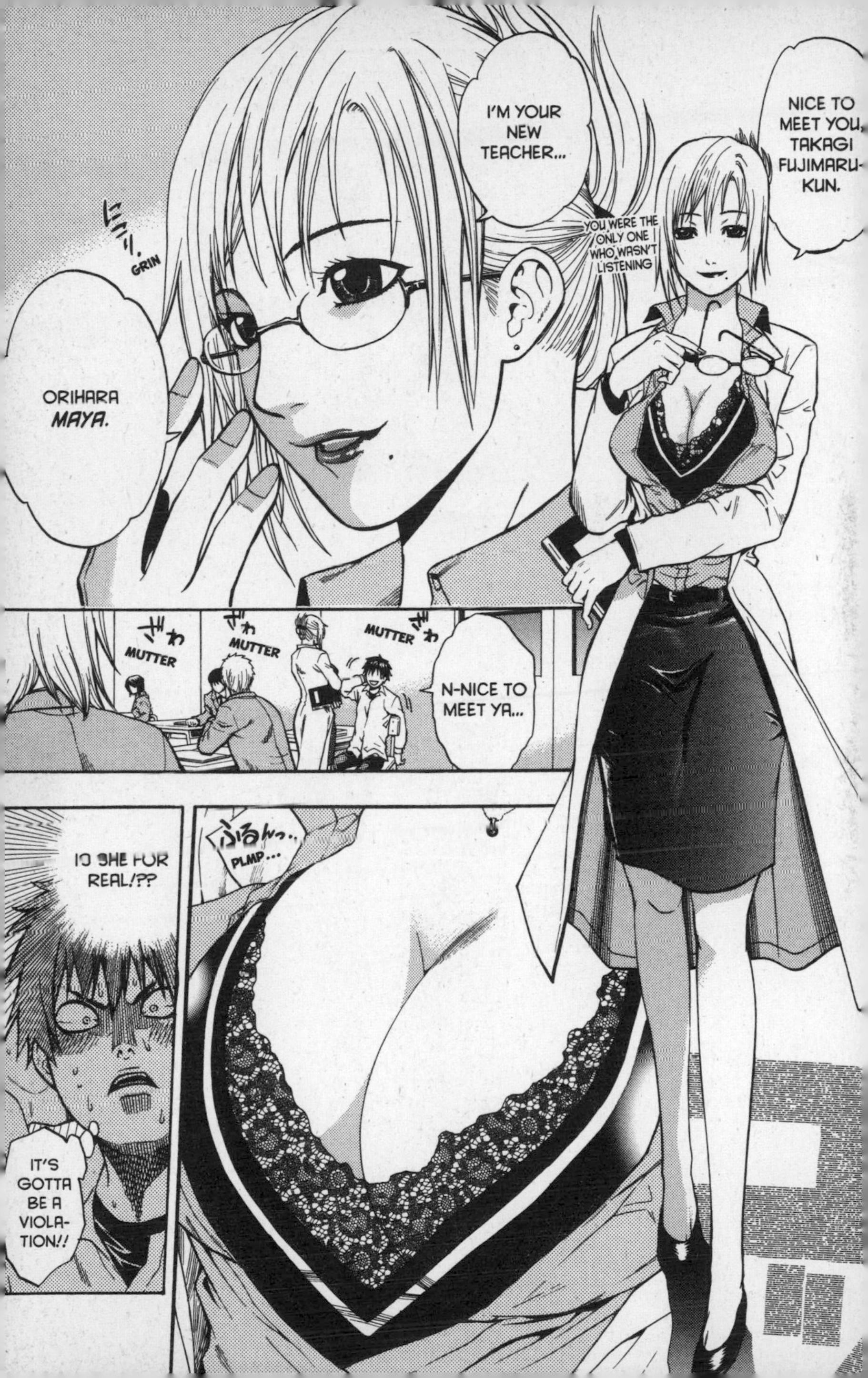
NICE TO MEET YOU, TAKAGI FUJIMARU-KUN.
YOU WERE THE ONLY ONE WHO WASN'T LISTENING
I'M YOUR NEW TEACHER...
ニヤリ。
GRIN
ORIHARA MAYA.
N-NICE TO MEET YA...
ざわ
MUTTER
ざわ
MUTTER
ざわ
MUTTER
ふるんっ...
PLMP...
IS SHE FOR REAL!??
IT'S GOTTA BE A VIOLATION!!

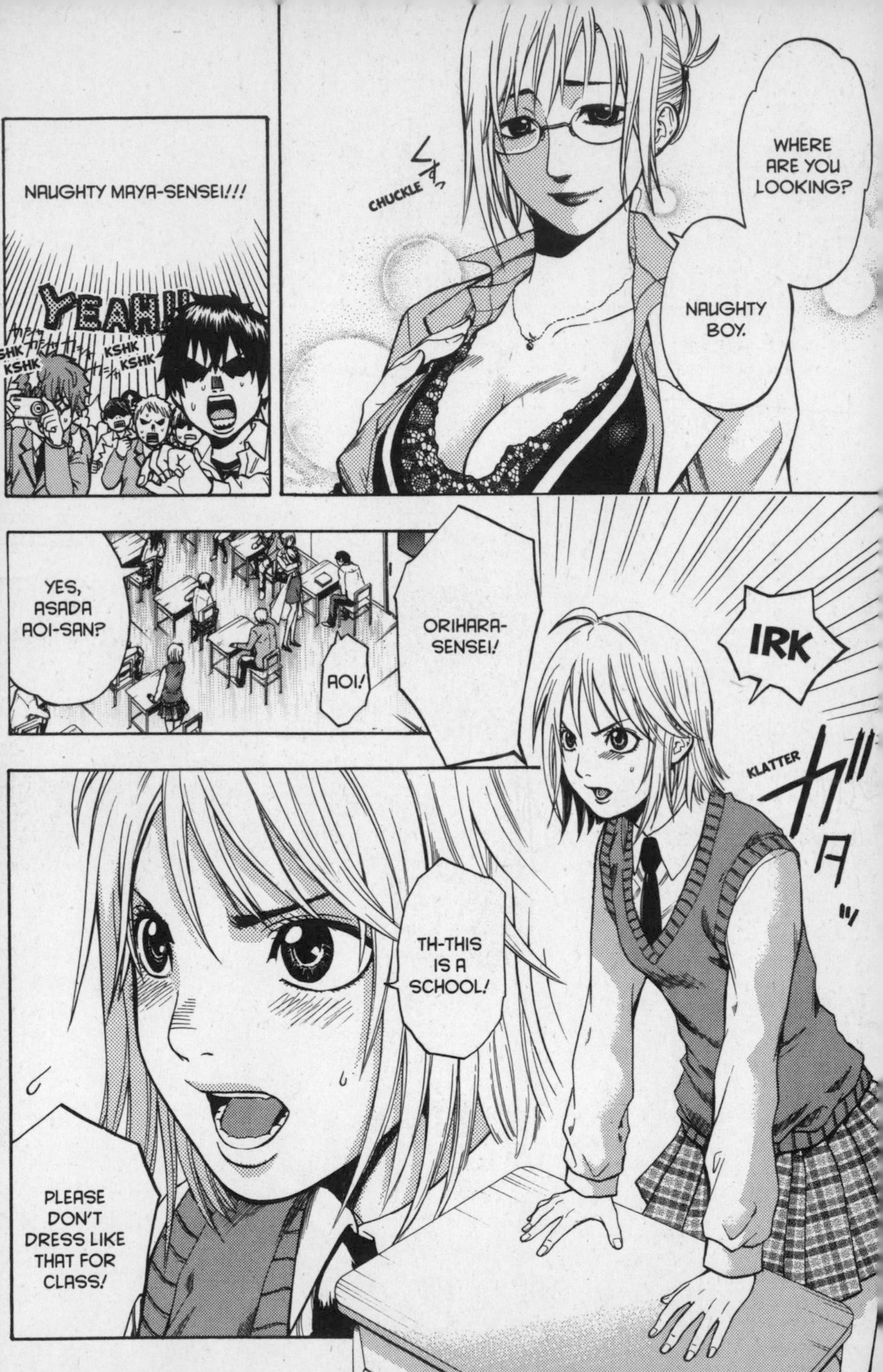
WHERE ARE YOU LOOKING?
NAUGHTY BOY.
くすっ
CHUCKLE
NAUGHTY MAYA-SENSEI!!!
YEAH!!
KSHK KSHK
KSHK KSHK
IRK
ORIHARA-SENSEI!
ガタッ
KLATTER
AOI!
YES, ASADA AOI-SAN?
TH-THIS IS A SCHOOL!
PLEASE DON'T DRESS LIKE THAT FOR CLASS!

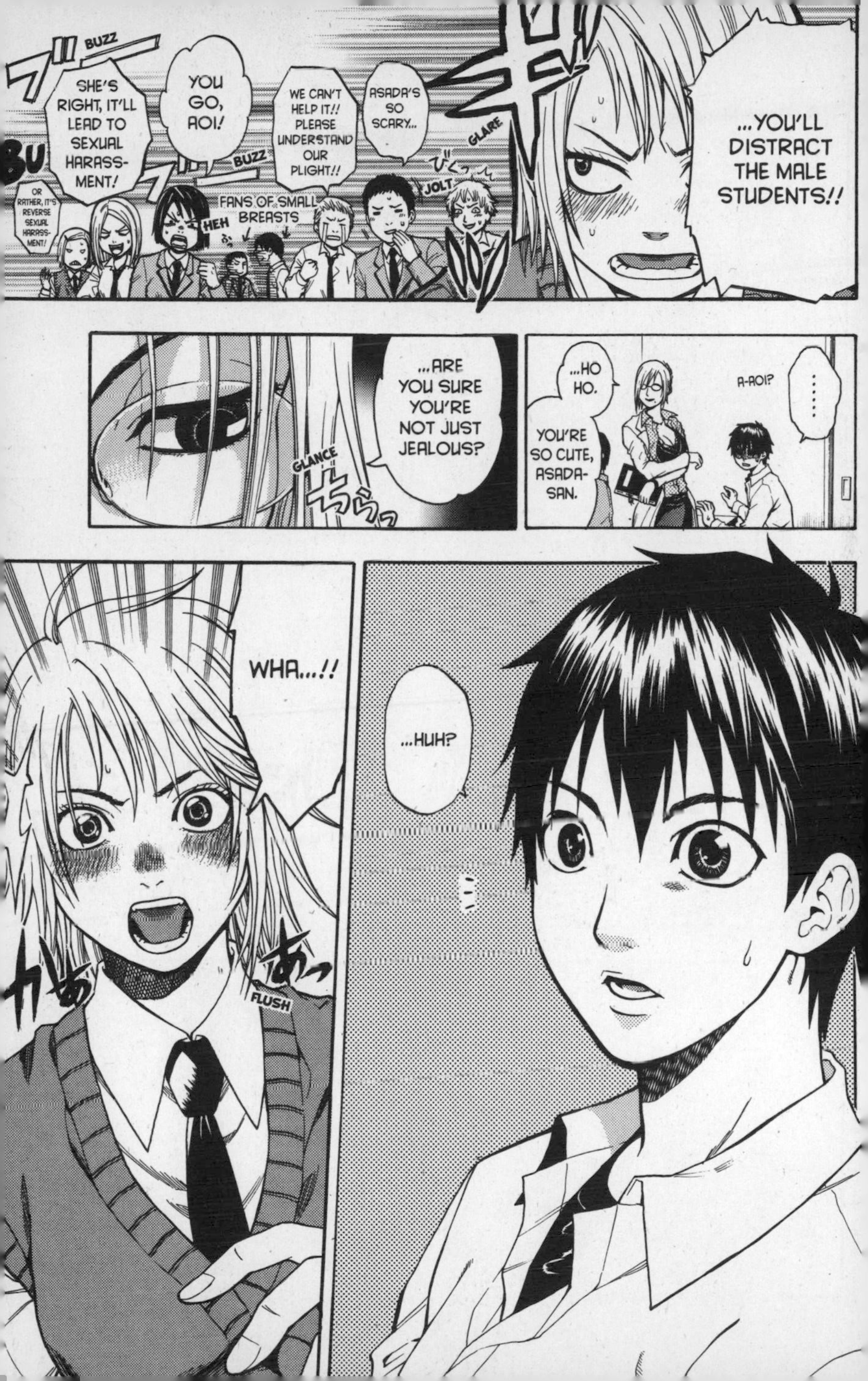
...YOU'LL DISTRACT THE MALE STUDENTS!!
GLARE
JOLT
ASADA'S SO SCARY...
WE CAN'T HELP IT!! PLEASE UNDERSTAND OUR PLIGHT!!
FANS OF SMALL BREASTS
BUZZ
YOU GO, AOI!
HEH
BUZZ
SHE'S RIGHT, IT'LL LEAD TO SEXUAL HARASSMENT!
BU
OR RATHER, IT'S REVERSE SEXUAL HARASSMENT!
......
A-AOI?
...HO HO.
YOU'RE SO CUTE, ASADA-SAN.
...ARE YOU SURE YOU'RE NOT JUST JEALOUS?
GLANCE
...HUH?
...
WHA...!!
FLUSH

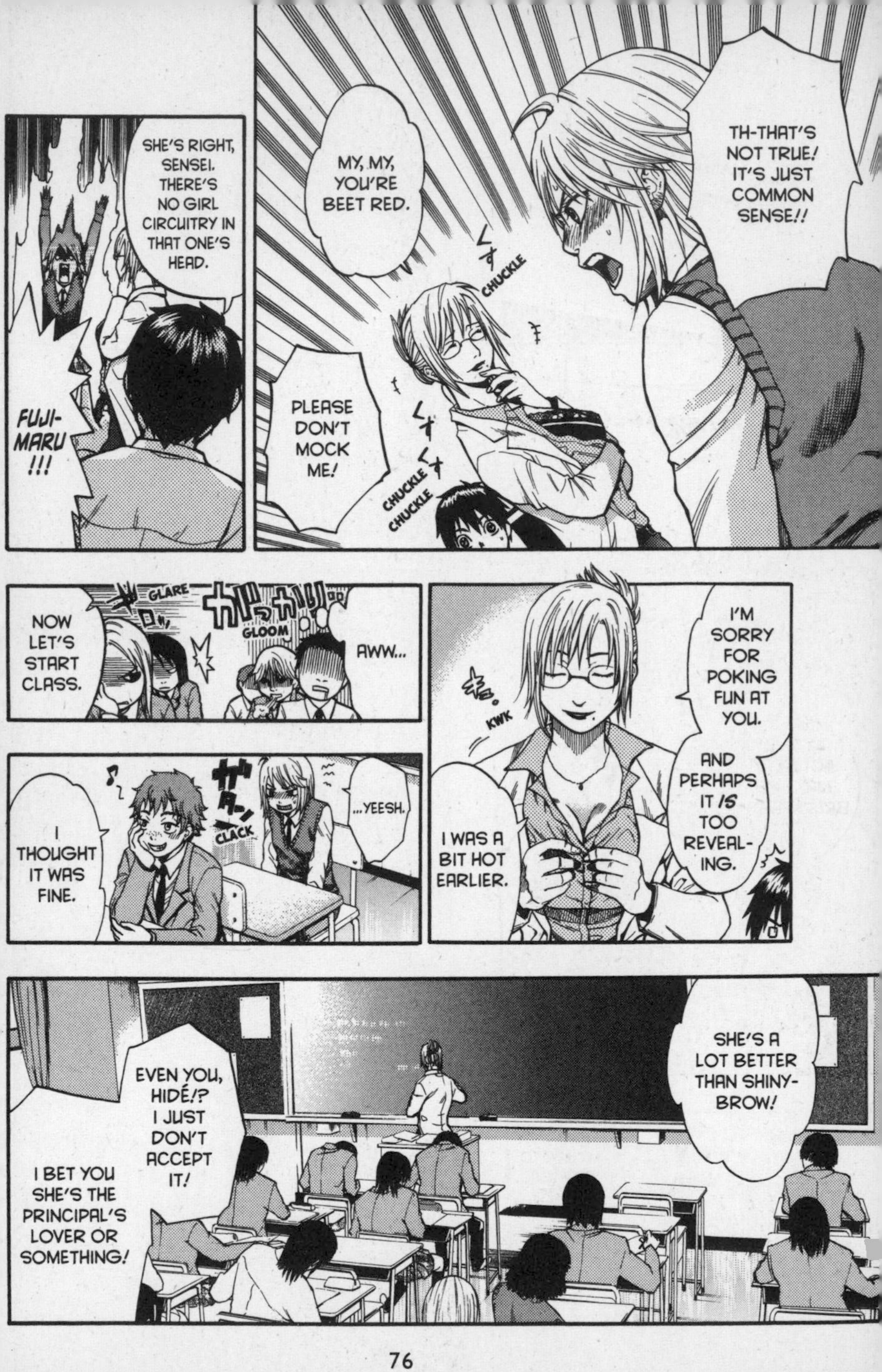
TH-THAT'S NOT TRUE! IT'S JUST COMMON SENSE!!
MY, MY, YOU'RE BEET RED.
くす
CHUCKLE
PLEASE DON'T MOCK ME!
くすくす
CHUCKLE CHUCKLE
SHE'S RIGHT, SENSEI. THERE'S NO GIRL CIRCUITRY IN THAT ONE'S HEAD.
FUJI-MARU!!!
I'M SORRY FOR POKING FUN AT YOU.
AND PERHAPS IT IS TOO REVEAL-ING.
KWK
I WAS A BIT HOT EARLIER.
AWW...
GLOOM
GLARE
NOW LET'S START CLASS.
...YEESH.
CLACK
I THOUGHT IT WAS FINE.
SHE'S A LOT BETTER THAN SHINY-BROW!
EVEN YOU, HIDÉ!? I JUST DON'T ACCEPT IT!
I BET YOU SHE'S THE PRINCIPAL'S LOVER OR SOMETHING!

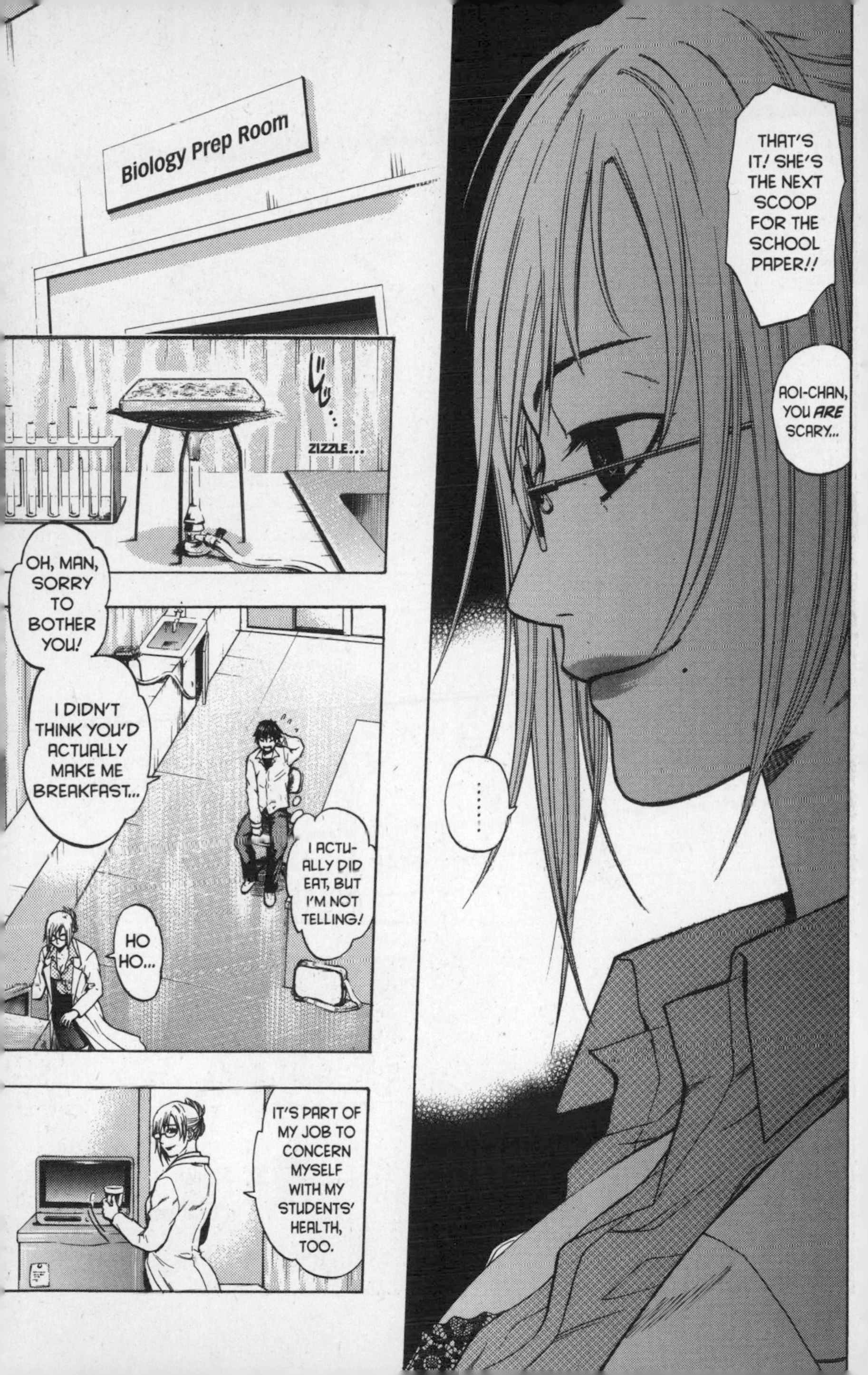
THAT'S IT! SHE'S THE NEXT SCOOP FOR THE SCHOOL PAPER!!
AOI-CHAN, YOU *ARE* SCARY...
......
Biology Prep Room
じじ...
ZIZZLE...
OH, MAN, SORRY TO BOTHER YOU!
I DIDN'T THINK YOU'D ACTUALLY MAKE ME BREAKFAST...
I ACTUALLY DID EAT, BUT I'M NOT TELLING!
HO HO...
IT'S PART OF MY JOB TO CONCERN MYSELF WITH MY STUDENTS' HEALTH, TOO.

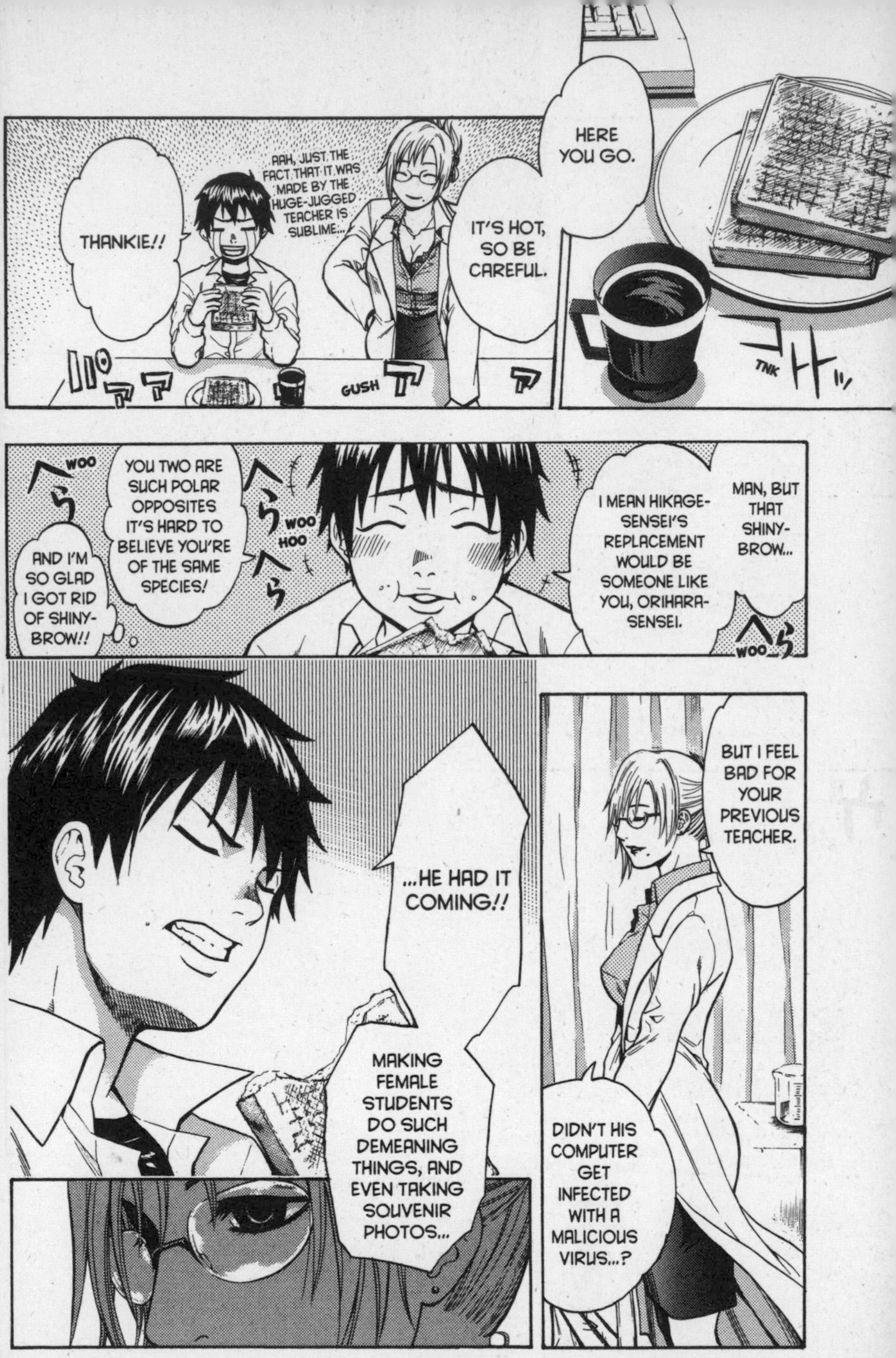
HERE YOU GO.
TNK
IT'S HOT, SO BE CAREFUL.
AAH, JUST THE FACT THAT IT WAS MADE BY THE HUGE-JUGGED TEACHER IS SUBLIME...
THANKIE!!
GUSH
MAN, BUT THAT SHINY-BROW...
WOO
I MEAN HIKAGE-SENSEI'S REPLACEMENT WOULD BE SOMEONE LIKE YOU, ORIHARA-SENSEI.
WOO HOO
YOU TWO ARE SUCH POLAR OPPOSITES IT'S HARD TO BELIEVE YOU'RE OF THE SAME SPECIES!
WOO
AND I'M SO GLAD I GOT RID OF SHINY-BROW!!
BUT I FEEL BAD FOR YOUR PREVIOUS TEACHER.
DIDN'T HIS COMPUTER GET INFECTED WITH A MALICIOUS VIRUS...?
...HE HAD IT COMING!!
MAKING FEMALE STUDENTS DO SUCH DEMEANING THINGS, AND EVEN TAKING SOUVENIR PHOTOS...

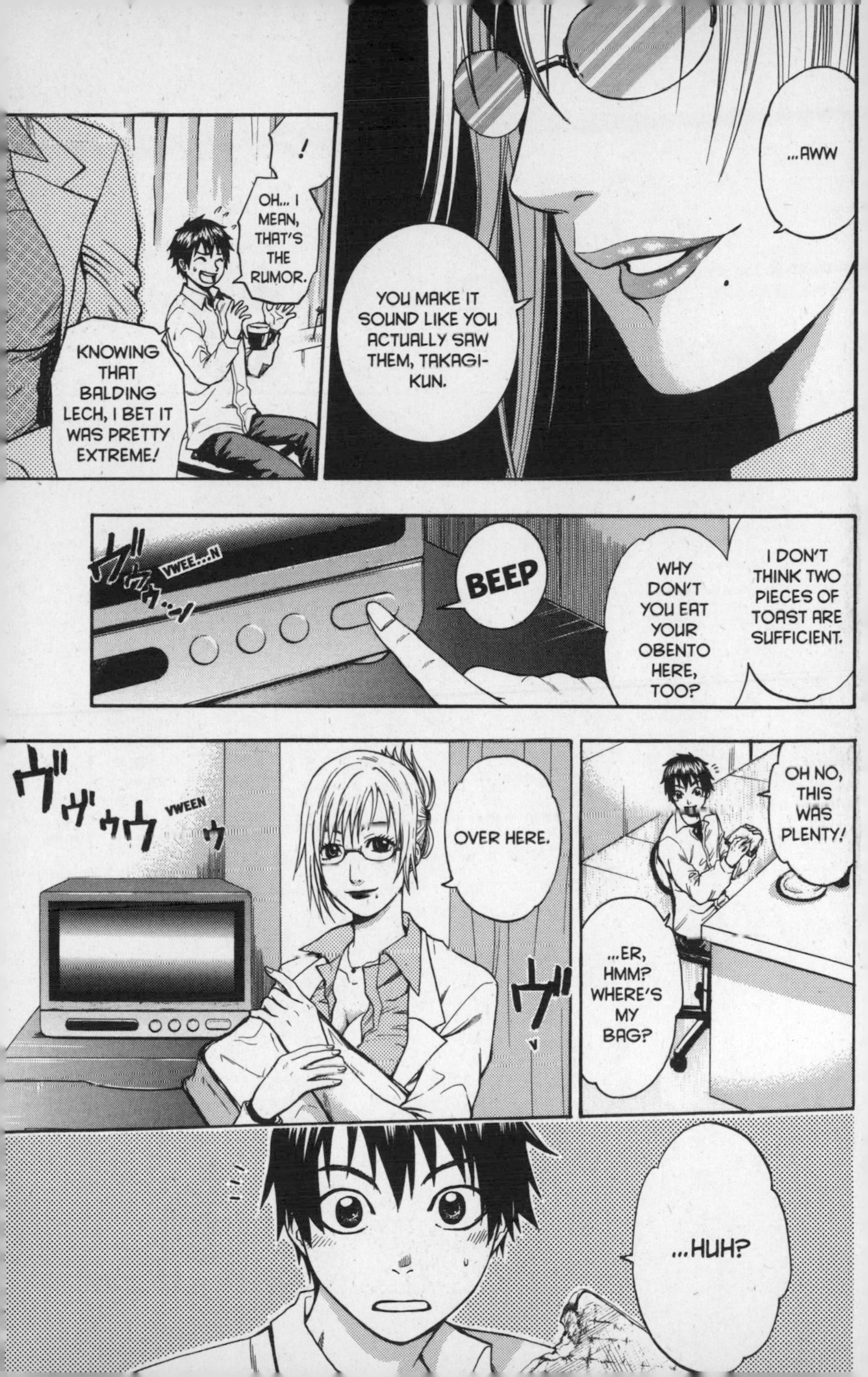
...AWW
YOU MAKE IT SOUND LIKE YOU ACTUALLY SAW THEM, TAKAGI-KUN.
!
OH... I MEAN, THAT'S THE RUMOR.
KNOWING THAT BALDING LECH, I BET IT WAS PRETTY EXTREME!
I DON'T THINK TWO PIECES OF TOAST ARE SUFFICIENT.
WHY DON'T YOU EAT YOUR OBENTO HERE, TOO?
BEEP
VWEE...N
OH NO, THIS WAS PLENTY!
...ER, HMM? WHERE'S MY BAG?
OVER HERE.
VWEEN
...HUH?

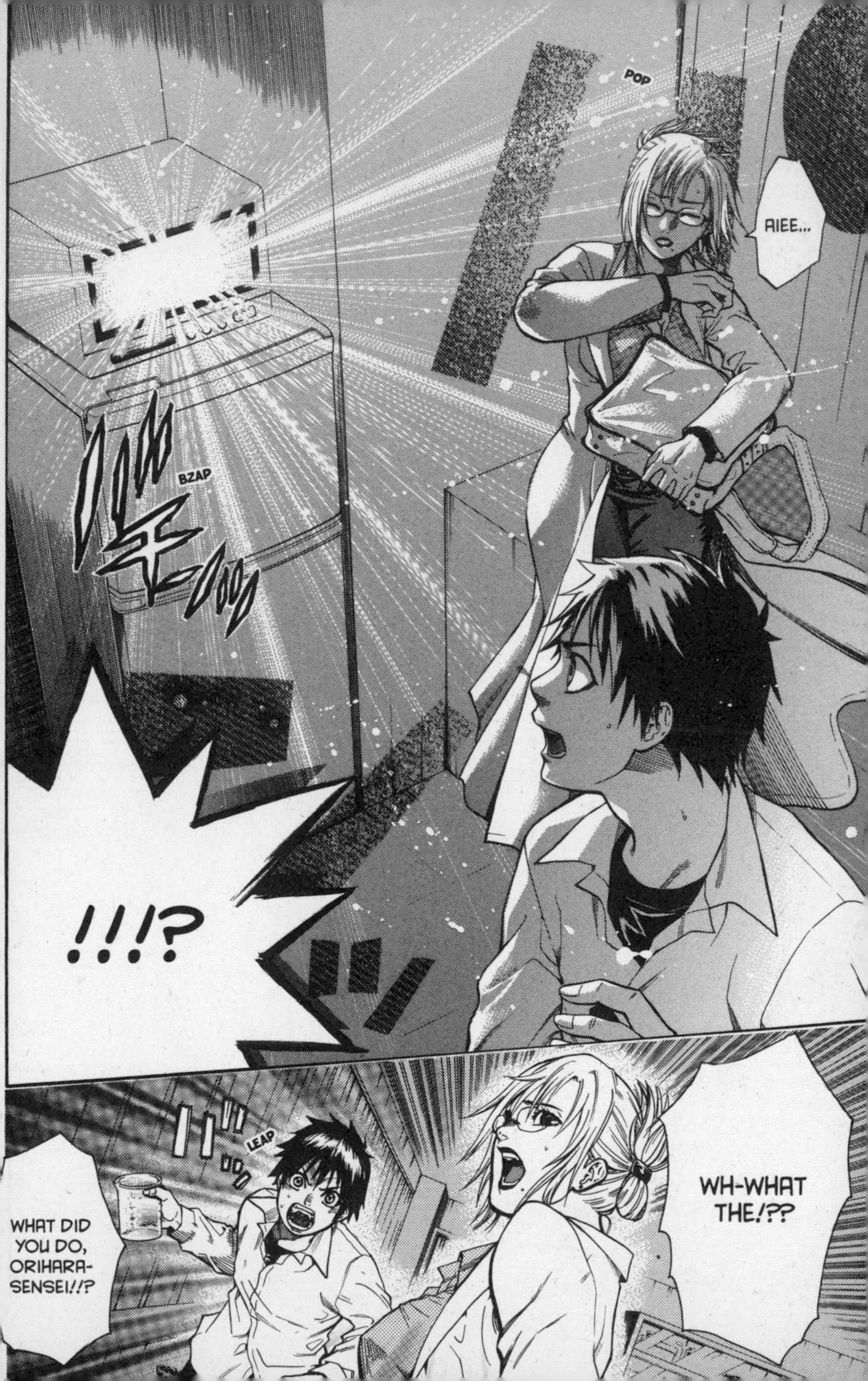
POP
AIEE...
BZAP
!!!?
WH-WHAT THE!??
LEAP
WHAT DID YOU DO, ORIHARA-SENSEI!!?

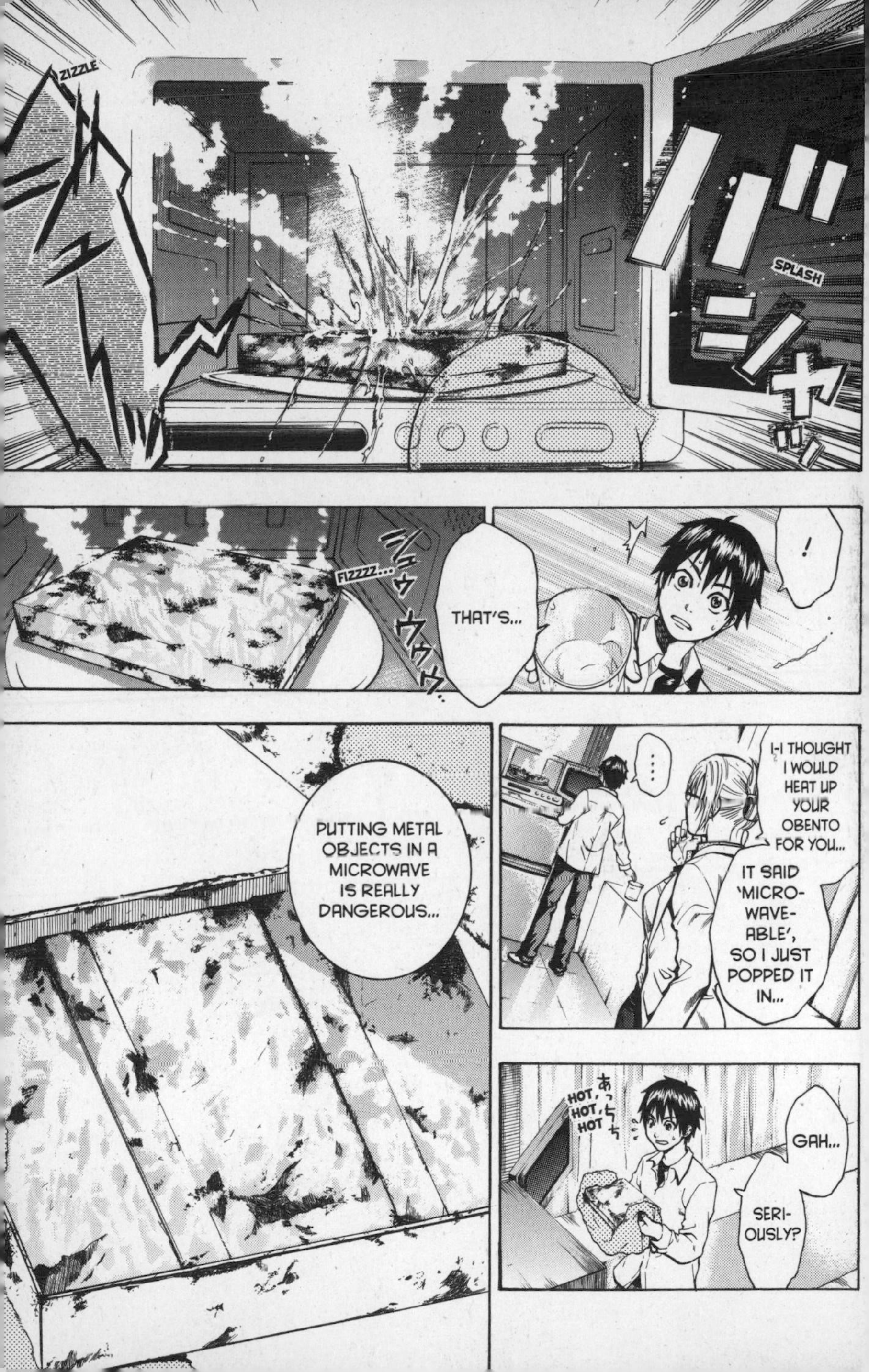
SPLASH
ZIZZLE
!
THAT'S...
FIZZZZ...
I-I THOUGHT I WOULD HEAT UP YOUR OBENTO FOR YOU...
IT SAID 'MICROWAVE-ABLE', SO I JUST POPPED IT IN...
....
GAH...
SERIOUSLY?
HOT, HOT, HOT
PUTTING METAL OBJECTS IN A MICROWAVE IS REALLY DANGEROUS...

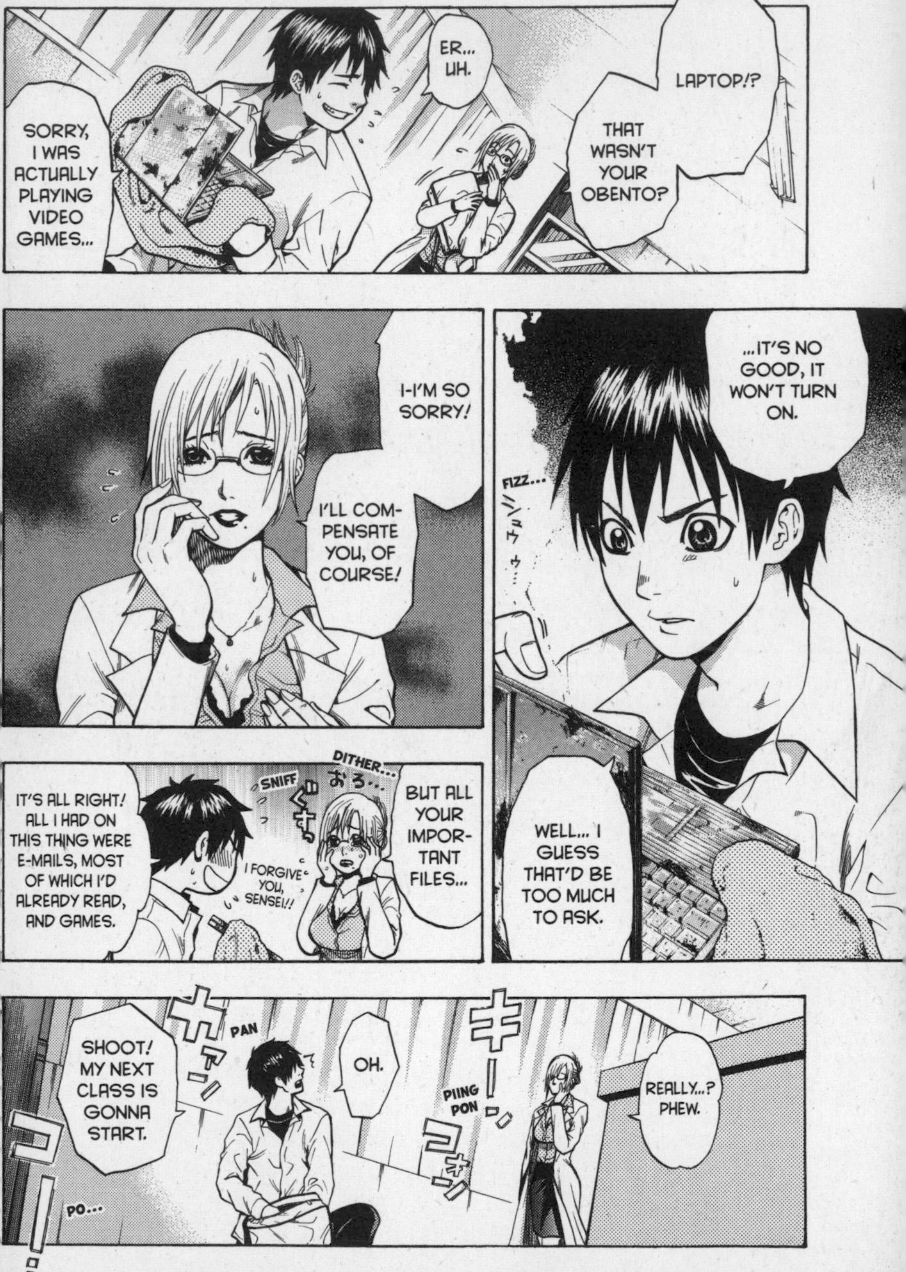
LAPTOP!?
THAT WASN'T YOUR OBENTO?
ER... UH.
SORRY, I WAS ACTUALLY PLAYING VIDEO GAMES...
...IT'S NO GOOD, IT WON'T TURN ON.
FIZZ...
WELL... I GUESS THAT'D BE TOO MUCH TO ASK.
I-I'M SO SORRY!
I'LL COMPENSATE YOU, OF COURSE!
DITHER...
BUT ALL YOUR IMPORTANT FILES...
SNIFF
I FORGIVE YOU, SENSEI!!
IT'S ALL RIGHT! ALL I HAD ON THIS THING WERE E-MAILS, MOST OF WHICH I'D ALREADY READ, AND GAMES.
REALLY...? PHEW.
PIING PON
OH.
PAN
SHOOT! MY NEXT CLASS IS GONNA START.
PO...

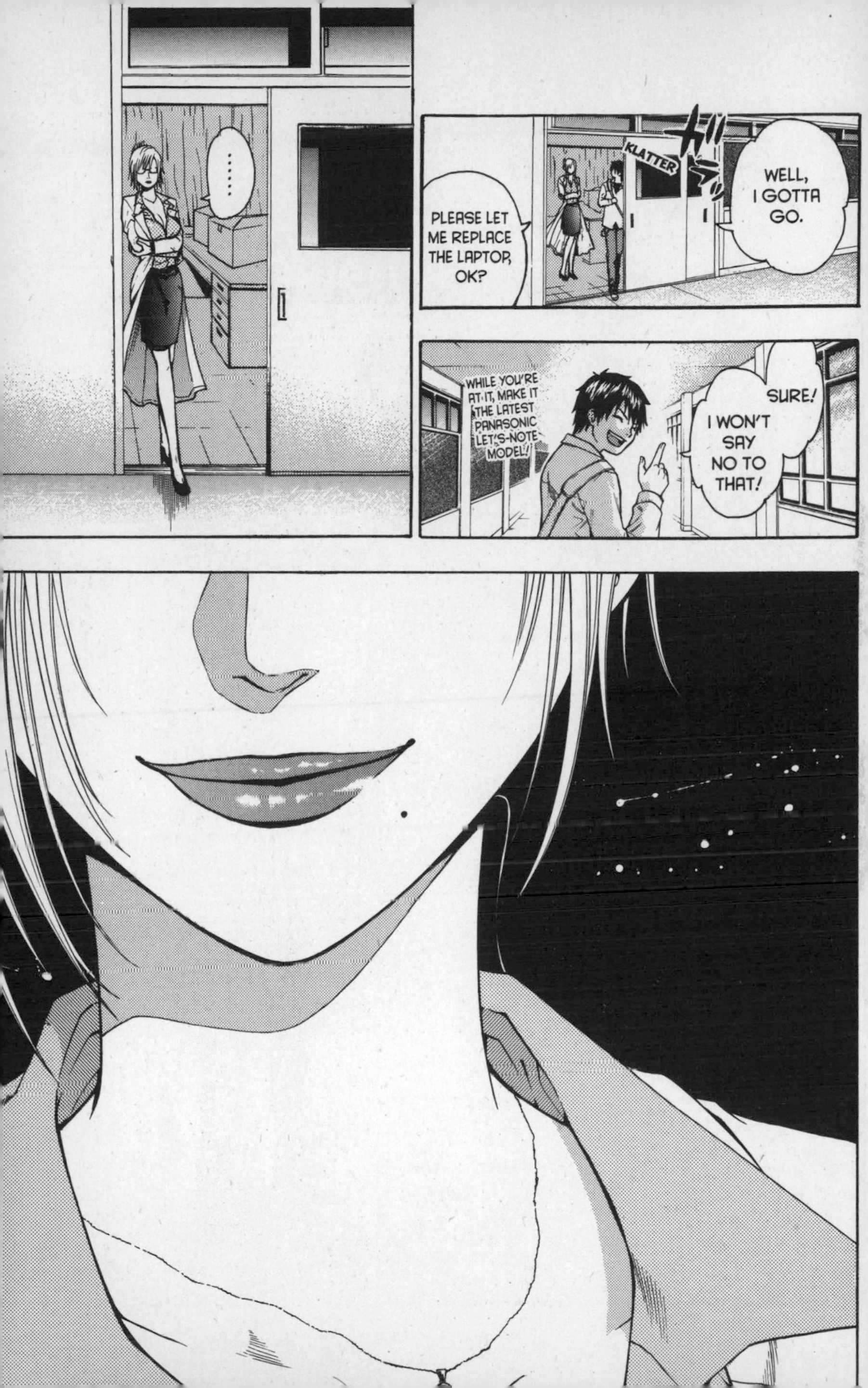
KLATTER
WELL, I GOTTA GO.
PLEASE LET ME REPLACE THE LAPTOP, OK?
SURE! I WON'T SAY NO TO THAT!
WHILE YOU'RE AT IT, MAKE IT THE LATEST PANASONIC LET'S-NOTE MODEL!
......

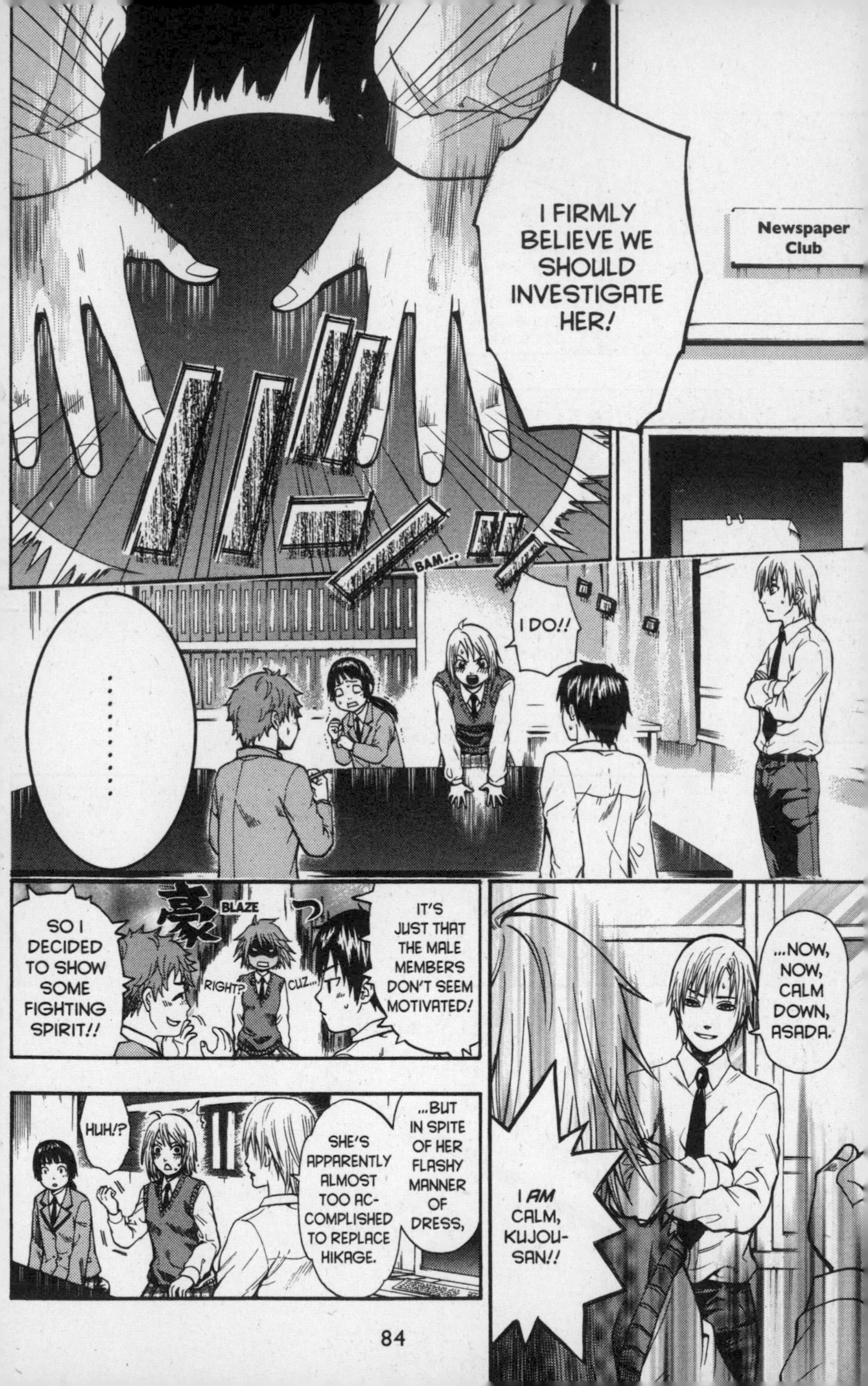
Newspaper Club
I FIRMLY BELIEVE WE SHOULD INVESTIGATE HER!
BAM...
I DO!!
......
...NOW, NOW, CALM DOWN, ASADA.
I AM CALM, KUJOU-SAN!!
IT'S JUST THAT THE MALE MEMBERS DON'T SEEM MOTIVATED!
CUZ...
RIGHT?
BLAZE
SO I DECIDED TO SHOW SOME FIGHTING SPIRIT!!
...BUT IN SPITE OF HER FLASHY MANNER OF DRESS,
SHE'S APPARENTLY ALMOST TOO AC-COMPLISHED TO REPLACE HIKAGE.
HUH!?

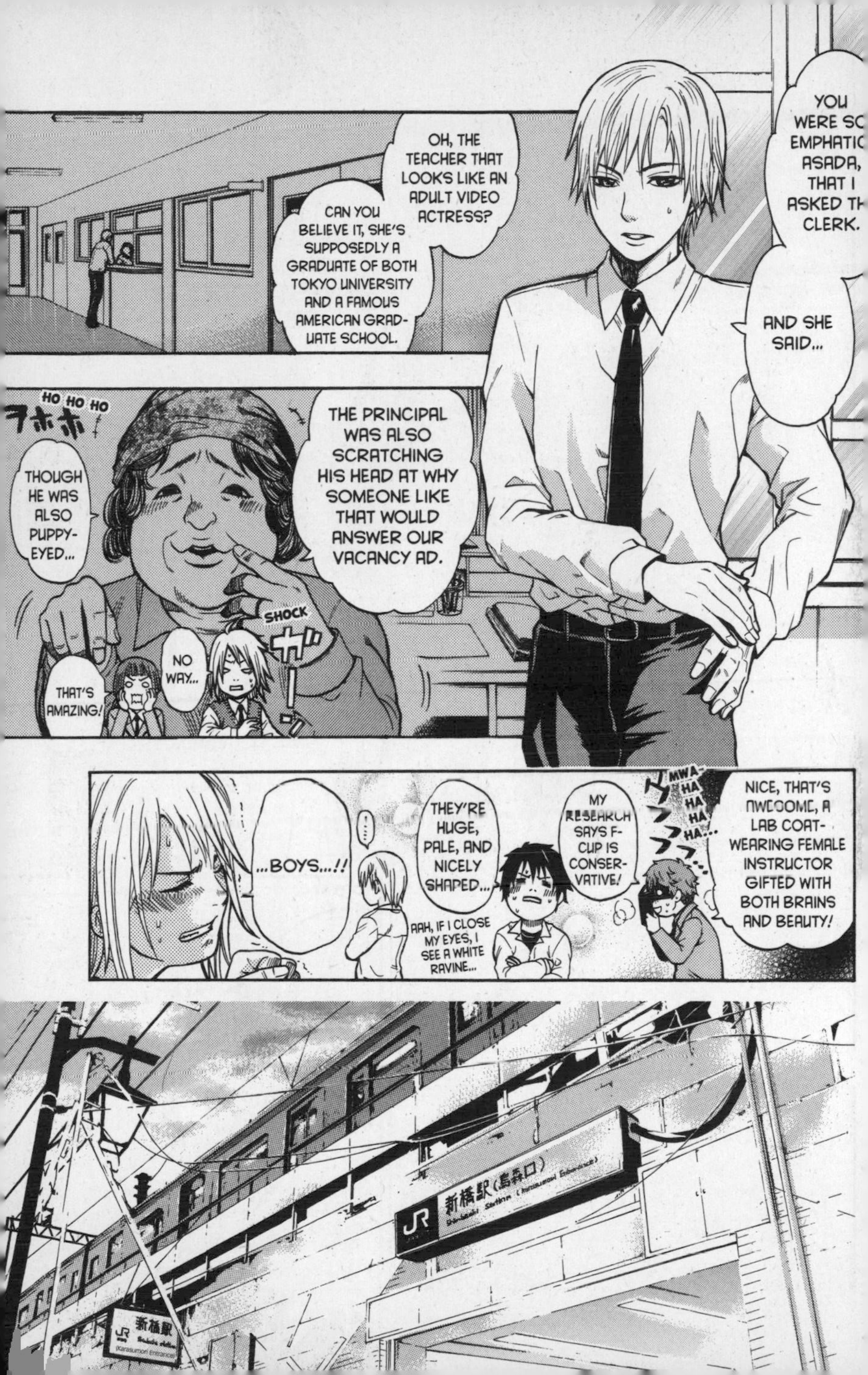
YOU WERE SO EMPHATIC ASADA, THAT I ASKED THE CLERK.
AND SHE SAID...
OH, THE TEACHER THAT LOOKS LIKE AN ADULT VIDEO ACTRESS?
CAN YOU BELIEVE IT, SHE'S SUPPOSEDLY A GRADUATE OF BOTH TOKYO UNIVERSITY AND A FAMOUS AMERICAN GRAD-UATE SCHOOL.
THE PRINCIPAL WAS ALSO SCRATCHING HIS HEAD AT WHY SOMEONE LIKE THAT WOULD ANSWER OUR VACANCY AD.
HO HO HO
THOUGH HE WAS ALSO PUPPY-EYED...
SHOCK
NO WAY...
THAT'S AMAZING!
NICE, THAT'S AWESOME, A LAB COAT-WEARING FEMALE INSTRUCTOR GIFTED WITH BOTH BRAINS AND BEAUTY!
MWA-HA HA HA HA...
MY RESEARCH SAYS F-CUP IS CONSER-VATIVE!
THEY'RE HUGE, PALE, AND NICELY SHAPED...
AAH, IF I CLOSE MY EYES, I SEE A WHITE RAVINE...
...!
...BOYS...!!
JR
新橋駅(烏森口)
JR
新橋駅
(Karasumori Entrance)

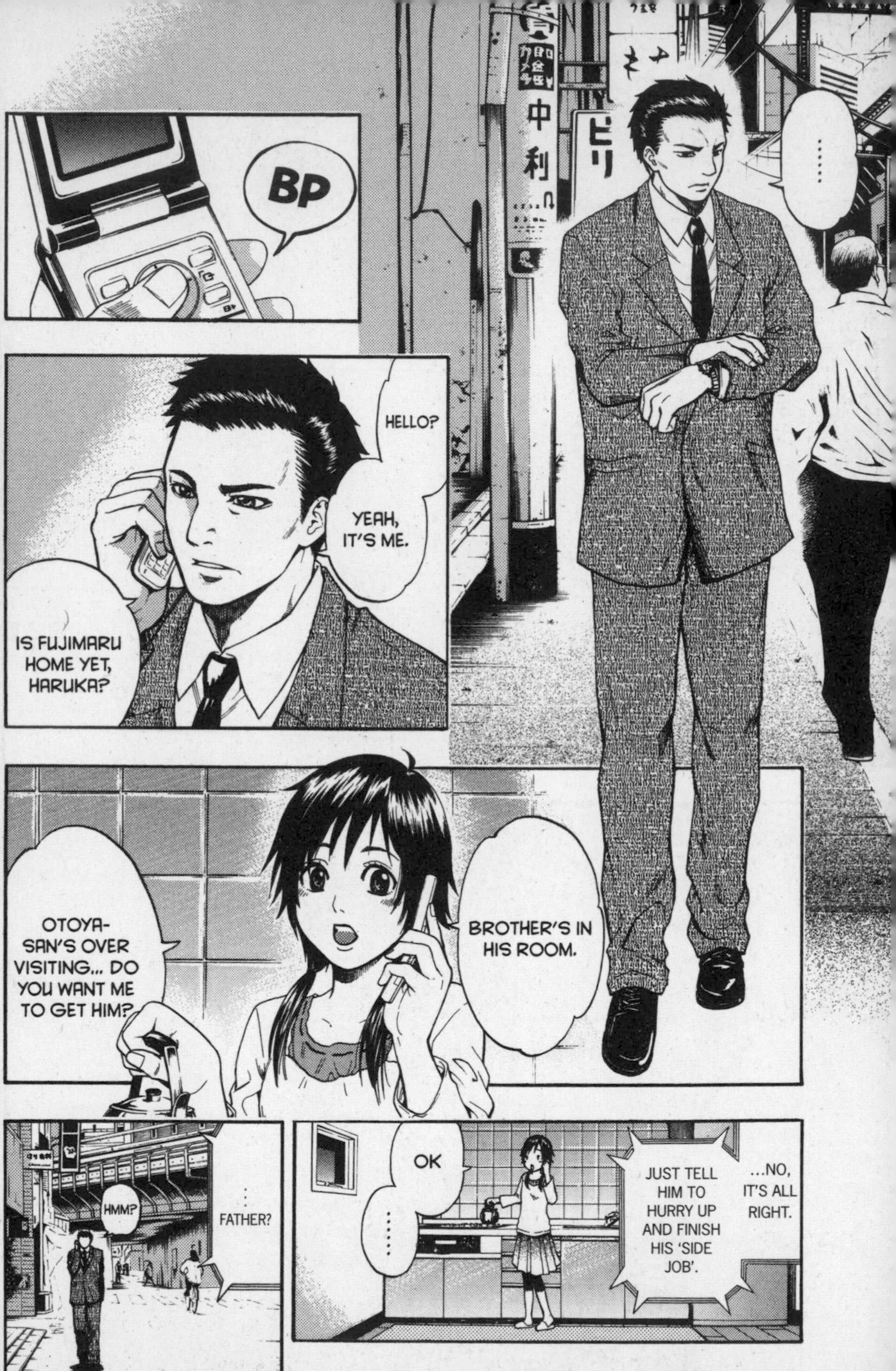
……
BP
HELLO?
YEAH, IT'S ME.
IS FUJIMARU HOME YET, HARUKA?
BROTHER'S IN HIS ROOM.
OTOYA-SAN'S OVER VISITING... DO YOU WANT ME TO GET HIM?
...NO, IT'S ALL RIGHT.
JUST TELL HIM TO HURRY UP AND FINISH HIS 'SIDE JOB'.
OK
……
…FATHER?
HMM?

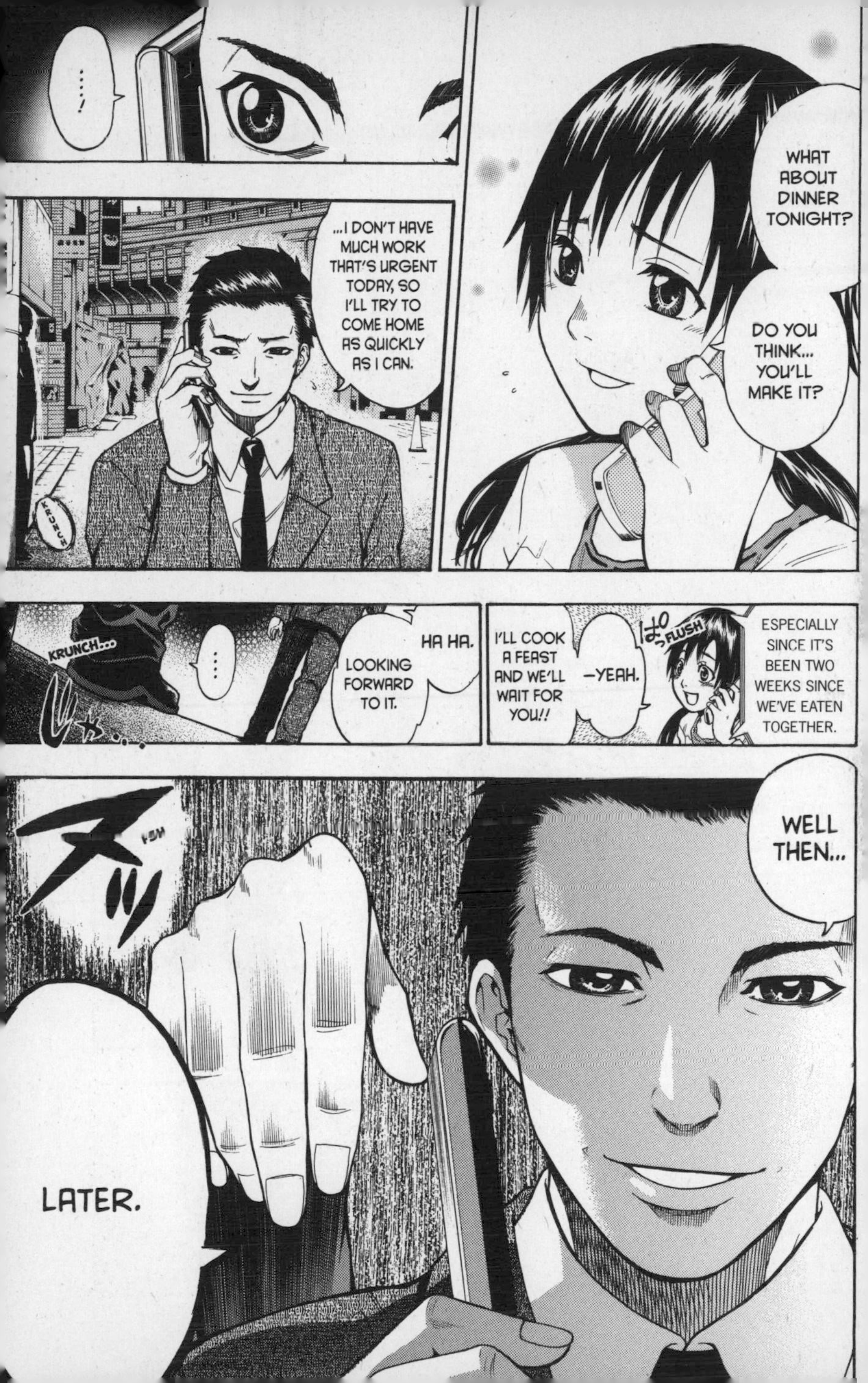
WHAT ABOUT DINNER TONIGHT?
DO YOU THINK... YOU'LL MAKE IT?
....!
...I DON'T HAVE MUCH WORK THAT'S URGENT TODAY, SO I'LL TRY TO COME HOME AS QUICKLY AS I CAN.
KRUNCH
ESPECIALLY SINCE IT'S BEEN TWO WEEKS SINCE WE'VE EATEN TOGETHER.
FLUSH
—YEAH.
I'LL COOK A FEAST AND WE'LL WAIT FOR YOU!!
HA HA.
LOOKING FORWARD TO IT.
.....
KRUNCH...
WELL THEN...
LATER.

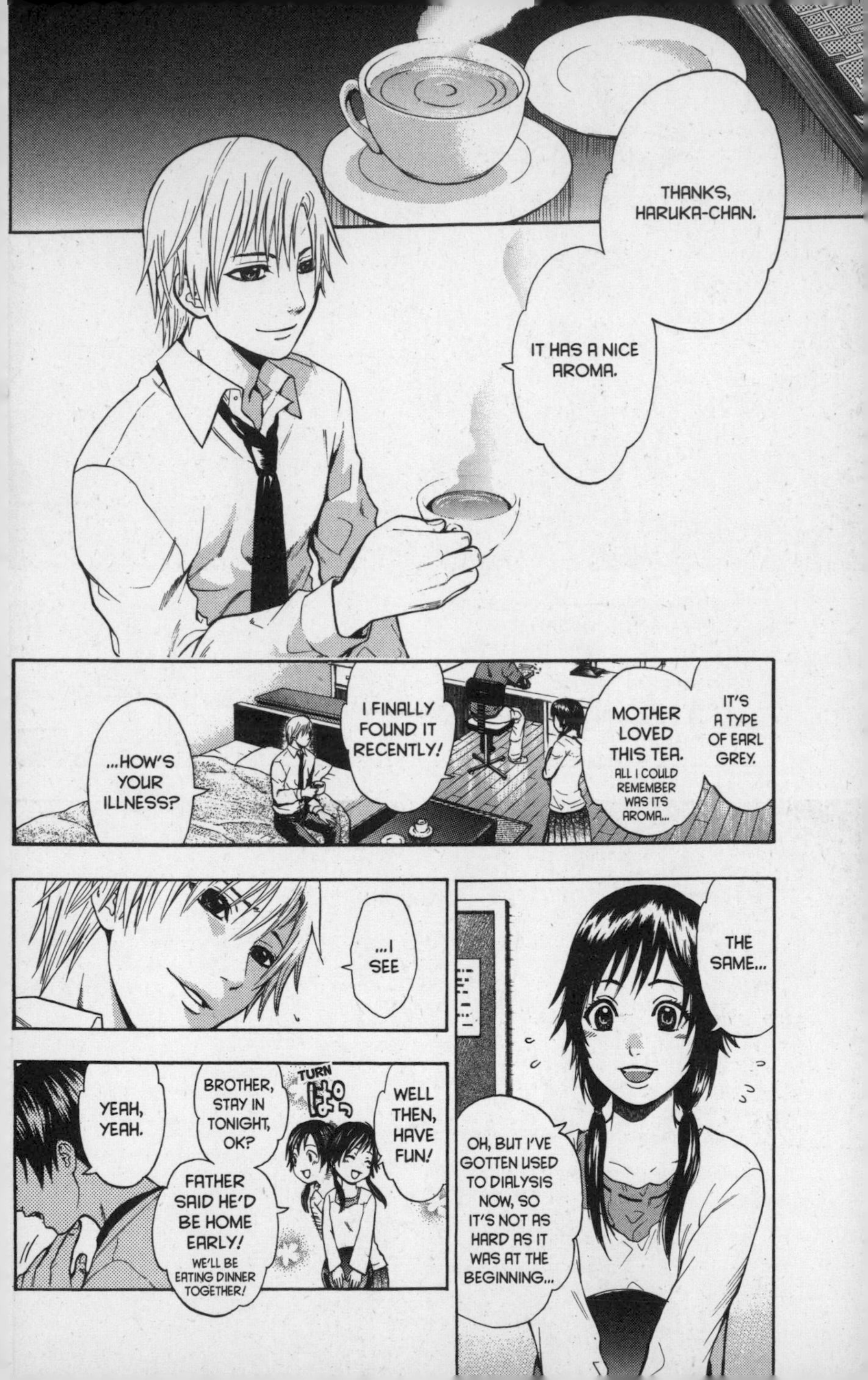
THANKS, HARUKA-CHAN.
IT HAS A NICE AROMA.
IT'S A TYPE OF EARL GREY.
MOTHER LOVED THIS TEA.
ALL I COULD REMEMBER WAS ITS AROMA...
I FINALLY FOUND IT RECENTLY!
...HOW'S YOUR ILLNESS?
THE SAME...
OH, BUT I'VE GOTTEN USED TO DIALYSIS NOW, SO IT'S NOT AS HARD AS IT WAS AT THE BEGINNING...
...I SEE
WELL THEN, HAVE FUN!
TURN
BROTHER, STAY IN TONIGHT, OK?
FATHER SAID HE'D BE HOME EARLY!
WE'LL BE EATING DINNER TOGETHER!
YEAH, YEAH.

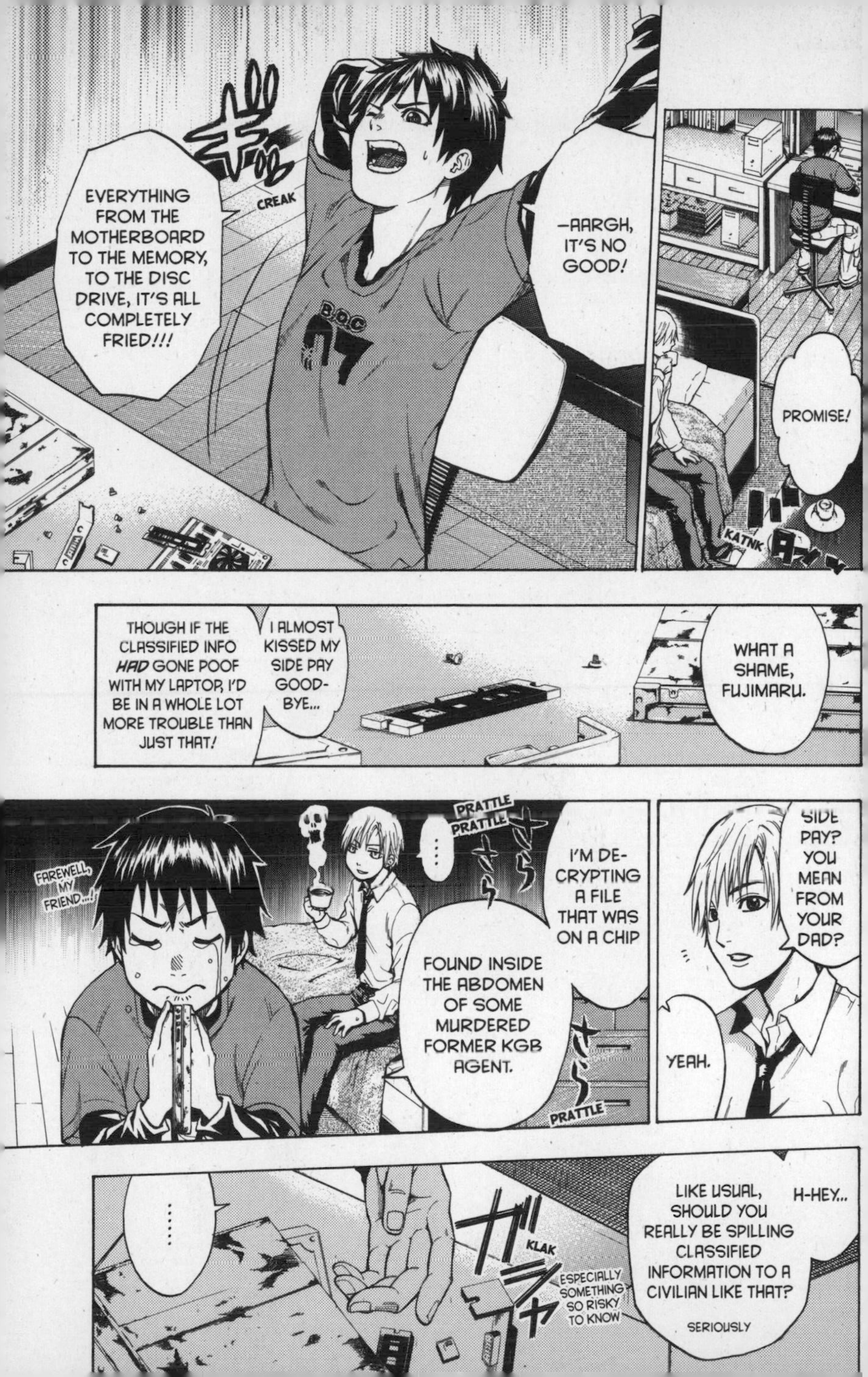
PROMISE!
KATNK
—AARGH, IT'S NO GOOD!
EVERYTHING FROM THE MOTHERBOARD TO THE MEMORY, TO THE DISC DRIVE, IT'S ALL COMPLETELY FRIED!!!
CREAK
WHAT A SHAME, FUJIMARU.
I ALMOST KISSED MY SIDE PAY GOOD-BYE...
THOUGH IF THE CLASSIFIED INFO *HAD* GONE POOF WITH MY LAPTOP, I'D BE IN A WHOLE LOT MORE TROUBLE THAN JUST THAT!
SIDE PAY? YOU MEAN FROM YOUR DAD?
YEAH.
I'M DE-CRYPTING A FILE THAT WAS ON A CHIP
FOUND INSIDE THE ABDOMEN OF SOME MURDERED FORMER KGB AGENT.
PRATTLE PRATTLE
PRATTLE
.....
FAREWELL, MY FRIEND...!
H-HEY...
LIKE USUAL, SHOULD YOU REALLY BE SPILLING CLASSIFIED INFORMATION TO A CIVILIAN LIKE THAT?
SERIOUSLY
ESPECIALLY SOMETHING SO RISKY TO KNOW
KLAK
......

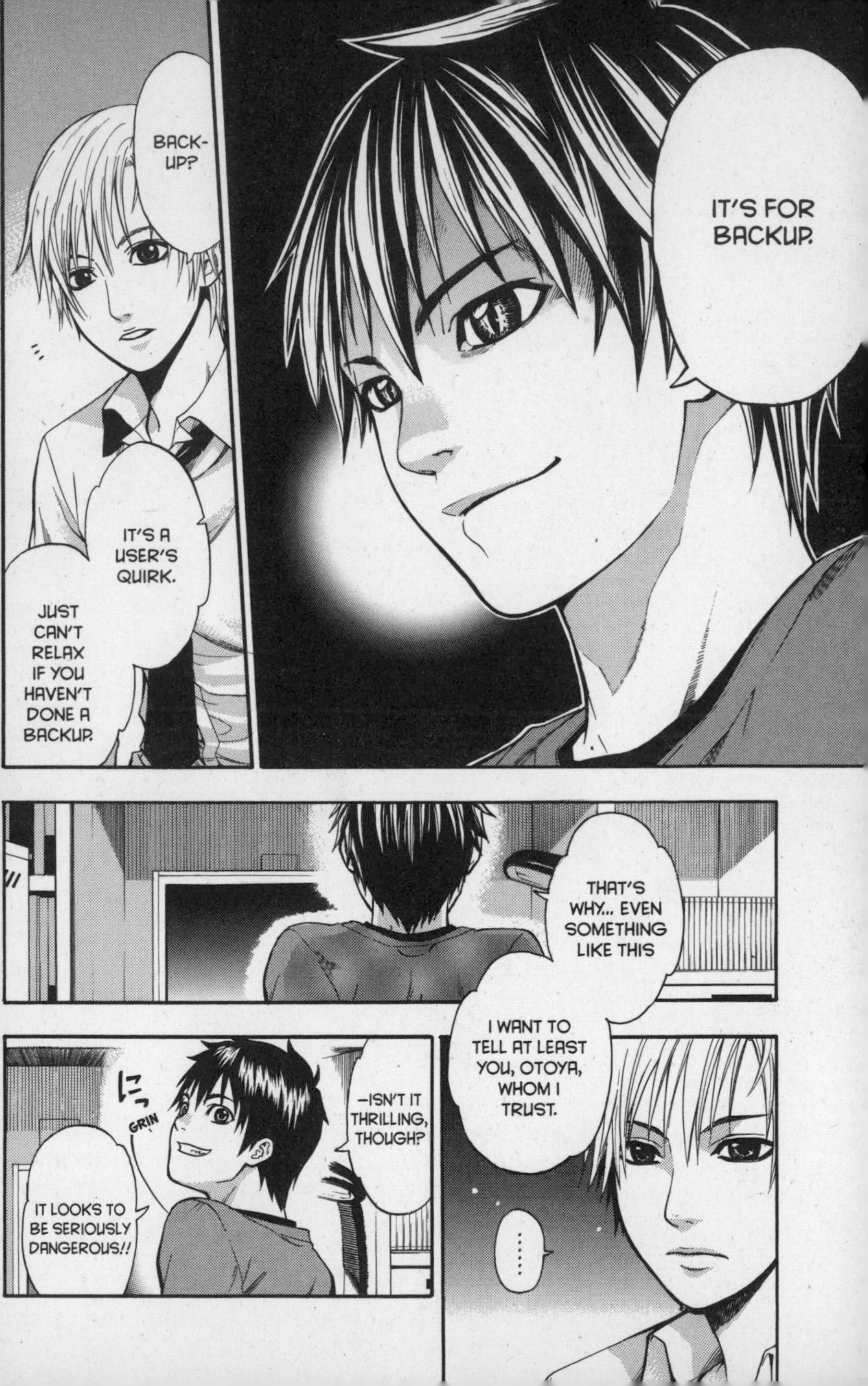
IT'S FOR BACKUP.
BACK-UP?
IT'S A USER'S QUIRK.
JUST CAN'T RELAX IF YOU HAVEN'T DONE A BACKUP.
THAT'S WHY... EVEN SOMETHING LIKE THIS
I WANT TO TELL AT LEAST YOU, OTOYA, WHOM I TRUST.
......
—ISN'T IT THRILLING, THOUGH?
にっ
GRIN
IT LOOKS TO BE SERIOUSLY DANGEROUS!!

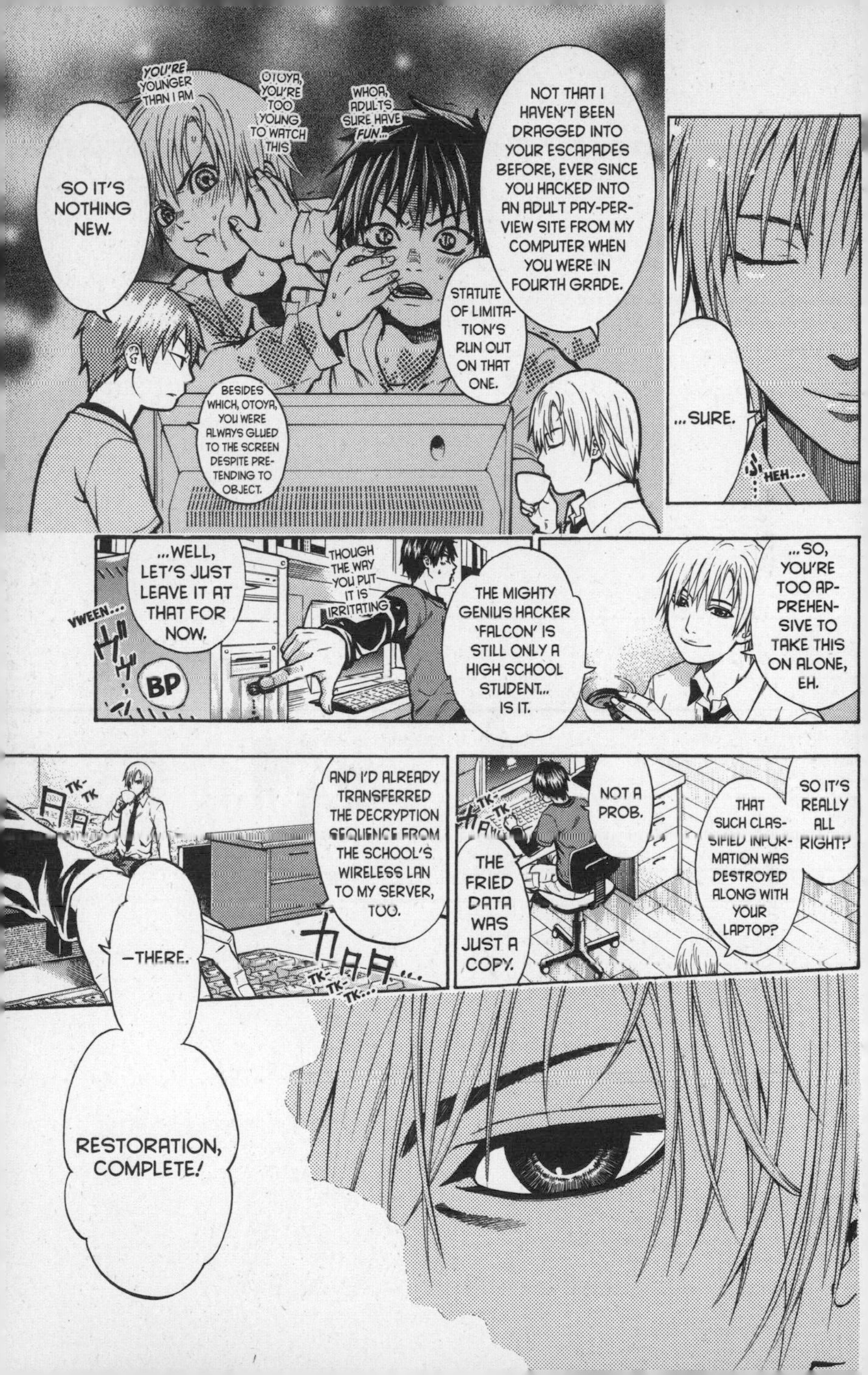
...SURE.
HEH...
NOT THAT I HAVEN'T BEEN DRAGGED INTO YOUR ESCAPADES BEFORE, EVER SINCE YOU HACKED INTO AN ADULT PAY-PER-VIEW SITE FROM MY COMPUTER WHEN YOU WERE IN FOURTH GRADE.
WHOA, ADULTS SURE HAVE *FUN*...
OTOYA, YOU'RE TOO YOUNG TO WATCH THIS
YOU'RE YOUNGER THAN I AM
STATUTE OF LIMITATION'S RUN OUT ON THAT ONE.
SO IT'S NOTHING NEW.
BESIDES WHICH, OTOYA, YOU WERE ALWAYS GLUED TO THE SCREEN DESPITE PRETENDING TO OBJECT.
...SO, YOU'RE TOO APPREHENSIVE TO TAKE THIS ON ALONE, EH.
THE MIGHTY GENIUS HACKER 'FALCON' IS STILL ONLY A HIGH SCHOOL STUDENT... IS IT.
THOUGH THE WAY YOU PUT IT IS IRRITATING
...WELL, LET'S JUST LEAVE IT AT THAT FOR NOW.
VWEEN...
BP
SO IT'S REALLY ALL RIGHT?
THAT SUCH CLASSIFIED INFORMATION WAS DESTROYED ALONG WITH YOUR LAPTOP?
NOT A PROB.
THE FRIED DATA WAS JUST A COPY.
TK-TK
AND I'D ALREADY TRANSFERRED THE DECRYPTION SEQUENCE FROM THE SCHOOL'S WIRELESS LAN TO MY SERVER, TOO.
TK-TK
—THERE.
TK-TK...
RESTORATION, COMPLETE!

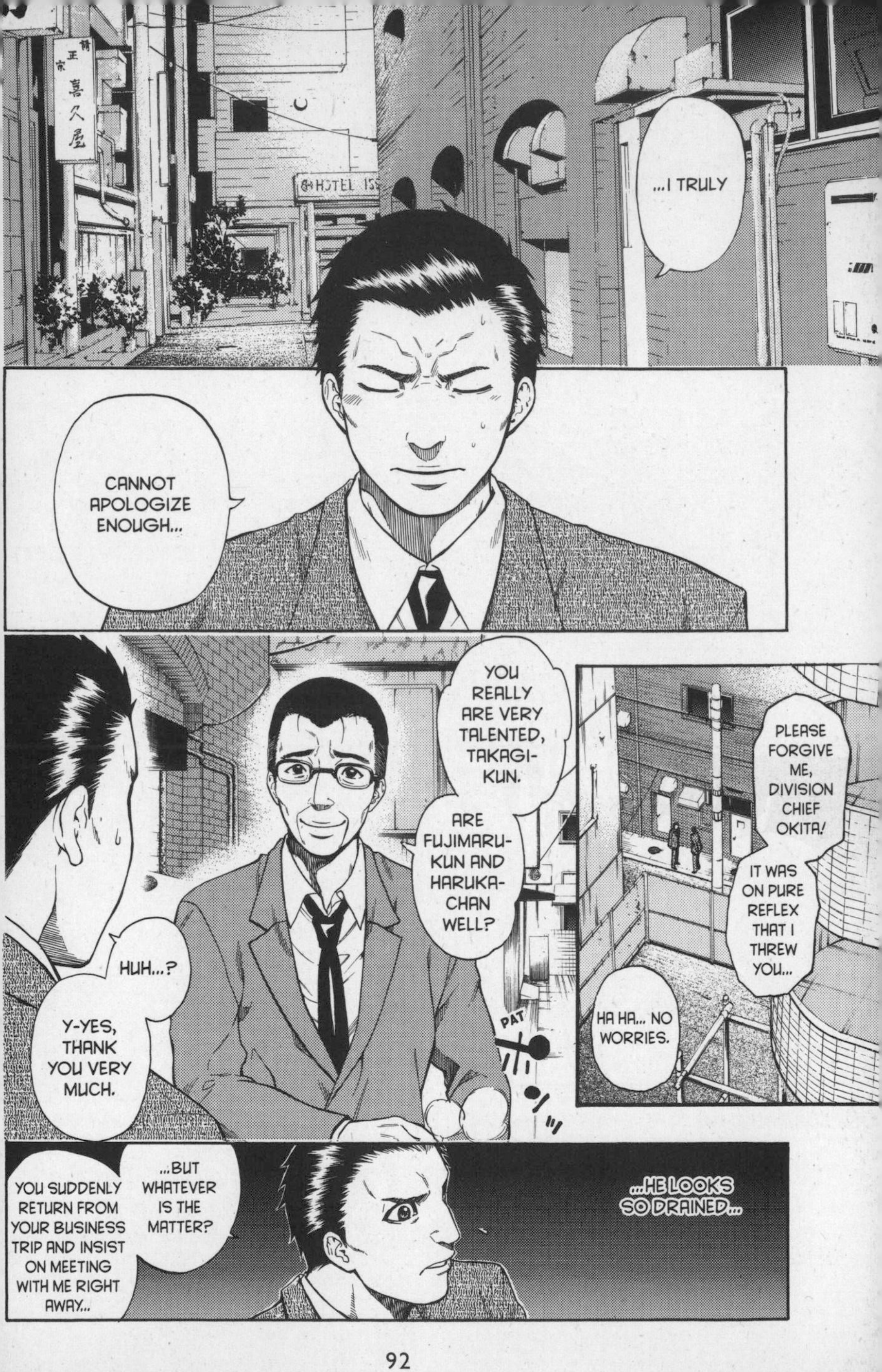
...I TRULY
CANNOT APOLOGIZE ENOUGH...
PLEASE FORGIVE ME, DIVISION CHIEF OKITA!
IT WAS ON PURE REFLEX THAT I THREW YOU...
HA HA... NO WORRIES.
YOU REALLY ARE VERY TALENTED, TAKAGI-KUN.
ARE FUJIMARU-KUN AND HARUKA-CHAN WELL?
PAT
HUH...?
Y-YES, THANK YOU VERY MUCH.
...HE LOOKS SO DRAINED...
...BUT WHATEVER IS THE MATTER?
YOU SUDDENLY RETURN FROM YOUR BUSINESS TRIP AND INSIST ON MEETING WITH ME RIGHT AWAY...

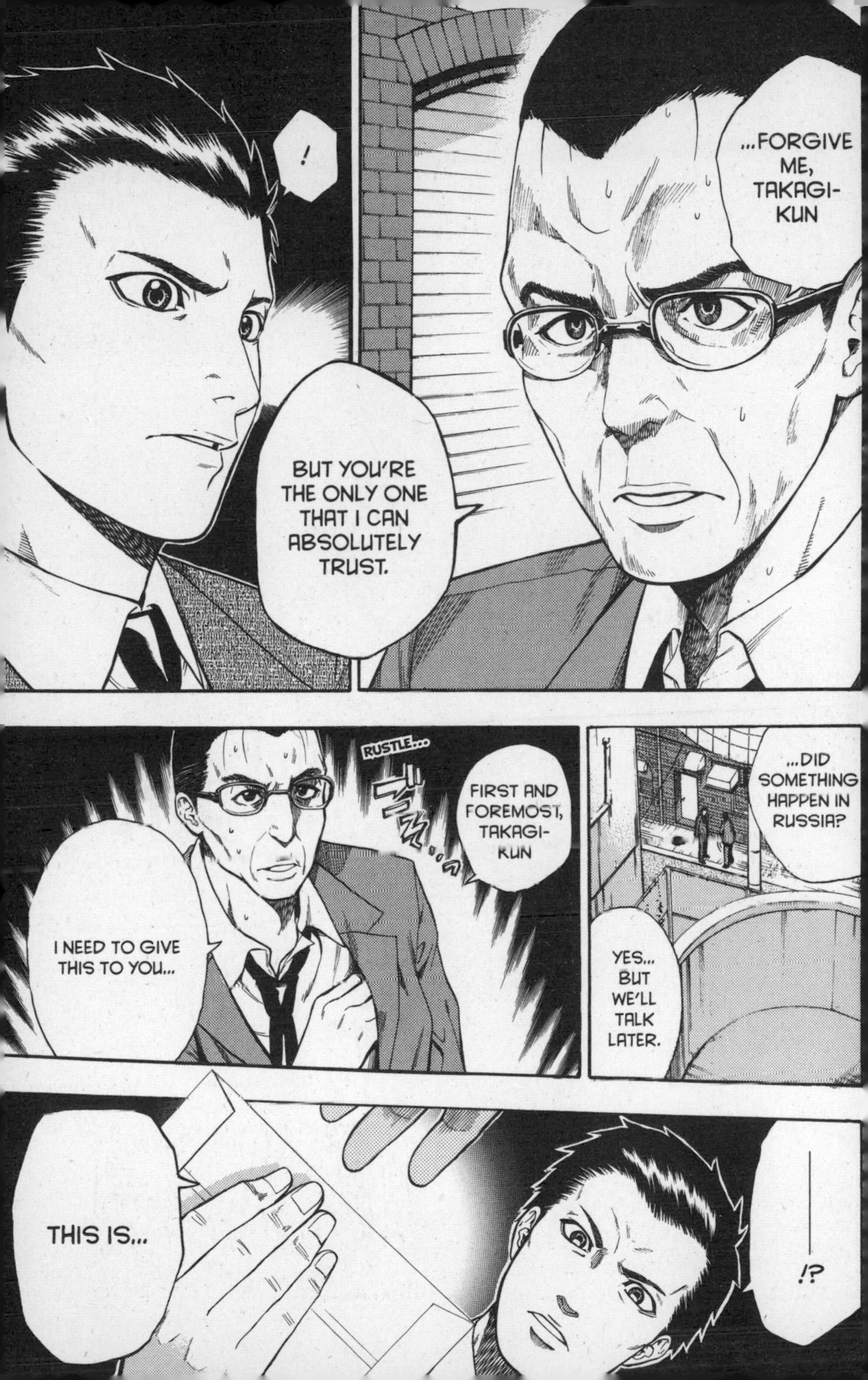
...FORGIVE ME, TAKAGI-KUN
BUT YOU'RE THE ONLY ONE THAT I CAN ABSOLUTELY TRUST.
!
...DID SOMETHING HAPPEN IN RUSSIA?
YES... BUT WE'LL TALK LATER.
FIRST AND FOREMOST, TAKAGI-KUN
RUSTLE...
I NEED TO GIVE THIS TO YOU...
——!?
THIS IS...

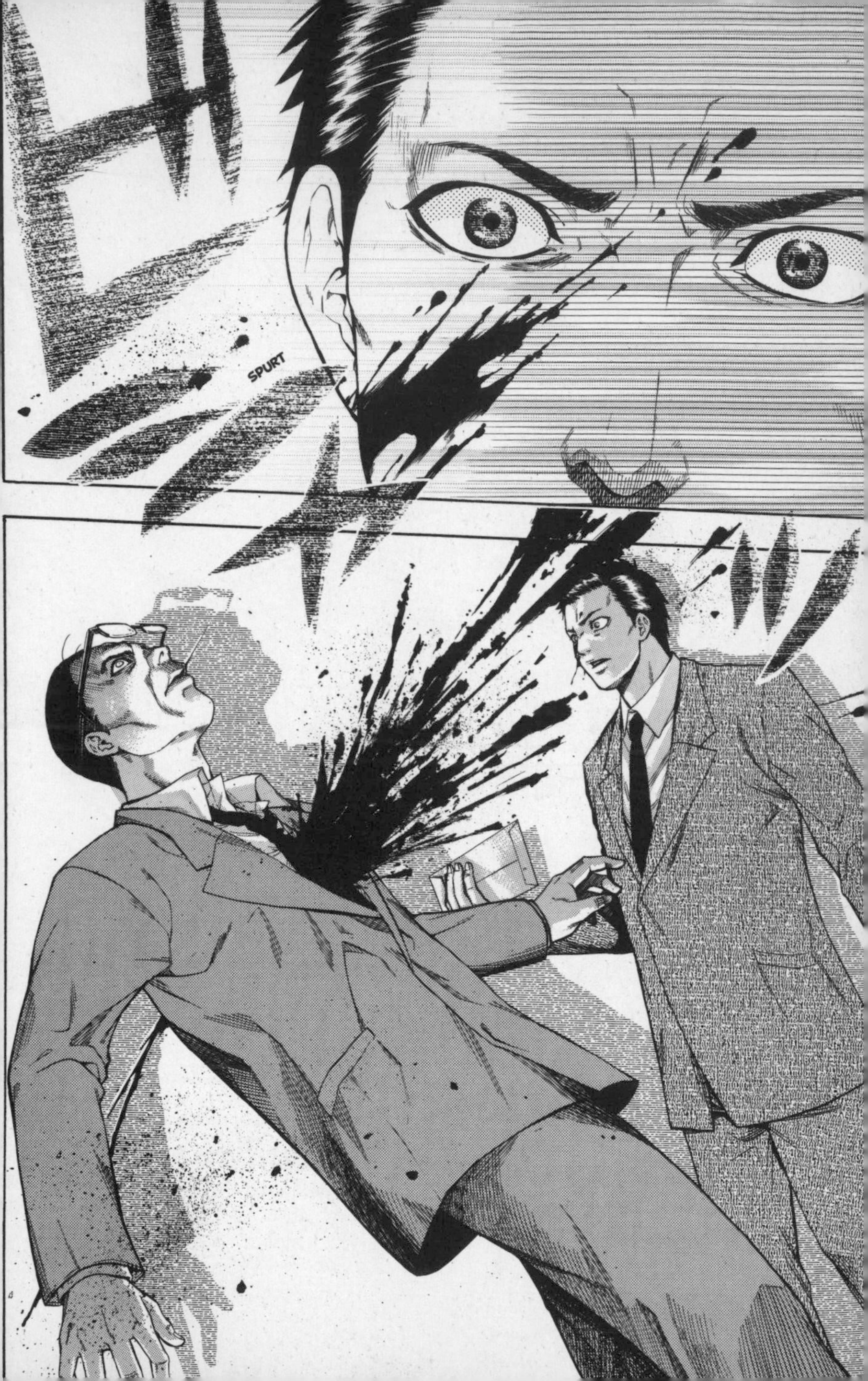
SPURT

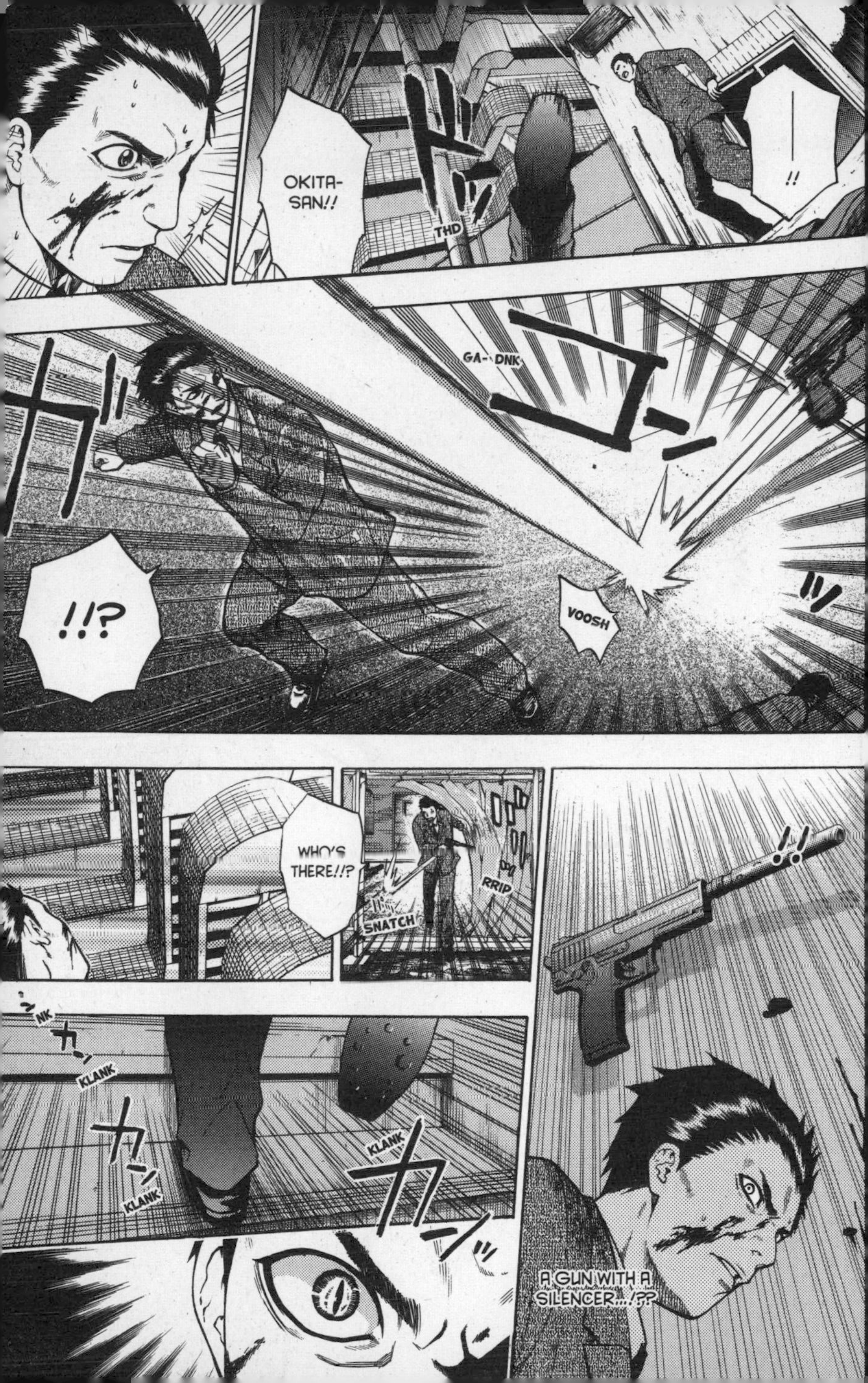
!!
OKITA-SAN!!
THD
GA-DNK
VOOSH
!!?
!!
A GUN WITH A SILENCER...!??
RRIP
SNATCH
WHO'S THERE!!?
KLANK
NK
KLANK
KLANK

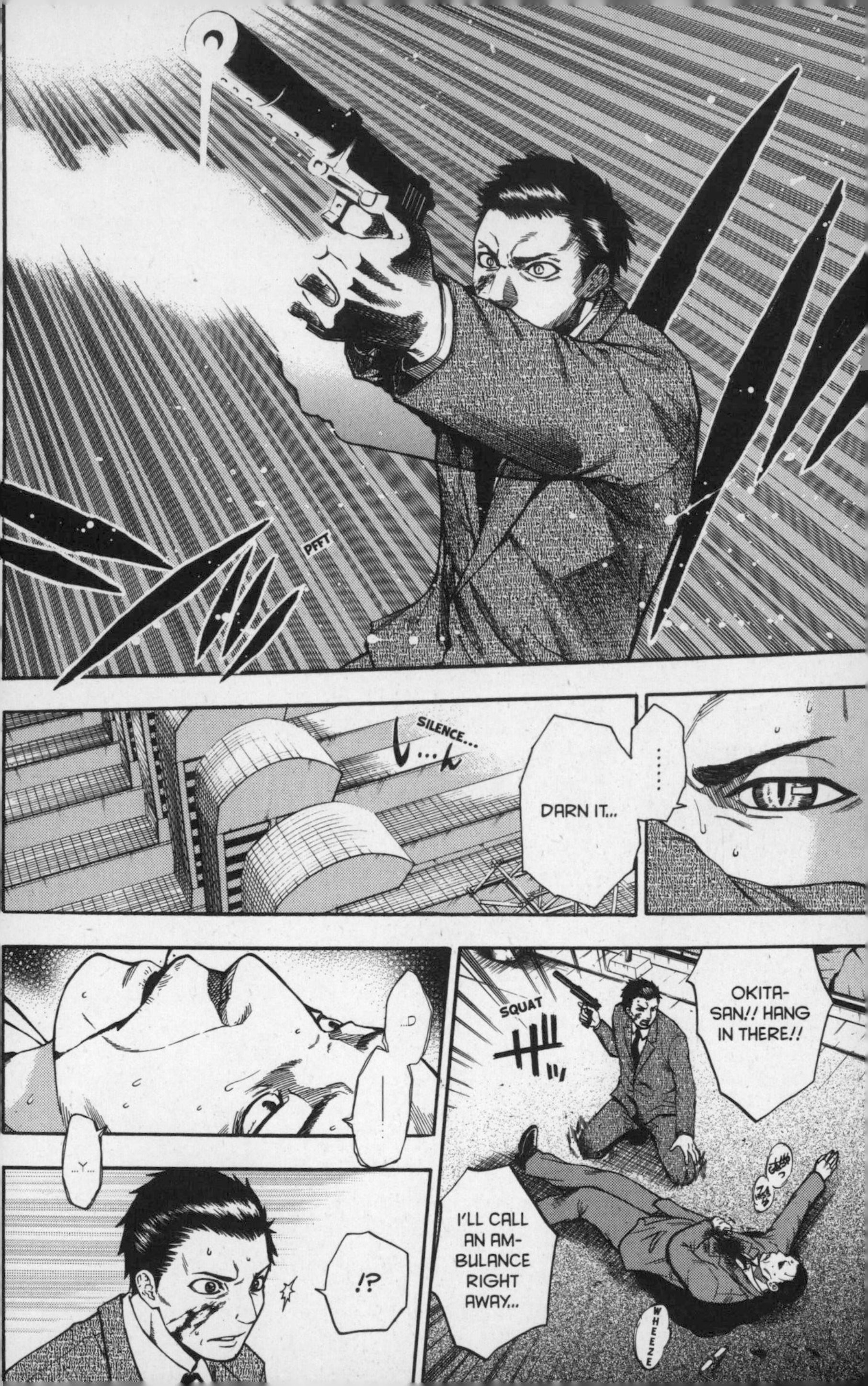

PFFT
......
DARN IT...
SILENCE...
OKITA-SAN!! HANG IN THERE!!
SQUAT
I'LL CALL AN AM-BULANCE RIGHT AWAY...
WHEEZE
...D
......
...Y...
!?

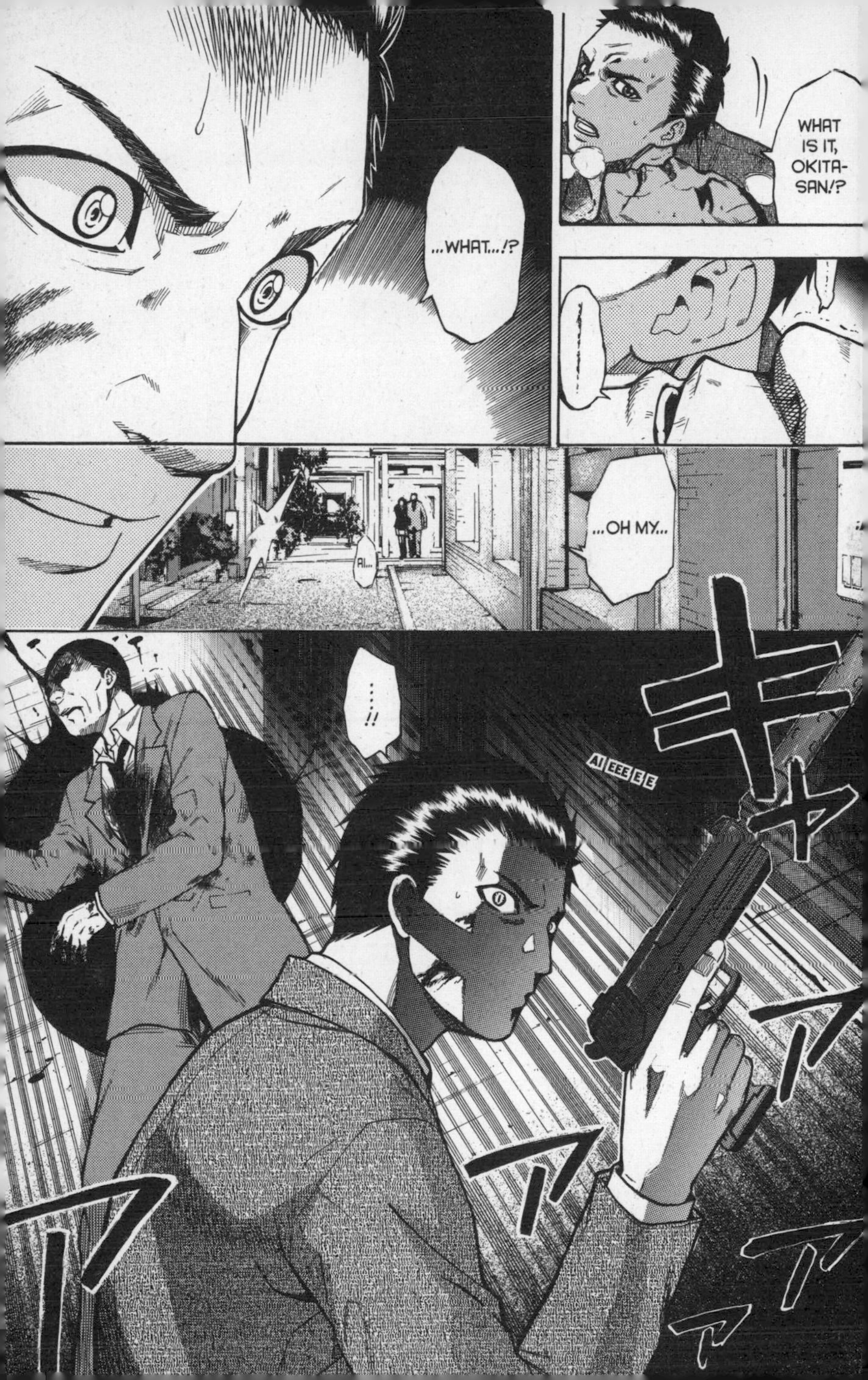
WHAT IS IT, OKITA-SAN!?
...
...WHAT...!?
...OH MY...
AI...
...!!
AI EEE E E
キャアアア

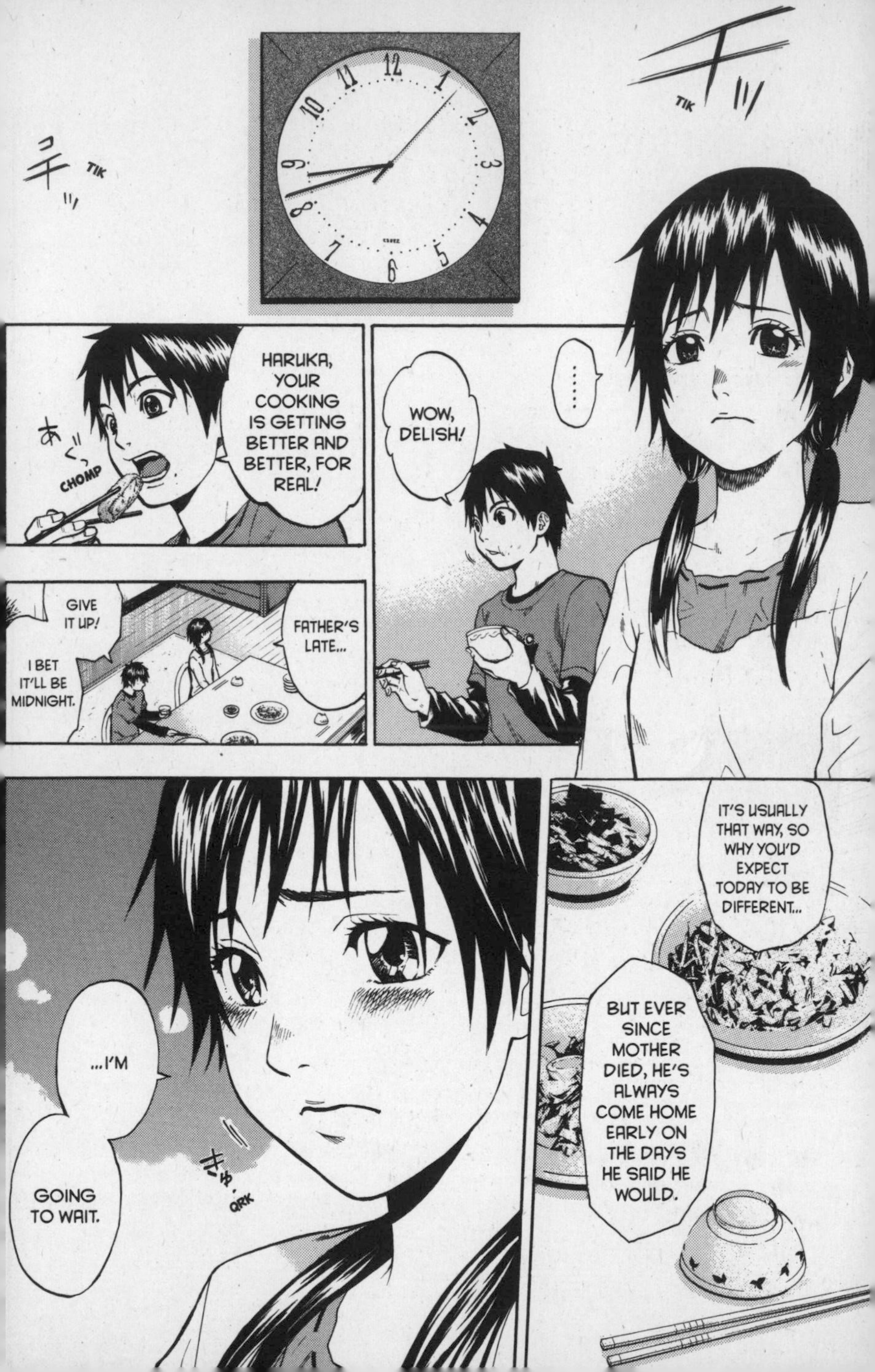

チッ TIK
チッ TIK
......
WOW, DELISH!
HARUKA, YOUR COOKING IS GETTING BETTER AND BETTER, FOR REAL!
あぐっ CHOMP
FATHER'S LATE...
GIVE IT UP!
I BET IT'LL BE MIDNIGHT.
IT'S USUALLY THAT WAY, SO WHY YOU'D EXPECT TODAY TO BE DIFFERENT...
BUT EVER SINCE MOTHER DIED, HE'S ALWAYS COME HOME EARLY ON THE DAYS HE SAID HE WOULD.
きゅ QRK
...I'M
GOING TO WAIT.

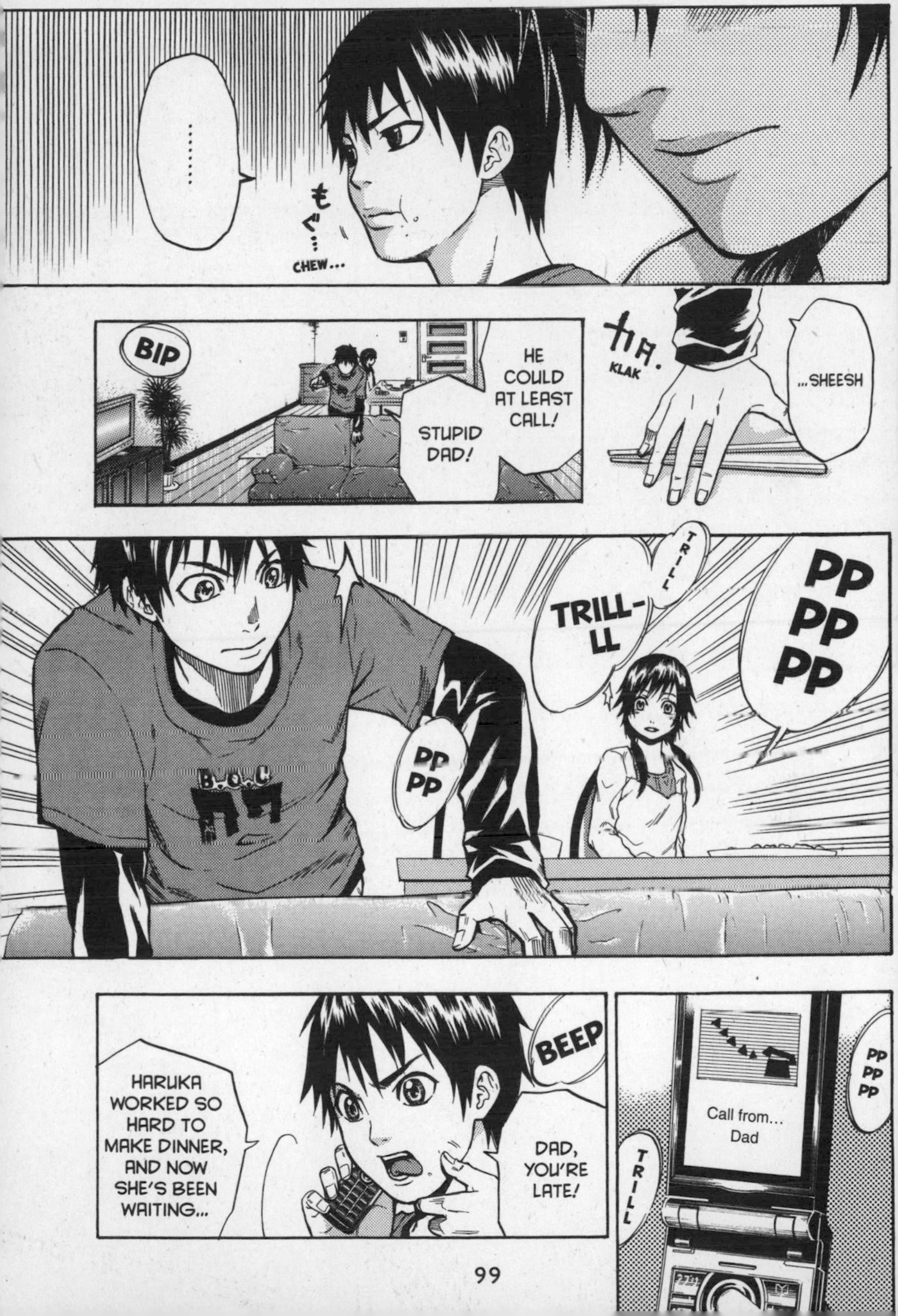
……
もぐ…
CHEW…
カチ
KLAK
…SHEESH
HE COULD AT LEAST CALL!
STUPID DAD!
BIP
TRILL
PP PP PP
TRILL-LL
PP PP
PP PP PP
Call from… Dad
TRILL
BEEP
DAD, YOU'RE LATE!
HARUKA WORKED SO HARD TO MAKE DINNER, AND NOW SHE'S BEEN WAITING…

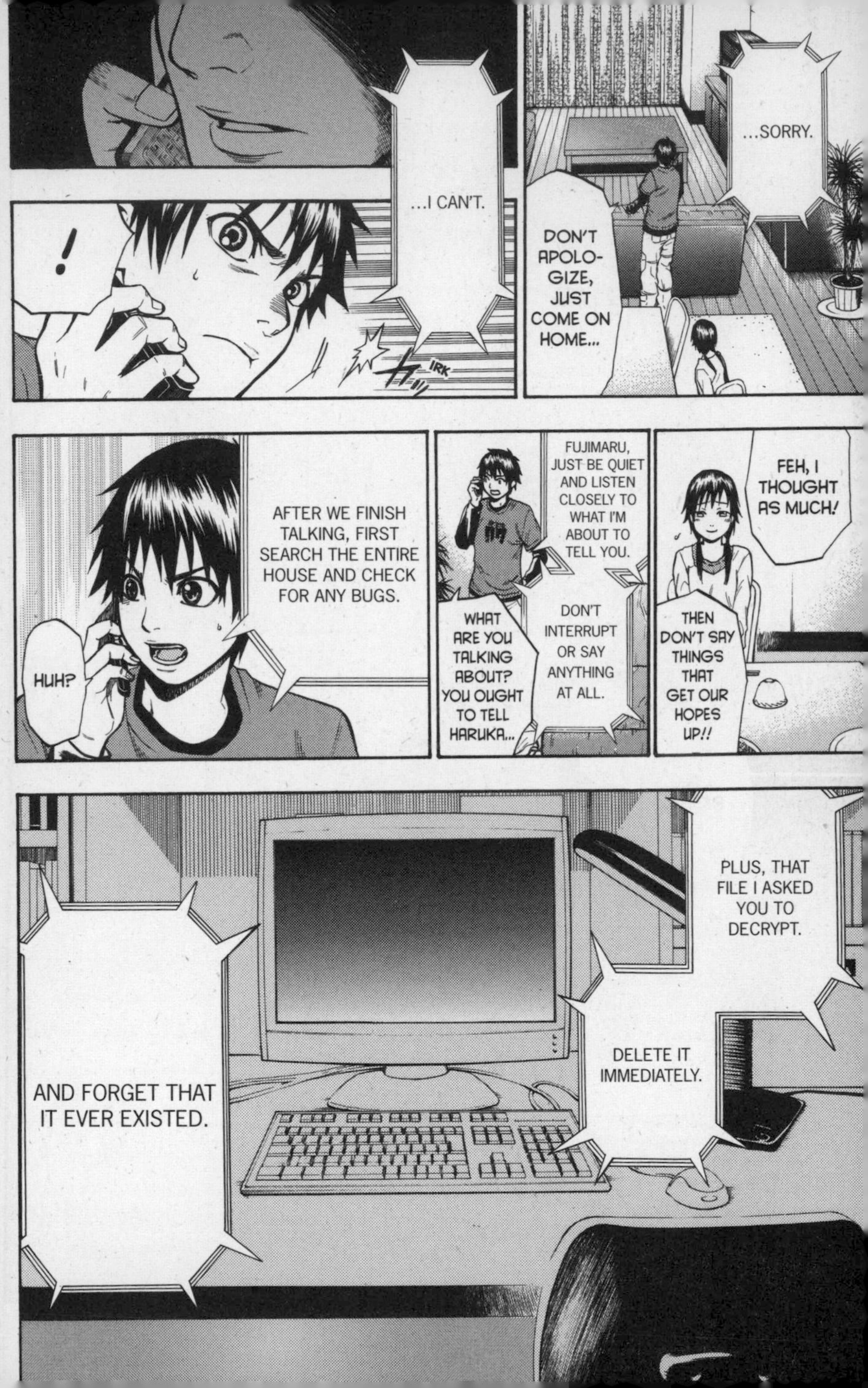
...SORRY.
DON'T APOLOGIZE, JUST COME ON HOME...
...I CAN'T.
!
IRK
FEH, I THOUGHT AS MUCH!
THEN DON'T SAY THINGS THAT GET OUR HOPES UP!!
FUJIMARU, JUST BE QUIET AND LISTEN CLOSELY TO WHAT I'M ABOUT TO TELL YOU.
DON'T INTERRUPT OR SAY ANYTHING AT ALL.
WHAT ARE YOU TALKING ABOUT? YOU OUGHT TO TELL HARUKA...
AFTER WE FINISH TALKING, FIRST SEARCH THE ENTIRE HOUSE AND CHECK FOR ANY BUGS.
HUH?
PLUS, THAT FILE I ASKED YOU TO DECRYPT.
DELETE IT IMMEDIATELY.
AND FORGET THAT IT EVER EXISTED.

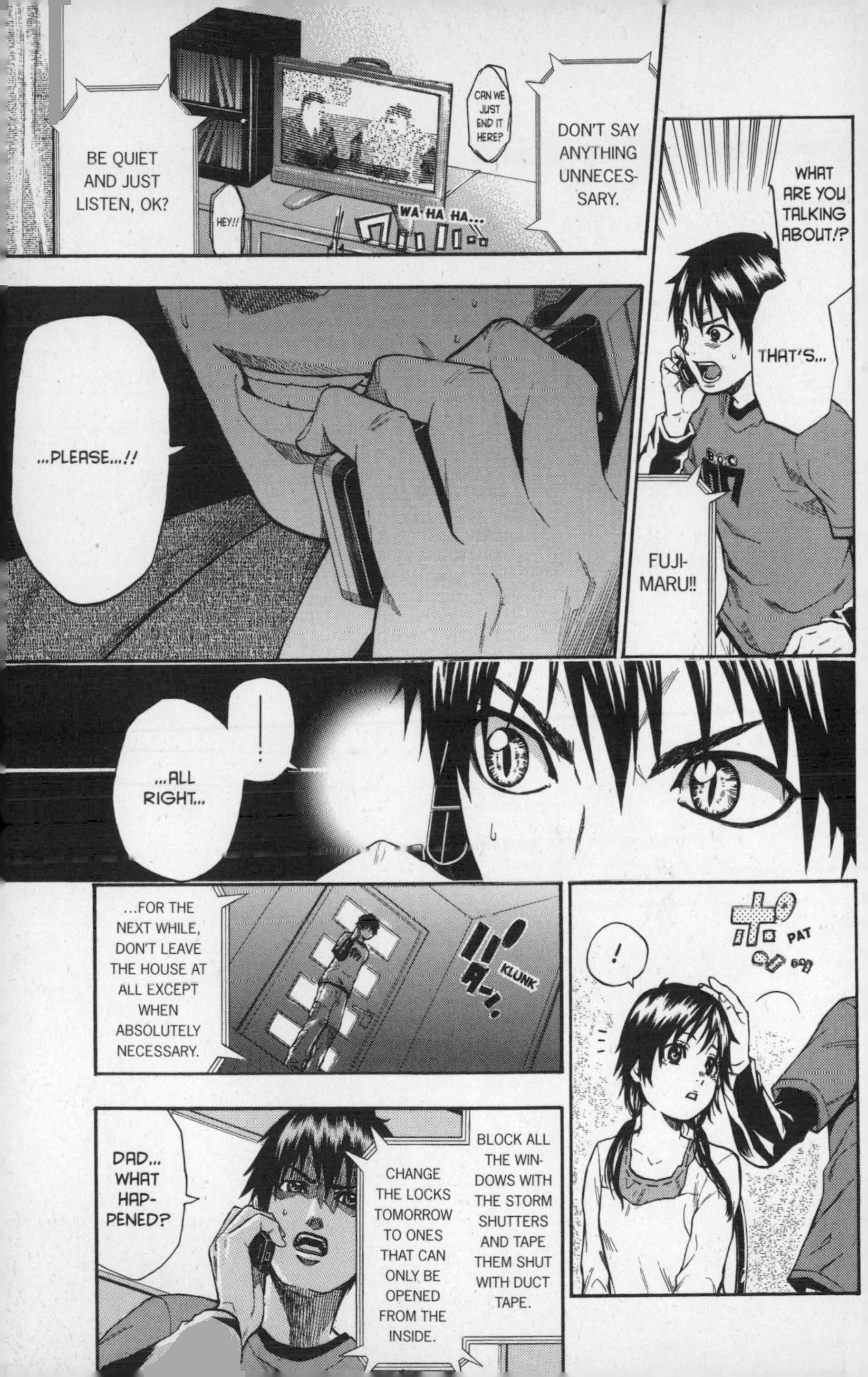
DON'T SAY ANYTHING UNNECES-SARY.
CAN WE JUST END IT HERE?
BE QUIET AND JUST LISTEN, OK?
HEY!!
WA HA HA...
WHAT ARE YOU TALKING ABOUT!?
THAT'S...
FUJI-MARU!!
...PLEASE...!!
!
...ALL RIGHT...
PAT
!
...FOR THE NEXT WHILE, DON'T LEAVE THE HOUSE AT ALL EXCEPT WHEN ABSOLUTELY NECESSARY.
KLUNK
BLOCK ALL THE WIN-DOWS WITH THE STORM SHUTTERS AND TAPE THEM SHUT WITH DUCT TAPE.
CHANGE THE LOCKS TOMORROW TO ONES THAT CAN ONLY BE OPENED FROM THE INSIDE.
DAD... WHAT HAP-PENED?

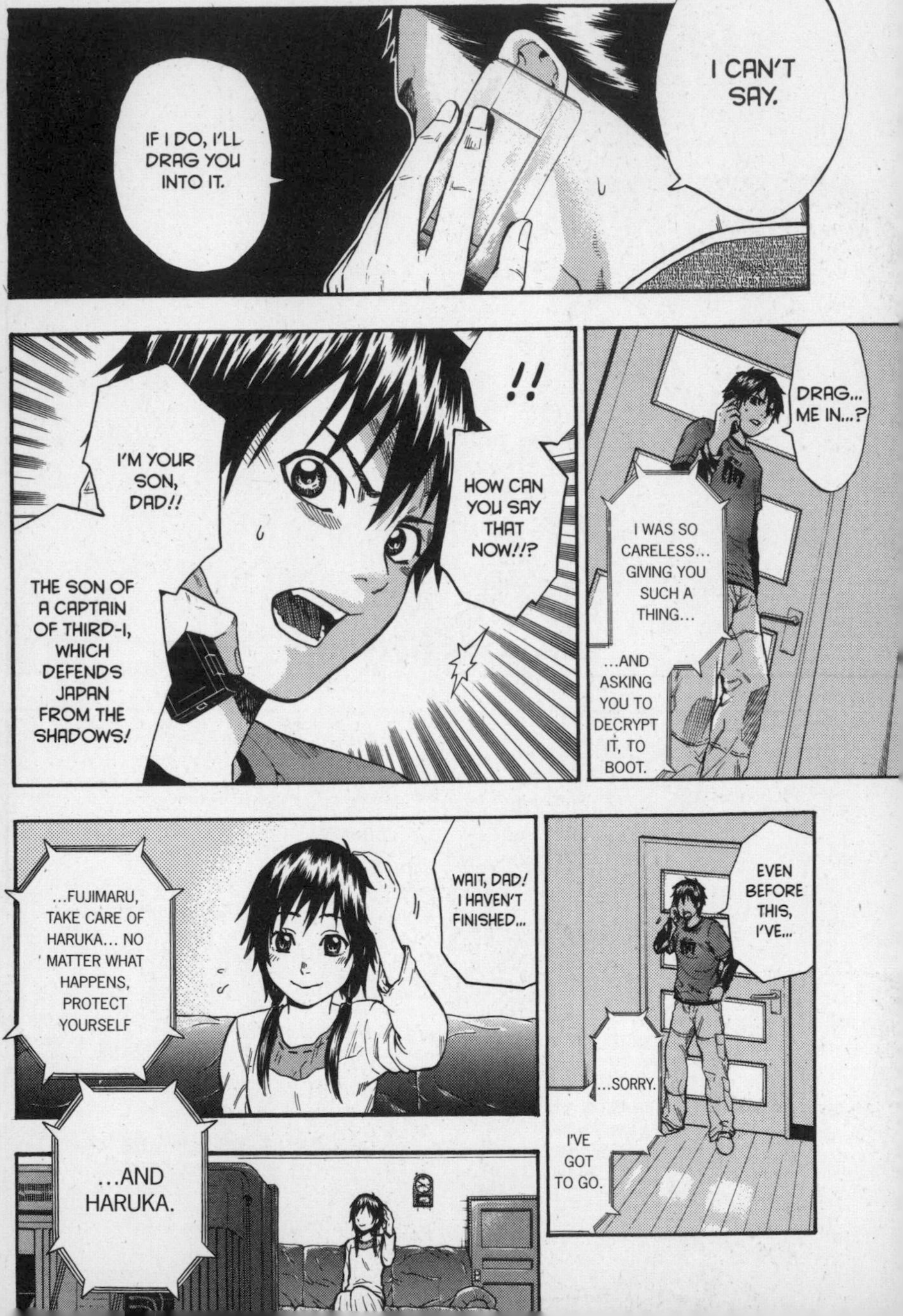
I CAN'T SAY.
IF I DO, I'LL DRAG YOU INTO IT.
DRAG... ME IN...?
I WAS SO CARELESS... GIVING YOU SUCH A THING...
...AND ASKING YOU TO DECRYPT IT, TO BOOT.
!!
HOW CAN YOU SAY THAT NOW!!?
I'M YOUR SON, DAD!!
THE SON OF A CAPTAIN OF THIRD-I, WHICH DEFENDS JAPAN FROM THE SHADOWS!
EVEN BEFORE THIS, I'VE...
...SORRY.
I'VE GOT TO GO.
WAIT, DAD! I HAVEN'T FINISHED...
...FUJIMARU, TAKE CARE OF HARUKA... NO MATTER WHAT HAPPENS, PROTECT YOURSELF
...AND HARUKA.

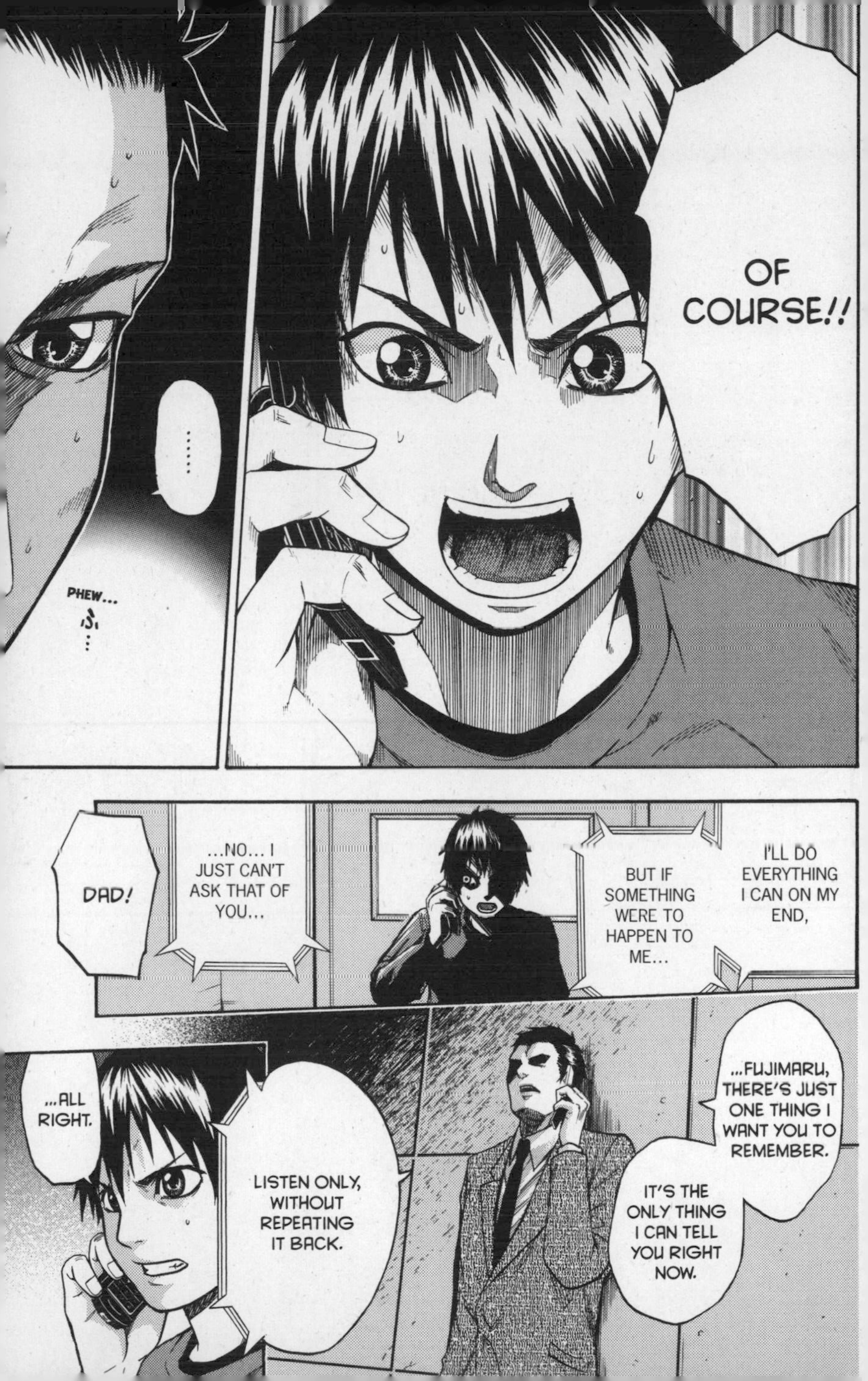
OF COURSE!!
......
PHEW...
ふ…
I'LL DO EVERYTHING I CAN ON MY END,
BUT IF SOMETHING WERE TO HAPPEN TO ME...
...NO... I JUST CAN'T ASK THAT OF YOU...
DAD!
...FUJIMARU, THERE'S JUST ONE THING I WANT YOU TO REMEMBER.
IT'S THE ONLY THING I CAN TELL YOU RIGHT NOW.
LISTEN ONLY, WITHOUT REPEATING IT BACK.
...ALL RIGHT.

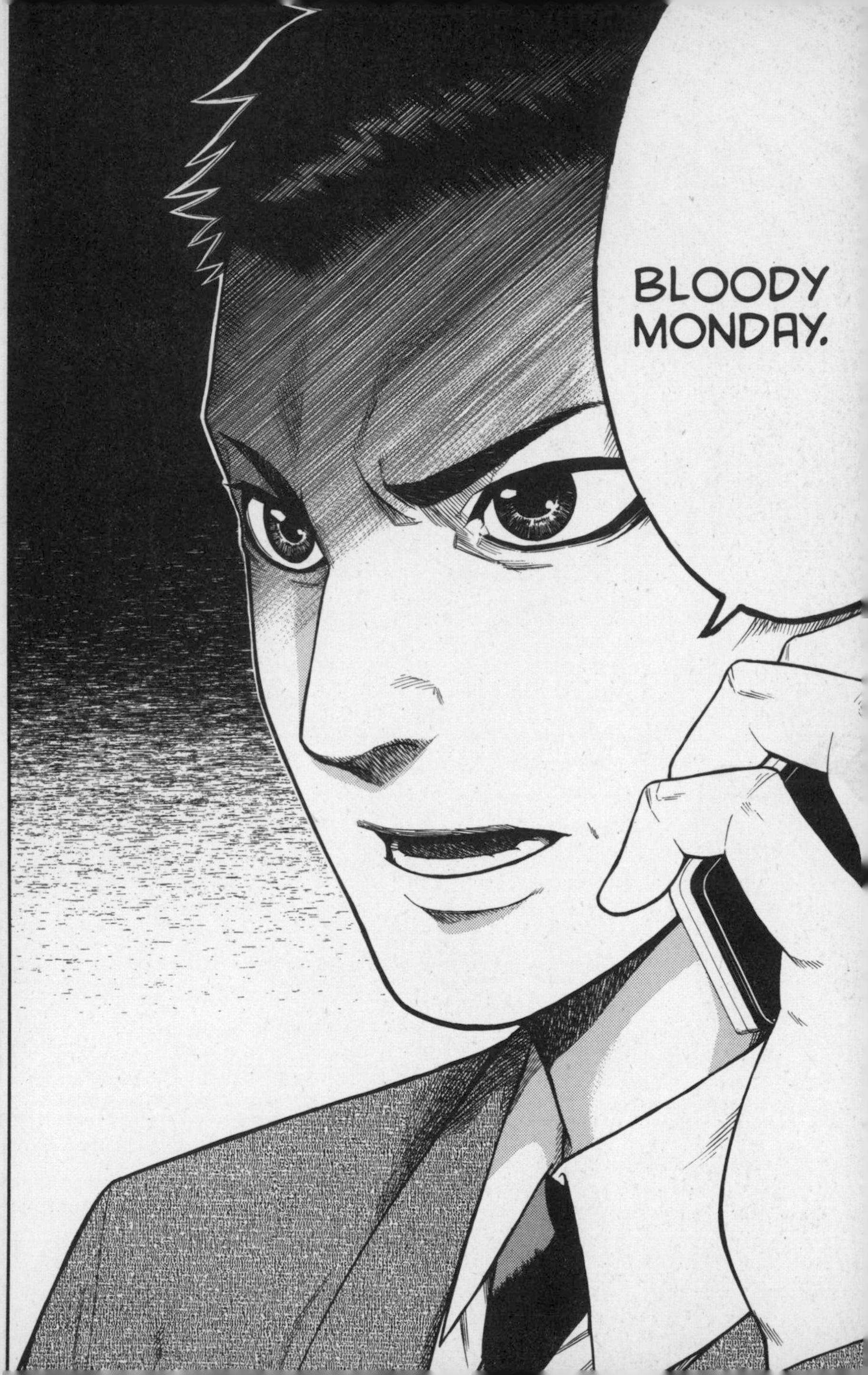
BLOODY MONDAY.

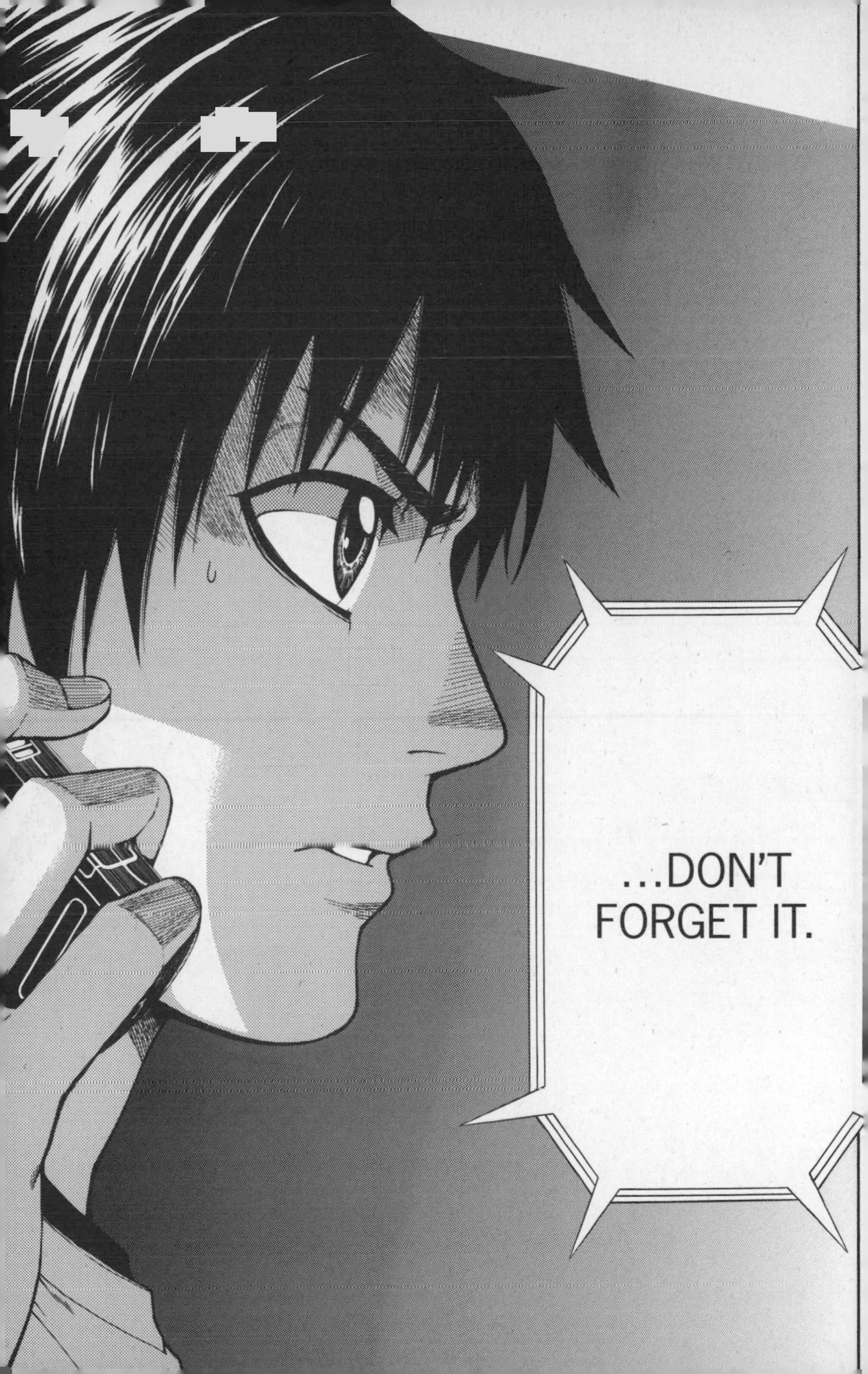
...DON’T FORGET IT.

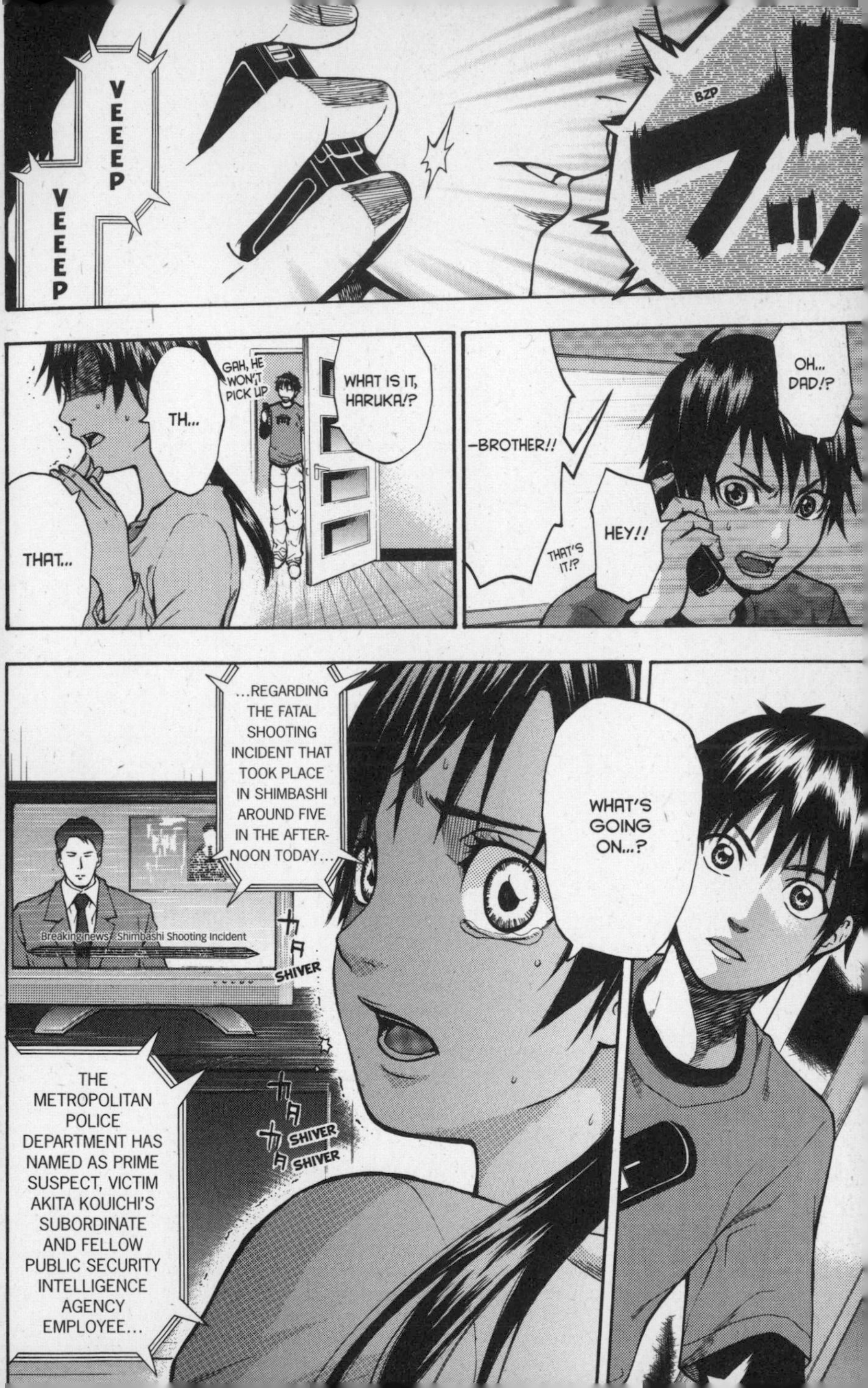
BZP
VEEEP
VEEEP
OH... DAD!?
-BROTHER!!
HEY!!
THAT'S IT!?
WHAT IS IT, HARUKA!?
GAH, HE WON'T PICK UP
TH...
THAT...
WHAT'S GOING ON...?
...REGARDING THE FATAL SHOOTING INCIDENT THAT TOOK PLACE IN SHIMBASHI AROUND FIVE IN THE AFTER-NOON TODAY...
Breaking news: Shimbashi Shooting Incident
SHIVER
SHIVER
SHIVER
THE METROPOLITAN POLICE DEPARTMENT HAS NAMED AS PRIME SUSPECT, VICTIM AKITA KOUICHI'S SUBORDINATE AND FELLOW PUBLIC SECURITY INTELLIGENCE AGENCY EMPLOYEE...

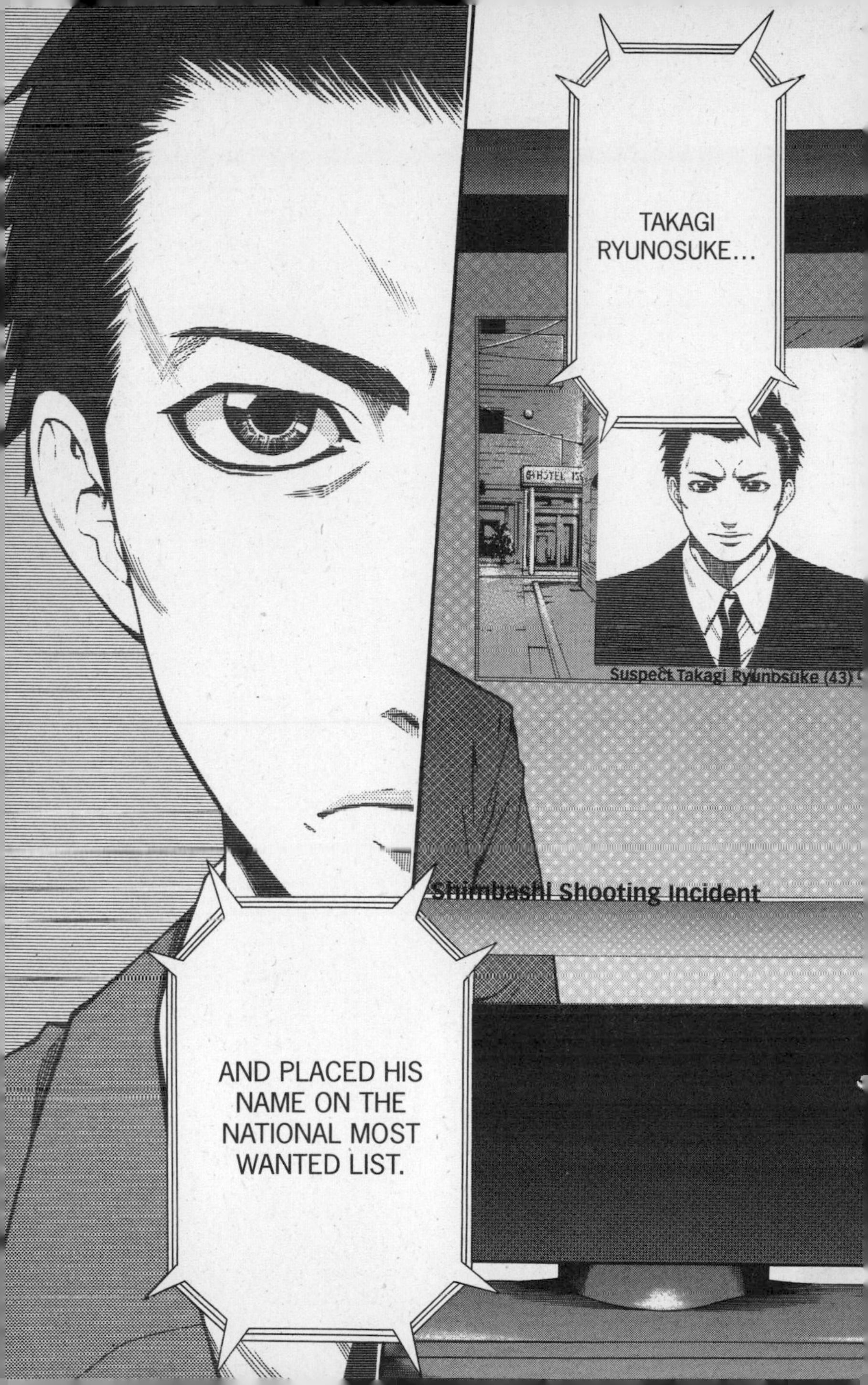
TAKAGI RYUNOSUKE...
Suspect Takagi Ryunosuke (43)
Shimbashi Shooting Incident
AND PLACED HIS NAME ON THE NATIONAL MOST WANTED LIST.

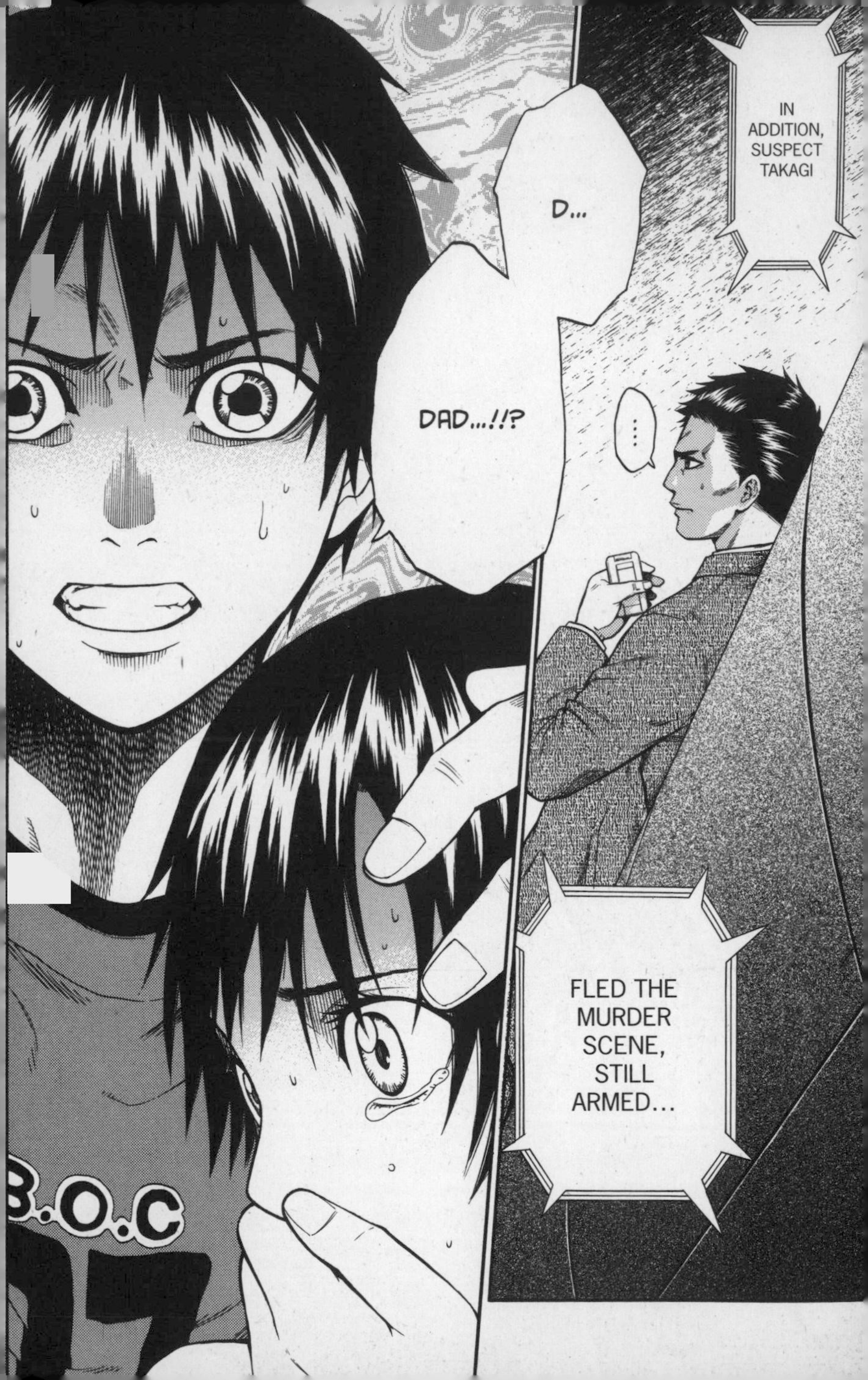
IN ADDITION, SUSPECT TAKAGI
...
FLED THE MURDER SCENE, STILL ARMED...
D...
DAD...!!?
B.O.C

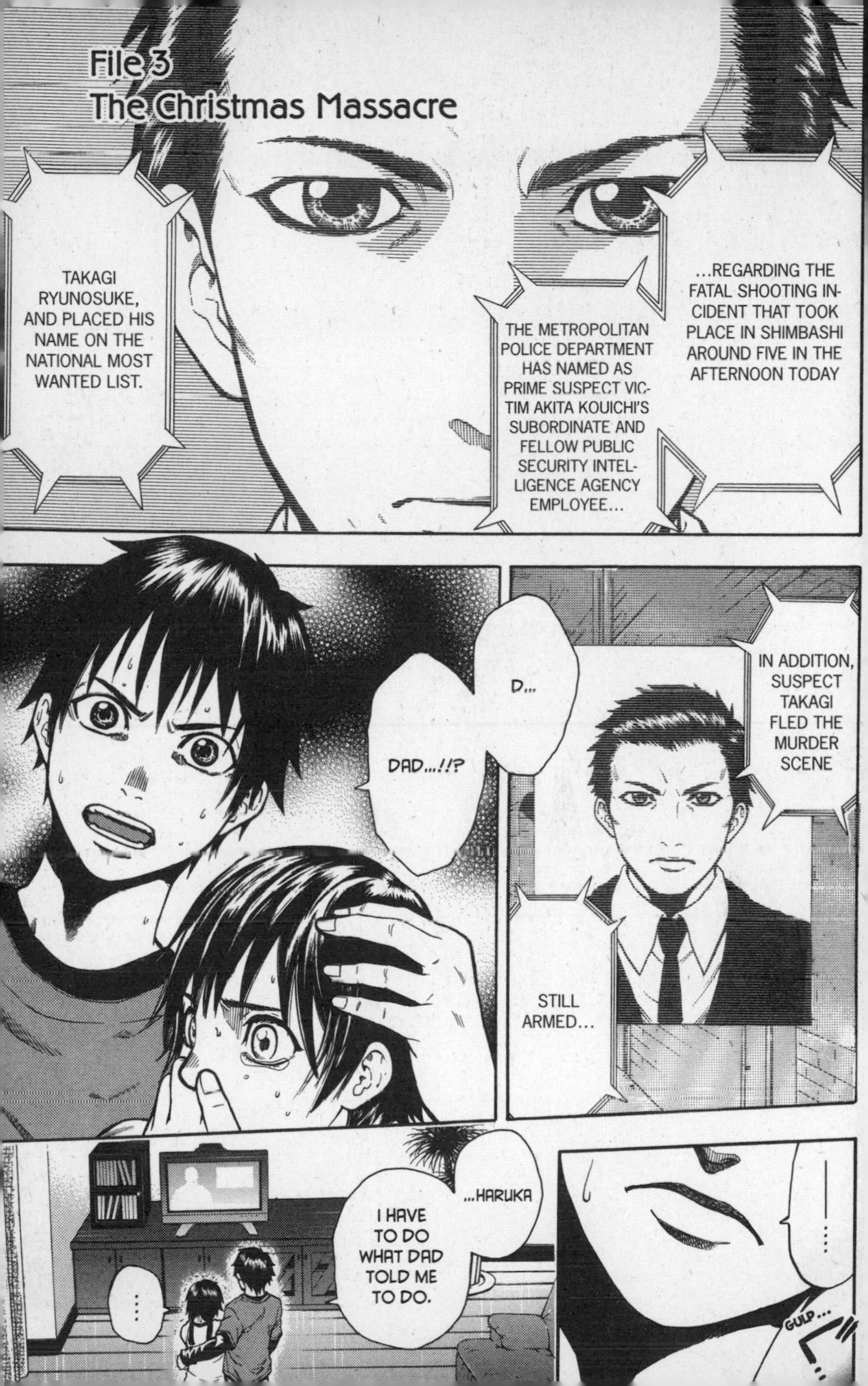
File 3
The Christmas Massacre
...REGARDING THE FATAL SHOOTING INCIDENT THAT TOOK PLACE IN SHIMBASHI AROUND FIVE IN THE AFTERNOON TODAY
THE METROPOLITAN POLICE DEPARTMENT HAS NAMED AS PRIME SUSPECT VICTIM AKITA KOUICHI'S SUBORDINATE AND FELLOW PUBLIC SECURITY INTELLIGENCE AGENCY EMPLOYEE...
TAKAGI RYUNOSUKE, AND PLACED HIS NAME ON THE NATIONAL MOST WANTED LIST.
IN ADDITION, SUSPECT TAKAGI FLED THE MURDER SCENE
STILL ARMED...
D...
DAD...!!?
......
GULP...
...HARUKA
I HAVE TO DO WHAT DAD TOLD ME TO DO.
......

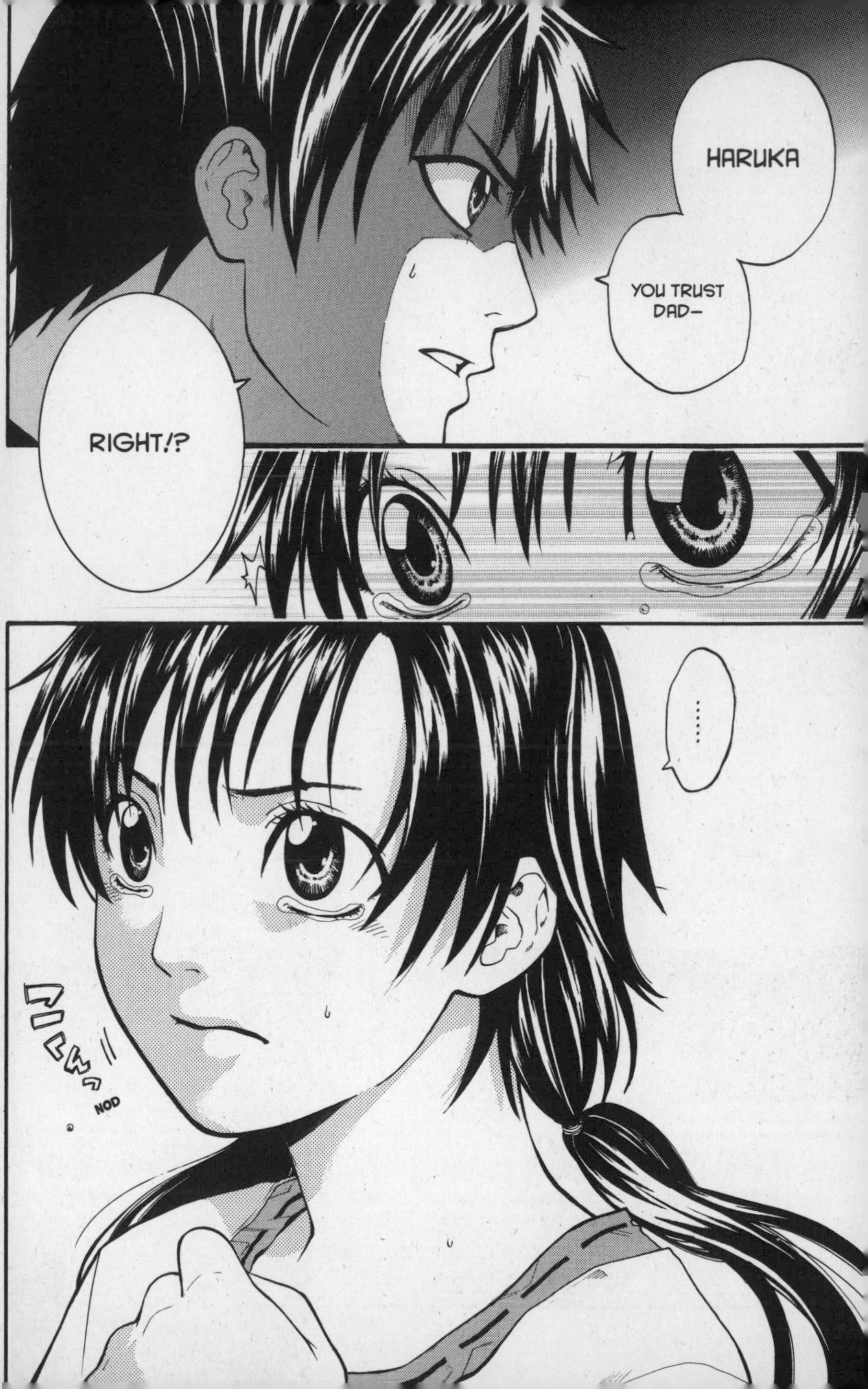
HARUKA
YOU TRUST DAD–
RIGHT!?
......
NOD

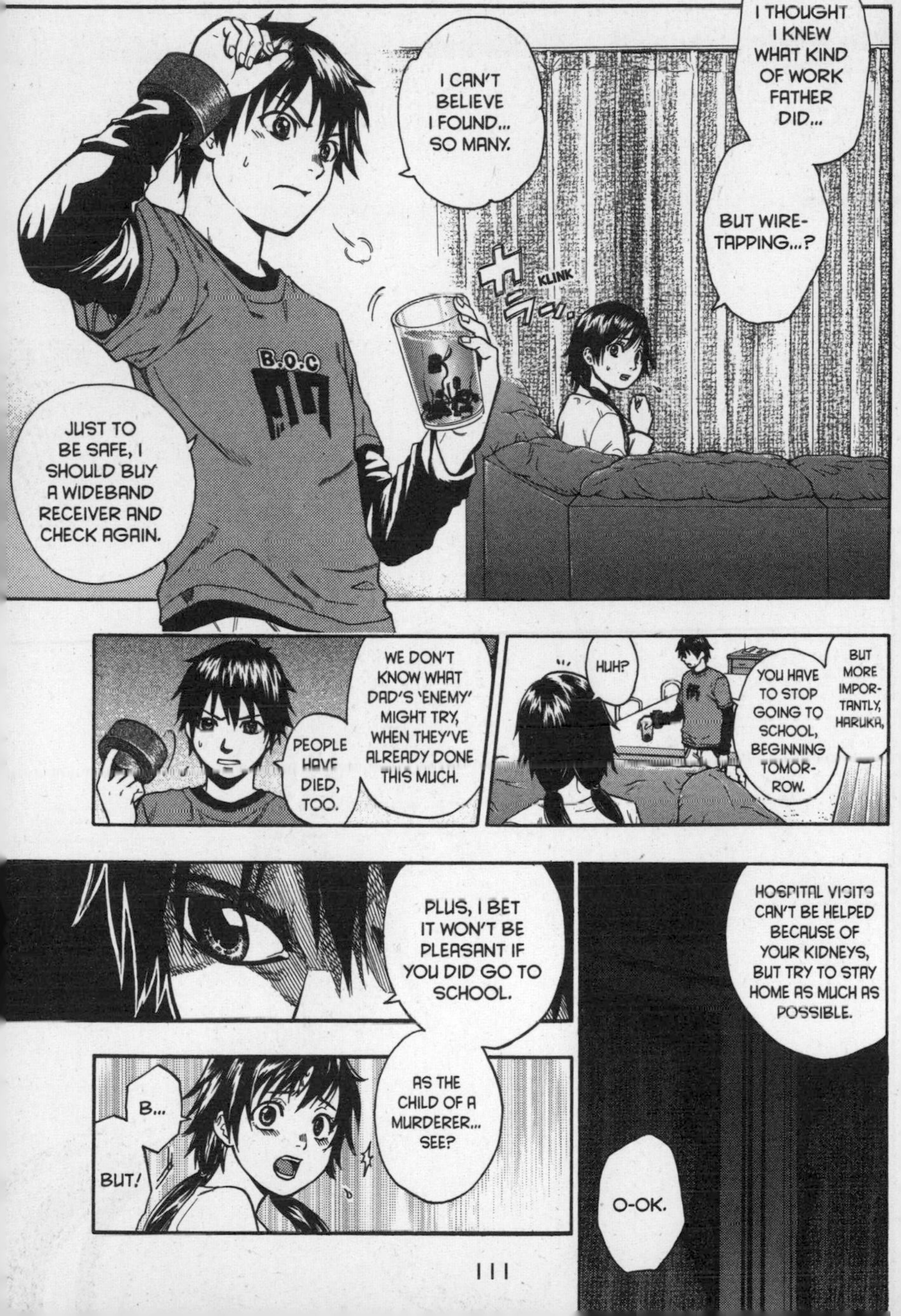
I THOUGHT I KNEW WHAT KIND OF WORK FATHER DID...
BUT WIRE-TAPPING...?
KLINK
I CAN'T BELIEVE I FOUND... SO MANY.
B.O.C
JUST TO BE SAFE, I SHOULD BUY A WIDEBAND RECEIVER AND CHECK AGAIN.
BUT MORE IMPORTANTLY, HARUKA,
YOU HAVE TO STOP GOING TO SCHOOL, BEGINNING TOMORROW.
HUH?
WE DON'T KNOW WHAT DAD'S 'ENEMY' MIGHT TRY, WHEN THEY'VE ALREADY DONE THIS MUCH.
PEOPLE HAVE DIED, TOO.
HOSPITAL VISITS CAN'T BE HELPED BECAUSE OF YOUR KIDNEYS, BUT TRY TO STAY HOME AS MUCH AS POSSIBLE.
O-OK.
PLUS, I BET IT WON'T BE PLEASANT IF YOU DID GO TO SCHOOL.
AS THE CHILD OF A MURDERER... SEE?
B...
BUT!

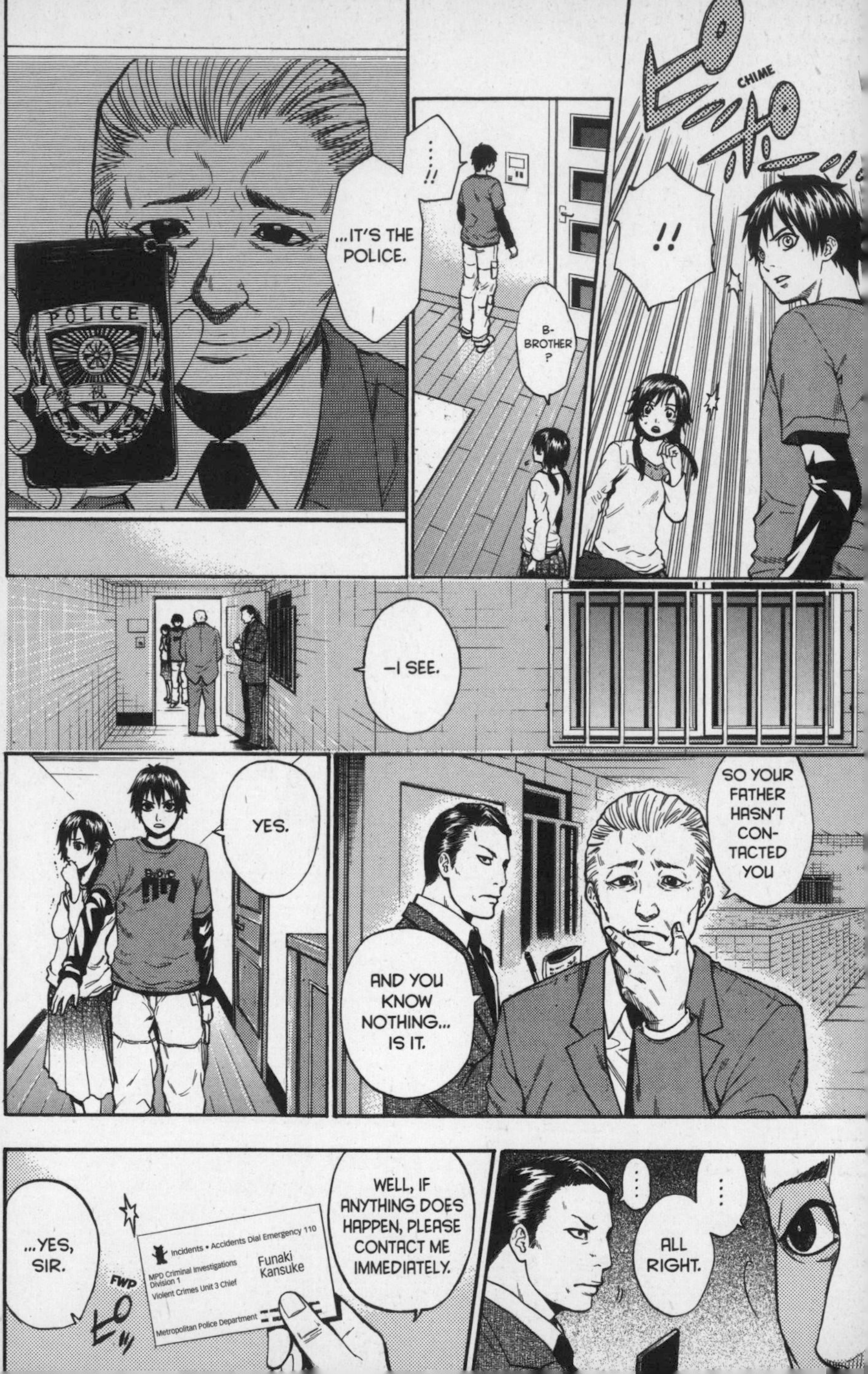
CHIME
!!
...!!
B-BROTHER?
...IT'S THE POLICE.
—I SEE.
SO YOUR FATHER HASN'T CON-TACTED YOU
AND YOU KNOW NOTHING... IS IT.
YES.
...
...
ALL RIGHT.
WELL, IF ANYTHING DOES HAPPEN, PLEASE CONTACT ME IMMEDIATELY.
Incidents • Accidents Dial Emergency 110
MPD Criminal Investigations Division 1
Violent Crimes Unit 3 Chief
Funaki Kansuke
Metropolitan Police Department
FWP
...YES, SIR.

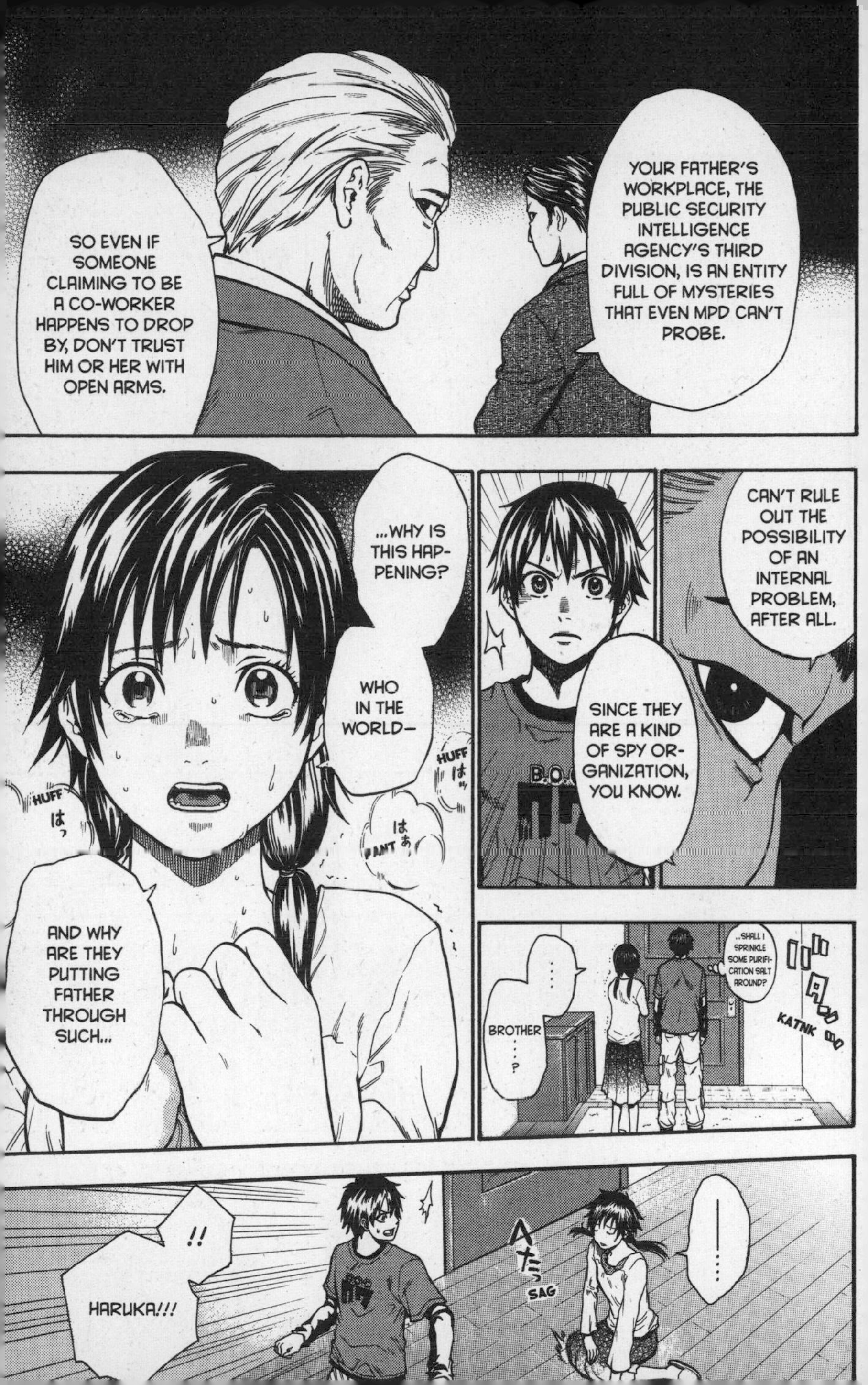
YOUR FATHER'S WORKPLACE, THE PUBLIC SECURITY INTELLIGENCE AGENCY'S THIRD DIVISION, IS AN ENTITY FULL OF MYSTERIES THAT EVEN MPD CAN'T PROBE.
SO EVEN IF SOMEONE CLAIMING TO BE A CO-WORKER HAPPENS TO DROP BY, DON'T TRUST HIM OR HER WITH OPEN ARMS.
CAN'T RULE OUT THE POSSIBILITY OF AN INTERNAL PROBLEM, AFTER ALL.
SINCE THEY ARE A KIND OF SPY ORGANIZATION, YOU KNOW.
...SHALL I SPRINKLE SOME PURIFICATION SALT AROUND?
KATNK
....
BROTHER....?
...WHY IS THIS HAPPENING?
WHO IN THE WORLD—
HUFF
PANT
HUFF
AND WHY ARE THEY PUTTING FATHER THROUGH SUCH...
......
SAG
!!
HARUKA!!!

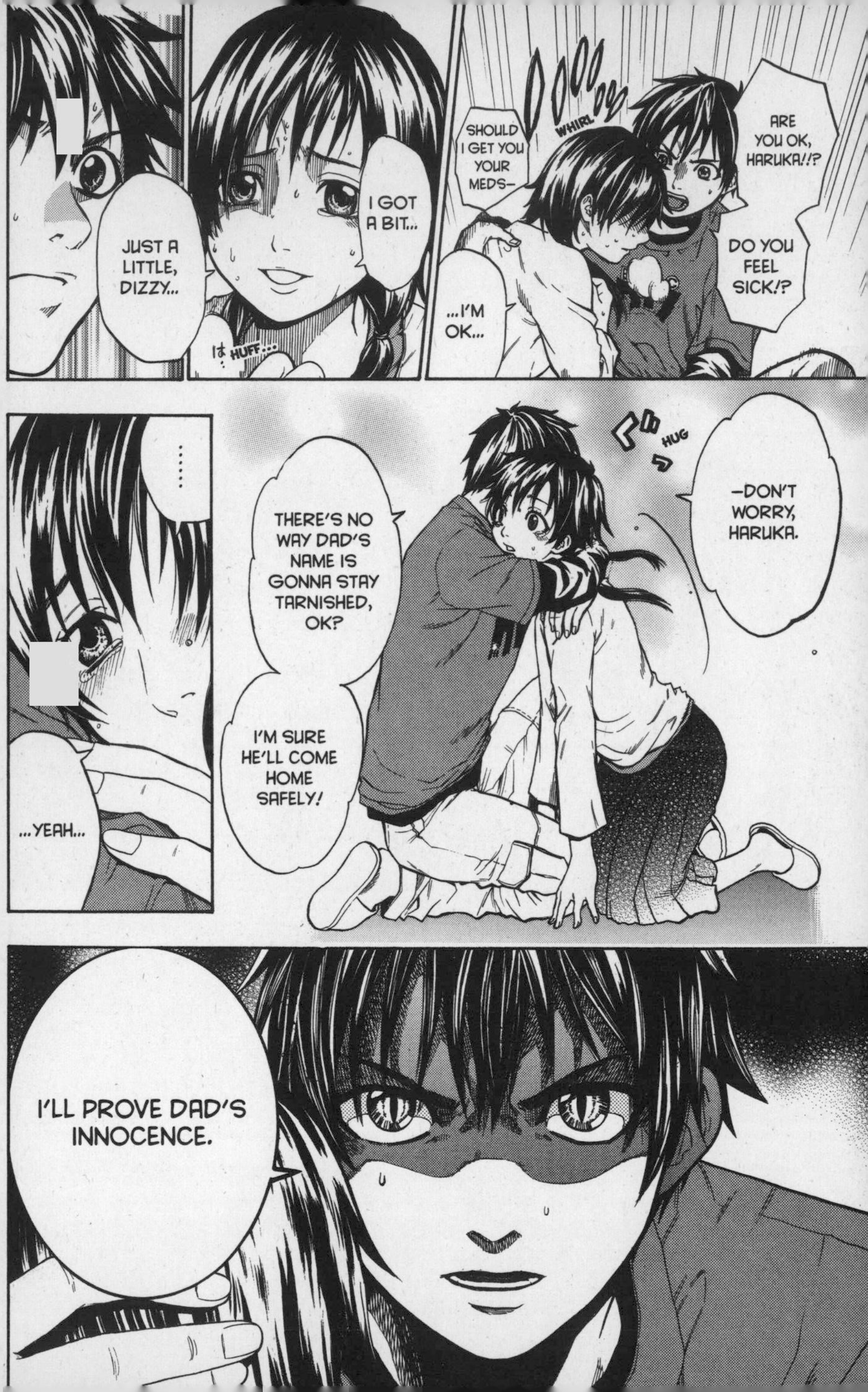
WHIRL
ARE YOU OK, HARUKA!!?
SHOULD I GET YOU YOUR MEDS—
DO YOU FEEL SICK!?
...I'M OK...
I GOT A BIT...
は HUFF...
JUST A LITTLE, DIZZY...
HUG
—DON'T WORRY, HARUKA.
THERE'S NO WAY DAD'S NAME IS GONNA STAY TARNISHED, OK?
I'M SURE HE'LL COME HOME SAFELY!
......
...YEAH...
I'LL PROVE DAD'S INNOCENCE.

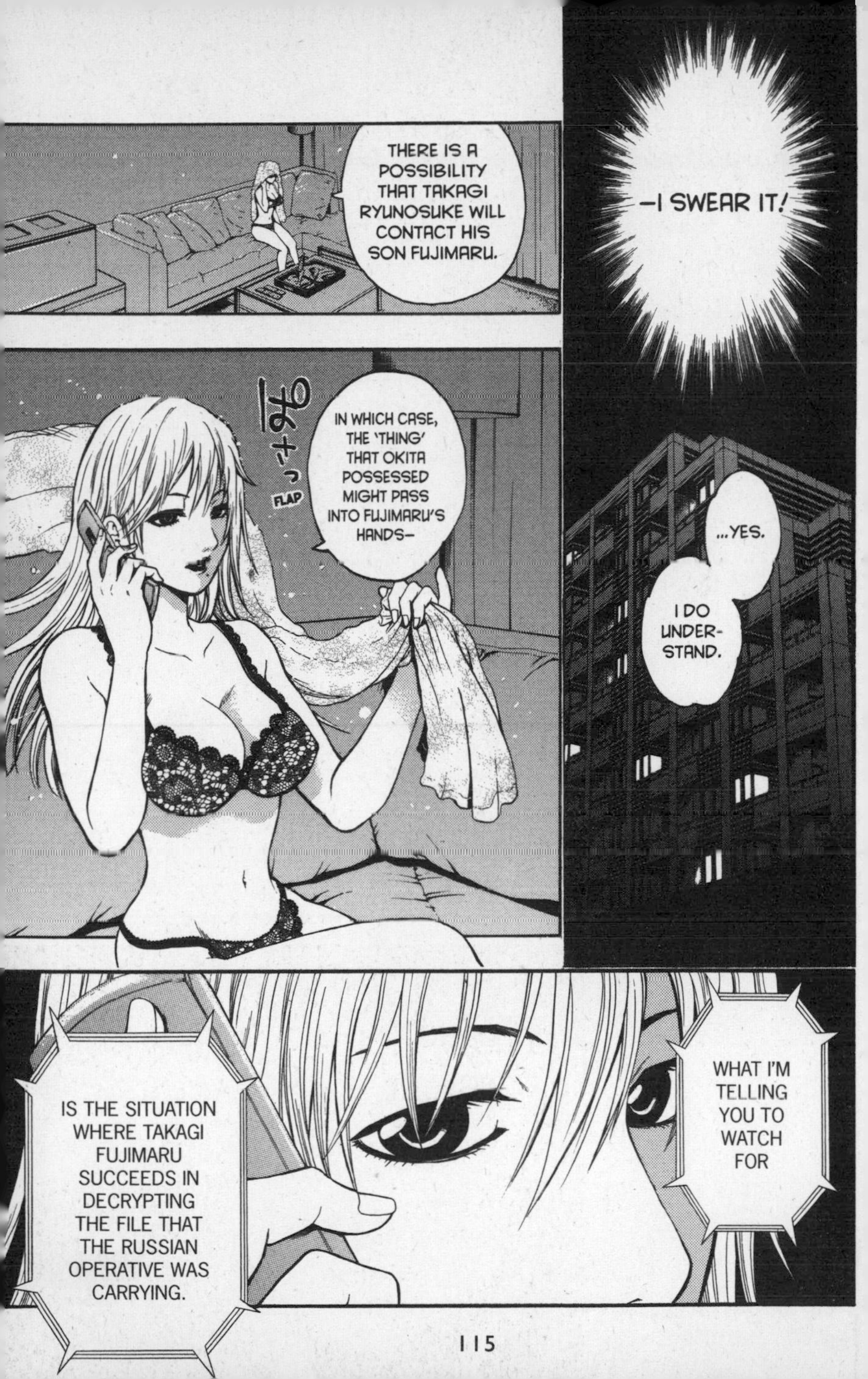
—I SWEAR IT!
THERE IS A POSSIBILITY THAT TAKAGI RYUNOSUKE WILL CONTACT HIS SON FUJIMARU.
...YES.
I DO UNDER-STAND.
ぱさっ
FLAP
IN WHICH CASE, THE 'THING' THAT OKITA POSSESSED MIGHT PASS INTO FUJIMARU'S HANDS—
WHAT I'M TELLING YOU TO WATCH FOR
IS THE SITUATION WHERE TAKAGI FUJIMARU SUCCEEDS IN DECRYPTING THE FILE THAT THE RUSSIAN OPERATIVE WAS CARRYING.

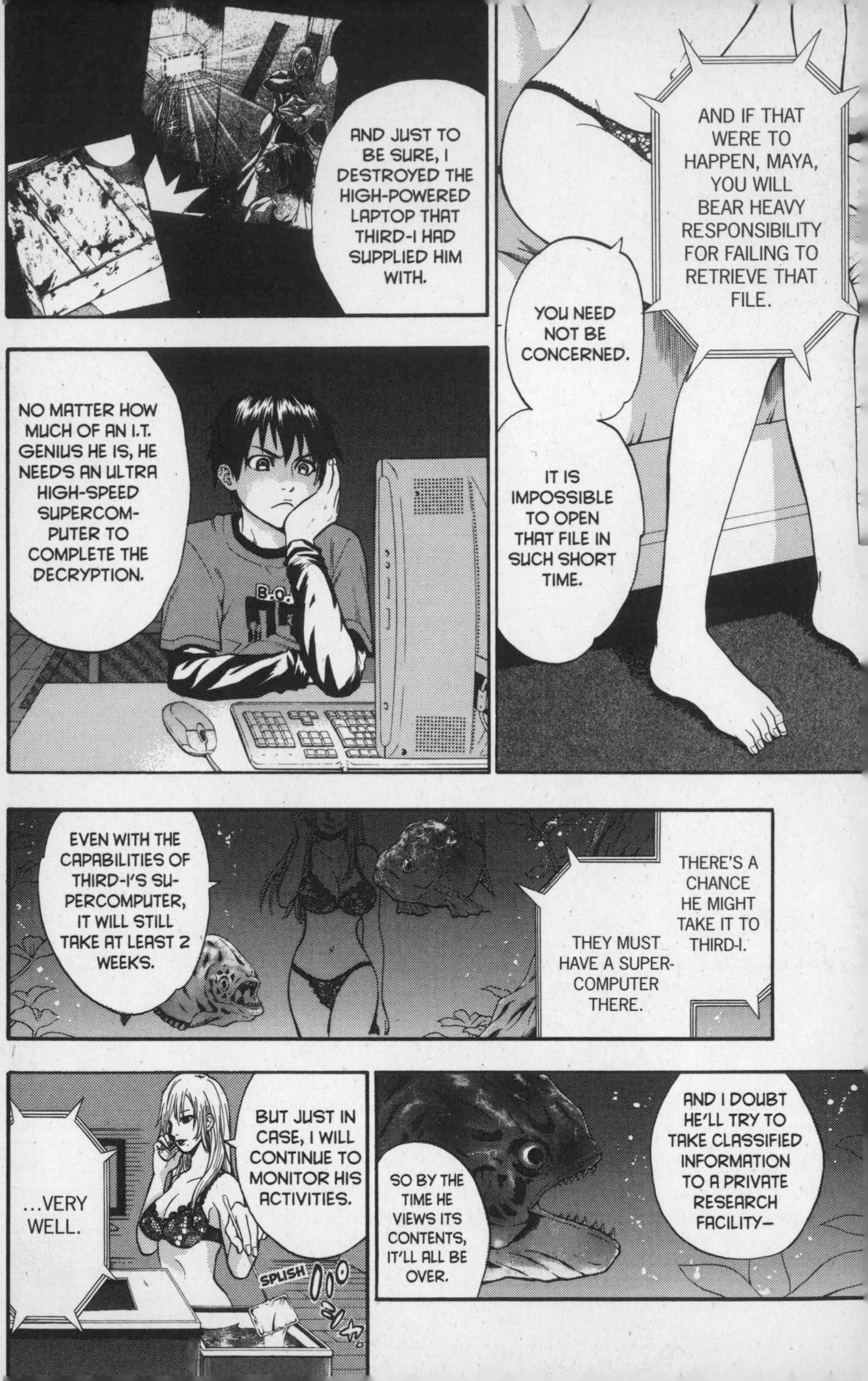
AND IF THAT WERE TO HAPPEN, MAYA, YOU WILL BEAR HEAVY RESPONSIBILITY FOR FAILING TO RETRIEVE THAT FILE.
YOU NEED NOT BE CONCERNED.
IT IS IMPOSSIBLE TO OPEN THAT FILE IN SUCH SHORT TIME.
AND JUST TO BE SURE, I DESTROYED THE HIGH-POWERED LAPTOP THAT THIRD-I HAD SUPPLIED HIM WITH.
NO MATTER HOW MUCH OF AN I.T. GENIUS HE IS, HE NEEDS AN ULTRA HIGH-SPEED SUPERCOMPUTER TO COMPLETE THE DECRYPTION.
THERE'S A CHANCE HE MIGHT TAKE IT TO THIRD-I.
THEY MUST HAVE A SUPERCOMPUTER THERE.
EVEN WITH THE CAPABILITIES OF THIRD-I'S SUPERCOMPUTER, IT WILL STILL TAKE AT LEAST 2 WEEKS.
AND I DOUBT HE'LL TRY TO TAKE CLASSIFIED INFORMATION TO A PRIVATE RESEARCH FACILITY—
SO BY THE TIME HE VIEWS ITS CONTENTS, IT'LL ALL BE OVER.
BUT JUST IN CASE, I WILL CONTINUE TO MONITOR HIS ACTIVITIES.
...VERY WELL.
SPLISH

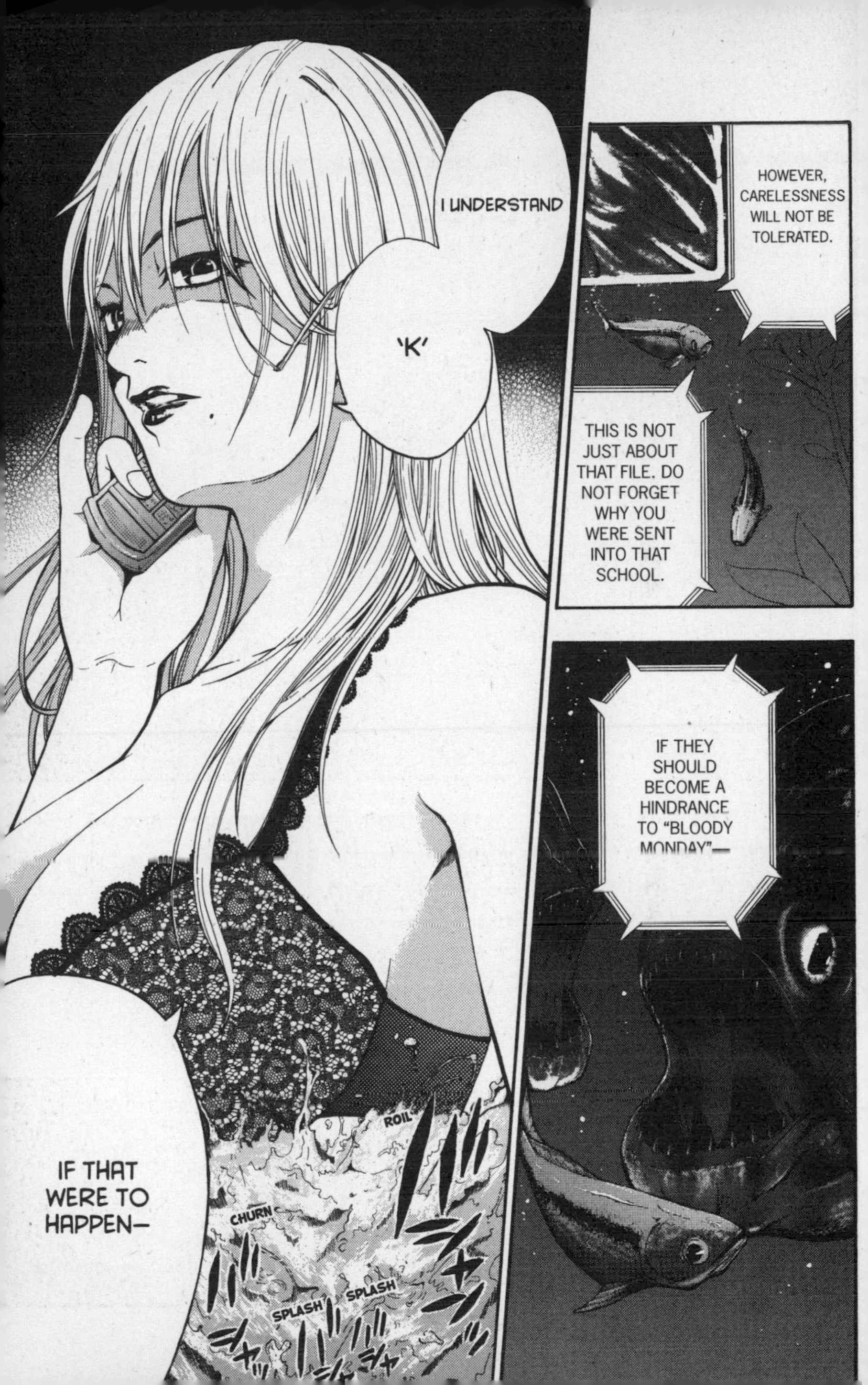
HOWEVER, CARELESSNESS WILL NOT BE TOLERATED.
THIS IS NOT JUST ABOUT THAT FILE. DO NOT FORGET WHY YOU WERE SENT INTO THAT SCHOOL.
IF THEY SHOULD BECOME A HINDRANCE TO "BLOODY MONDAY"—
I UNDERSTAND
'K'
IF THAT WERE TO HAPPEN—
ROIL
CHURN
SPLASH
SPLASH

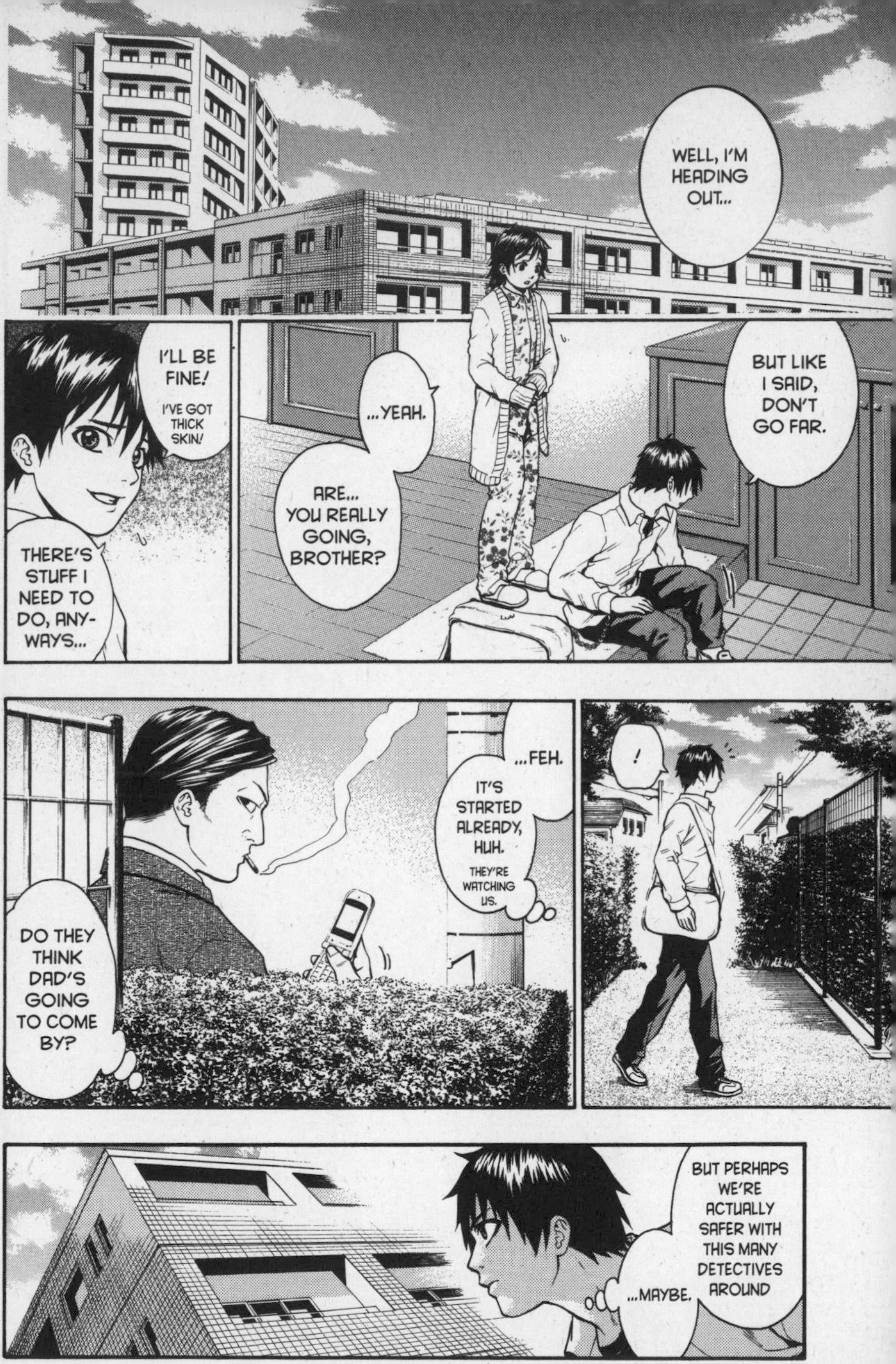
WELL, I'M HEADING OUT...
BUT LIKE I SAID, DON'T GO FAR.
...YEAH.
ARE... YOU REALLY GOING, BROTHER?
I'LL BE FINE!
I'VE GOT THICK SKIN!
THERE'S STUFF I NEED TO DO, ANY-WAYS...
!
...FEH.
IT'S STARTED ALREADY, HUH.
THEY'RE WATCHING US.
DO THEY THINK DAD'S GOING TO COME BY?
BUT PERHAPS WE'RE ACTUALLY SAFER WITH THIS MANY DETECTIVES AROUND
...MAYBE.

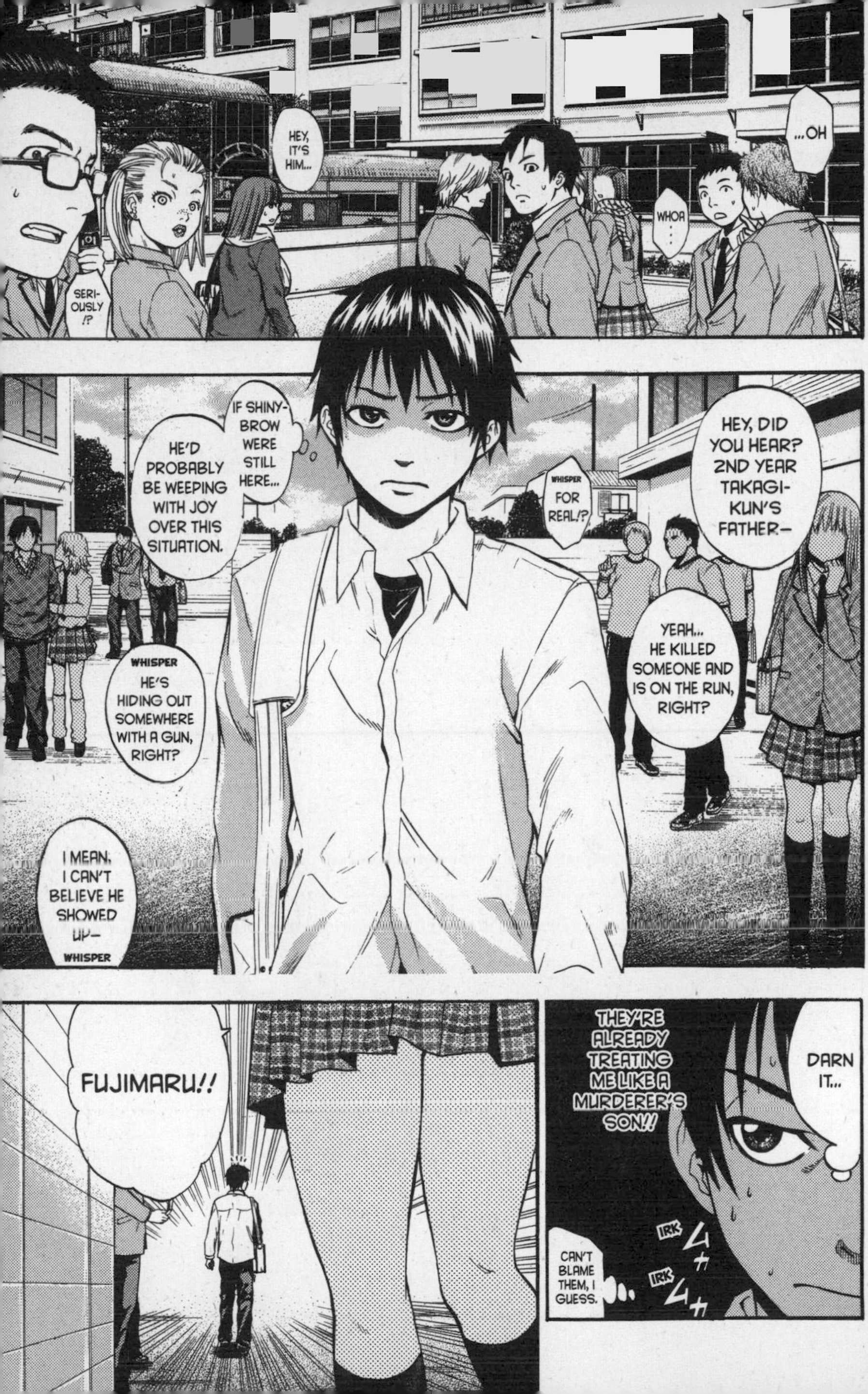
...OH
WHOA...
HEY, IT'S HIM...
SERI-OUSLY!?
HEY, DID YOU HEAR? 2ND YEAR TAKAGI-KUN'S FATHER—
WHISPER
FOR REAL!?
IF SHINY-BROW WERE STILL HERE...
HE'D PROBABLY BE WEEPING WITH JOY OVER THIS SITUATION.
YEAH... HE KILLED SOMEONE AND IS ON THE RUN, RIGHT?
WHISPER
HE'S HIDING OUT SOMEWHERE WITH A GUN, RIGHT?
I MEAN, I CAN'T BELIEVE HE SHOWED UP—
WHISPER
THEY'RE ALREADY TREATING ME LIKE A MURDERER'S SON!!
DARN IT...
IRK
IRK
CAN'T BLAME THEM, I GUESS.
FUJIMARU!!

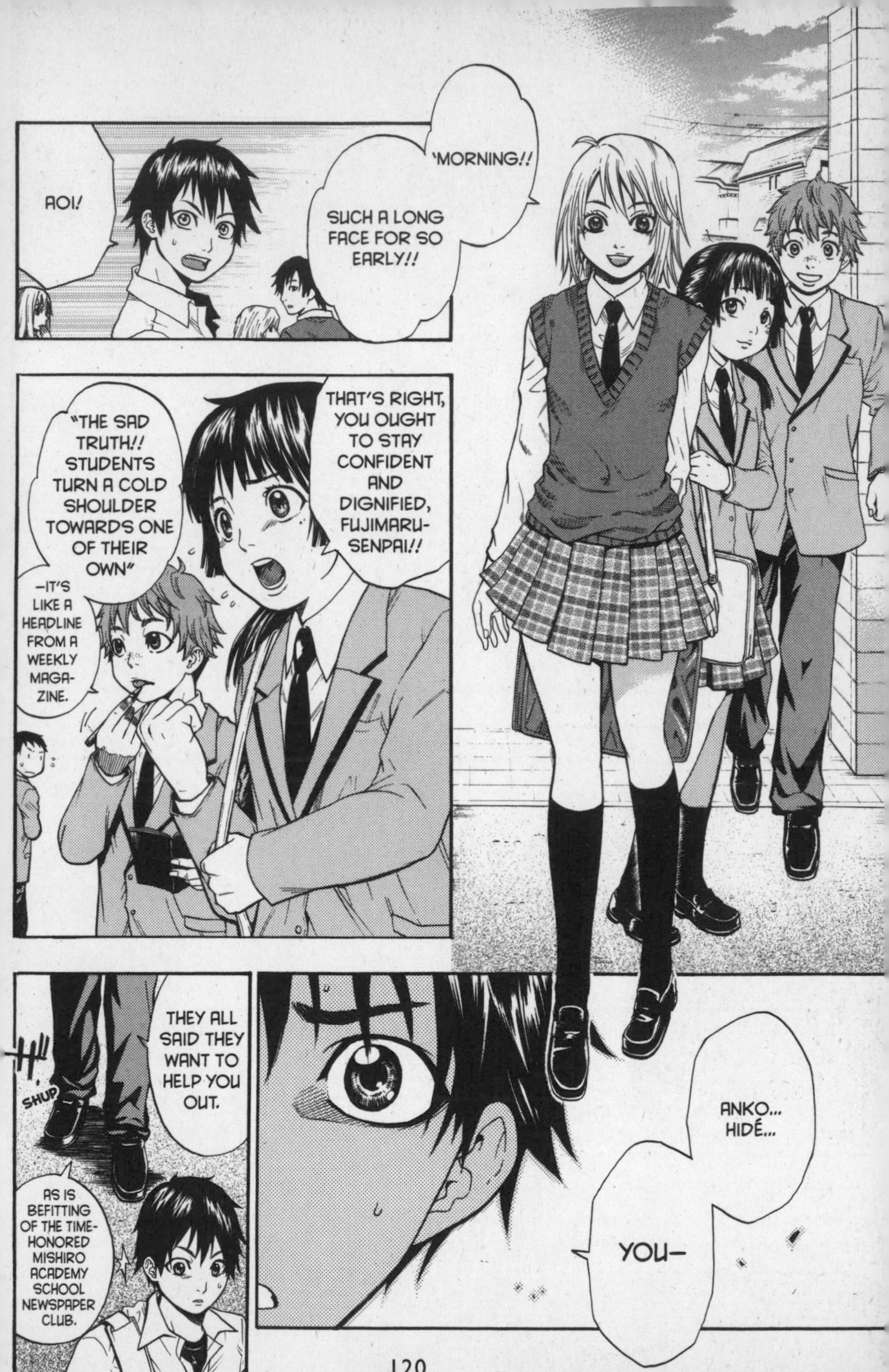
'MORNING!!
SUCH A LONG FACE FOR SO EARLY!!
AOI!
THAT'S RIGHT, YOU OUGHT TO STAY CONFIDENT AND DIGNIFIED, FUJIMARU-SENPAI!!
"THE SAD TRUTH!! STUDENTS TURN A COLD SHOULDER TOWARDS ONE OF THEIR OWN"
—IT'S LIKE A HEADLINE FROM A WEEKLY MAGAZINE.
ANKO... HIDÉ...
YOU—
THEY ALL SAID THEY WANT TO HELP YOU OUT.
SHUP
AS IS BEFITTING OF THE TIME-HONORED MISHIRO ACADEMY SCHOOL NEWSPAPER CLUB.

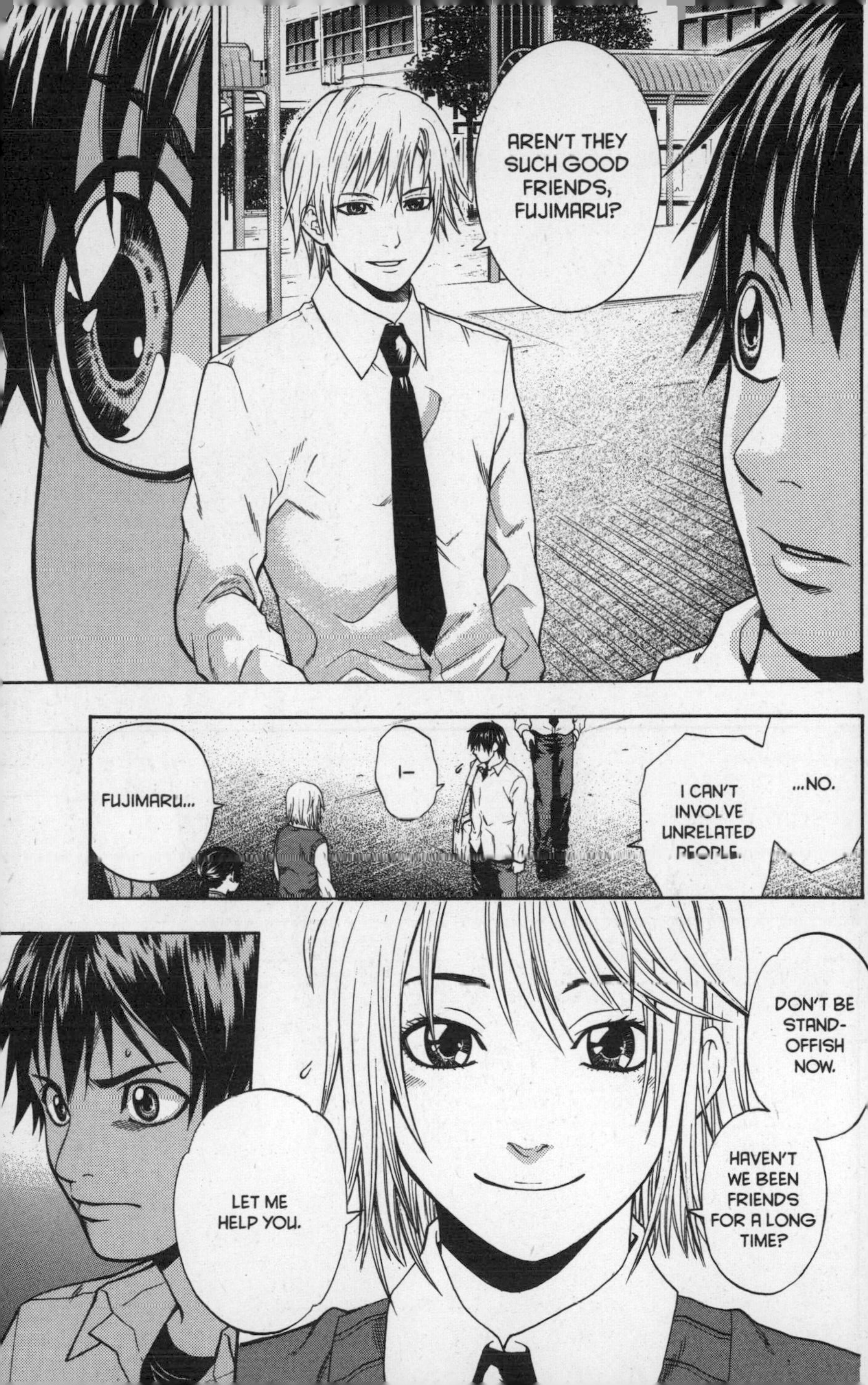
AREN'T THEY SUCH GOOD FRIENDS, FUJIMARU?
...NO.
I CAN'T INVOLVE UNRELATED PEOPLE.
I—
FUJIMARU...
DON'T BE STAND-OFFISH NOW.
HAVEN'T WE BEEN FRIENDS FOR A LONG TIME?
LET ME HELP YOU.

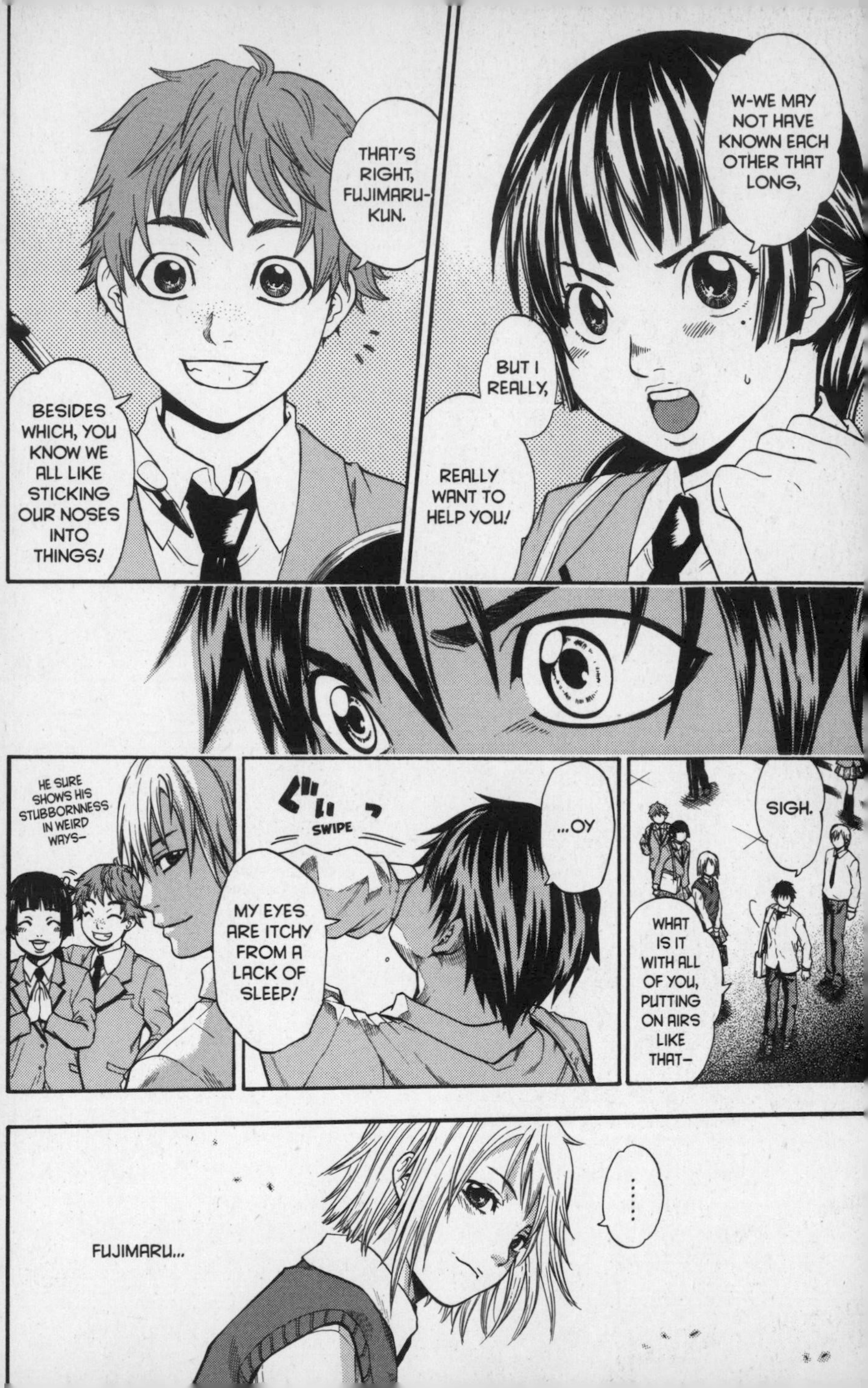
W-WE MAY NOT HAVE KNOWN EACH OTHER THAT LONG,
BUT I REALLY,
REALLY WANT TO HELP YOU!
THAT'S RIGHT, FUJIMARU-KUN.
BESIDES WHICH, YOU KNOW WE ALL LIKE STICKING OUR NOSES INTO THINGS!
SIGH.
WHAT IS IT WITH ALL OF YOU, PUTTING ON AIRS LIKE THAT–
...OY
SWIPE
MY EYES ARE ITCHY FROM A LACK OF SLEEP!
HE SURE SHOWS HIS STUBBORNNESS IN WEIRD WAYS–
......
FUJIMARU...

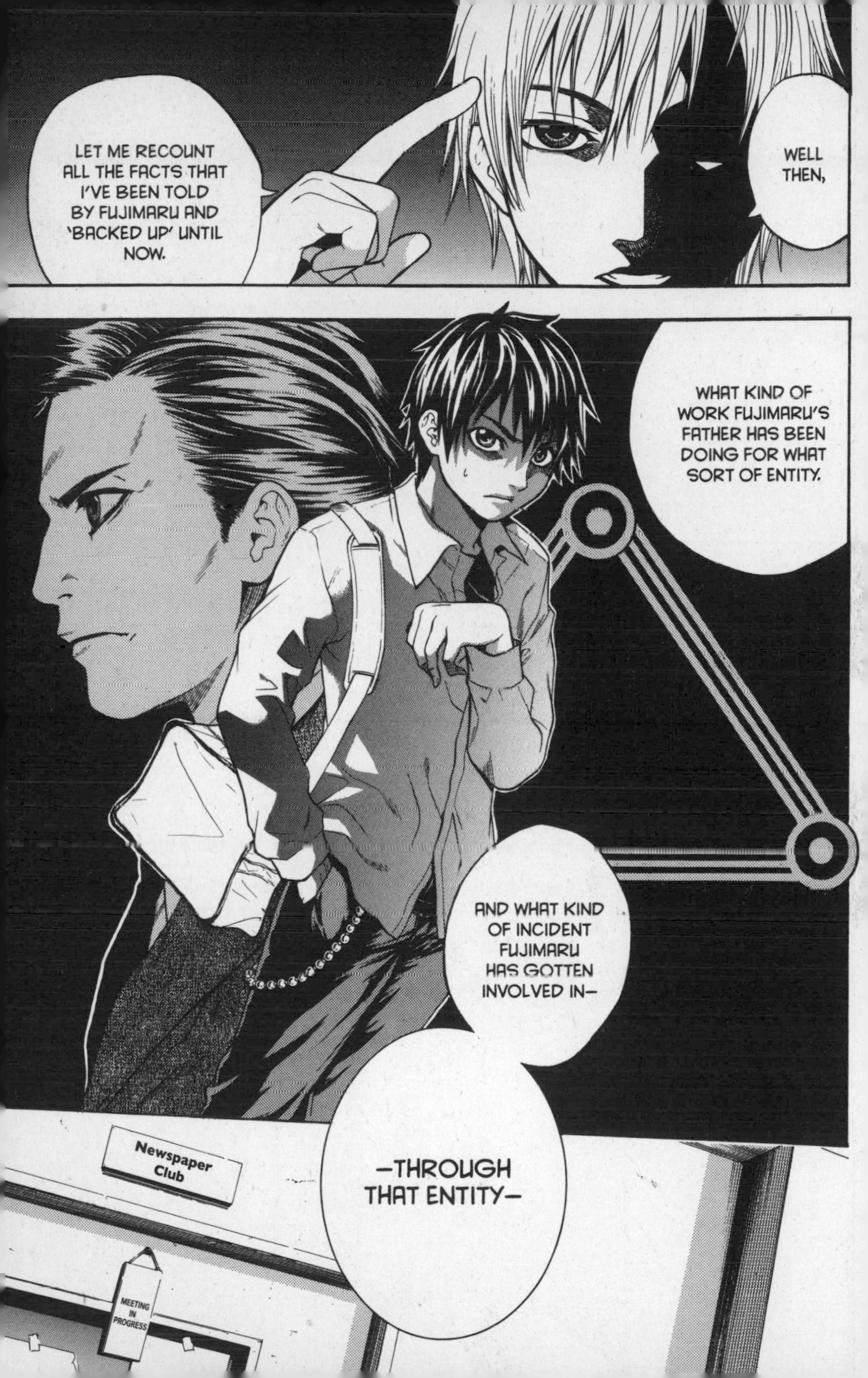
WELL THEN,
LET ME RECOUNT ALL THE FACTS THAT I'VE BEEN TOLD BY FUJIMARU AND 'BACKED UP' UNTIL NOW.
WHAT KIND OF WORK FUJIMARU'S FATHER HAS BEEN DOING FOR WHAT SORT OF ENTITY.
AND WHAT KIND OF INCIDENT FUJIMARU HAS GOTTEN INVOLVED IN—
Newspaper Club
—THROUGH THAT ENTITY—
MEETING IN PROGRESS

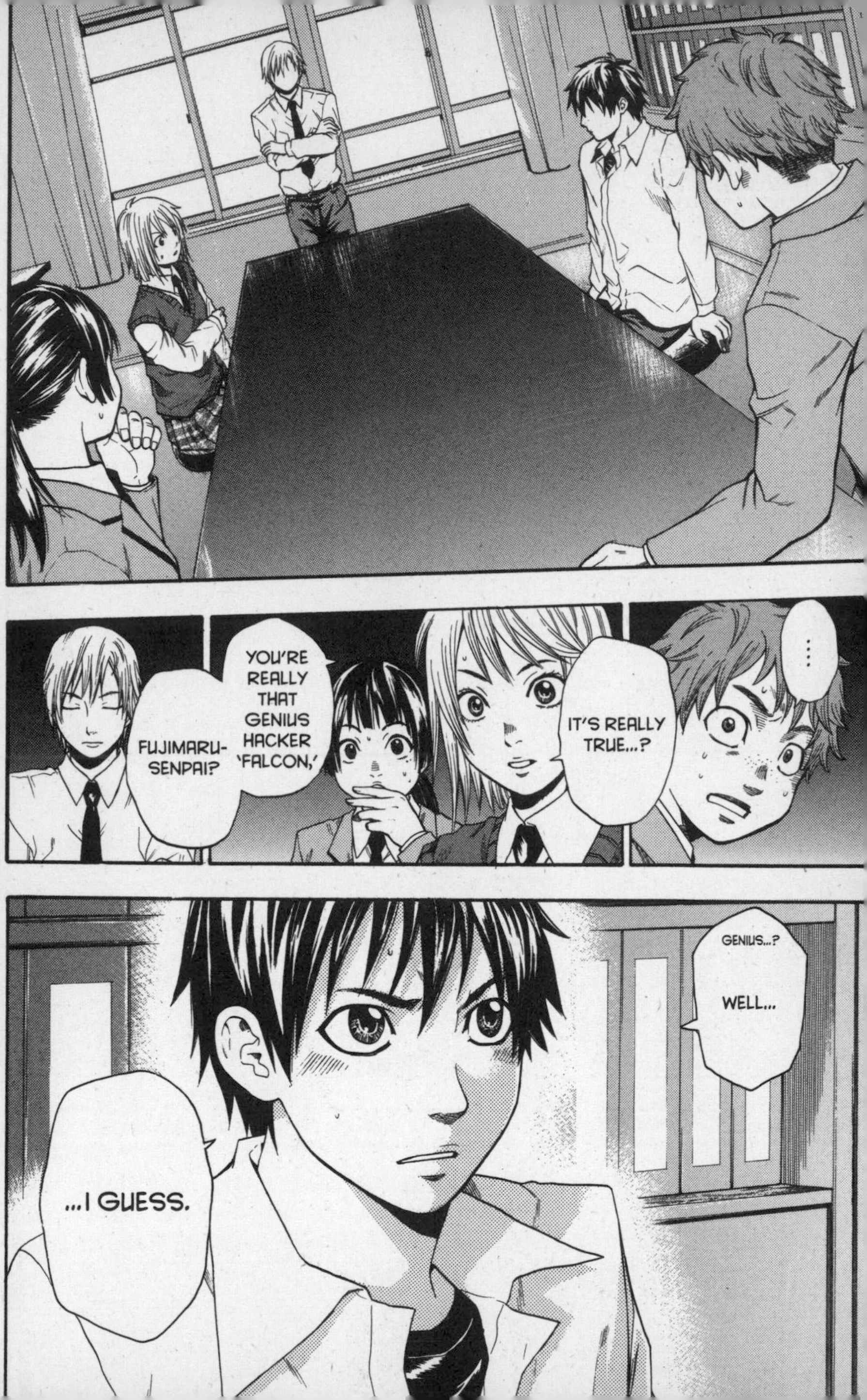
....
YOU'RE REALLY THAT GENIUS HACKER 'FALCON,'
FUJIMARU-SENPAI?
IT'S REALLY TRUE...?
GENIUS...?
WELL...
...I GUESS.

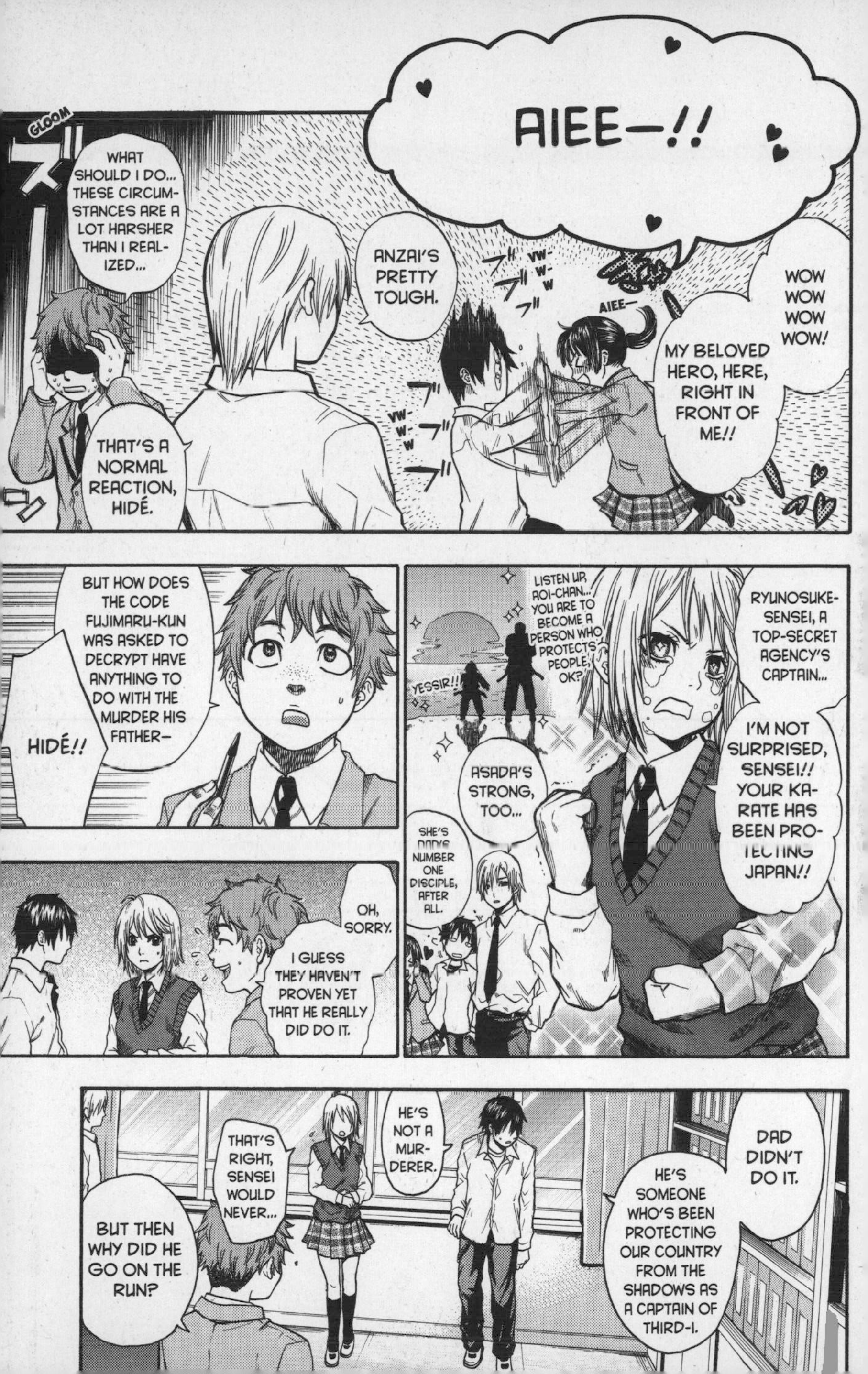
AIEE—!!
WOW WOW WOW WOW!
MY BELOVED HERO, HERE, RIGHT IN FRONT OF ME!!
AIEE—
VW-W-W
ANZAI'S PRETTY TOUGH.
VW-W-W
GLOOM
WHAT SHOULD I DO... THESE CIRCUMSTANCES ARE A LOT HARSHER THAN I REALIZED...
THAT'S A NORMAL REACTION, HIDÉ.
RYUNOSUKE-SENSEI, A TOP-SECRET AGENCY'S CAPTAIN...
LISTEN UP, AOI-CHAN... YOU ARE TO BECOME A PERSON WHO PROTECTS PEOPLE, OK?
YESSIR!!
I'M NOT SURPRISED, SENSEI!! YOUR KARATE HAS BEEN PROTECTING JAPAN!!
ASADA'S STRONG, TOO...
SHE'S NUMBER ONE DISCIPLE, AFTER ALL.
BUT HOW DOES THE CODE FUJIMARU-KUN WAS ASKED TO DECRYPT HAVE ANYTHING TO DO WITH THE MURDER HIS FATHER—
HIDÉ!!
OH, SORRY.
I GUESS THEY HAVEN'T PROVEN YET THAT HE REALLY DID DO IT.
DAD DIDN'T DO IT.
HE'S SOMEONE WHO'S BEEN PROTECTING OUR COUNTRY FROM THE SHADOWS AS A CAPTAIN OF THIRD-I.
HE'S NOT A MURDERER.
THAT'S RIGHT, SENSEI WOULD NEVER...
BUT THEN WHY DID HE GO ON THE RUN?

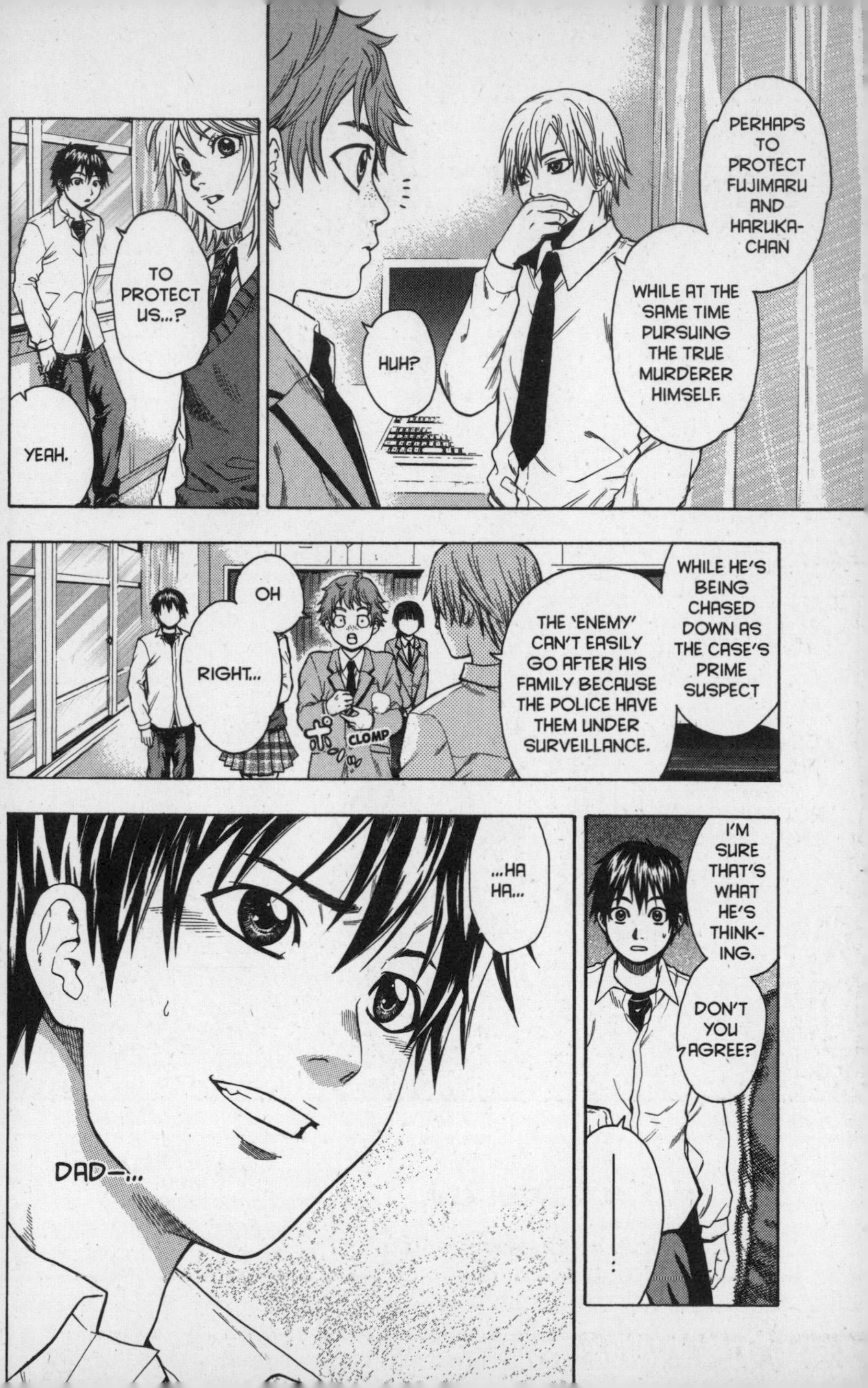
PERHAPS TO PROTECT FUJIMARU AND HARUKA-CHAN
WHILE AT THE SAME TIME PURSUING THE TRUE MURDERER HIMSELF.
HUH?
TO PROTECT US...?
YEAH.
WHILE HE'S BEING CHASED DOWN AS THE CASE'S PRIME SUSPECT
THE 'ENEMY' CAN'T EASILY GO AFTER HIS FAMILY BECAUSE THE POLICE HAVE THEM UNDER SURVEILLANCE.
OH RIGHT...
CLOMP
I'M SURE THAT'S WHAT HE'S THINKING.
DON'T YOU AGREE?
...HA HA...
DAD—...

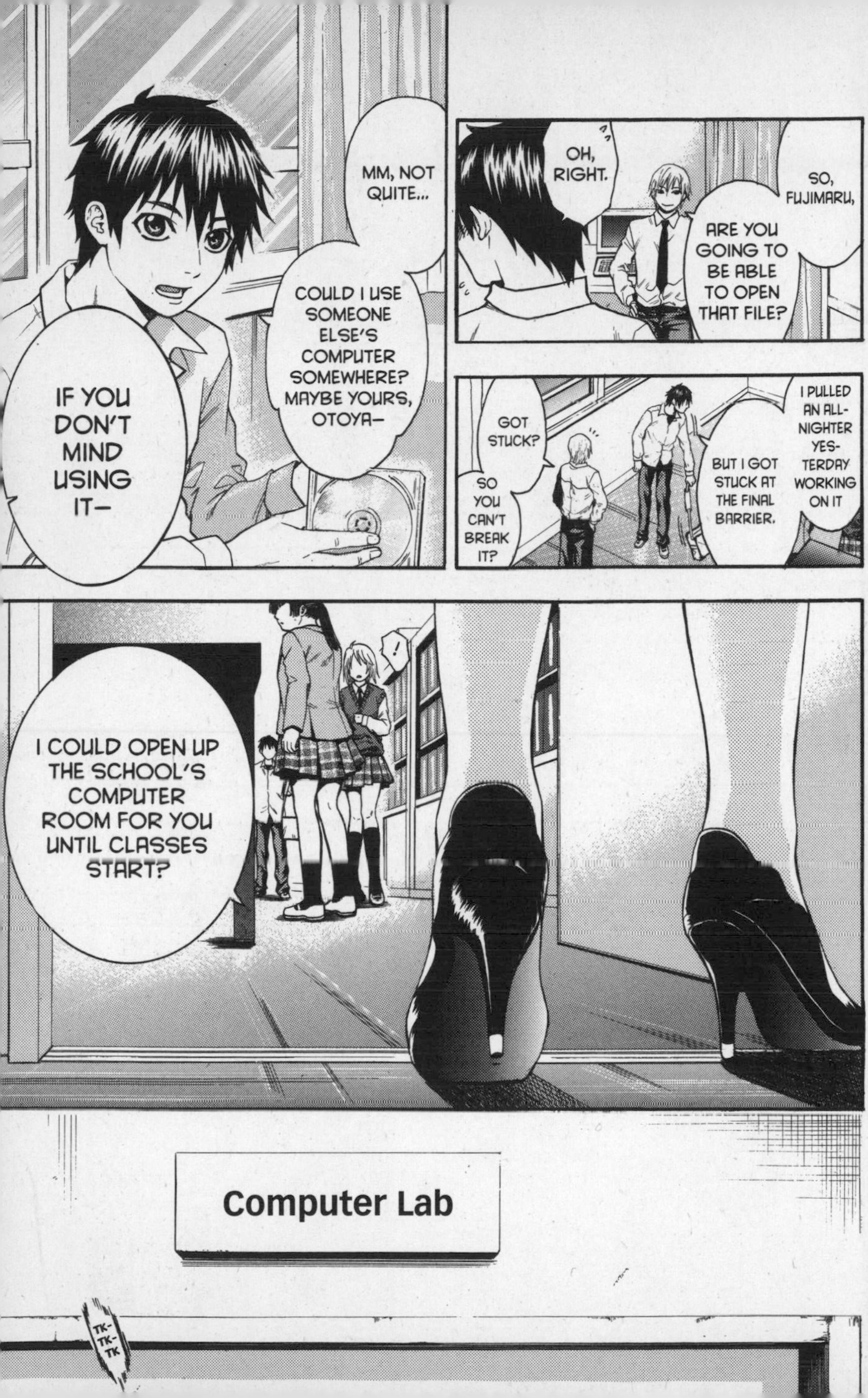
SO, FUJIMARU,
ARE YOU GOING TO BE ABLE TO OPEN THAT FILE?
OH, RIGHT.
I PULLED AN ALL-NIGHTER YESTERDAY WORKING ON IT
BUT I GOT STUCK AT THE FINAL BARRIER.
GOT STUCK?
SO YOU CAN'T BREAK IT?
MM, NOT QUITE...
COULD I USE SOMEONE ELSE'S COMPUTER SOMEWHERE? MAYBE YOURS, OTOYA—
IF YOU DON'T MIND USING IT—
!
I COULD OPEN UP THE SCHOOL'S COMPUTER ROOM FOR YOU UNTIL CLASSES START?
Computer Lab
TK-TK-TK

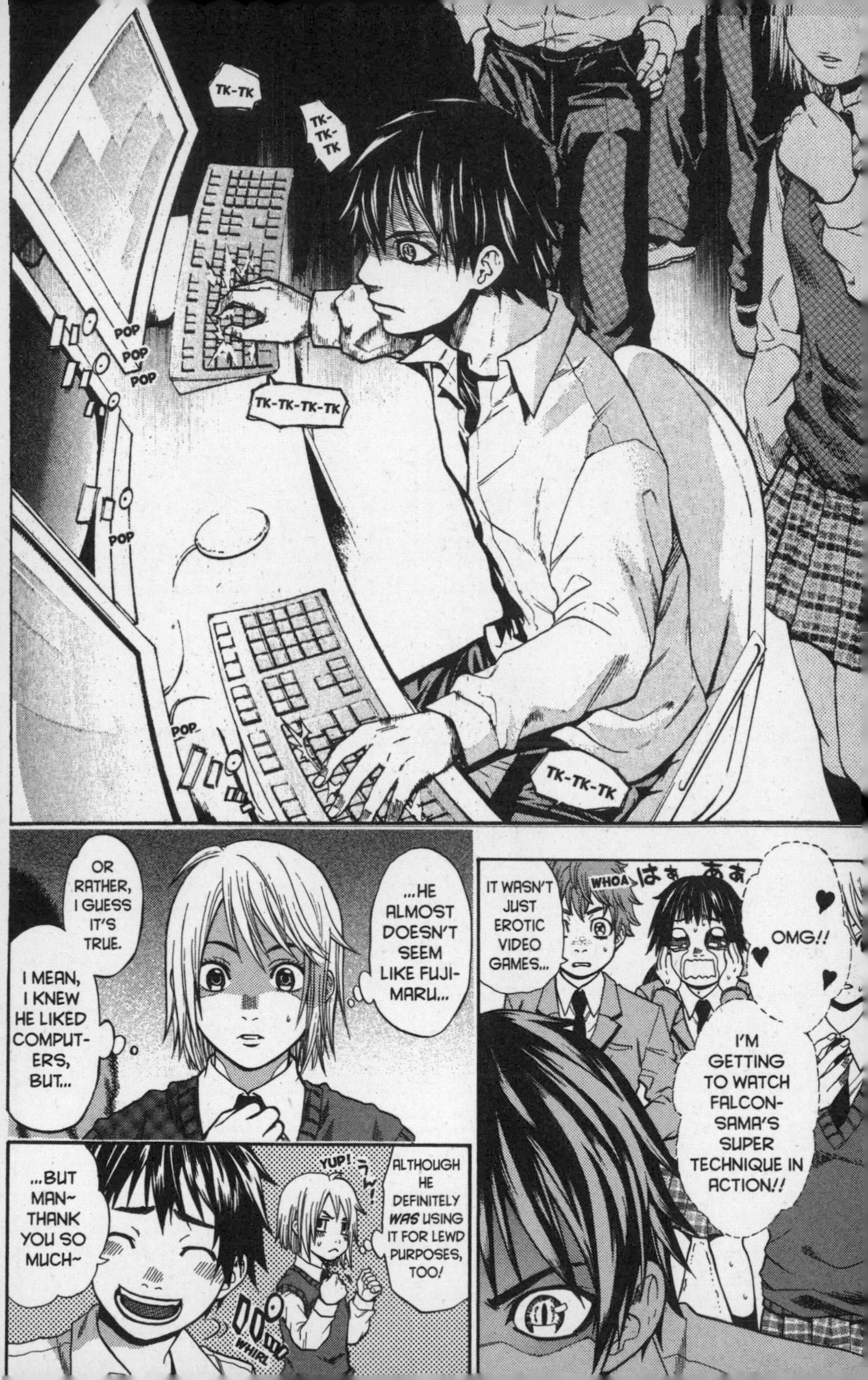
TK-TK
TK-TK-TK
POP
POP
POP
TK-TK-TK-TK
POP
POP
TK-TK-TK
OMG!!
はぁ あぁ
WHOA
IT WASN'T JUST EROTIC VIDEO GAMES...
I'M GETTING TO WATCH FALCON-SAMA'S SUPER TECHNIQUE IN ACTION!!
...HE ALMOST DOESN'T SEEM LIKE FUJI-MARU...
OR RATHER, I GUESS IT'S TRUE.
I MEAN, I KNEW HE LIKED COMPUTERS, BUT...
ALTHOUGH HE DEFINITELY *WAS* USING IT FOR LEWD PURPOSES, TOO!
YUP!
うん
...BUT MAN~ THANK YOU SO MUCH~
WHIRL

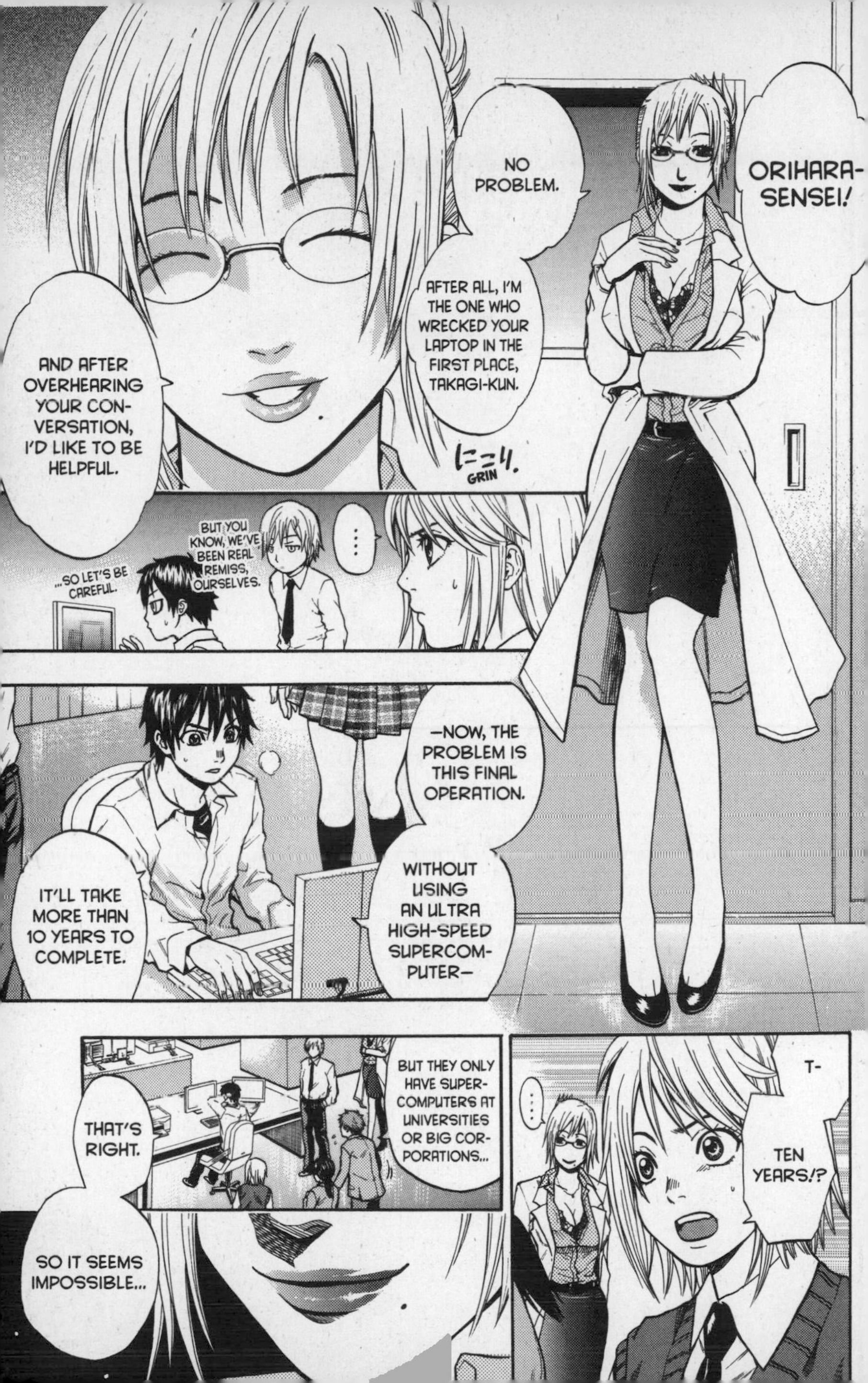
ORIHARA-SENSEI!
NO PROBLEM.
AFTER ALL, I'M THE ONE WHO WRECKED YOUR LAPTOP IN THE FIRST PLACE, TAKAGI-KUN.
AND AFTER OVERHEARING YOUR CONVERSATION, I'D LIKE TO BE HELPFUL.
にこり
GRIN
....
BUT YOU KNOW, WE'VE BEEN REAL REMISS, OURSELVES.
...SO LET'S BE CAREFUL.
—NOW, THE PROBLEM IS THIS FINAL OPERATION.
WITHOUT USING AN ULTRA HIGH-SPEED SUPERCOMPUTER—
IT'LL TAKE MORE THAN 10 YEARS TO COMPLETE.
T-
TEN YEARS!?
....
BUT THEY ONLY HAVE SUPERCOMPUTERS AT UNIVERSITIES OR BIG CORPORATIONS...
THAT'S RIGHT.
SO IT SEEMS IMPOSSIBLE...

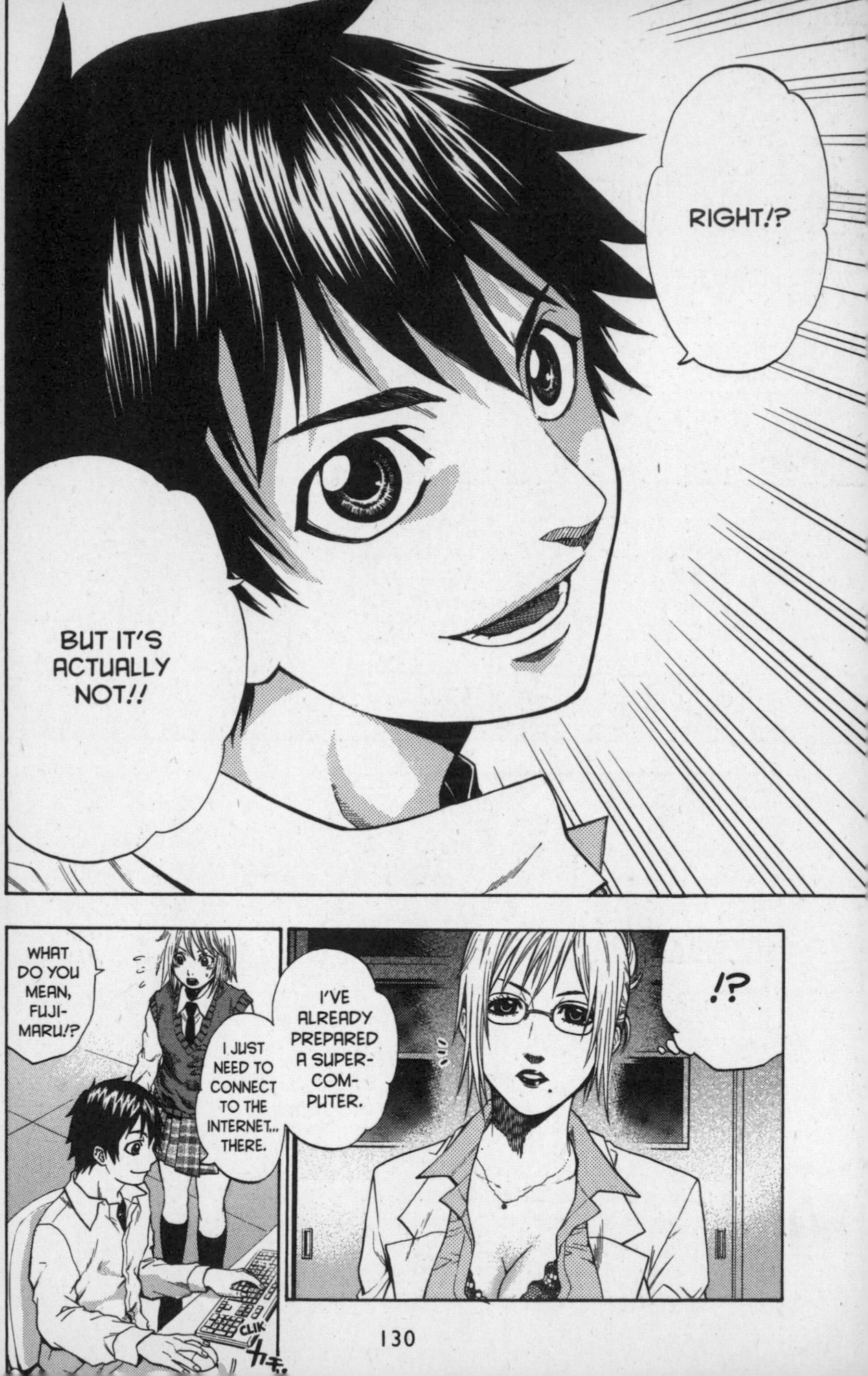
RIGHT!?
BUT IT'S ACTUALLY NOT!!
!?
I'VE ALREADY PREPARED A SUPER-COMPUTER.
I JUST NEED TO CONNECT TO THE INTERNET... THERE.
WHAT DO YOU MEAN, FUJI-MARU!?
CLIK

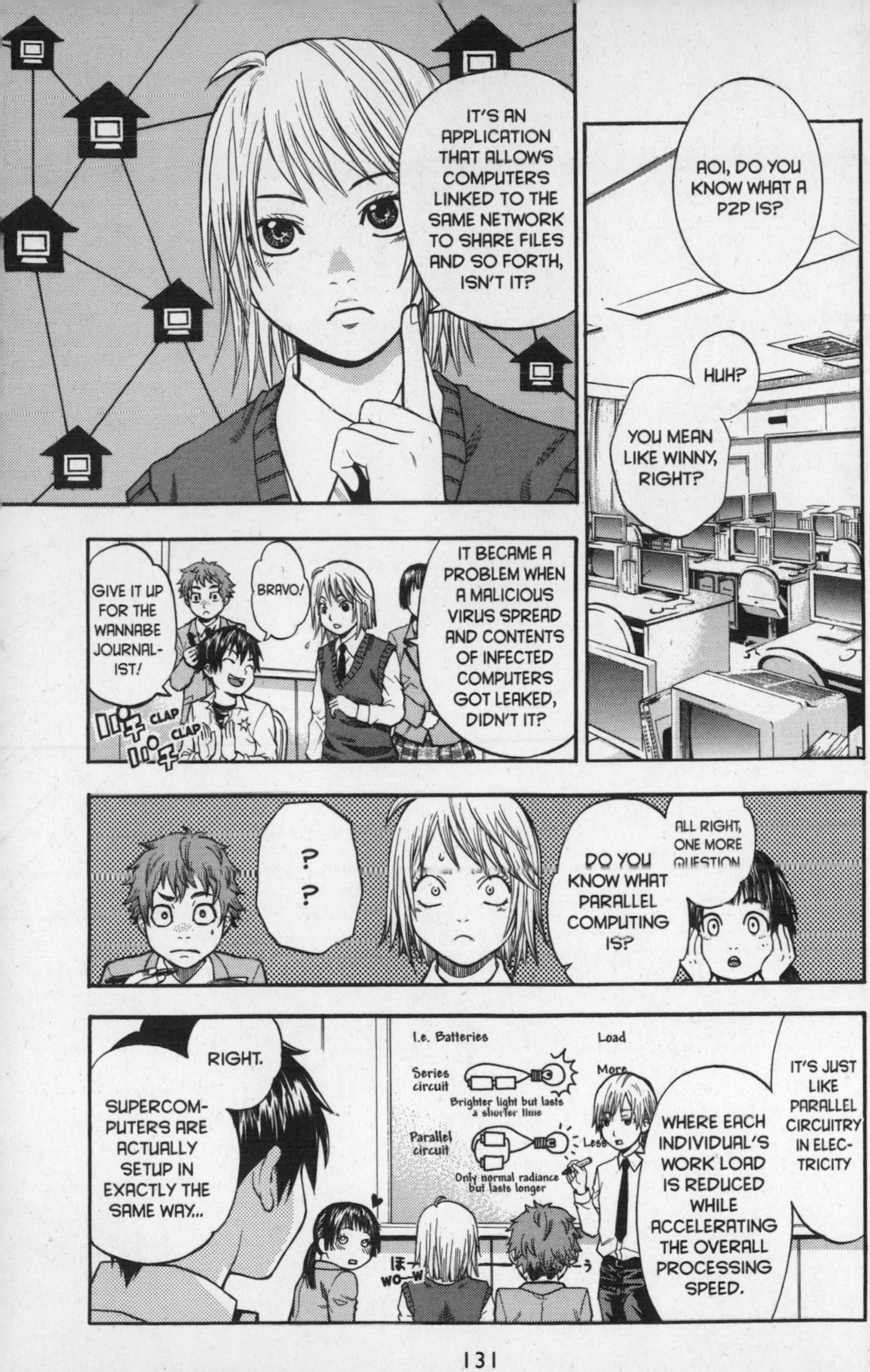
AOI, DO YOU KNOW WHAT A P2P IS?
HUH?
YOU MEAN LIKE WINNY, RIGHT?
IT'S AN APPLICATION THAT ALLOWS COMPUTERS LINKED TO THE SAME NETWORK TO SHARE FILES AND SO FORTH, ISN'T IT?
IT BECAME A PROBLEM WHEN A MALICIOUS VIRUS SPREAD AND CONTENTS OF INFECTED COMPUTERS GOT LEAKED, DIDN'T IT?
BRAVO!
GIVE IT UP FOR THE WANNABE JOURNAL-IST!
パチ CLAP
パチ CLAP
ALL RIGHT, ONE MORE QUESTION
DO YOU KNOW WHAT PARALLEL COMPUTING IS?
? ?
IT'S JUST LIKE PARALLEL CIRCUITRY IN ELECTRICITY
WHERE EACH INDIVIDUAL'S WORK LOAD IS REDUCED WHILE ACCELERATING THE OVERALL PROCESSING SPEED.
I.e. Batteries
Load
Series circuit
More
Brighter light but lasts a shorter time
Parallel circuit
Less
Only normal radiance but lasts longer
RIGHT.
SUPERCOM-PUTERS ARE ACTUALLY SETUP IN EXACTLY THE SAME WAY...
ほー WO—W
ーう

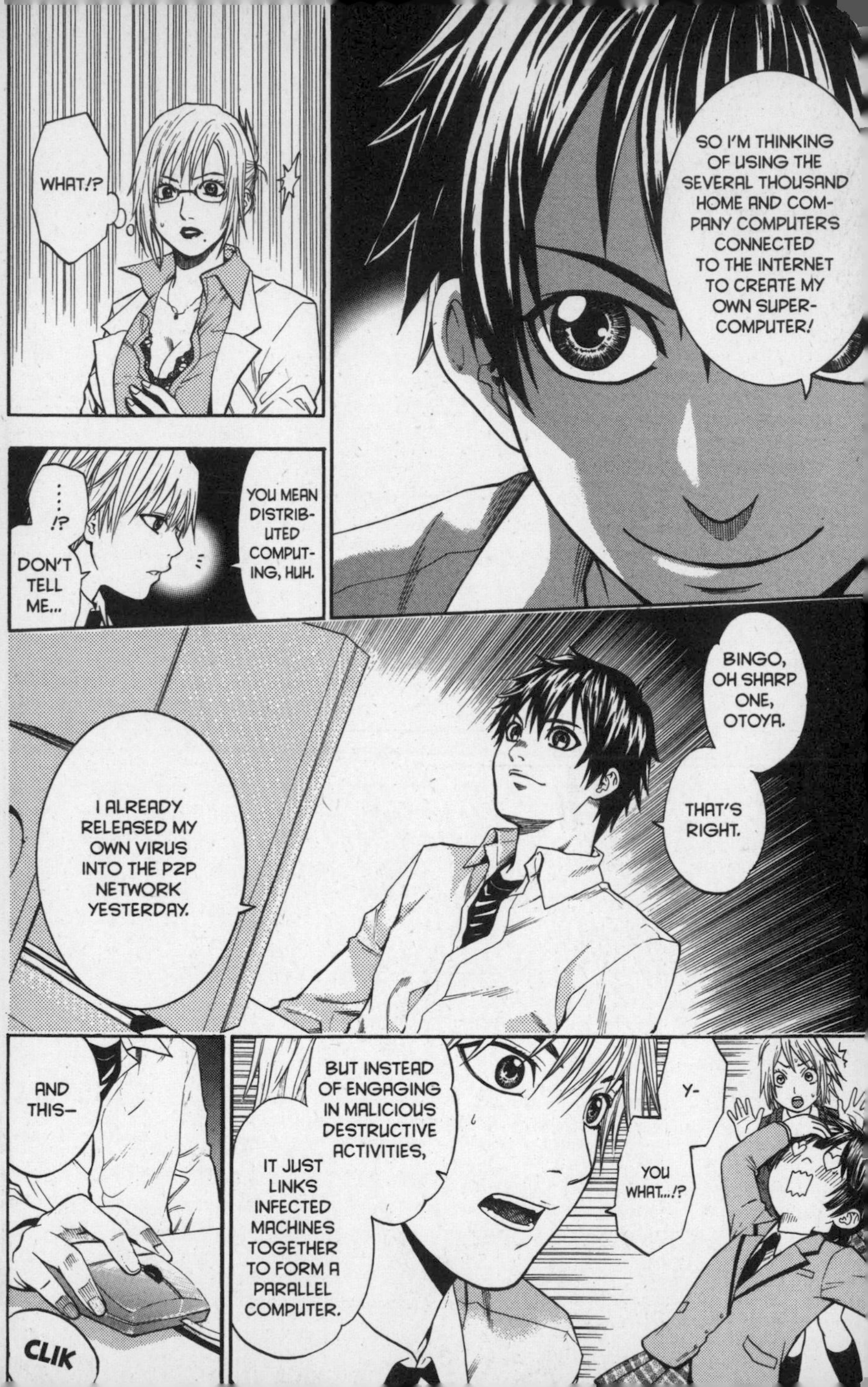
SO I'M THINKING OF USING THE SEVERAL THOUSAND HOME AND COMPANY COMPUTERS CONNECTED TO THE INTERNET TO CREATE MY OWN SUPER-COMPUTER!
WHAT!?
YOU MEAN DISTRIBUTED COMPUTING, HUH.
......!?
DON'T TELL ME...
BINGO, OH SHARP ONE, OTOYA.
THAT'S RIGHT.
I ALREADY RELEASED MY OWN VIRUS INTO THE P2P NETWORK YESTERDAY.
Y-
YOU WHAT...!?
BUT INSTEAD OF ENGAGING IN MALICIOUS DESTRUCTIVE ACTIVITIES,
IT JUST LINKS INFECTED MACHINES TOGETHER TO FORM A PARALLEL COMPUTER.
AND THIS—
CLIK

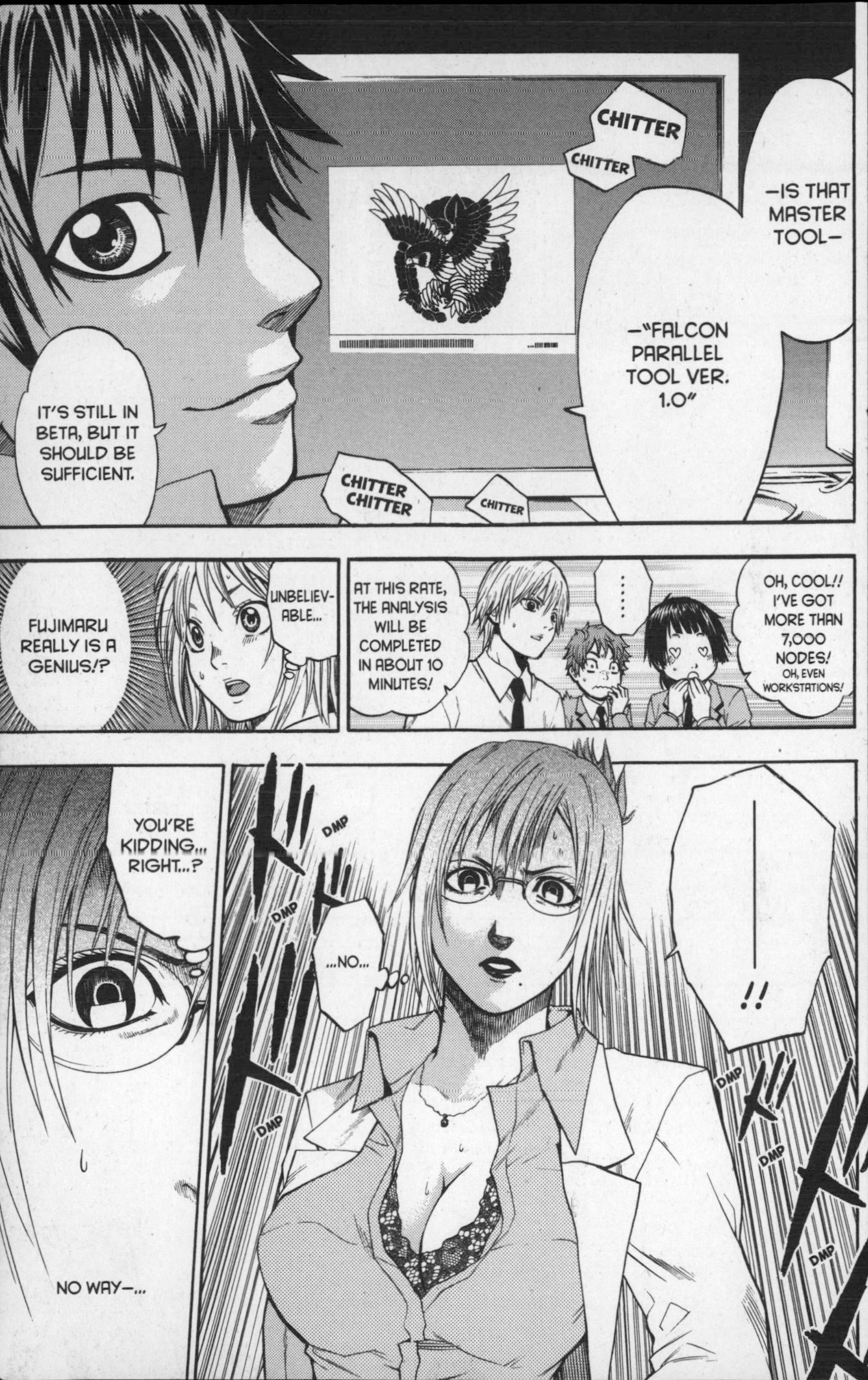
—IS THAT MASTER TOOL—
—"FALCON PARALLEL TOOL VER. 1.0"
CHITTER
CHITTER
IT'S STILL IN BETA, BUT IT SHOULD BE SUFFICIENT.
CHITTER CHITTER
CHITTER
OH, COOL!! I'VE GOT MORE THAN 7,000 NODES! OH, EVEN WORKSTATIONS!
......
AT THIS RATE, THE ANALYSIS WILL BE COMPLETED IN ABOUT 10 MINUTES!
UNBELIEV-ABLE...
FUJIMARU REALLY IS A GENIUS!?
—!!
DMP
DMP
DMP
...NO...
DMP
DMP
DMP
YOU'RE KIDDING... RIGHT...?
NO WAY—...

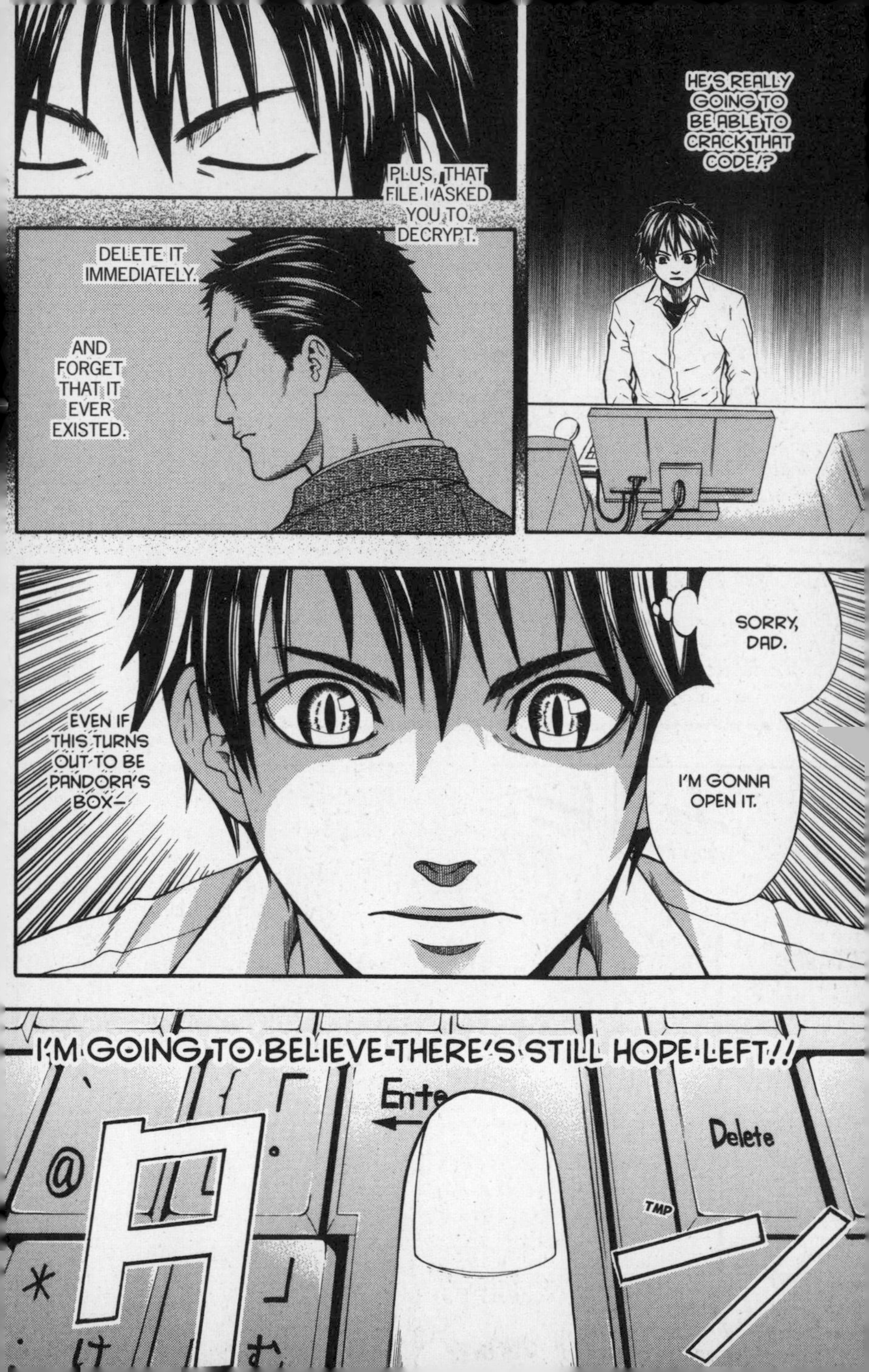
HE'S REALLY GOING TO BE ABLE TO CRACK THAT CODE!?
PLUS, THAT FILE I ASKED YOU TO DECRYPT.
DELETE IT IMMEDIATELY.
AND FORGET THAT IT EVER EXISTED.
SORRY, DAD.
I'M GONNA OPEN IT.
EVEN IF THIS TURNS OUT TO BE PANDORA'S BOX—
I'M GOING TO BELIEVE THERE'S STILL HOPE LEFT!!
Ente
Delete
TMP

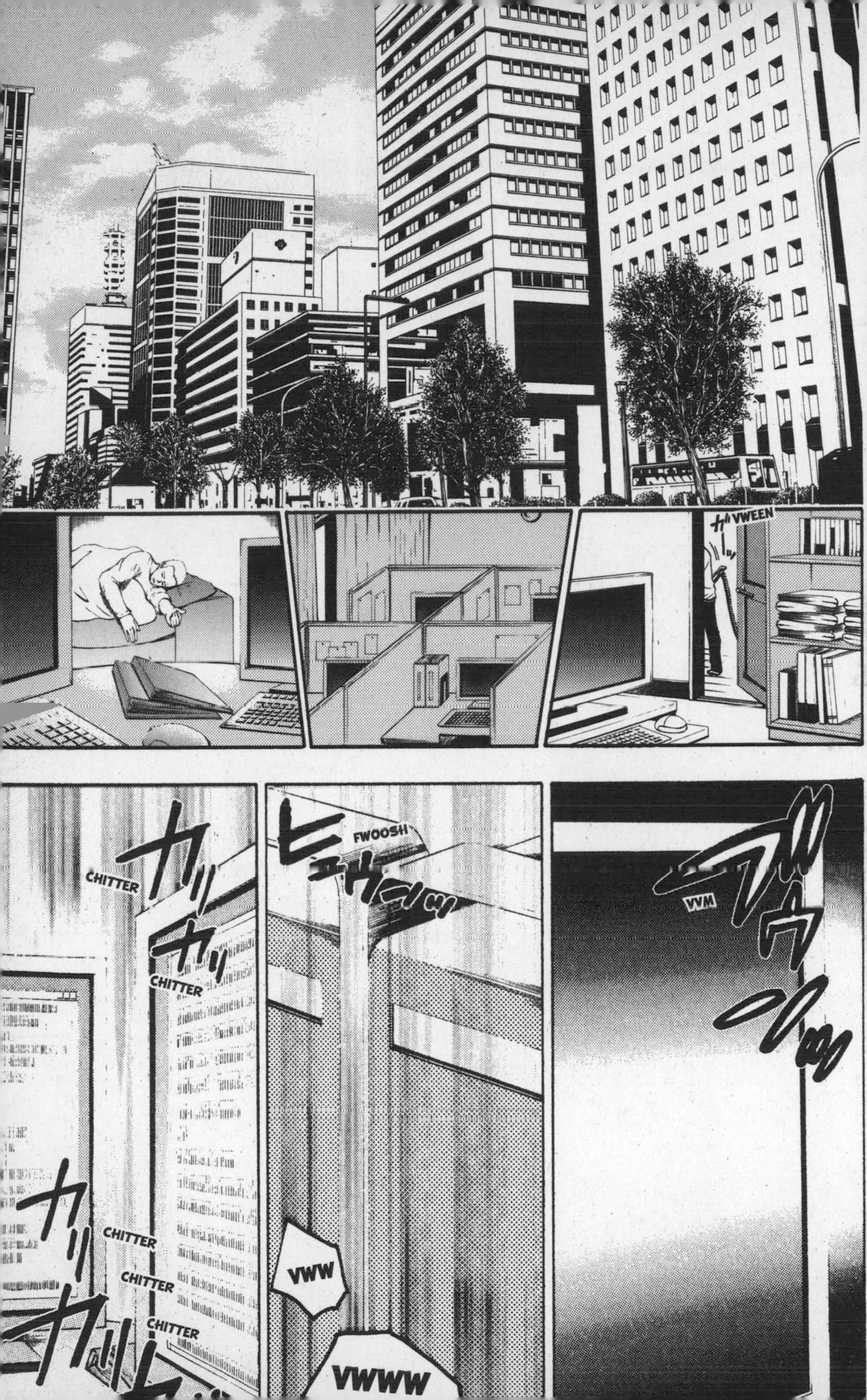
VWEEN
VVM
FWOOSH
VWW
VWWW
CHITTER
CHITTER
CHITTER
CHITTER
CHITTER

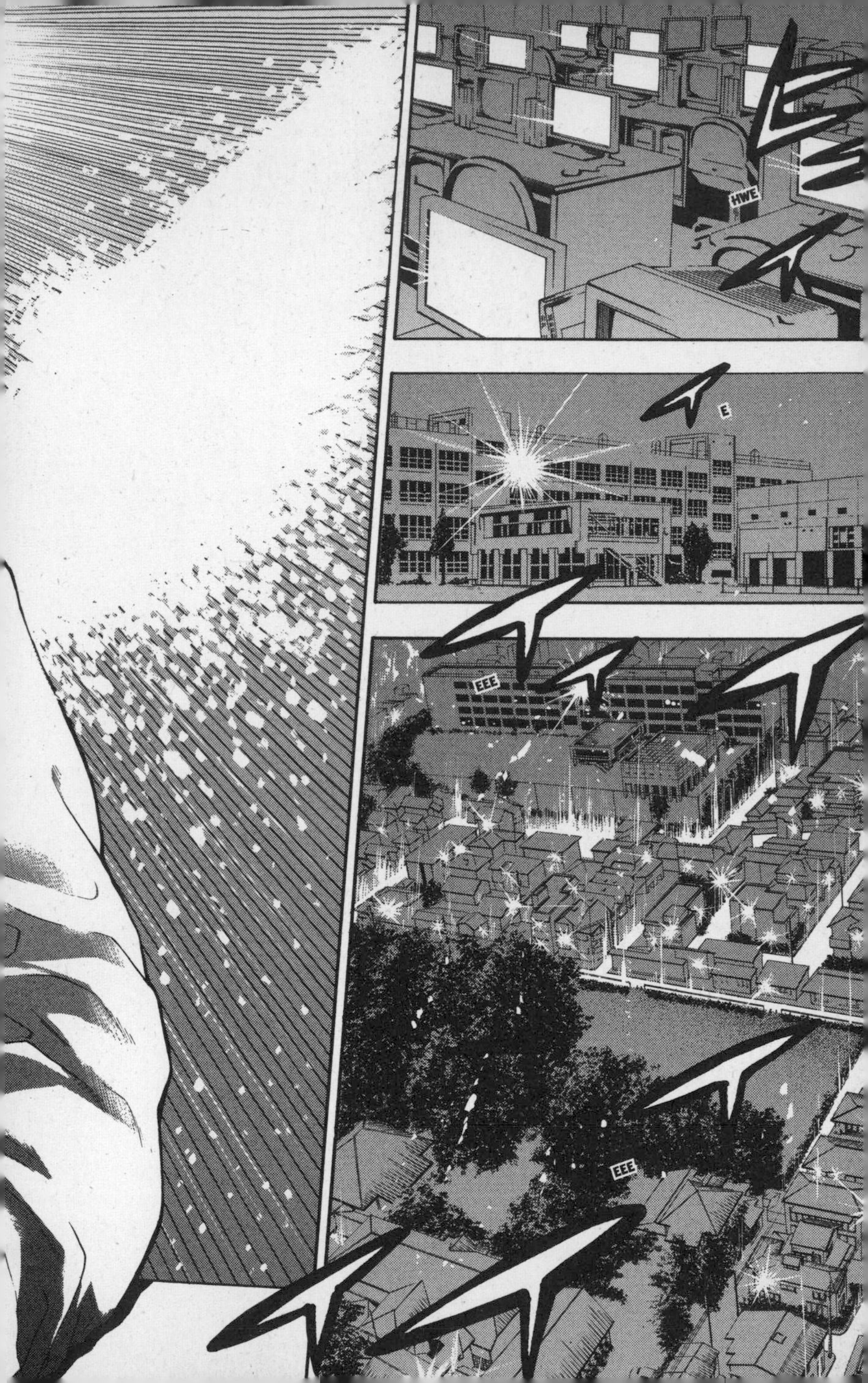
HWE
E
EEE
EEE

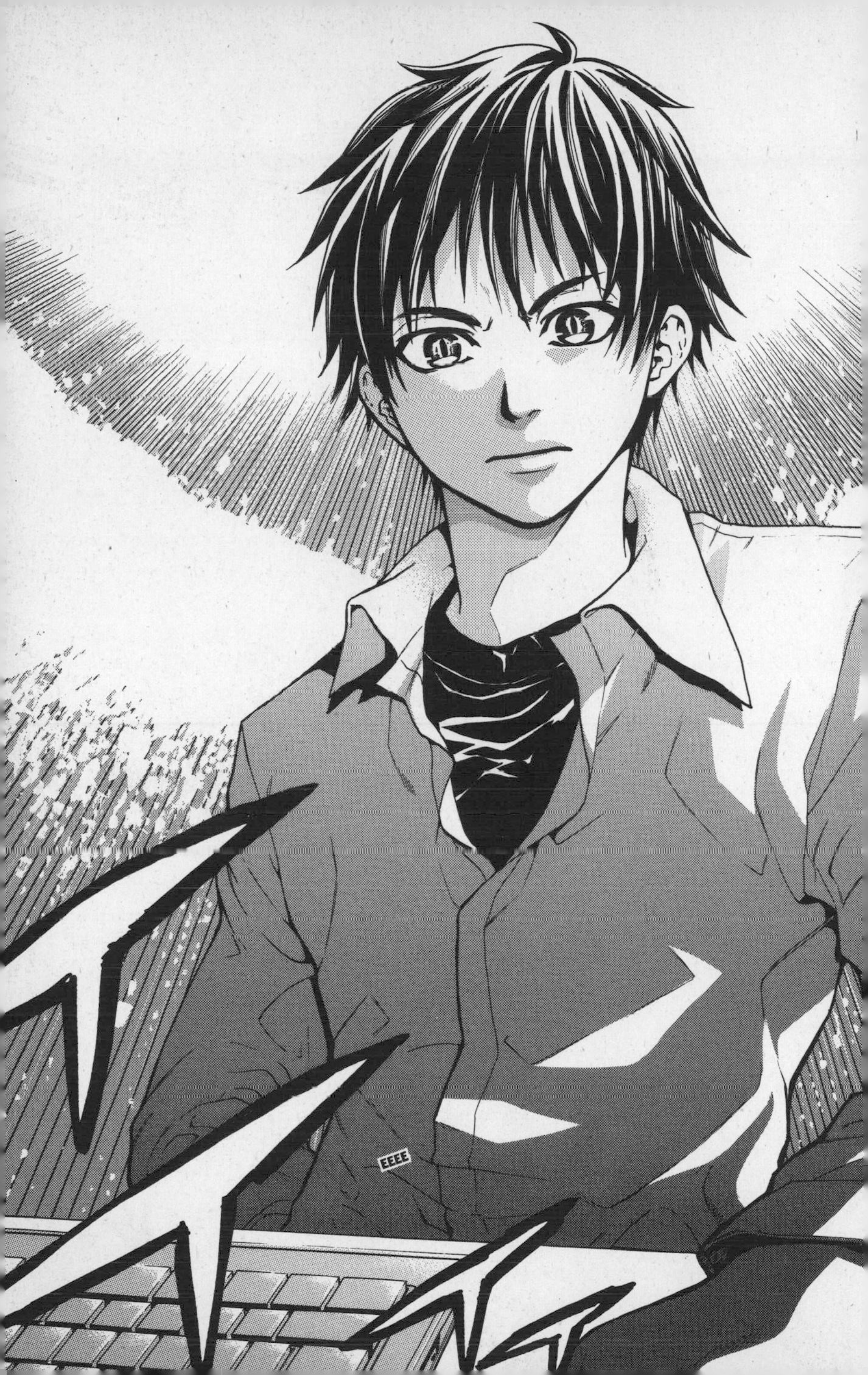
EEEE

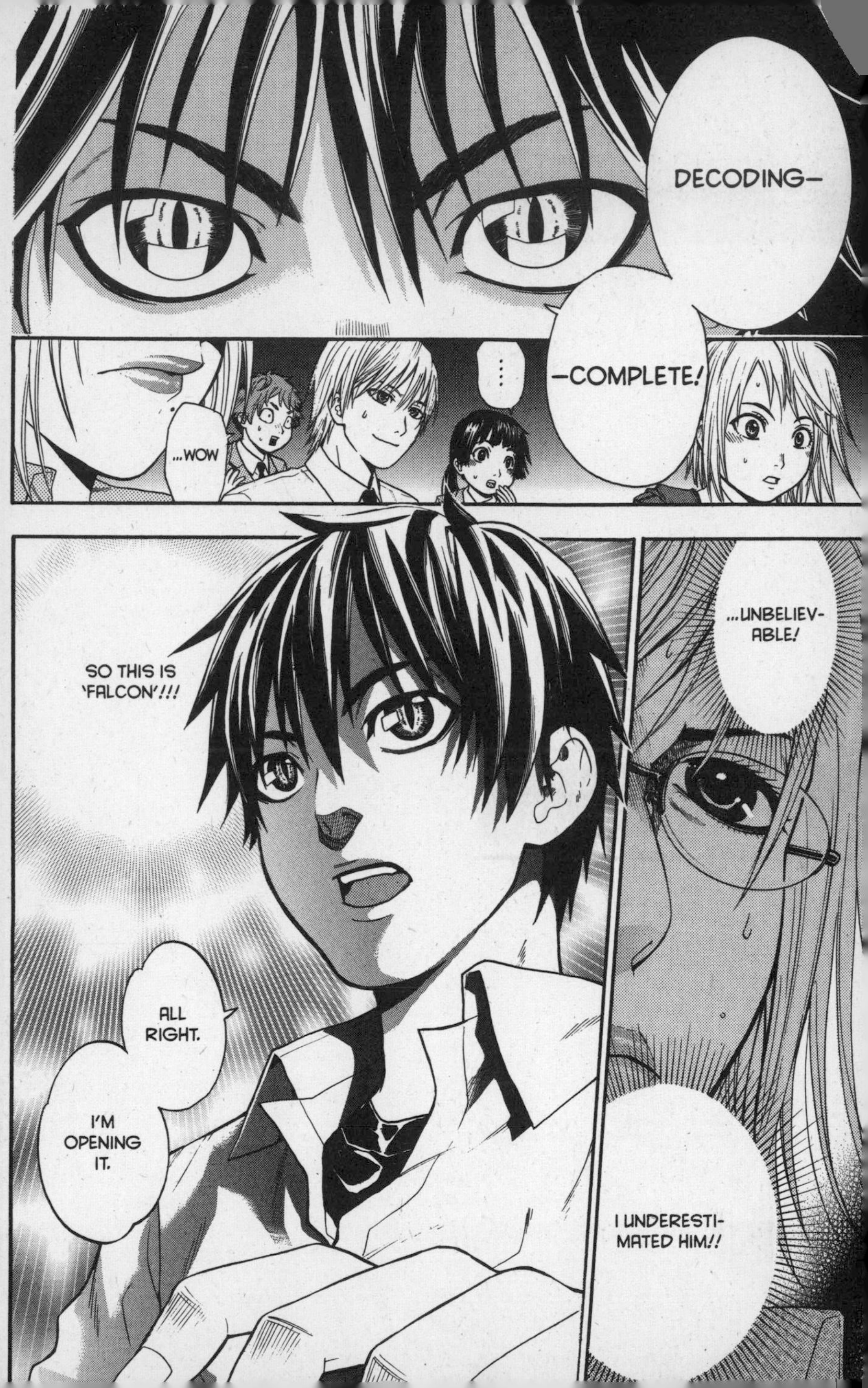
DECODING—
—COMPLETE!
......
...WOW
...UNBELIEVABLE!
I UNDERESTIMATED HIM!!
SO THIS IS 'FALCON'!!!
ALL RIGHT.
I'M OPENING IT.

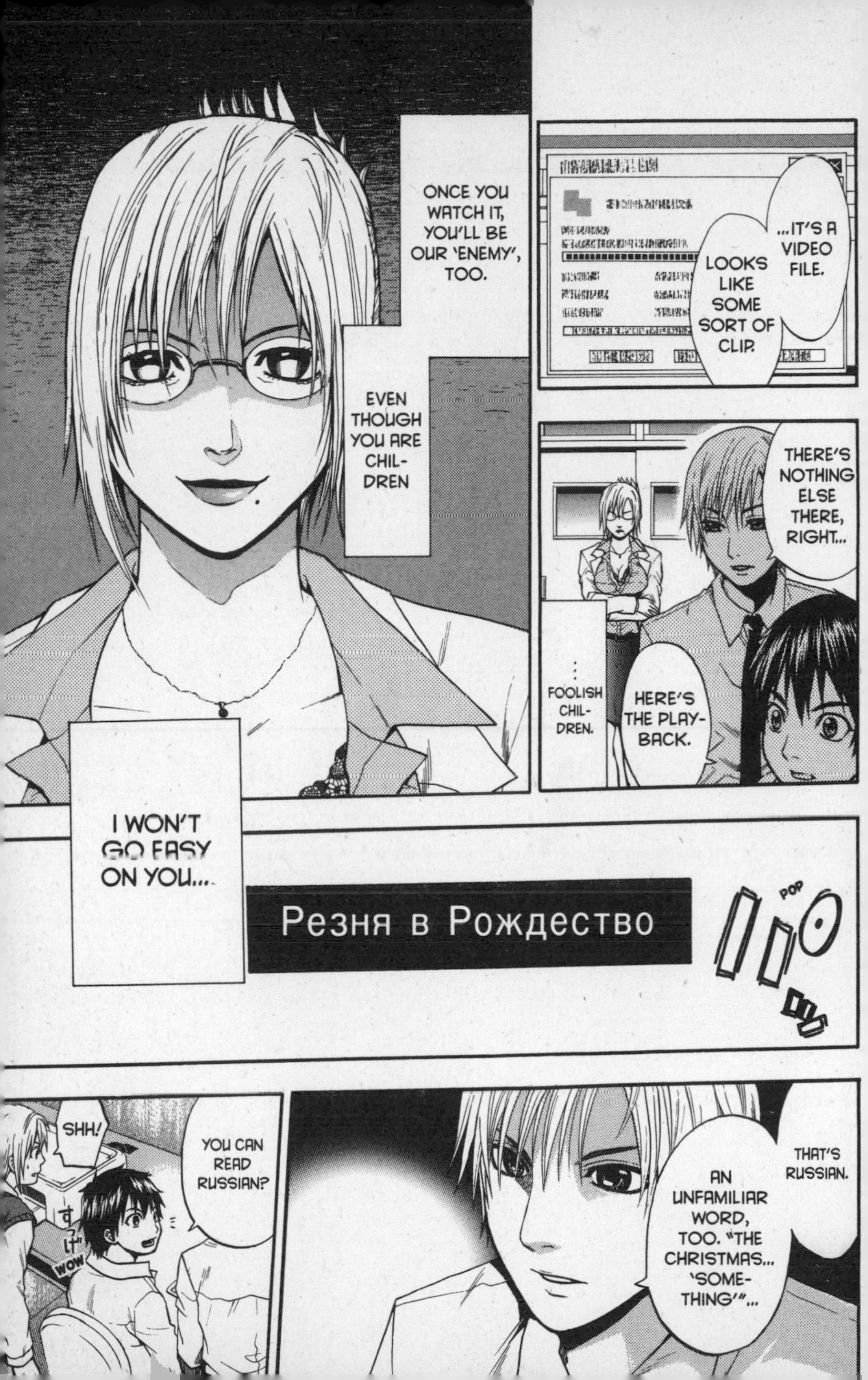
...IT'S A VIDEO FILE.
LOOKS LIKE SOME SORT OF CLIP.
THERE'S NOTHING ELSE THERE, RIGHT...
HERE'S THE PLAYBACK.
...FOOLISH CHILDREN.
ONCE YOU WATCH IT, YOU'LL BE OUR 'ENEMY', TOO.
EVEN THOUGH YOU ARE CHILDREN
I WON'T GO EASY ON YOU...
Резня в Рождество
POP
THAT'S RUSSIAN.
AN UNFAMILIAR WORD, TOO. "THE CHRISTMAS... 'SOMETHING'"...
YOU CAN READ RUSSIAN?
SHH!
すげ
WOW

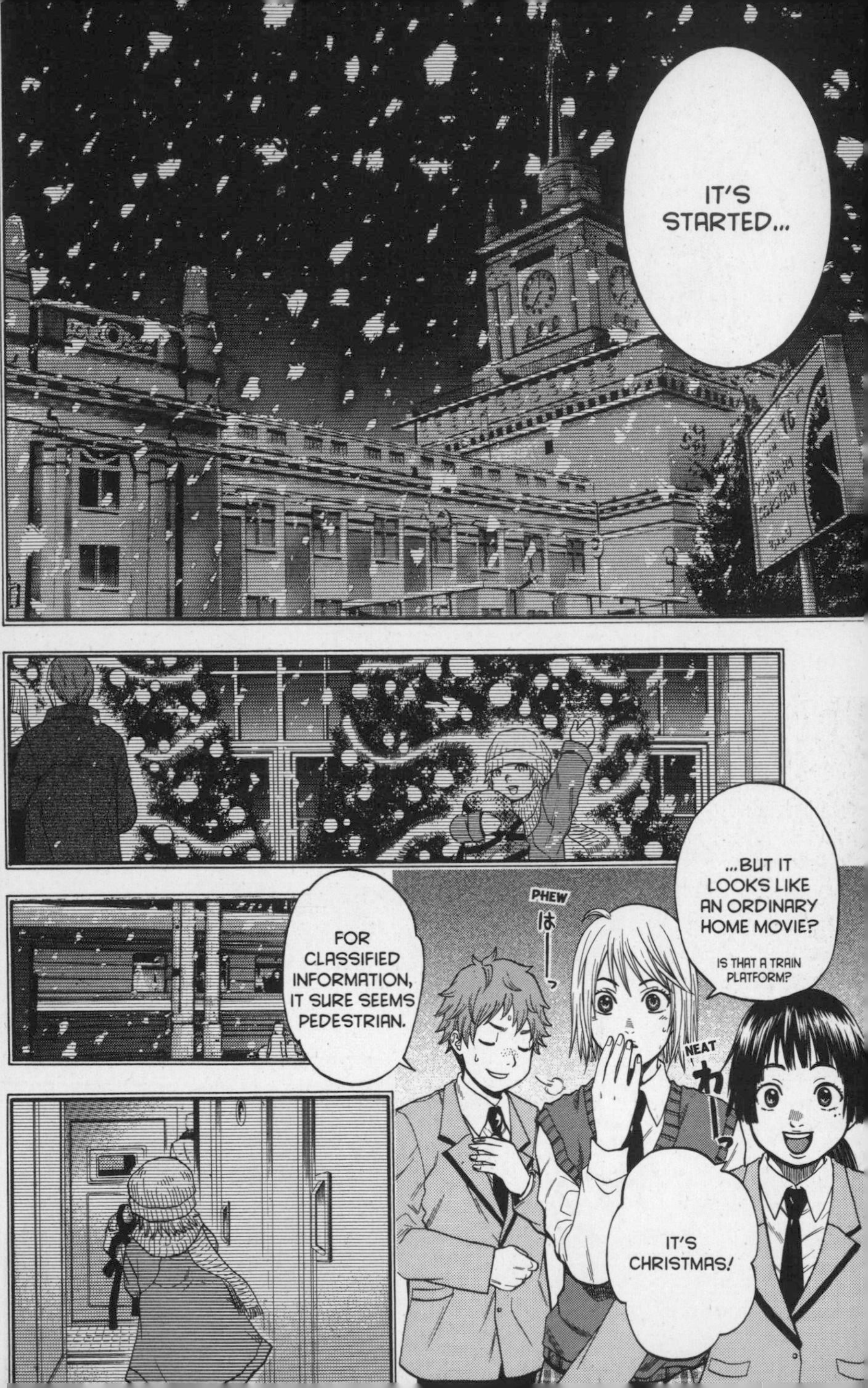
IT'S STARTED...
...BUT IT LOOKS LIKE AN ORDINARY HOME MOVIE?
IS THAT A TRAIN PLATFORM?
PHEW はーっ
FOR CLASSIFIED INFORMATION, IT SURE SEEMS PEDESTRIAN.
NEAT わーっ
IT'S CHRISTMAS!

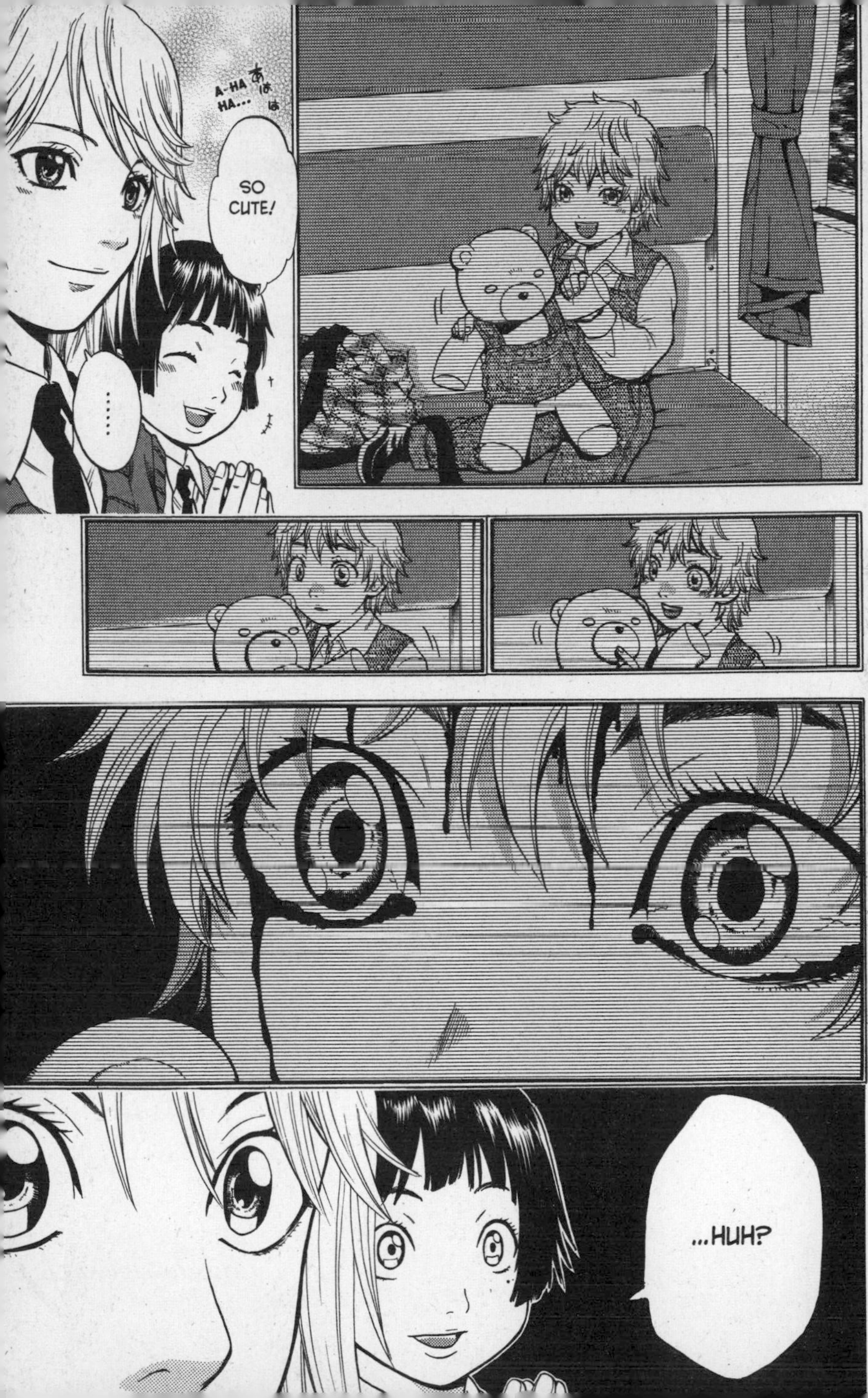
A-HA HA...
あはは
SO CUTE!
......
...HUH?

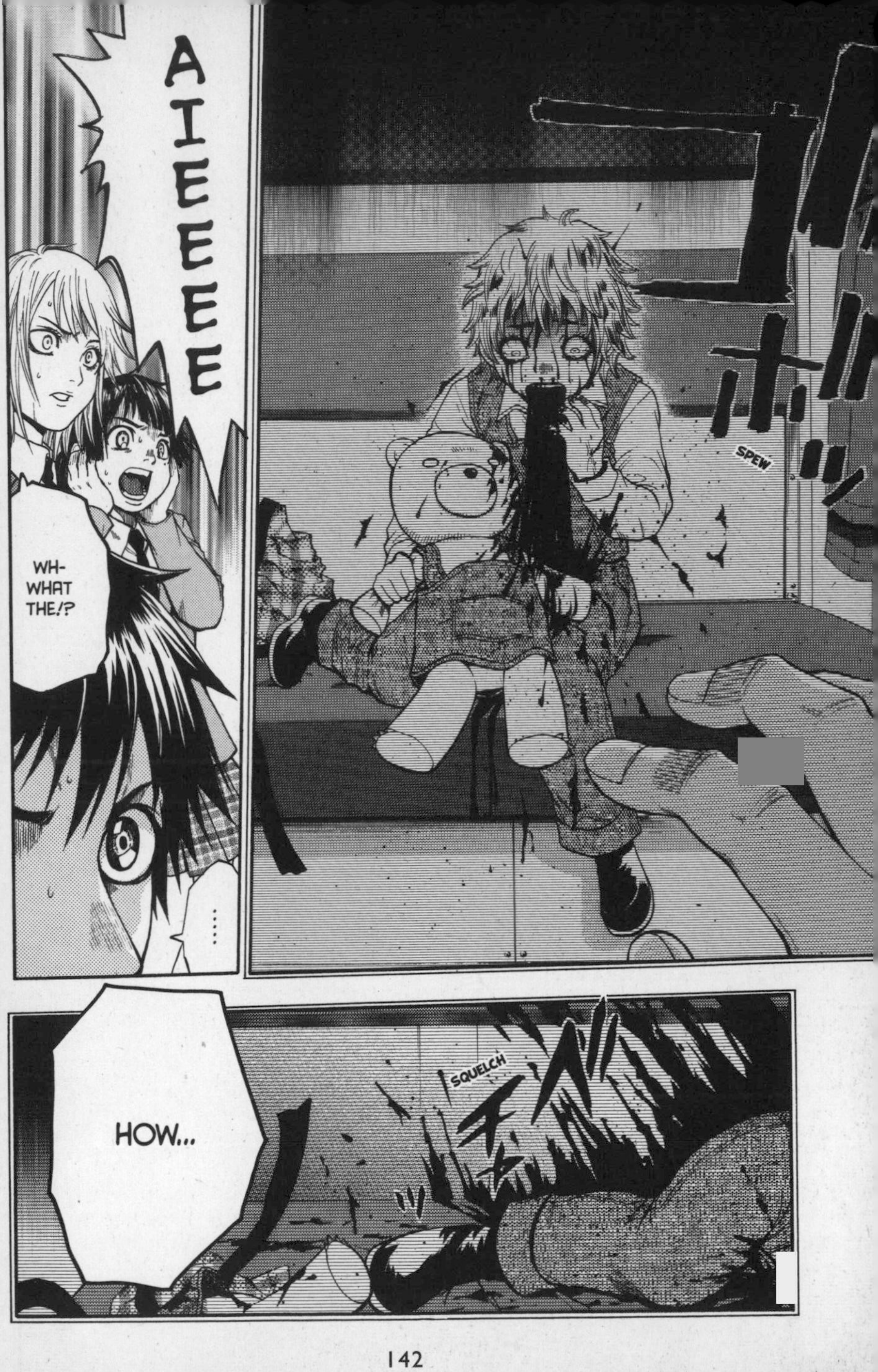
SPEW
AIEEEE
WH-WHAT THE!?
.....
HOW...
SQUELCH

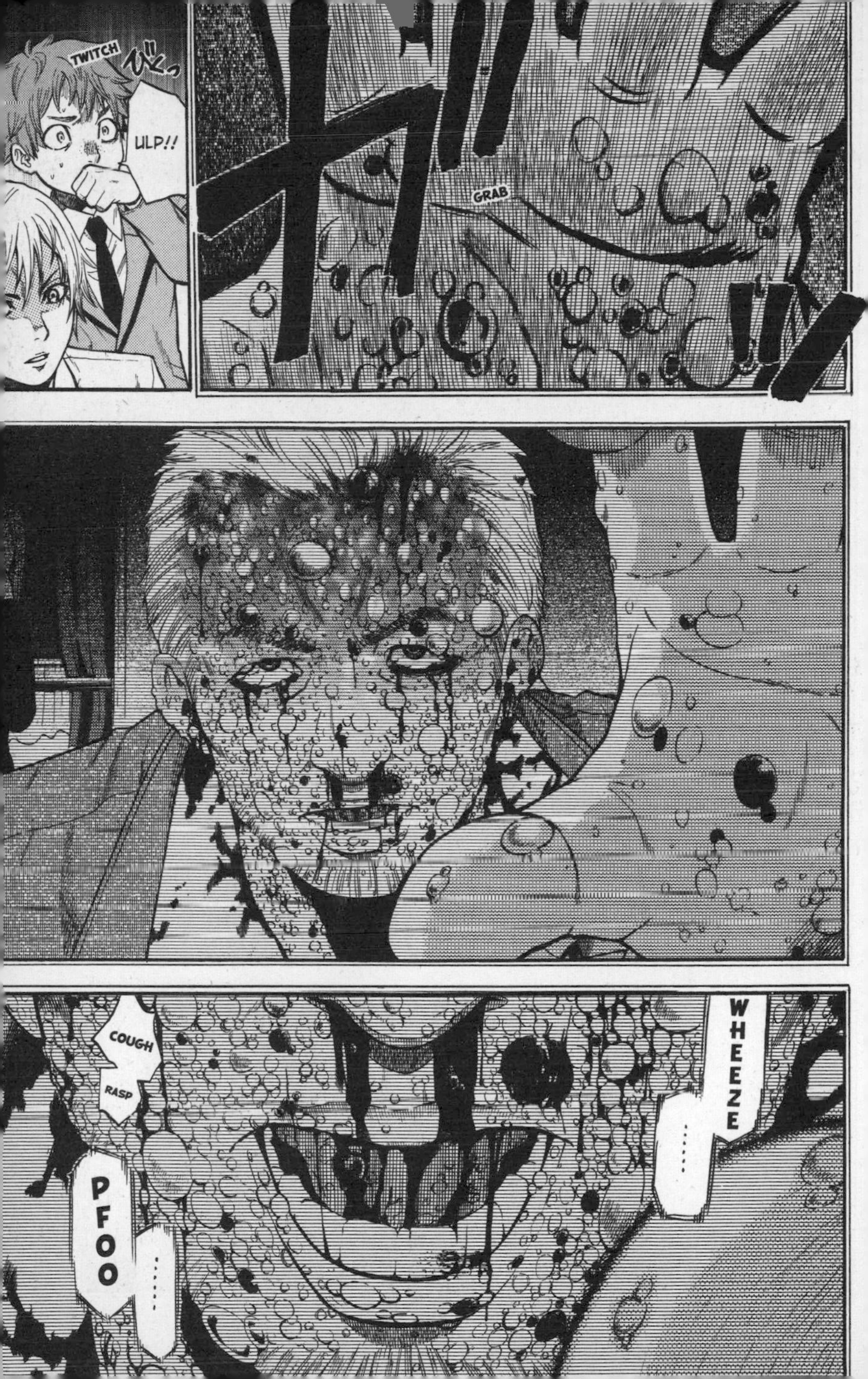
GRAB
TWITCH
ULP!!
WHEEZE
......
COUGH
RASP
PFOO
......

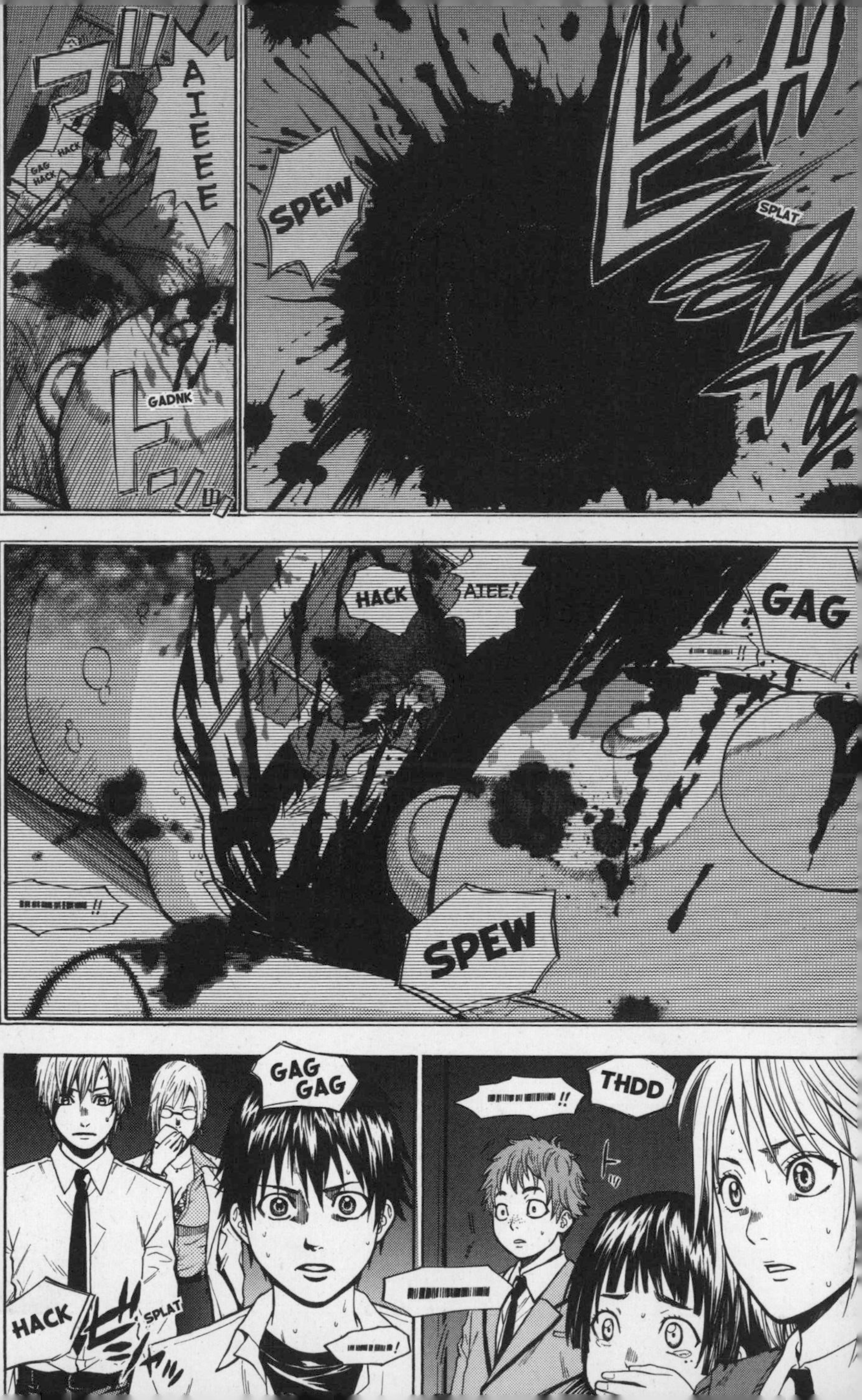
SPLAT
SPEW
AIEEE
HACK
GAG HACK
GADNK
GAG
ATEE!
HACK
SPEW
THDD
GAG GAG
SPLAT
HACK

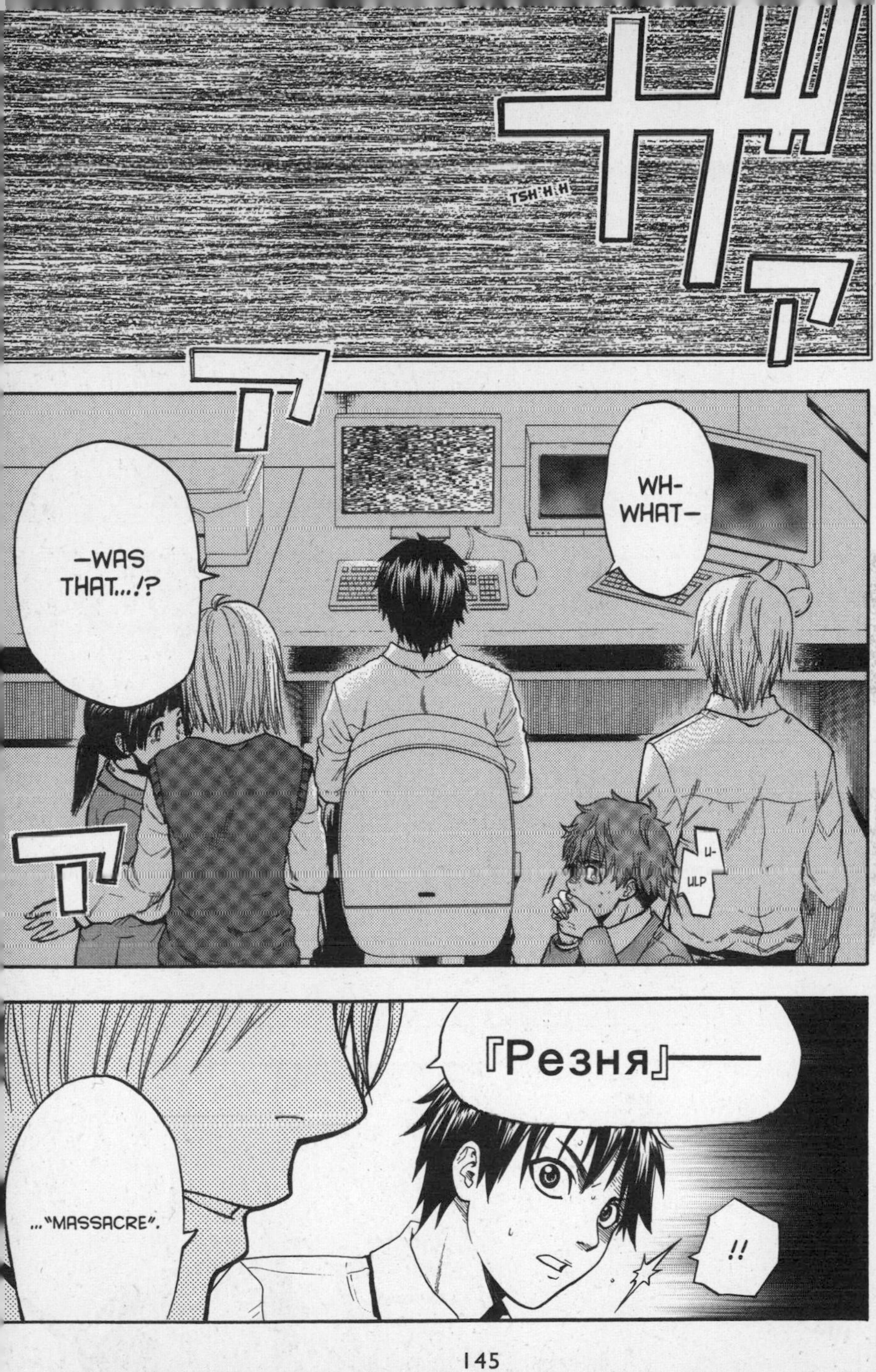
TSH'H'H
WH- WHAT—
—WAS THAT...!?
U- ULP
『Резня』——
..."MASSACRE".
!!

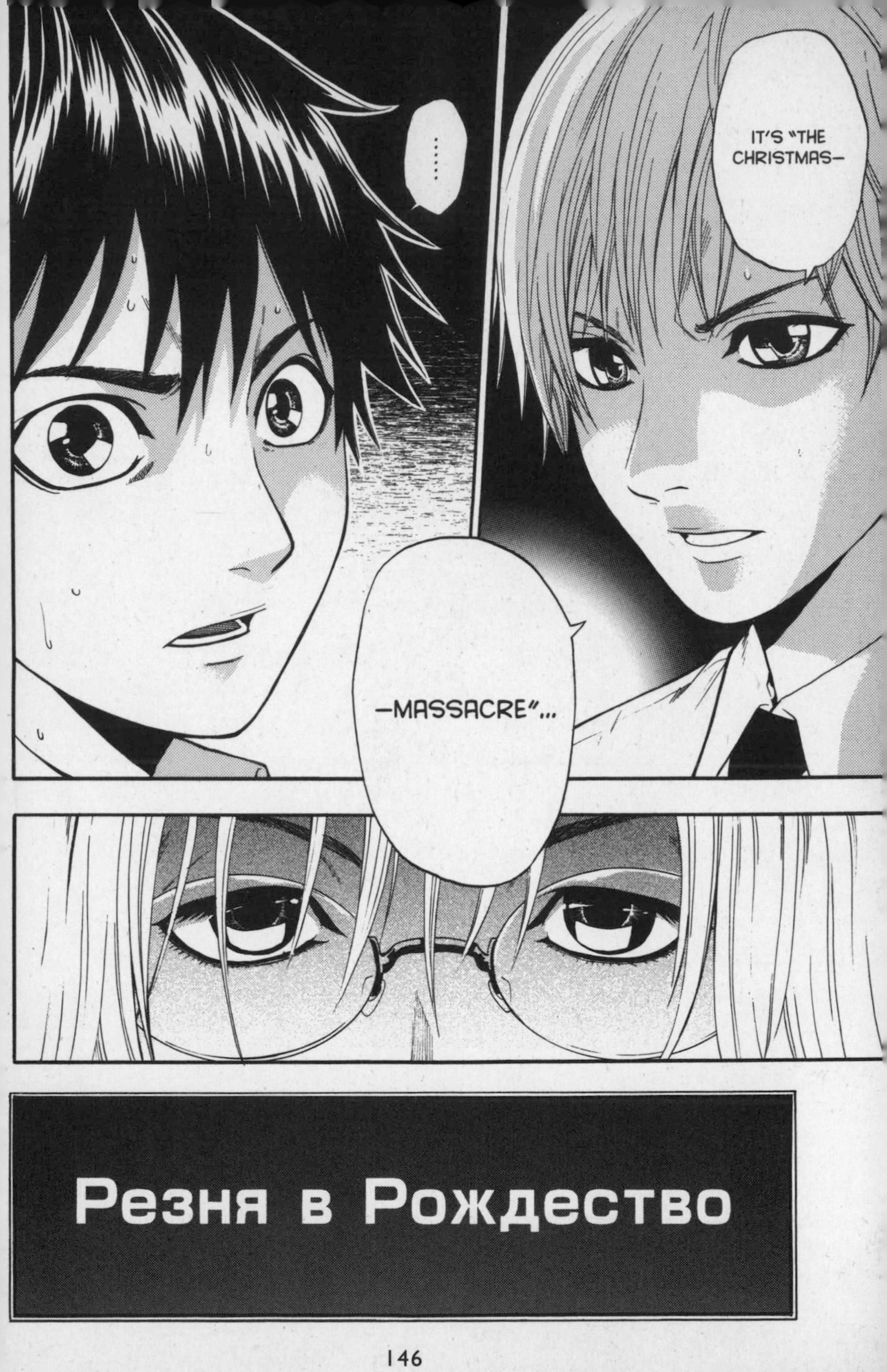
IT'S "THE CHRISTMAS—
......
—MASSACRE"...

Резня в Рождество

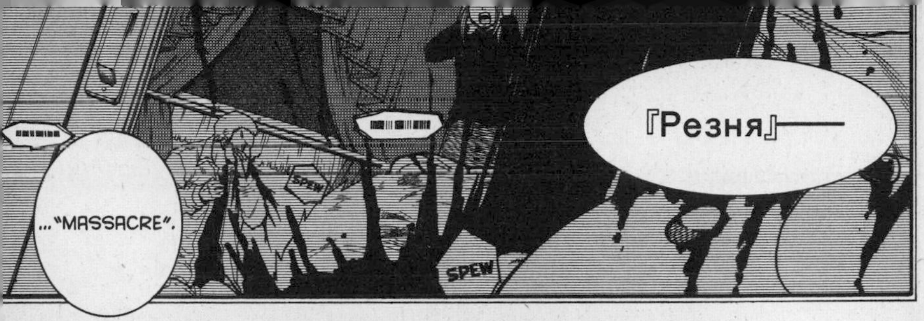
『Резня』——
..."MASSACRE".
SPEW
SPEW

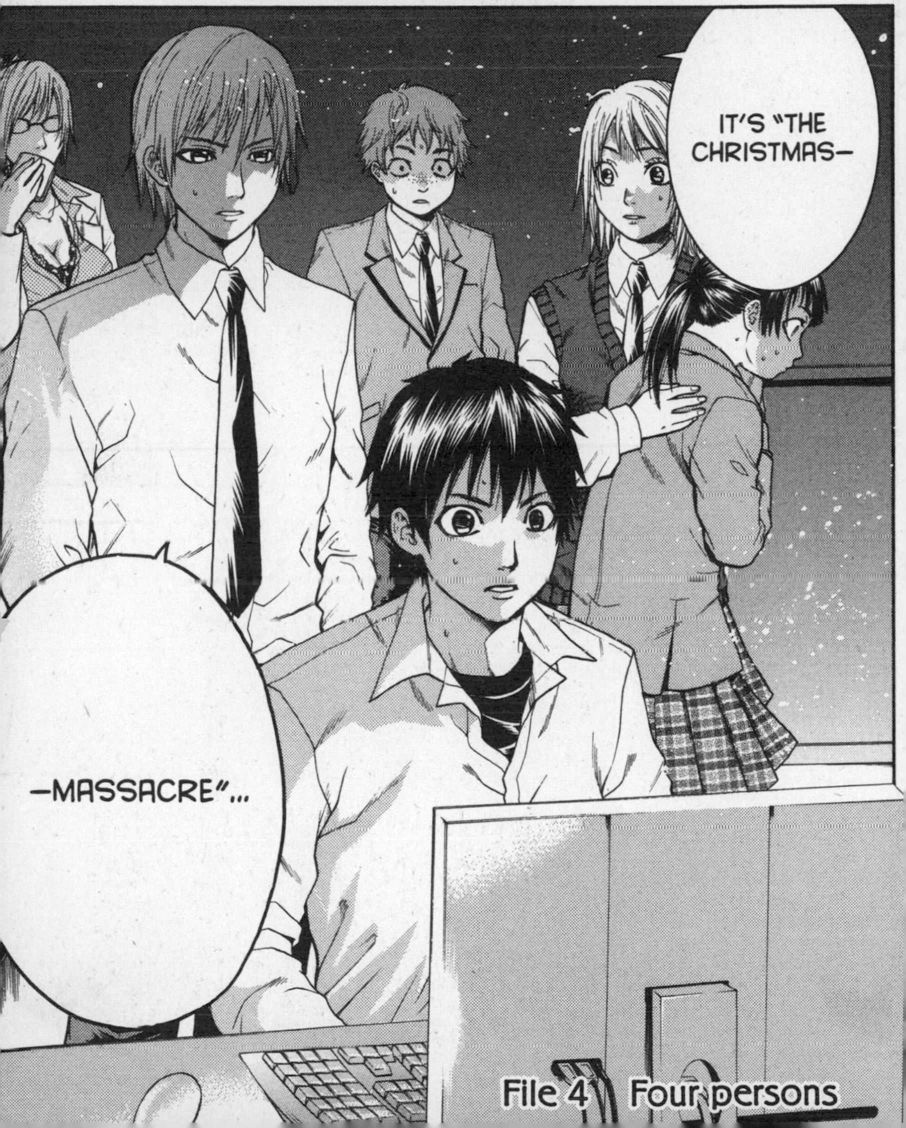
IT'S "THE CHRISTMAS-
-MASSACRE"...

File 4 Four persons

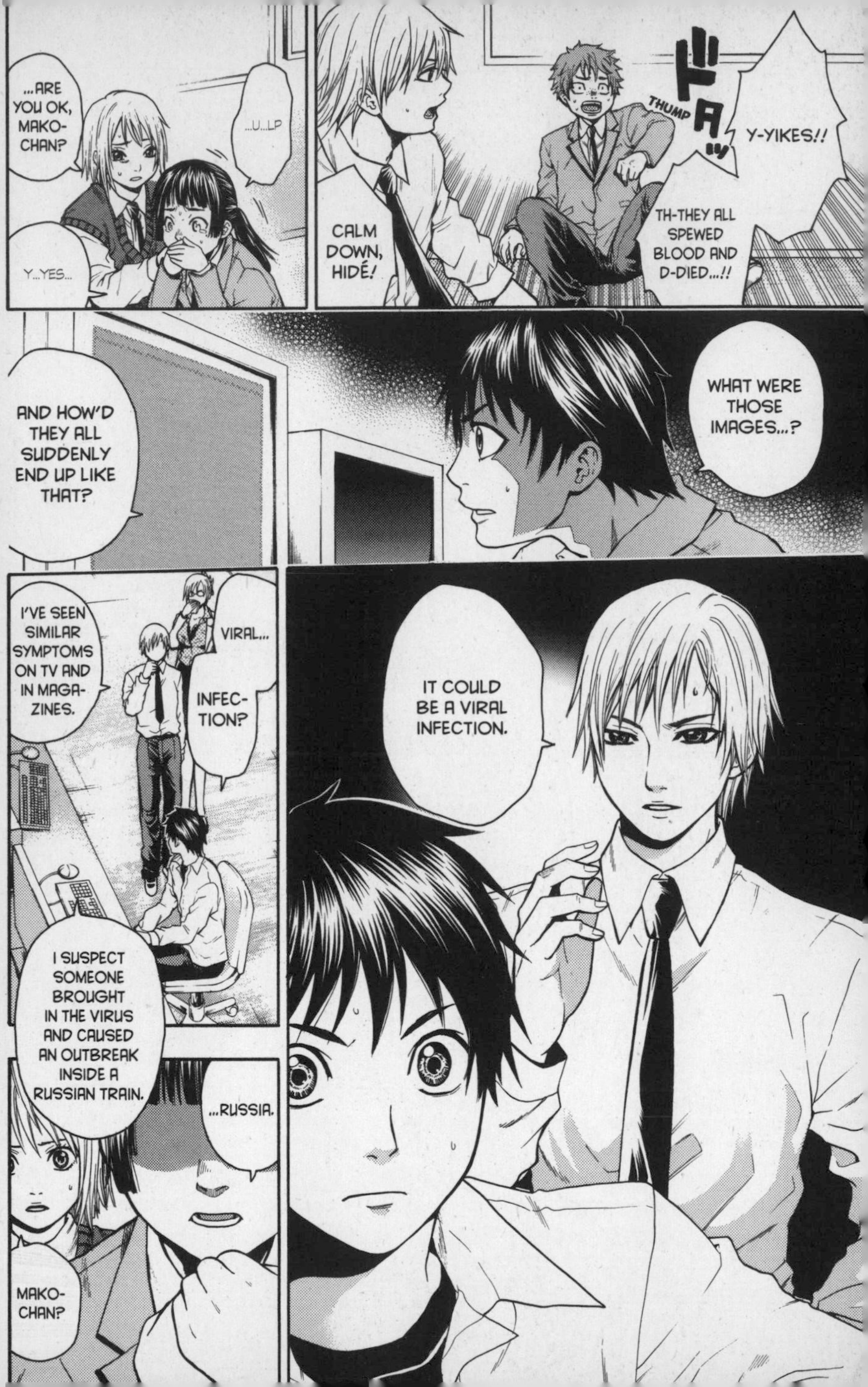
Y-YIKES!!
THUMP
TH-THEY ALL SPEWED BLOOD AND D-DIED...!!
CALM DOWN, HIDÉ!
...ARE YOU OK, MAKO-CHAN?
...U...LP
Y...YES...
WHAT WERE THOSE IMAGES...?
AND HOW'D THEY ALL SUDDENLY END UP LIKE THAT?
IT COULD BE A VIRAL INFECTION.
VIRAL... INFECTION?
I'VE SEEN SIMILAR SYMPTOMS ON TV AND IN MAGAZINES.
I SUSPECT SOMEONE BROUGHT IN THE VIRUS AND CAUSED AN OUTBREAK INSIDE A RUSSIAN TRAIN.
...RUSSIA.
MAKO-CHAN?

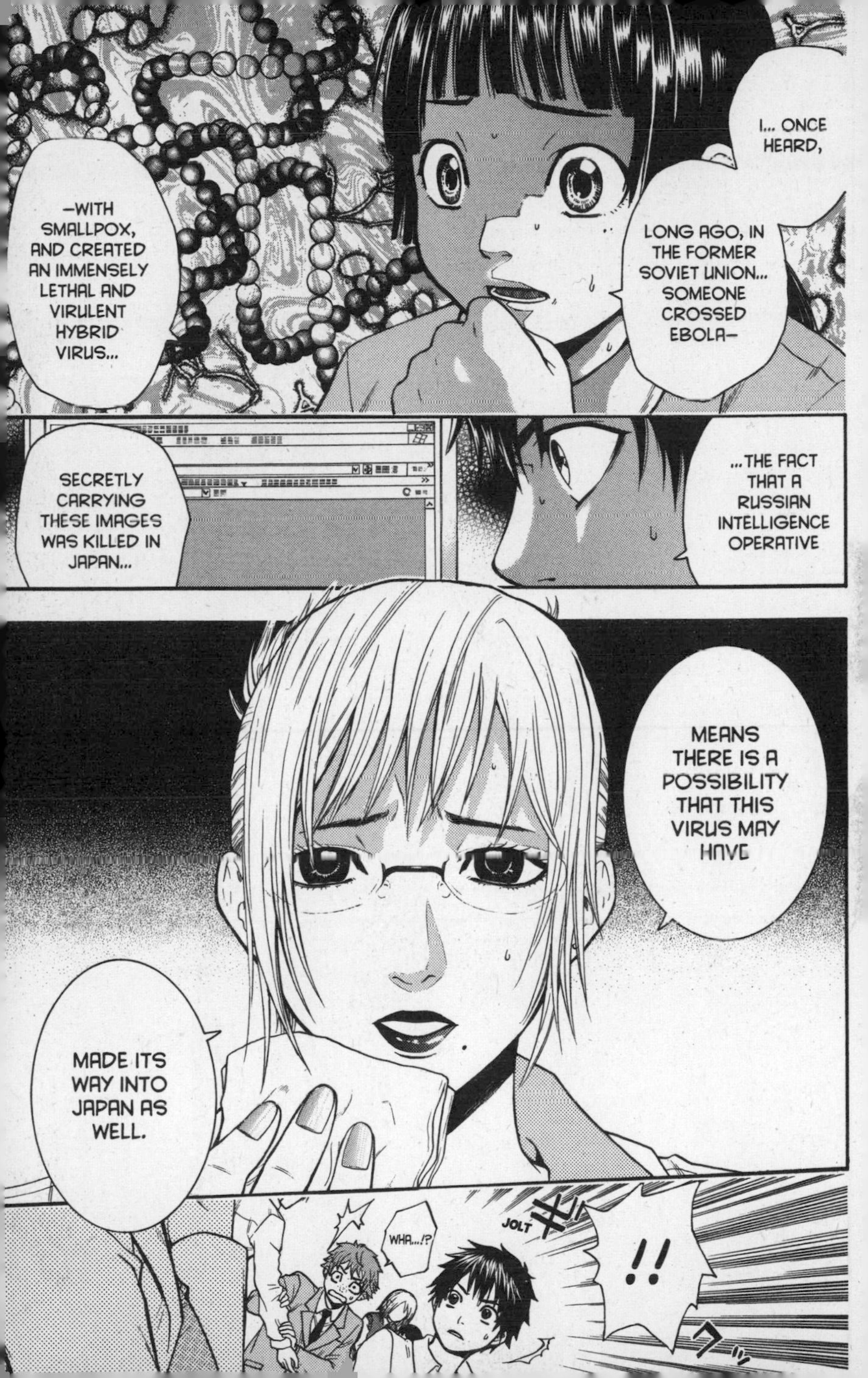
I... ONCE HEARD,
LONG AGO, IN THE FORMER SOVIET UNION... SOMEONE CROSSED EBOLA—
—WITH SMALLPOX, AND CREATED AN IMMENSELY LETHAL AND VIRULENT HYBRID VIRUS...
...THE FACT THAT A RUSSIAN INTELLIGENCE OPERATIVE
SECRETLY CARRYING THESE IMAGES WAS KILLED IN JAPAN...
MEANS THERE IS A POSSIBILITY THAT THIS VIRUS MAY HAVE
MADE ITS WAY INTO JAPAN AS WELL.
!!
JOLT
WHA...!?

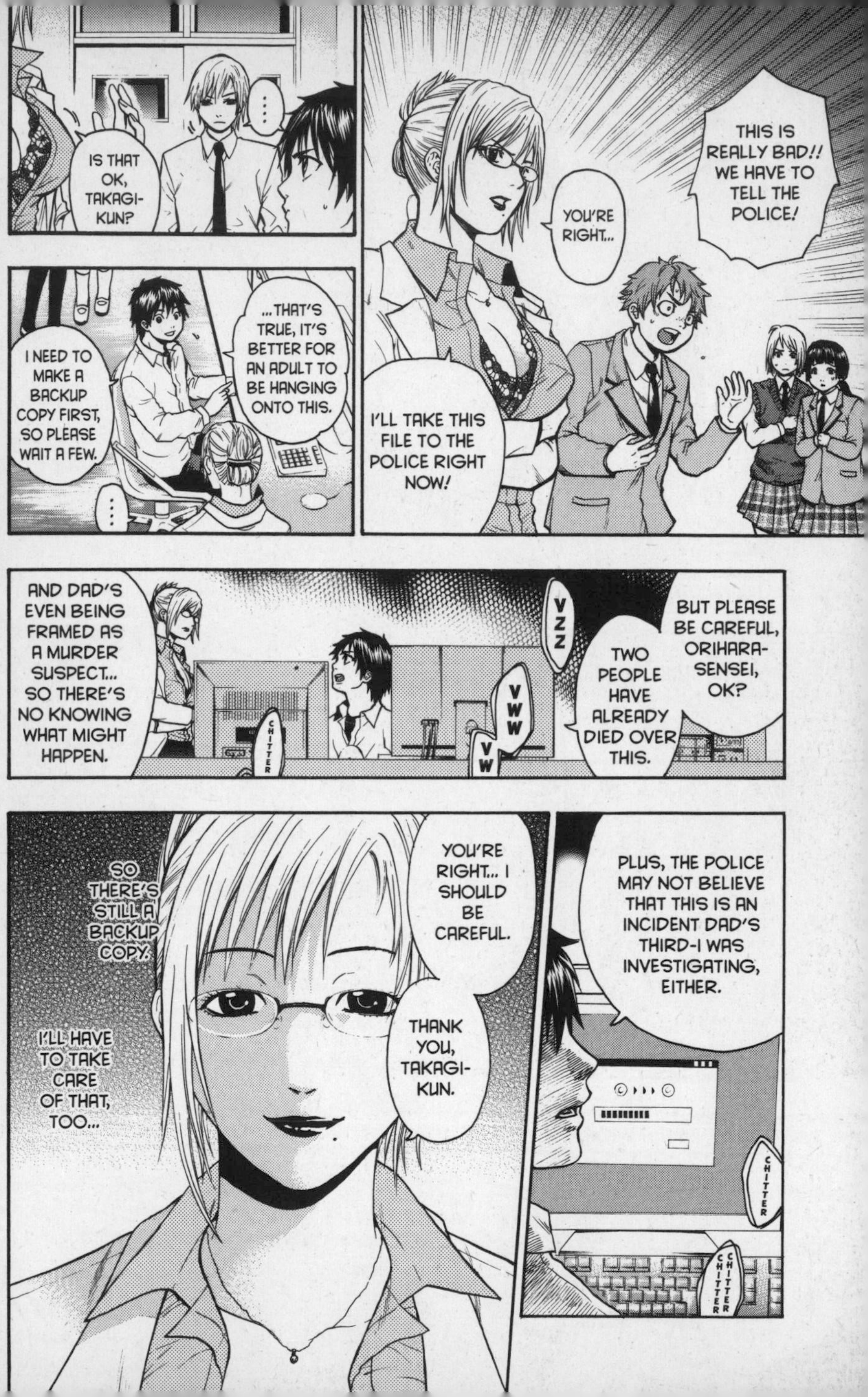
THIS IS REALLY BAD!! WE HAVE TO TELL THE POLICE!
YOU'RE RIGHT...
I'LL TAKE THIS FILE TO THE POLICE RIGHT NOW!
....
IS THAT OK, TAKAGI-KUN?
...THAT'S TRUE, IT'S BETTER FOR AN ADULT TO BE HANGING ONTO THIS.
I NEED TO MAKE A BACKUP COPY FIRST, SO PLEASE WAIT A FEW.
....
BUT PLEASE BE CAREFUL, ORIHARA-SENSEI, OK?
VZZ
TWO PEOPLE HAVE ALREADY DIED OVER THIS.
VWW
VW
CHITTER
AND DAD'S EVEN BEING FRAMED AS A MURDER SUSPECT... SO THERE'S NO KNOWING WHAT MIGHT HAPPEN.
PLUS, THE POLICE MAY NOT BELIEVE THAT THIS IS AN INCIDENT DAD'S THIRD-I WAS INVESTIGATING, EITHER.
CHITTER
CHITTER
CHITTER
YOU'RE RIGHT... I SHOULD BE CAREFUL.
THANK YOU, TAKAGI-KUN.
SO THERE'S STILL A BACKUP COPY.
I'LL HAVE TO TAKE CARE OF THAT, TOO...

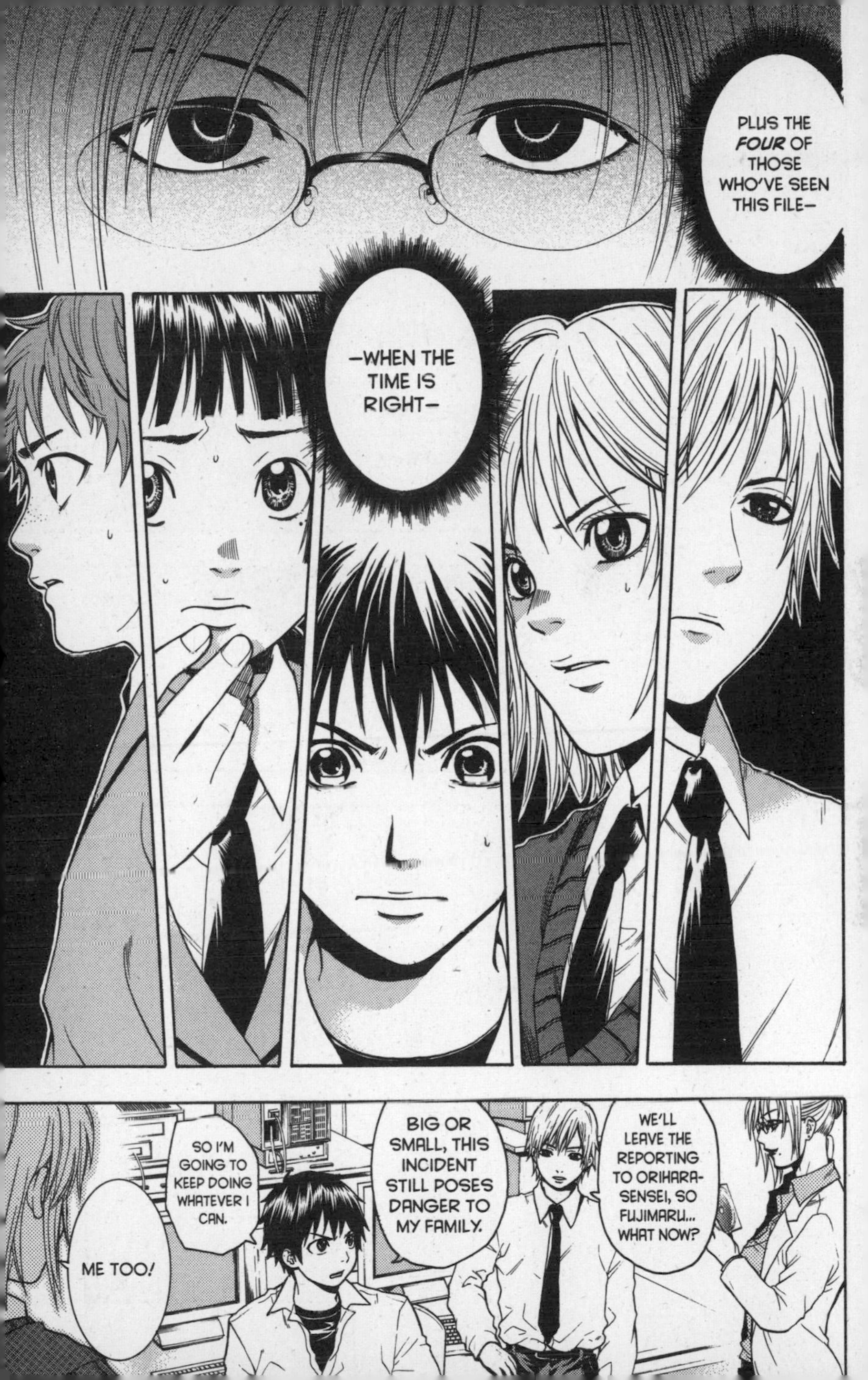
PLUS THE *FOUR* OF THOSE WHO'VE SEEN THIS FILE—
—WHEN THE TIME IS RIGHT—
WE'LL LEAVE THE REPORTING TO ORIHARA-SENSEI, SO FUJIMARU... WHAT NOW?
BIG OR SMALL, THIS INCIDENT STILL POSES DANGER TO MY FAMILY.
SO I'M GOING TO KEEP DOING WHATEVER I CAN.
ME TOO!

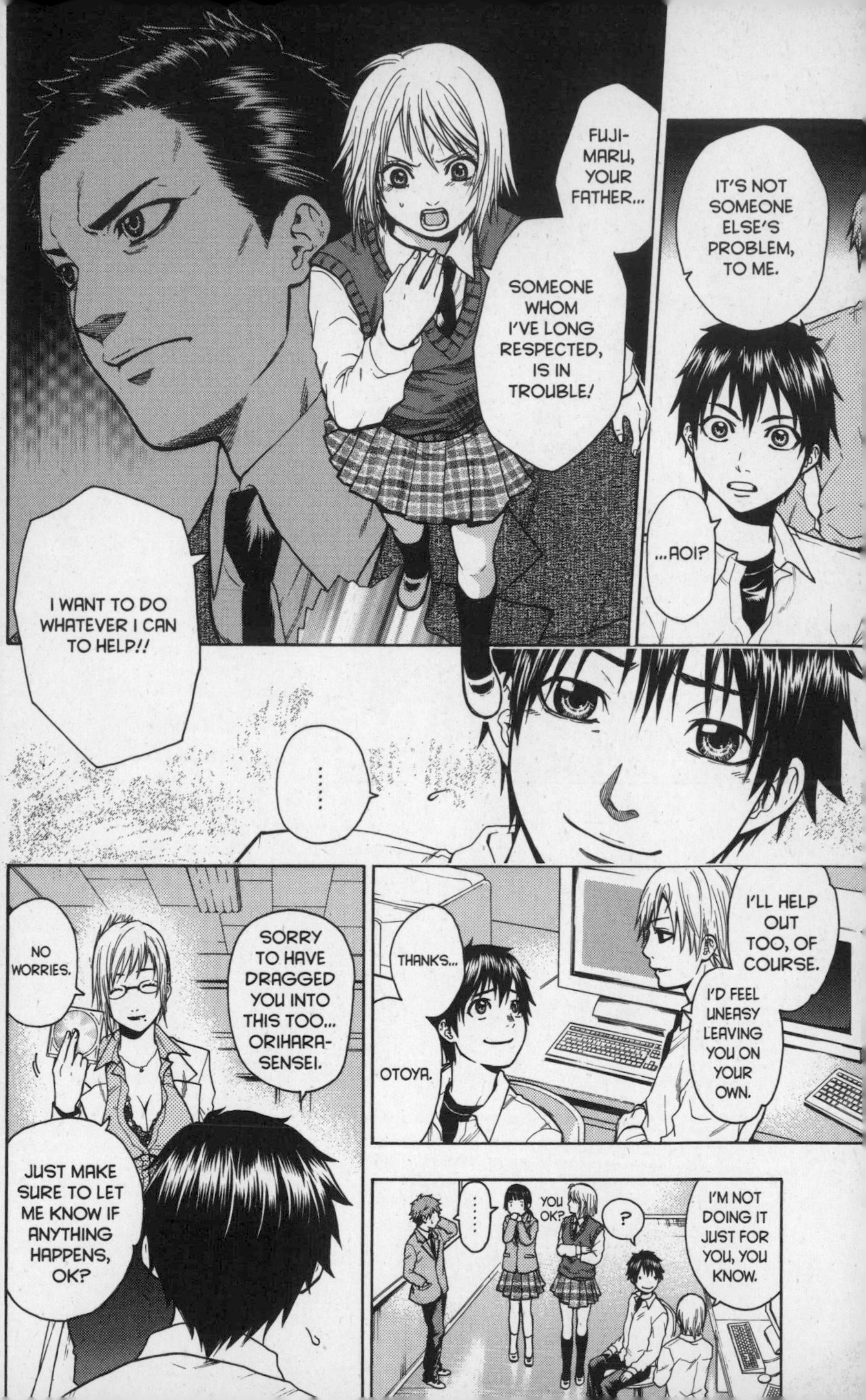
FUJI-MARU, YOUR FATHER...
SOMEONE WHOM I'VE LONG RESPECTED, IS IN TROUBLE!
IT'S NOT SOMEONE ELSE'S PROBLEM, TO ME.
...AOI?
I WANT TO DO WHATEVER I CAN TO HELP!!
......
I'LL HELP OUT TOO, OF COURSE.
I'D FEEL UNEASY LEAVING YOU ON YOUR OWN.
THANKS...
OTOYA.
I'M NOT DOING IT JUST FOR YOU, YOU KNOW.
?
YOU OK?
......
SORRY TO HAVE DRAGGED YOU INTO THIS TOO... ORIHARA-SENSEI.
NO WORRIES.
JUST MAKE SURE TO LET ME KNOW IF ANYTHING HAPPENS, OK?

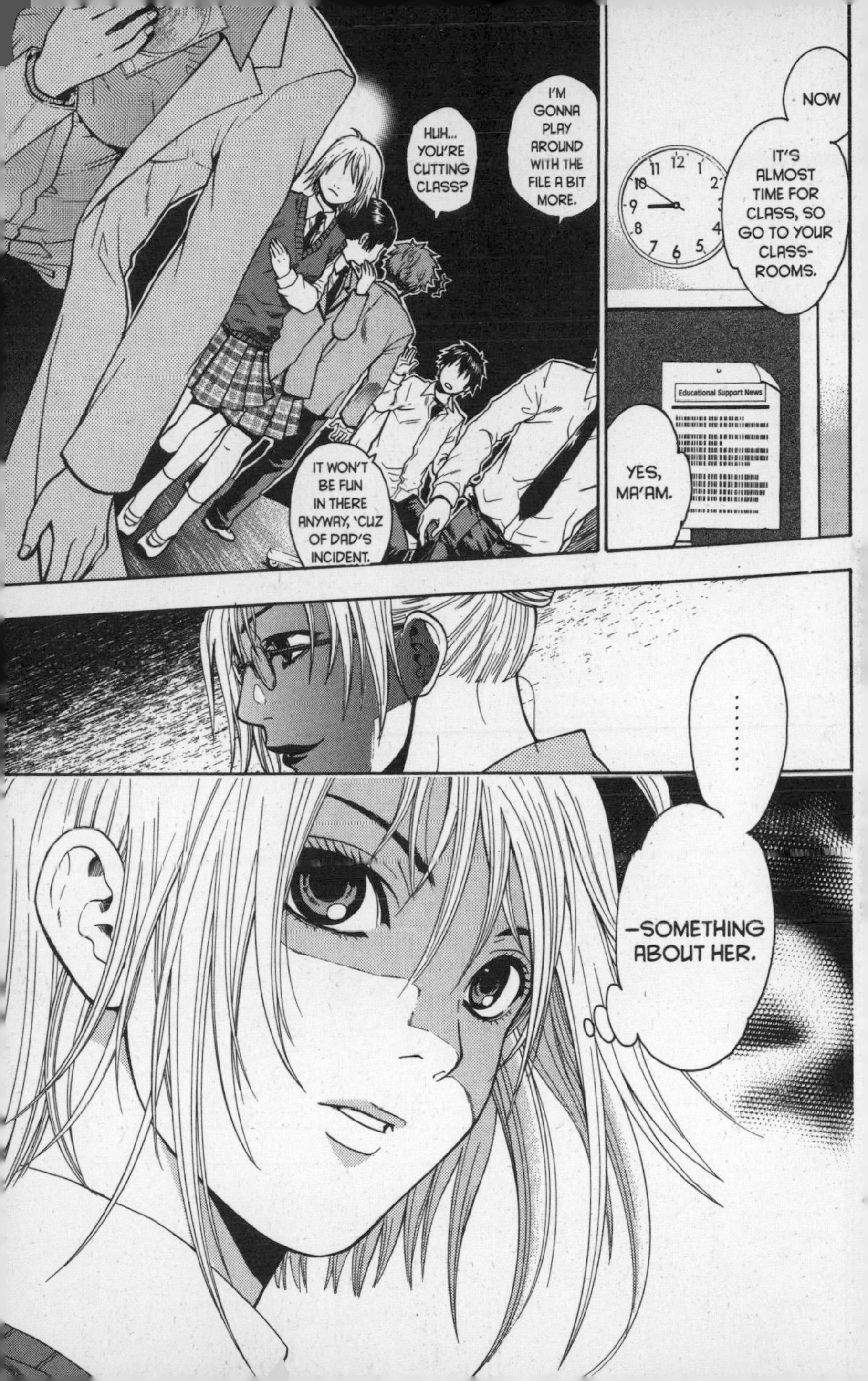
NOW
IT'S ALMOST TIME FOR CLASS, SO GO TO YOUR CLASS-ROOMS.
Educational Support News
YES, MA'AM.
I'M GONNA PLAY AROUND WITH THE FILE A BIT MORE.
HUH... YOU'RE CUTTING CLASS?
IT WON'T BE FUN IN THERE ANYWAY, 'CUZ OF DAD'S INCIDENT.
......
—SOMETHING ABOUT HER.

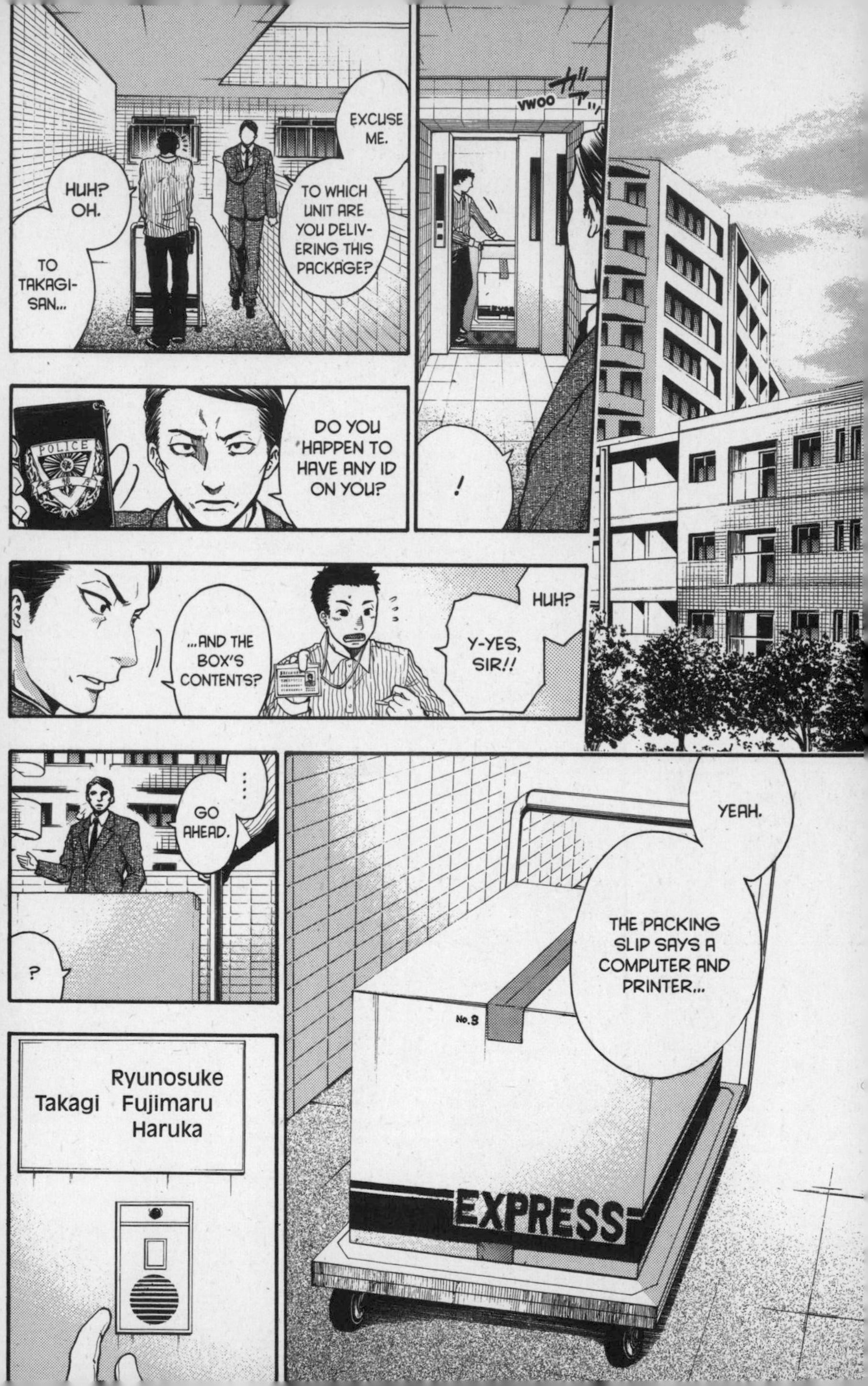
VWOO
!
EXCUSE ME.
TO WHICH UNIT ARE YOU DELIVERING THIS PACKAGE?
HUH? OH.
TO TAKAGI-SAN...
DO YOU HAPPEN TO HAVE ANY ID ON YOU?
POLICE
HUH?
Y-YES, SIR!!
...AND THE BOX'S CONTENTS?
YEAH.
THE PACKING SLIP SAYS A COMPUTER AND PRINTER...
No.3
EXPRESS
...
GO AHEAD.
?
Takagi
Ryunosuke
Fujimaru
Haruka

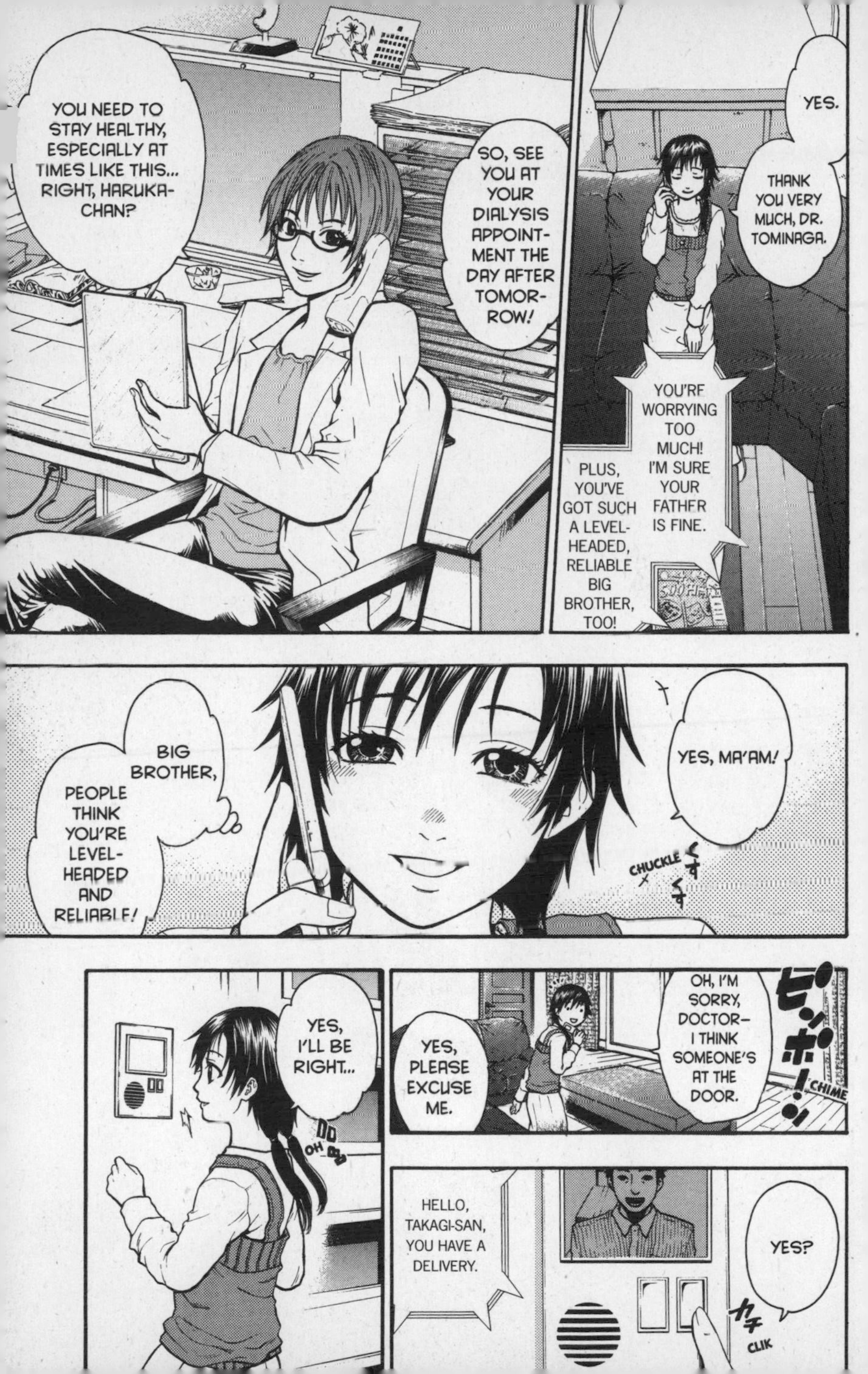
YES.
THANK YOU VERY MUCH, DR. TOMINAGA.
YOU'RE WORRYING TOO MUCH! I'M SURE YOUR FATHER IS FINE.
PLUS, YOU'VE GOT SUCH A LEVEL-HEADED, RELIABLE BIG BROTHER, TOO!
SO, SEE YOU AT YOUR DIALYSIS APPOINTMENT THE DAY AFTER TOMORROW!
YOU NEED TO STAY HEALTHY, ESPECIALLY AT TIMES LIKE THIS... RIGHT, HARUKA-CHAN?
YES, MA'AM!
CHUCKLE
BIG BROTHER, PEOPLE THINK YOU'RE LEVEL-HEADED AND RELIABLE!
CHIME
OH, I'M SORRY, DOCTOR— I THINK SOMEONE'S AT THE DOOR.
YES, PLEASE EXCUSE ME.
YES?
CLIK
HELLO, TAKAGI-SAN, YOU HAVE A DELIVERY.
YES, I'LL BE RIGHT...

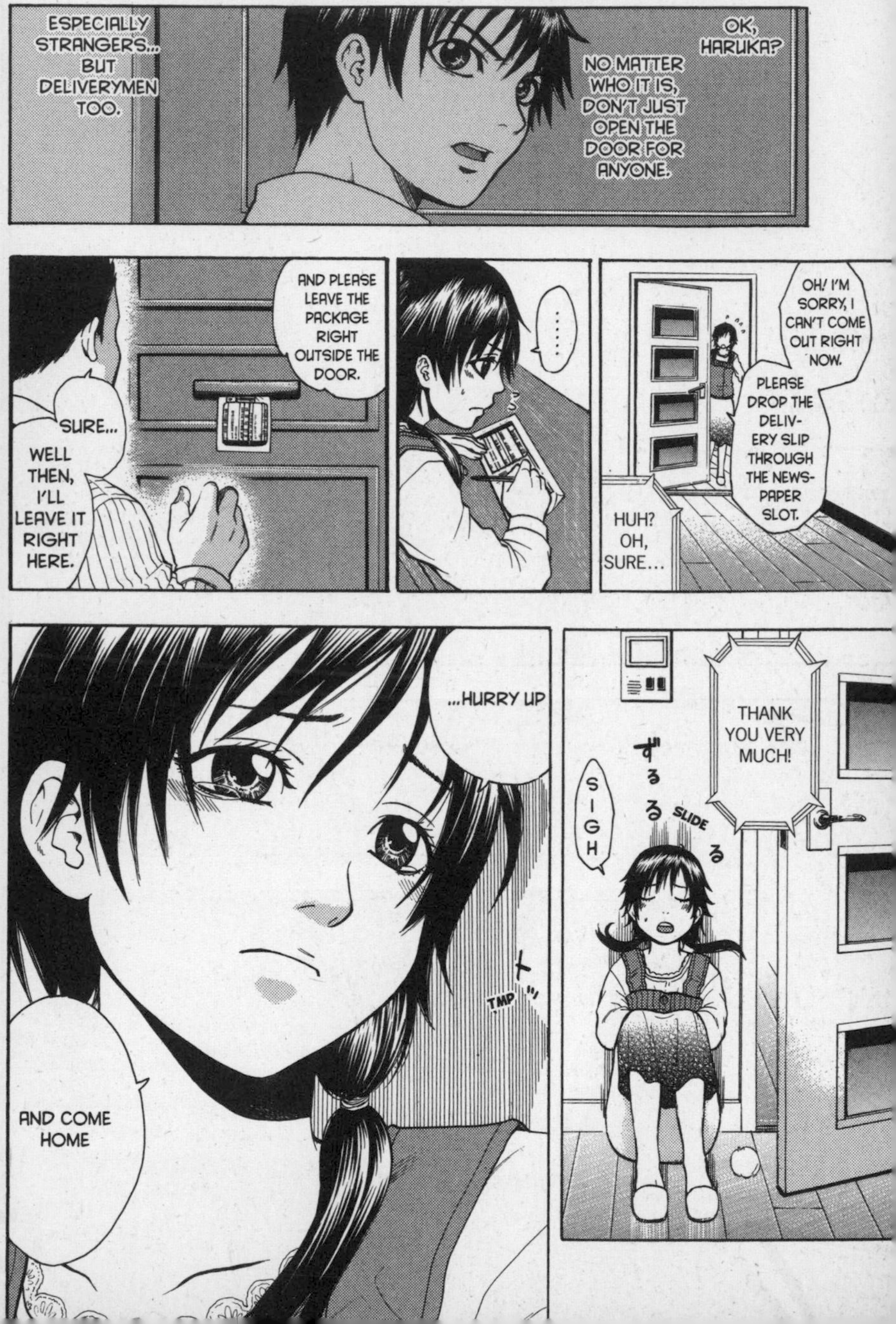
OK, HARUKA?
NO MATTER WHO IT IS, DON'T JUST OPEN THE DOOR FOR ANYONE.
ESPECIALLY STRANGERS... BUT DELIVERYMEN TOO.
OH! I'M SORRY, I CAN'T COME OUT RIGHT NOW.
PLEASE DROP THE DELIVERY SLIP THROUGH THE NEWSPAPER SLOT.
HUH? OH, SURE...
......
AND PLEASE LEAVE THE PACKAGE RIGHT OUTSIDE THE DOOR.
SURE...
WELL THEN, I'LL LEAVE IT RIGHT HERE.
THANK YOU VERY MUCH!
ずるるる
SLIDE
SIGH
...HURRY UP
TMP
AND COME HOME

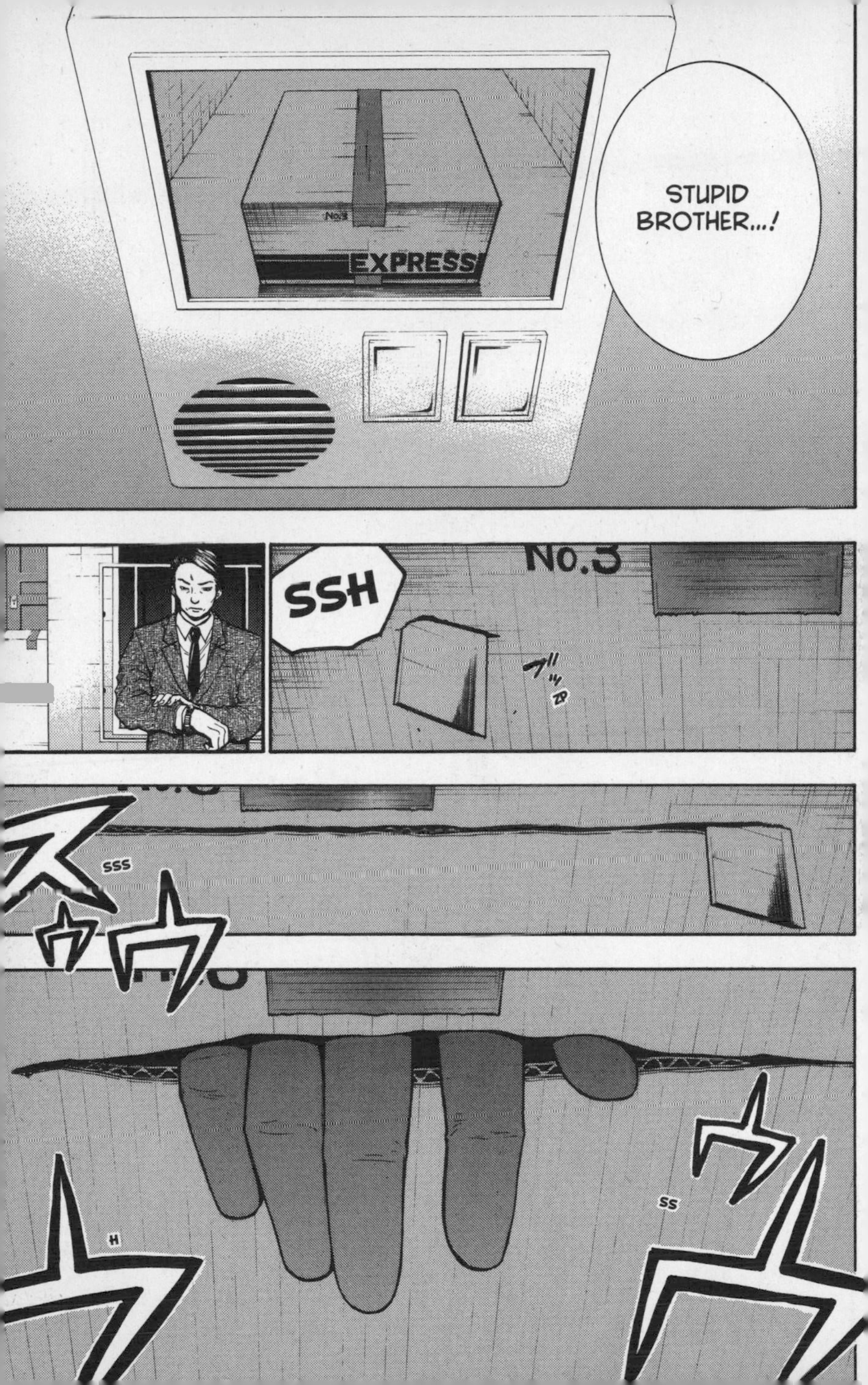
STUPID BROTHER...!
No.3
EXPRESS
No.3
SSH
ZP
SSS
SS
H

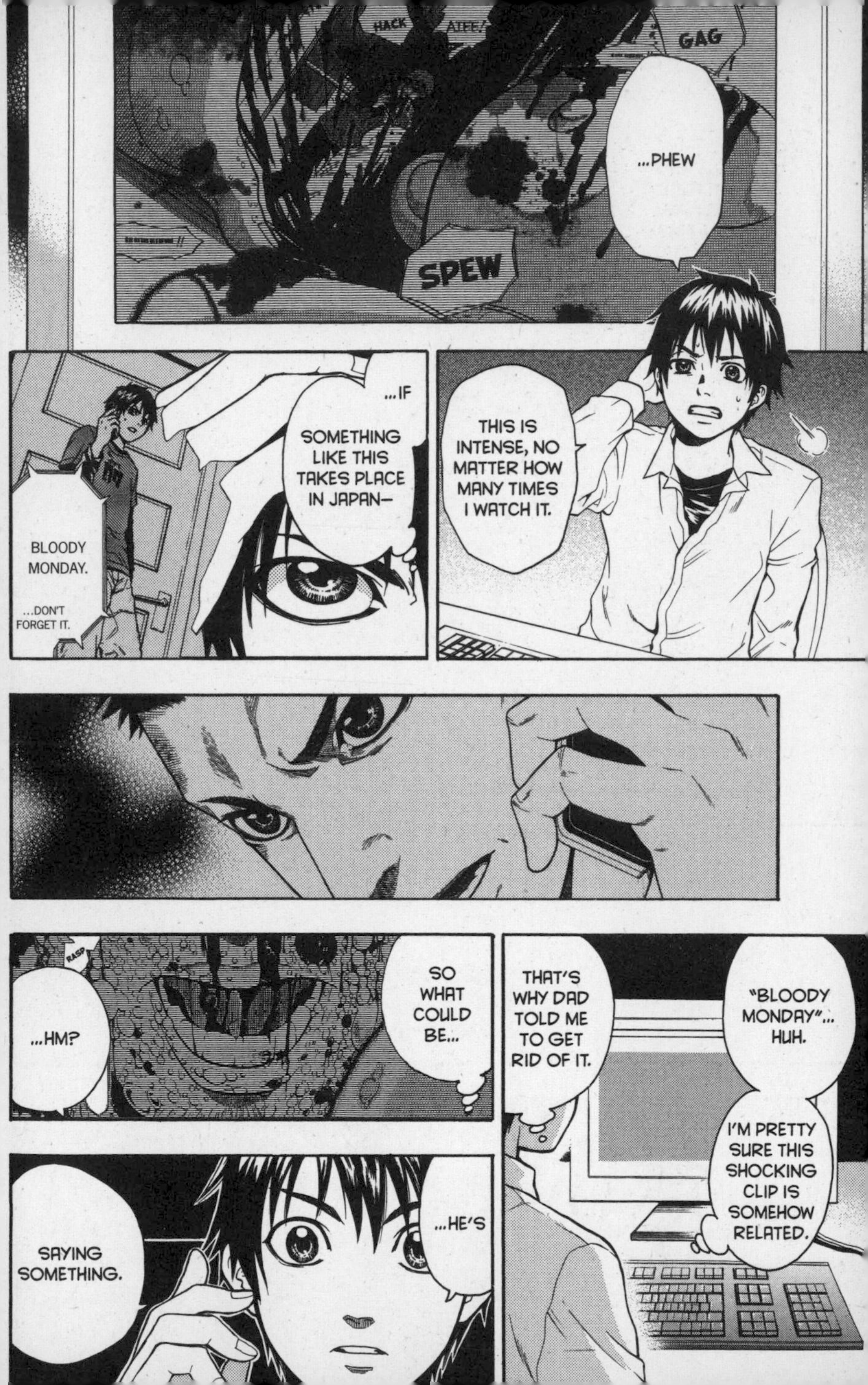
GAG
...PHEW
HACK
SPEW
THIS IS INTENSE, NO MATTER HOW MANY TIMES I WATCH IT.
...IF
SOMETHING LIKE THIS TAKES PLACE IN JAPAN—
BLOODY MONDAY.
...DON'T FORGET IT.
"BLOODY MONDAY"... HUH.
I'M PRETTY SURE THIS SHOCKING CLIP IS SOMEHOW RELATED.
THAT'S WHY DAD TOLD ME TO GET RID OF IT.
SO WHAT COULD BE...
RASP
...HM?
...HE'S
SAYING SOMETHING.

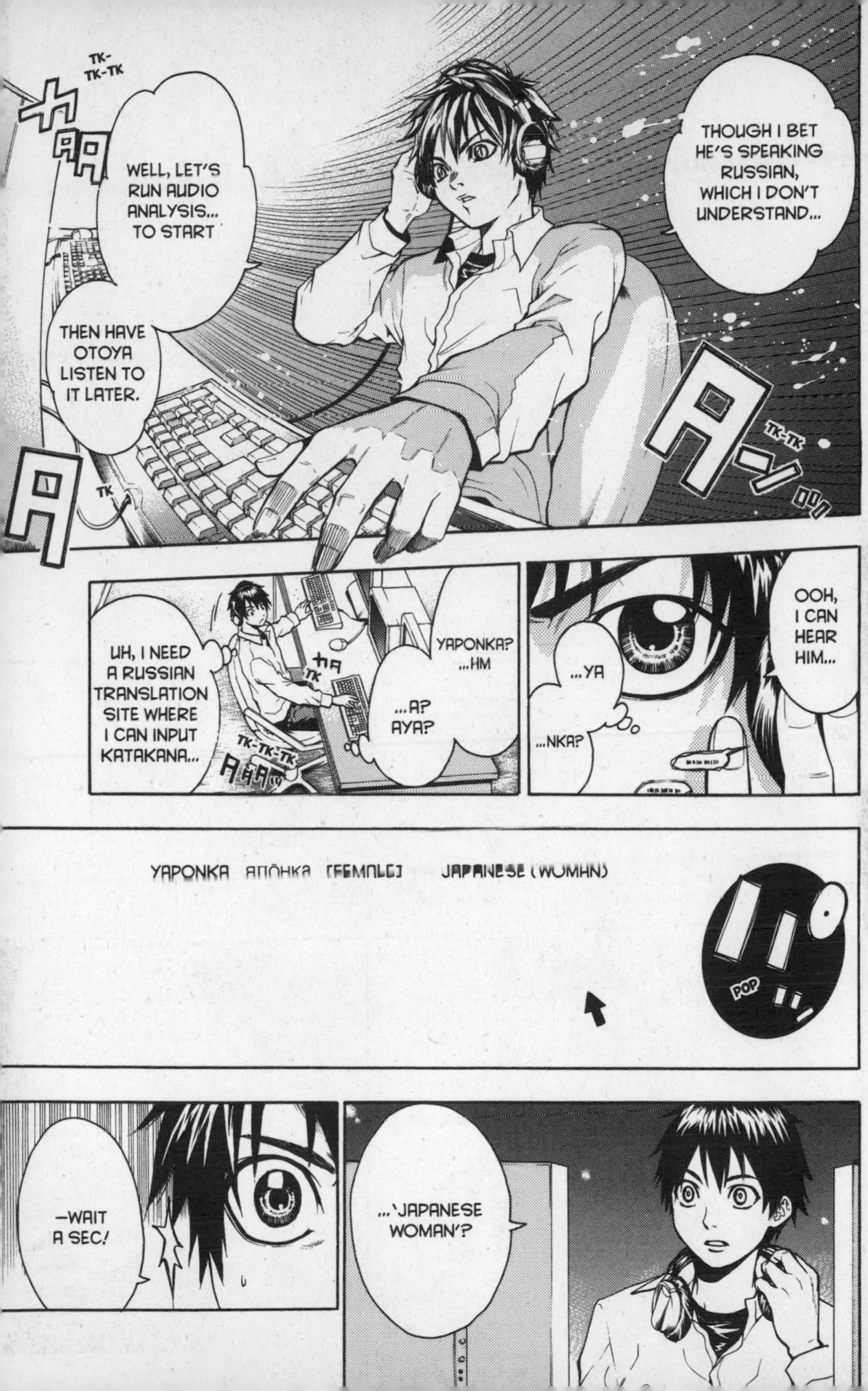
THOUGH I BET HE'S SPEAKING RUSSIAN, WHICH I DON'T UNDERSTAND...
TK-TK
WELL, LET'S RUN AUDIO ANALYSIS... TO START
TK-TK-TK
THEN HAVE OTOYA LISTEN TO IT LATER.
TK
OOH, I CAN HEAR HIM...
...YA
...NKA?
YAPONKA? ...HM
...A? AYA?
TK
UH, I NEED A RUSSIAN TRANSLATION SITE WHERE I CAN INPUT KATAKANA...
TK-TK-TK
YAPONKA япóнка [FEMALE] — JAPANESE (WOMAN)
POP
...'JAPANESE WOMAN'?
—WAIT A SEC!

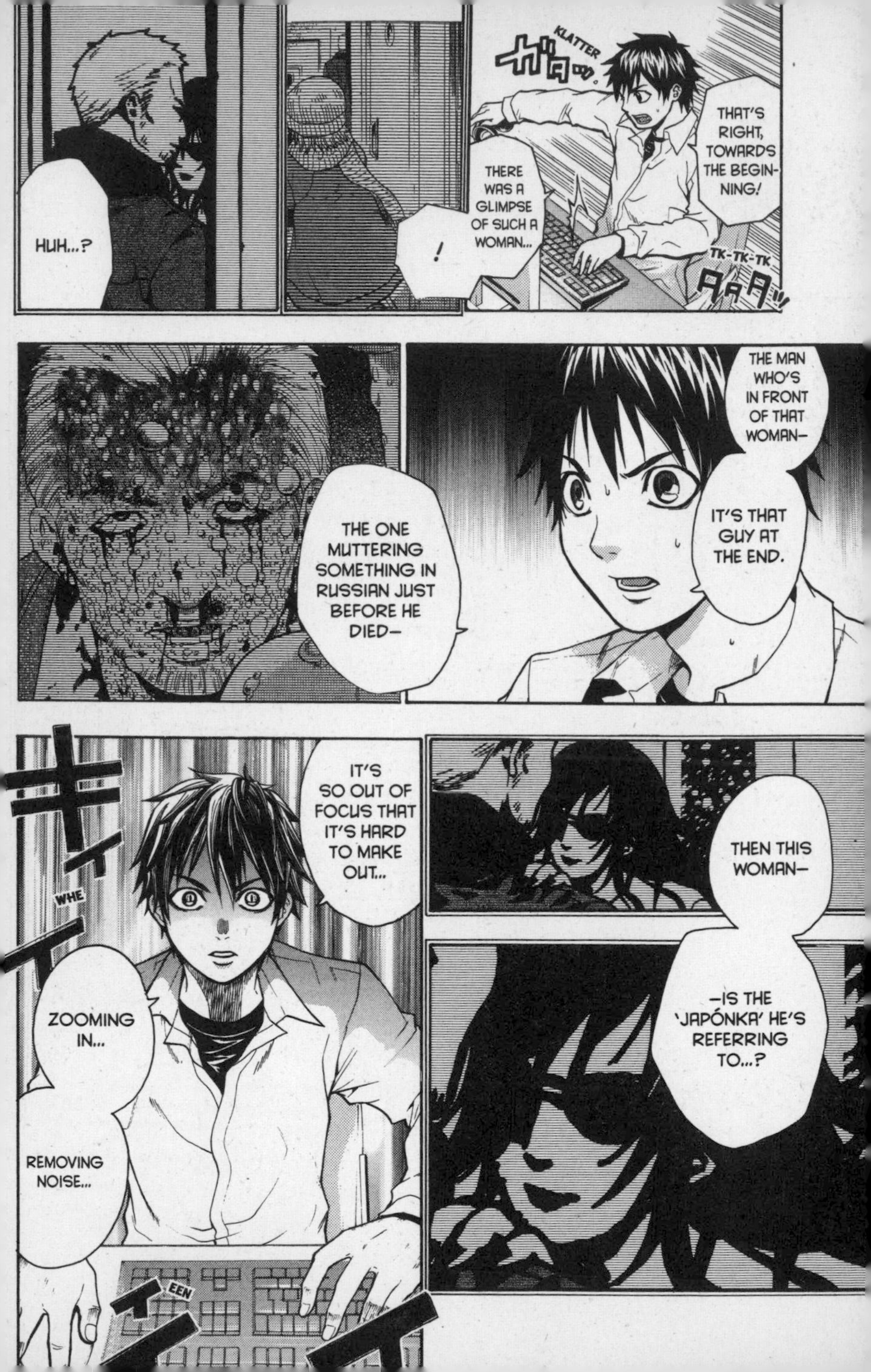
KLATTER
THAT'S RIGHT, TOWARDS THE BEGIN-NING!
THERE WAS A GLIMPSE OF SUCH A WOMAN...
TK-TK-TK
!
HUH...?
THE MAN WHO'S IN FRONT OF THAT WOMAN—
IT'S THAT GUY AT THE END.
THE ONE MUTTERING SOMETHING IN RUSSIAN JUST BEFORE HE DIED—
THEN THIS WOMAN—
—IS THE 'JAPÓNKA' HE'S REFERRING TO...?
IT'S SO OUT OF FOCUS THAT IT'S HARD TO MAKE OUT...
WHE
ZOOMING IN...
REMOVING NOISE...
EEN

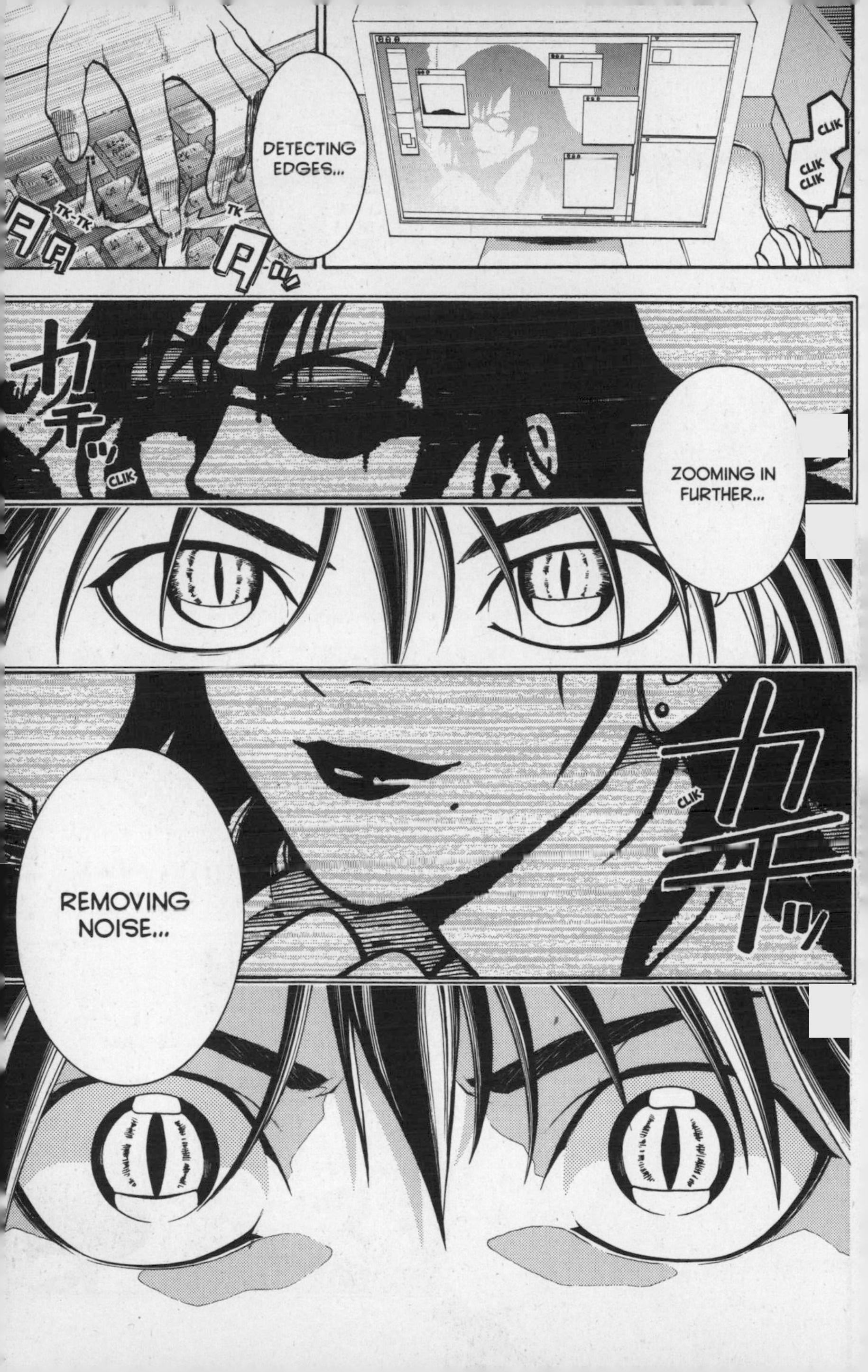
CLIK
CLIK CLIK
DETECTING EDGES...
TK
TK-TK
ZOOMING IN FURTHER...
カチッ
CLIK
カチッ
CLIK
REMOVING NOISE...

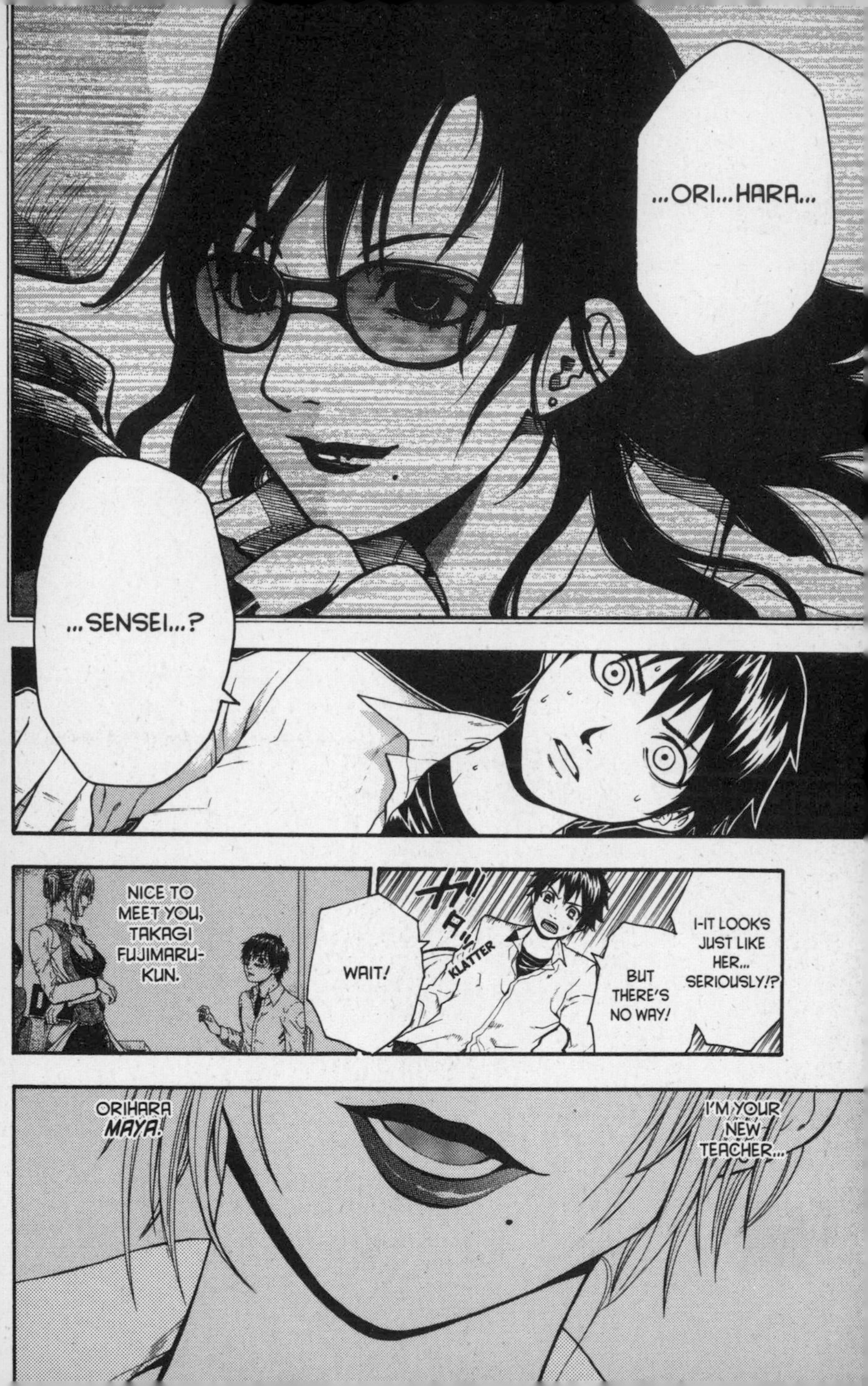
...ORI...HARA...
...SENSEI...?
I-IT LOOKS JUST LIKE HER... SERIOUSLY!?
BUT THERE'S NO WAY!
KLATTER
WAIT!
NICE TO MEET YOU, TAKAGI FUJIMARU-KUN.
I'M YOUR NEW TEACHER...
ORIHARA MAYA!

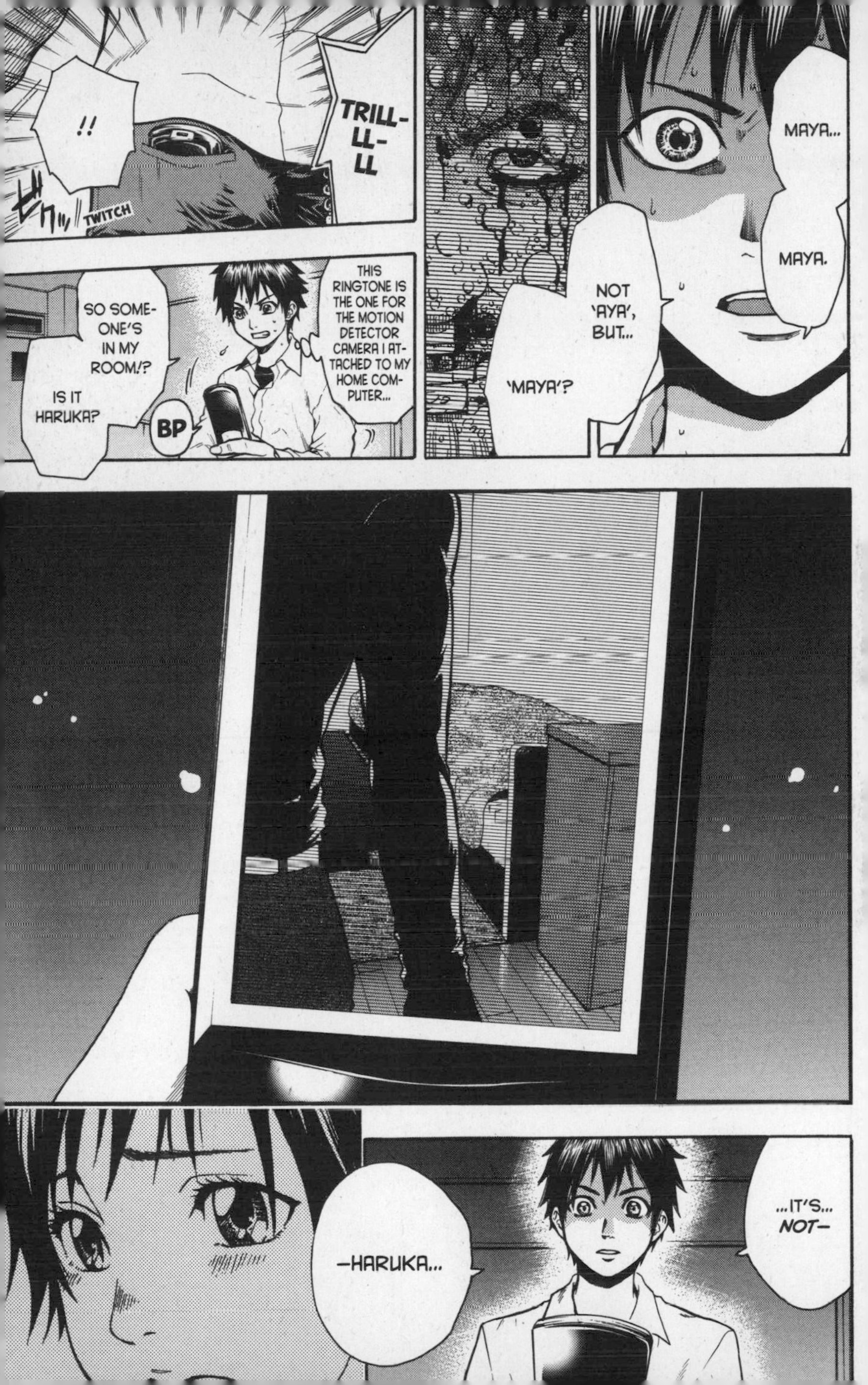
MAYA...
MAYA.
NOT 'AYA', BUT... 'MAYA'?
TRILL-LL-LL
!!
TWITCH
THIS RINGTONE IS THE ONE FOR THE MOTION DETECTOR CAMERA I ATTACHED TO MY HOME COMPUTER...
SO SOMEONE'S IN MY ROOM!?
IS IT HARUKA?
BP
...IT'S... *NOT*—
—HARUKA...

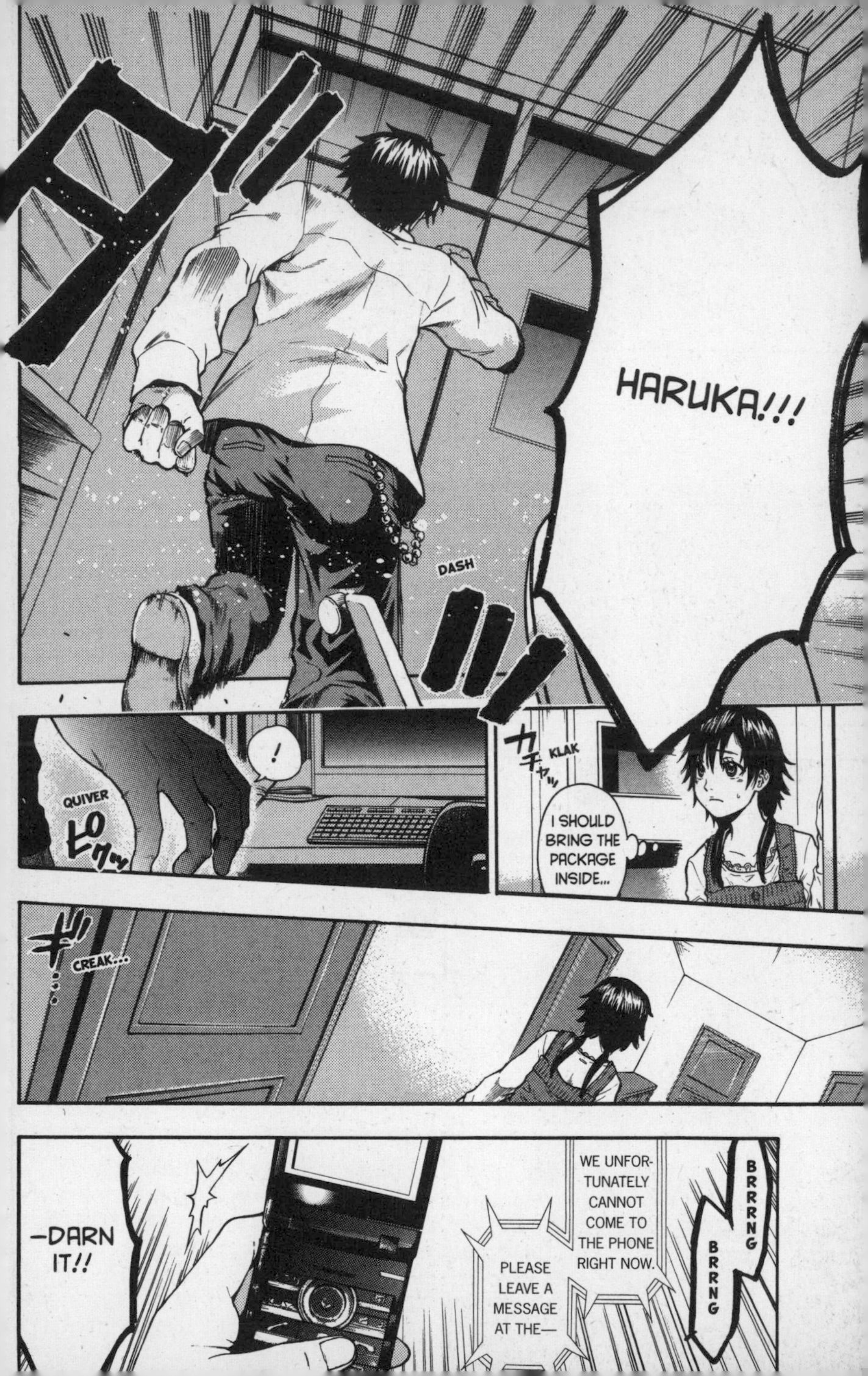
HARUKA!!!
DASH
KLAK
I SHOULD BRING THE PACKAGE INSIDE...
!
QUIVER
CREAK...
BRRRNG
BRRNG
WE UNFOR-TUNATELY CANNOT COME TO THE PHONE RIGHT NOW.
PLEASE LEAVE A MESSAGE AT THE—
—DARN IT!!

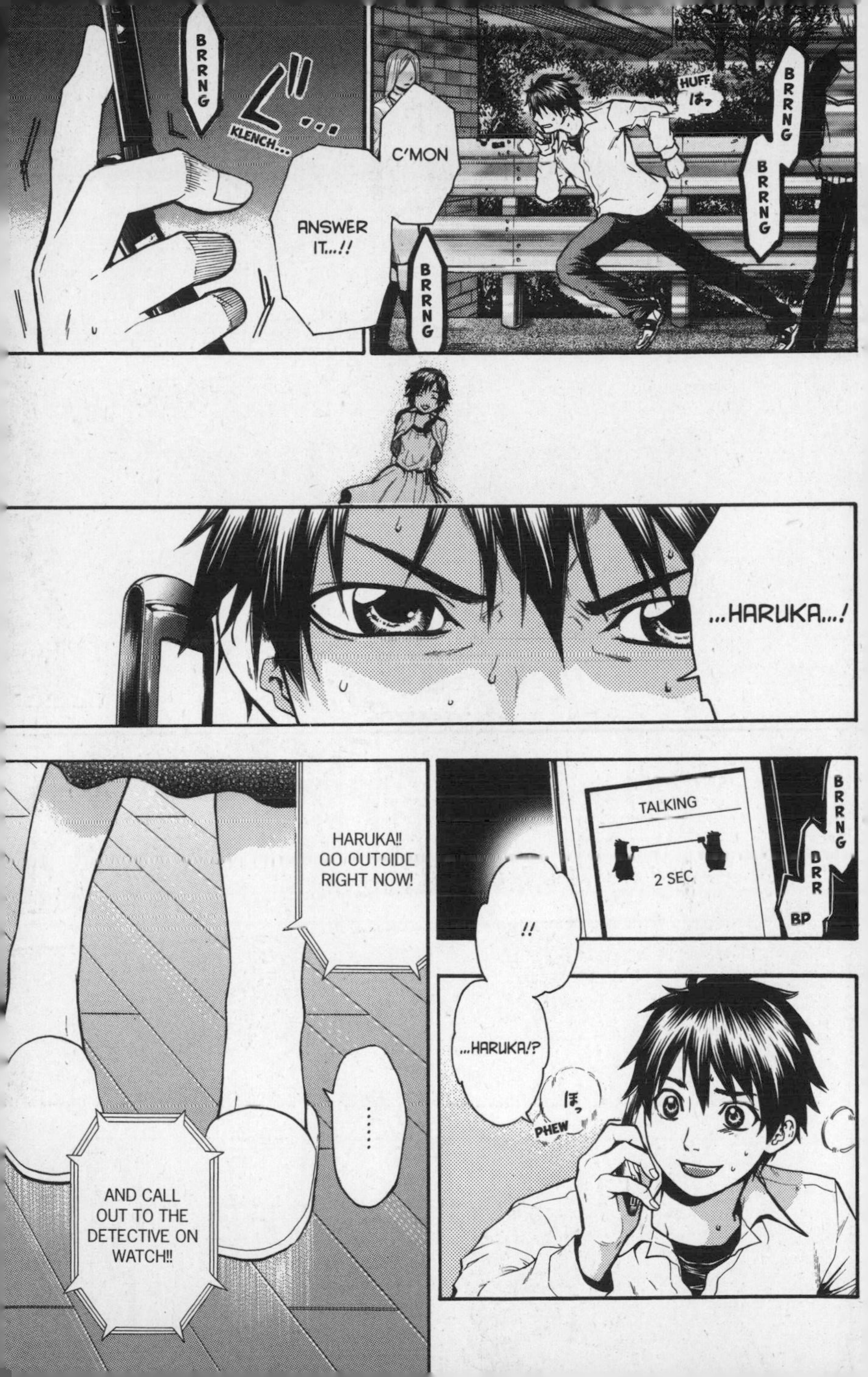
BRRNG
BRRNG
BRRNG
HUFF
はっ
BRRNG
ぐ...
KLENCH...
C'MON
ANSWER IT...!!
BRRNG
...HARUKA...!
BRRNG
BRR
BP
TALKING
2 SEC
!!
...HARUKA!?
ほっ
PHEW
HARUKA!! GO OUTSIDE RIGHT NOW!
......
AND CALL OUT TO THE DETECTIVE ON WATCH!!

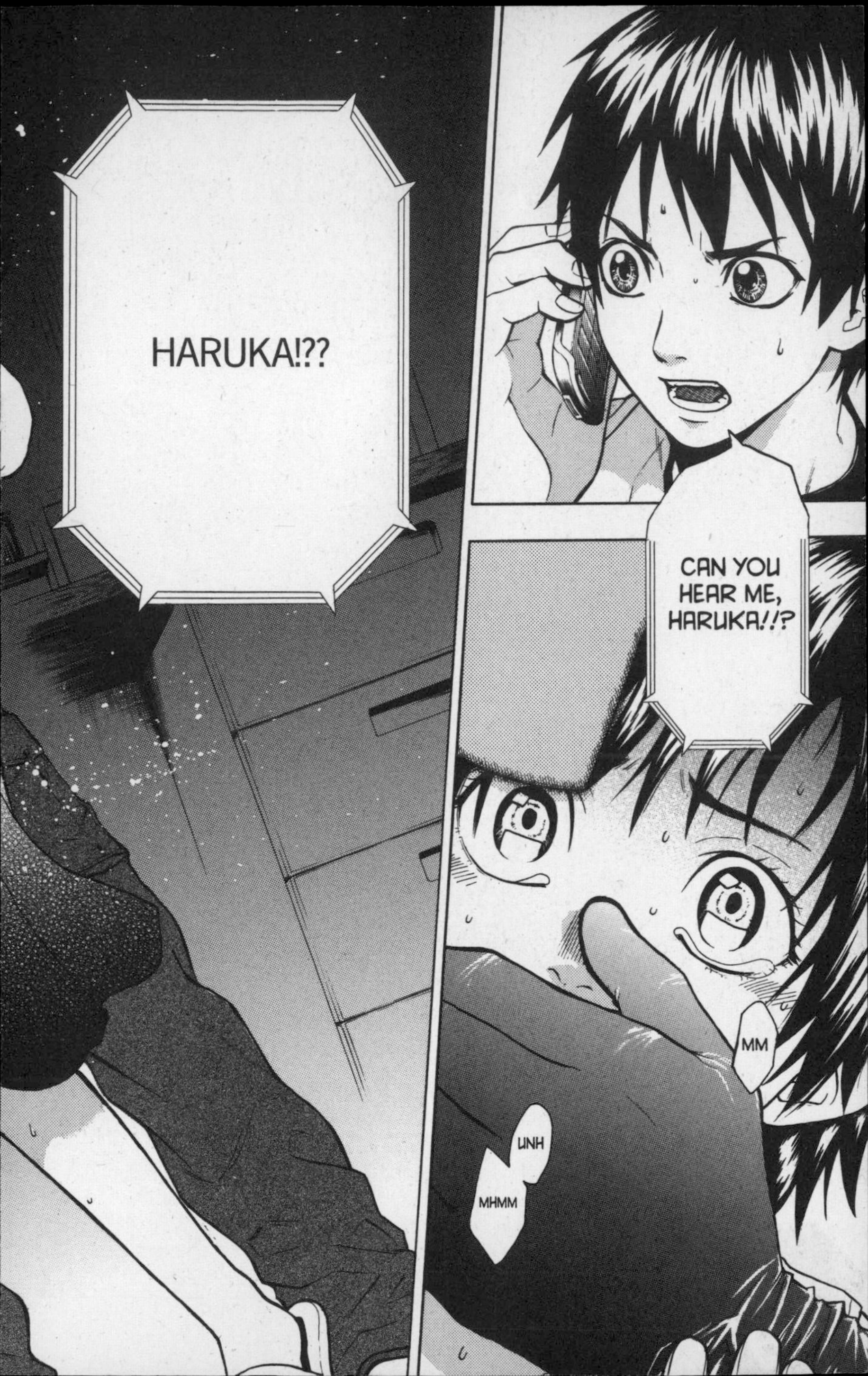
CAN YOU HEAR ME, HARUKA!!?
MM
UNH
MHMM
HARUKA!??

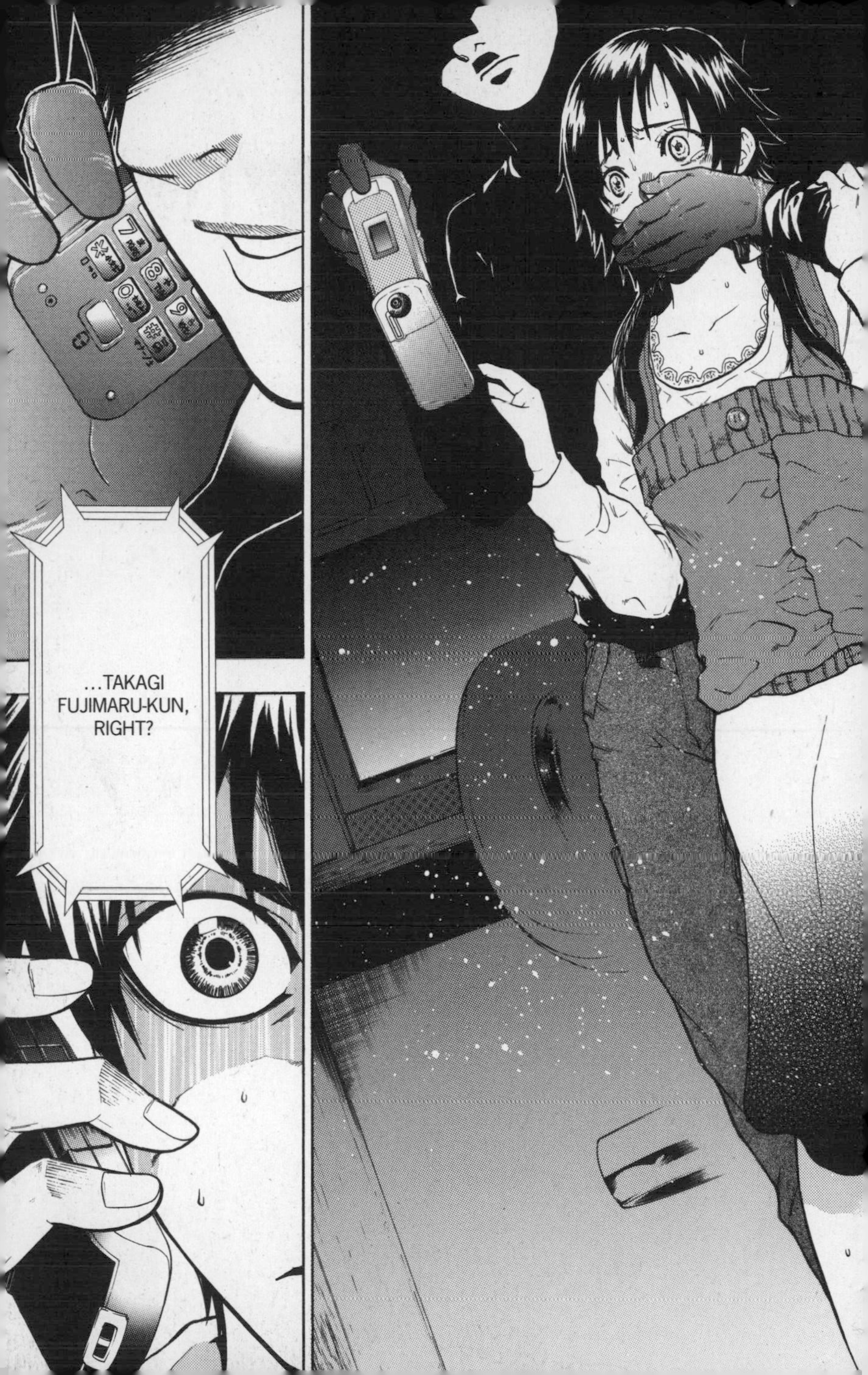
…TAKAGI FUJIMARU-KUN, RIGHT?

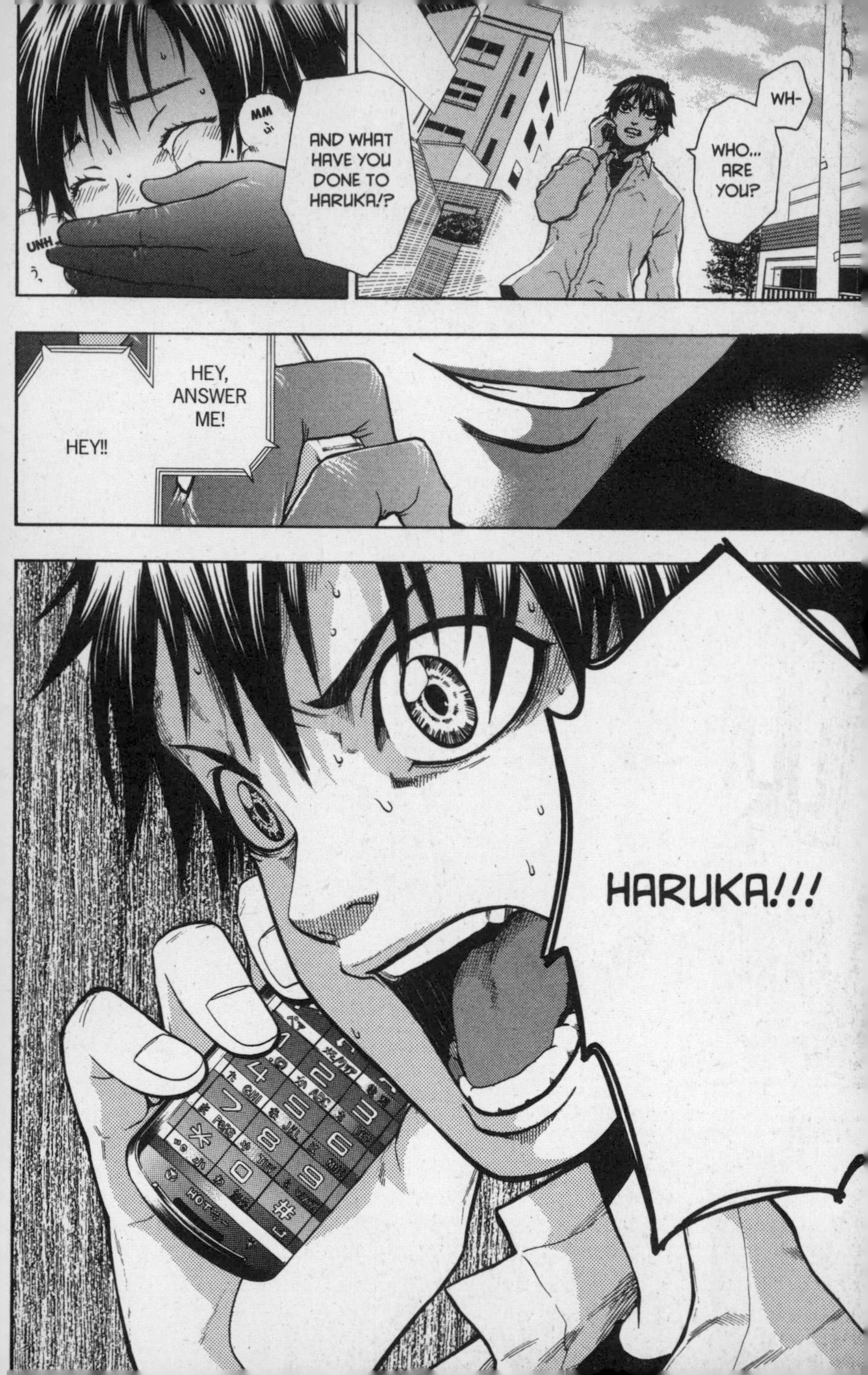
WH-
WHO... ARE YOU?
AND WHAT HAVE YOU DONE TO HARUKA!?
MM
UNH
HEY, ANSWER ME!
HEY!!
HARUKA!!!

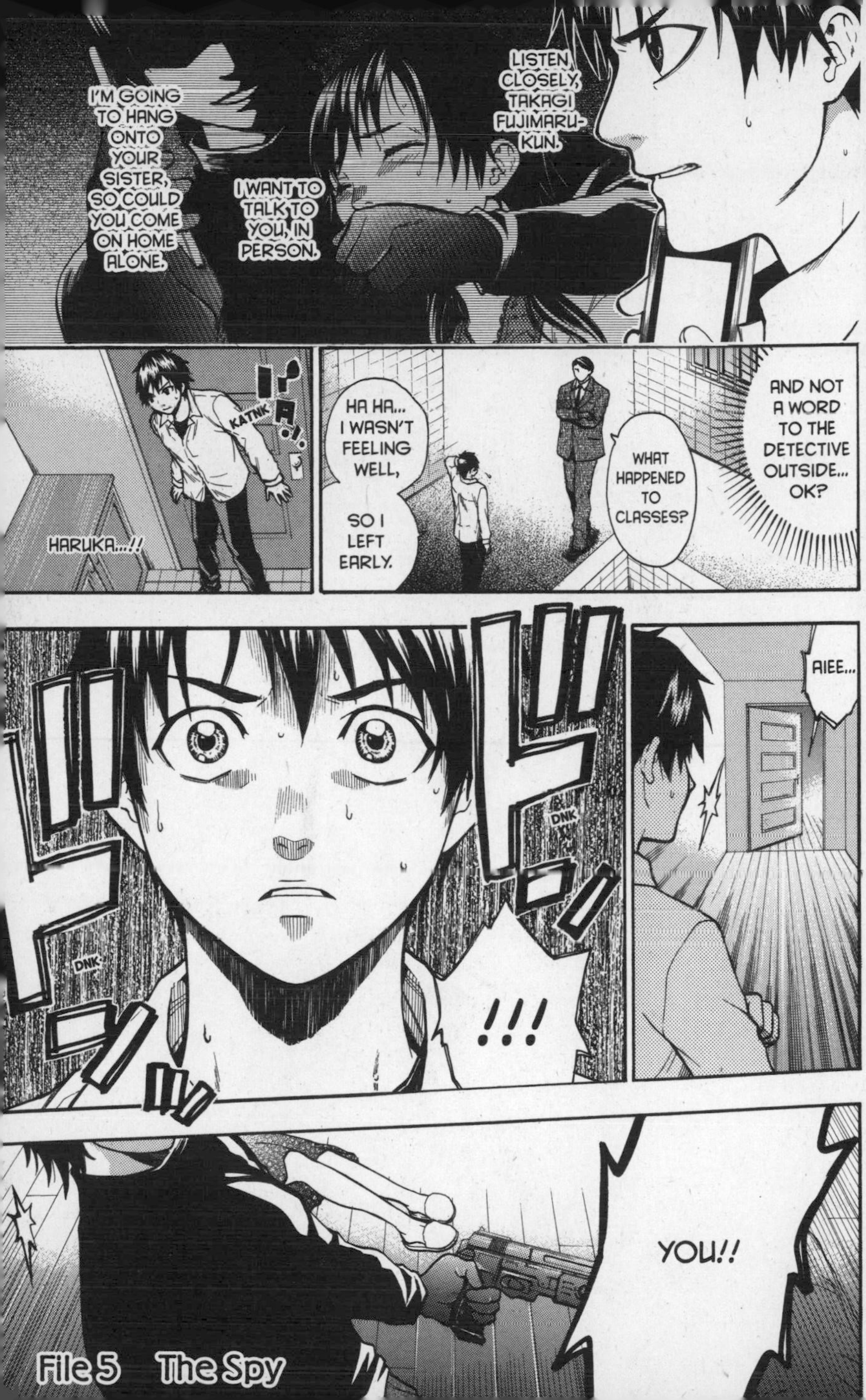
LISTEN CLOSELY, TAKAGI FUJIMARU-KUN.
I WANT TO TALK TO YOU, IN PERSON.
I'M GOING TO HANG ONTO YOUR SISTER, SO COULD YOU COME ON HOME ALONE.
AND NOT A WORD TO THE DETECTIVE OUTSIDE... OK?
WHAT HAPPENED TO CLASSES?
HA HA... I WASN'T FEELING WELL,
SO I LEFT EARLY.
KATNK
HARUKA...!!
AIEE...
DNK
!!!
DNK
YOU!!

File 5 The Spy

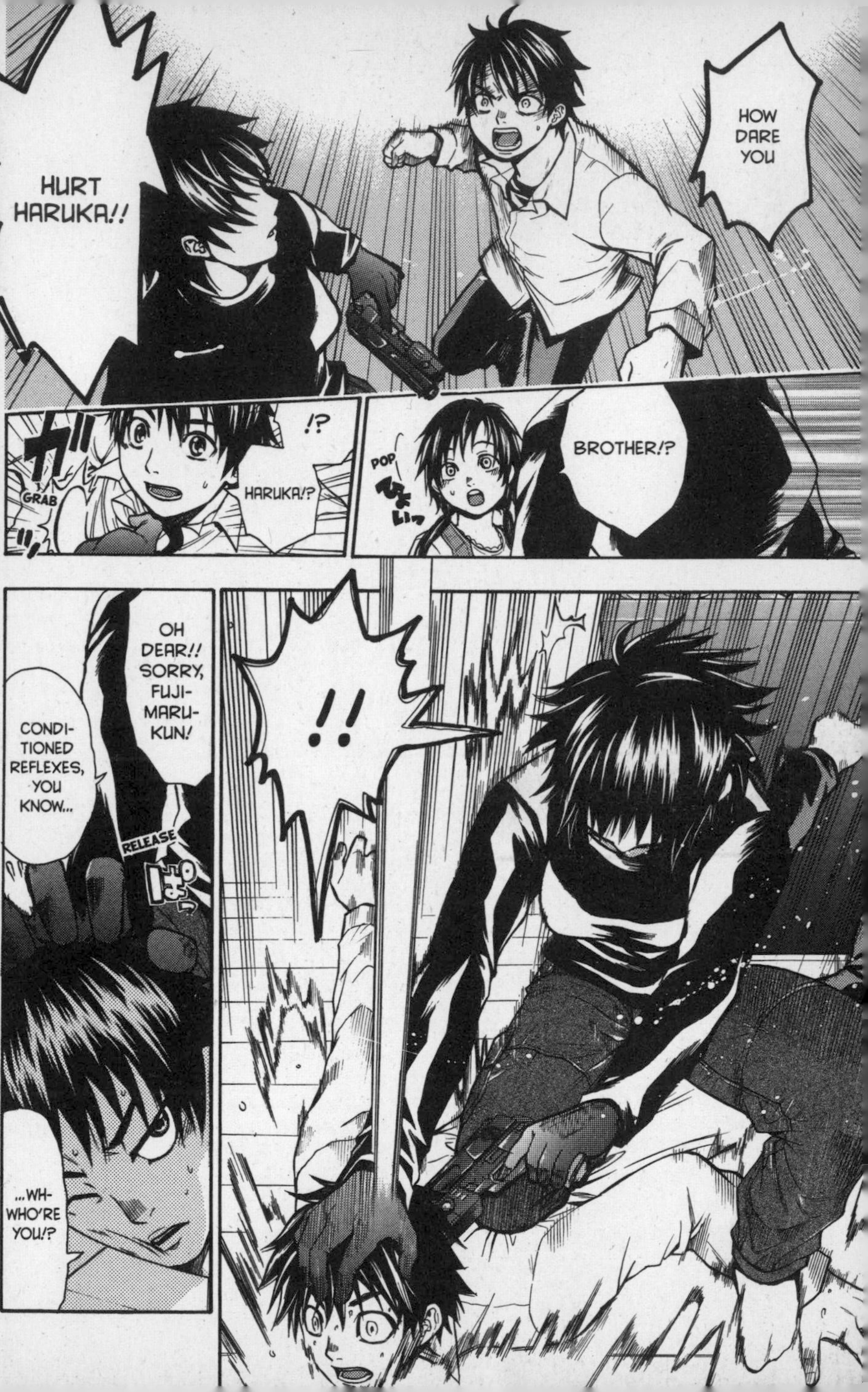
HOW DARE YOU
HURT HARUKA!!
BROTHER!?
POP
!?
HARUKA!?
GRAB
!!
OH DEAR!! SORRY, FUJI-MARU-KUN!
CONDI-TIONED REFLEXES, YOU KNOW...
RELEASE
...WH-WHO'RE YOU!?

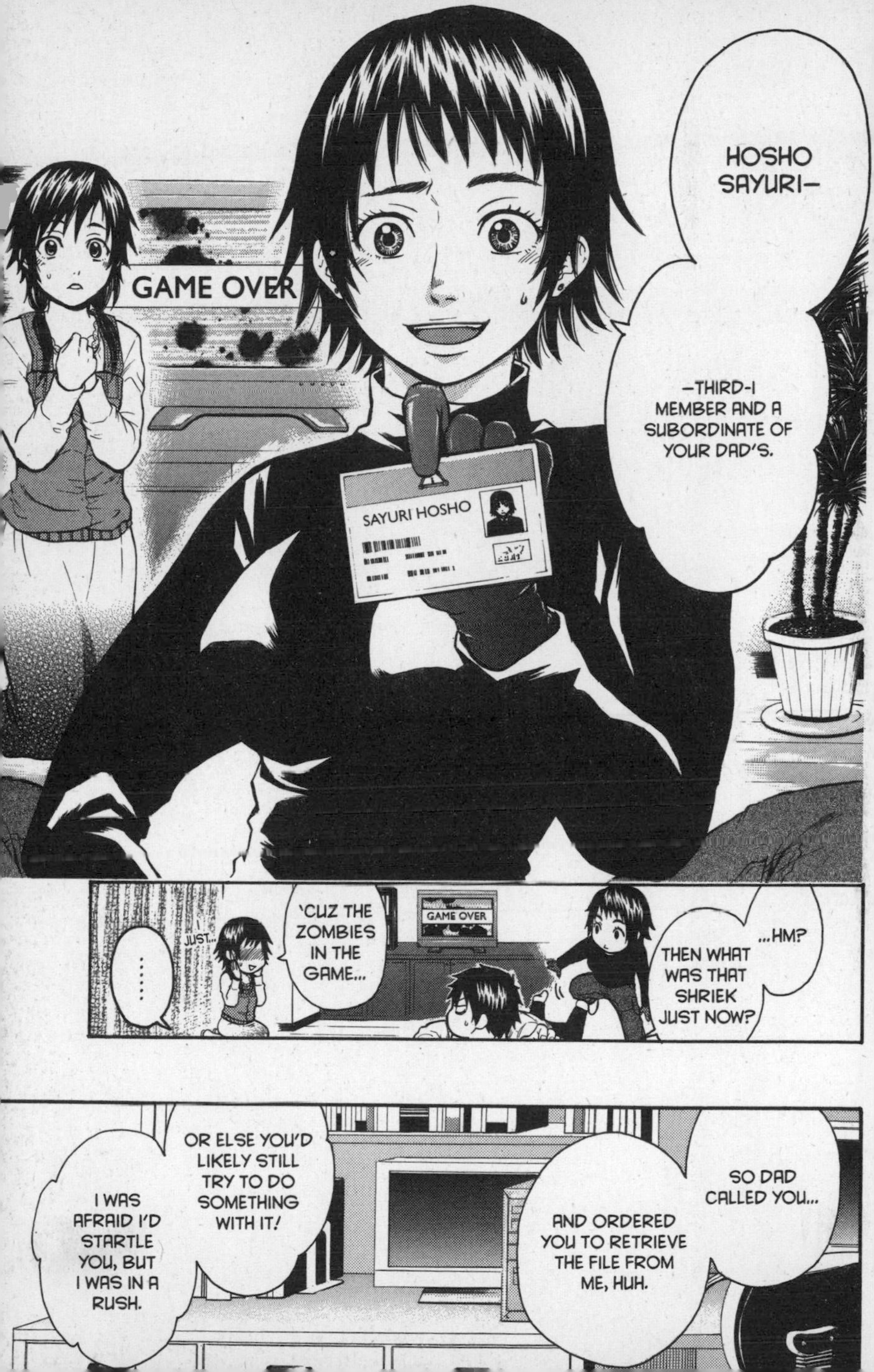
HOSHO SAYURI—
—THIRD-I MEMBER AND A SUBORDINATE OF YOUR DAD'S.
SAYURI HOSHO
GAME OVER
...HM?
THEN WHAT WAS THAT SHRIEK JUST NOW?
GAME OVER
'CUZ THE ZOMBIES IN THE GAME...
JUST...
......
SO DAD CALLED YOU...
AND ORDERED YOU TO RETRIEVE THE FILE FROM ME, HUH.
I WAS AFRAID I'D STARTLE YOU, BUT I WAS IN A RUSH.
OR ELSE YOU'D LIKELY STILL TRY TO DO SOMETHING WITH IT!

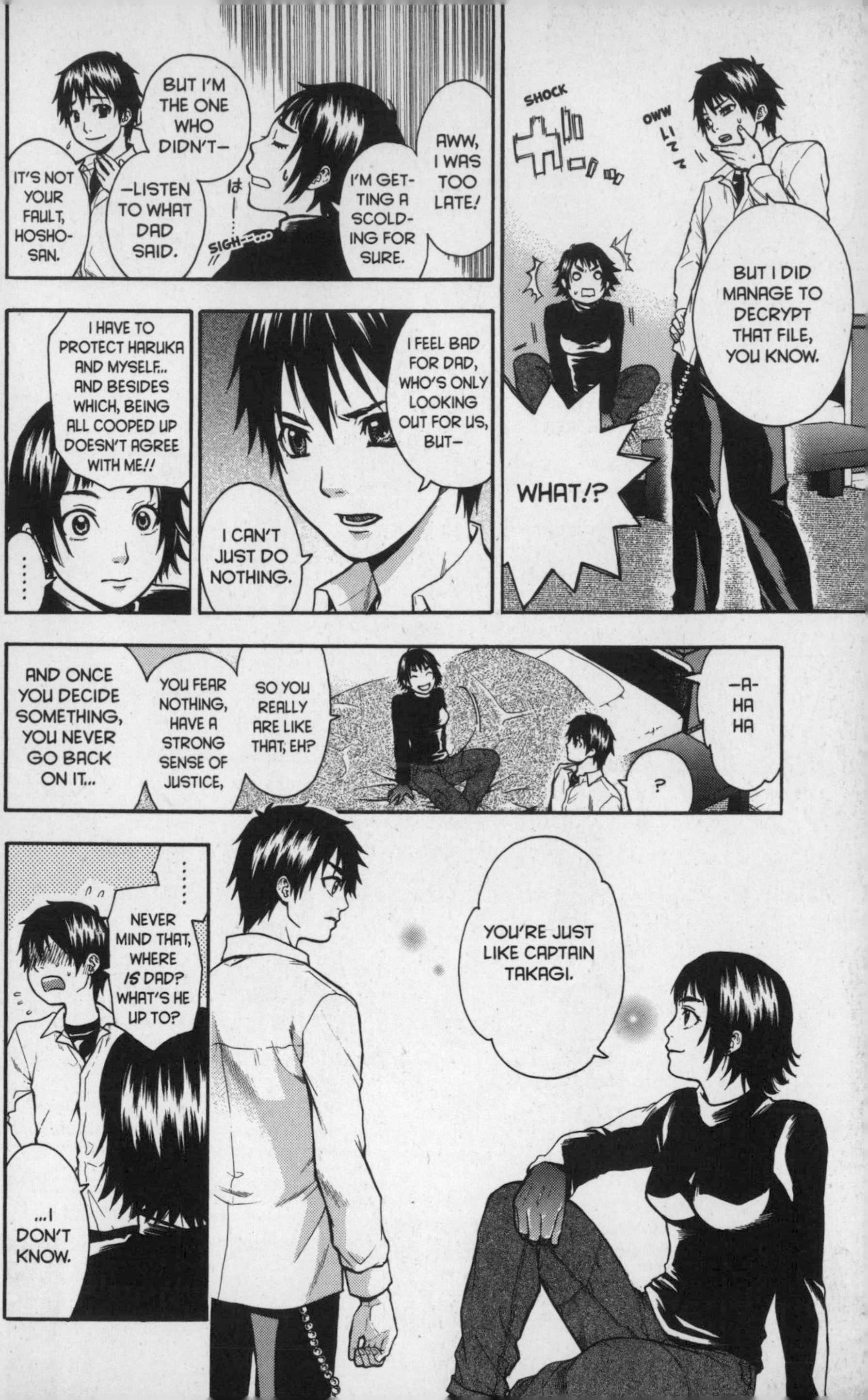
SHOCK
OWW
BUT I DID MANAGE TO DECRYPT THAT FILE, YOU KNOW.
WHAT!?
AWW, I WAS TOO LATE!
I'M GETTING A SCOLDING FOR SURE.
SIGH...
—LISTEN TO WHAT DAD SAID.
BUT I'M THE ONE WHO DIDN'T—
IT'S NOT YOUR FAULT, HOSHO-SAN.
I FEEL BAD FOR DAD, WHO'S ONLY LOOKING OUT FOR US, BUT—
I CAN'T JUST DO NOTHING.
I HAVE TO PROTECT HARUKA AND MYSELF... AND BESIDES WHICH, BEING ALL COOPED UP DOESN'T AGREE WITH ME!!
......
—A-HA HA
?
SO YOU REALLY ARE LIKE THAT, EH?
YOU FEAR NOTHING, HAVE A STRONG SENSE OF JUSTICE,
AND ONCE YOU DECIDE SOMETHING, YOU NEVER GO BACK ON IT...
YOU'RE JUST LIKE CAPTAIN TAKAGI.
......
NEVER MIND THAT, WHERE IS DAD? WHAT'S HE UP TO?
...I DON'T KNOW.

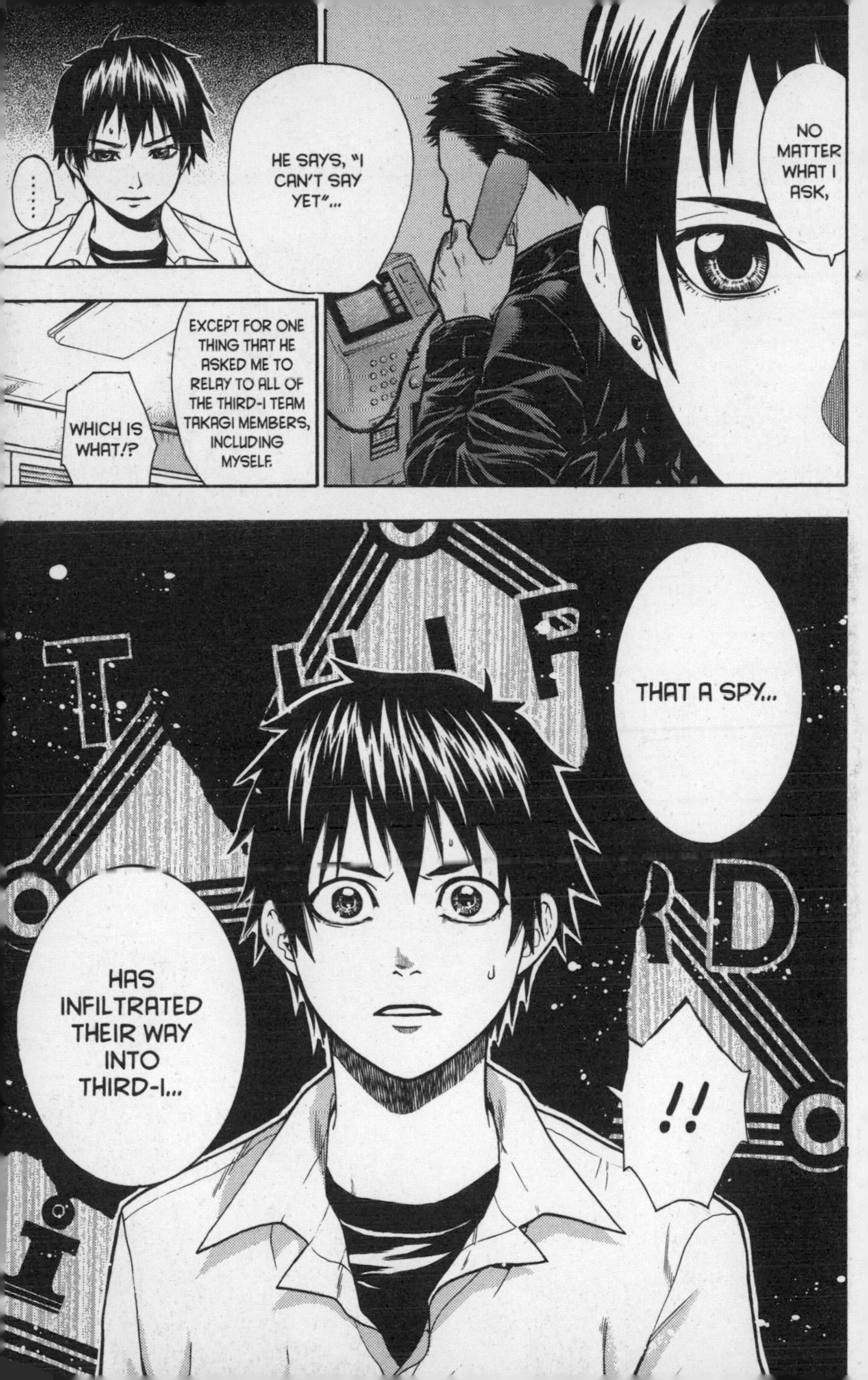
NO MATTER WHAT I ASK,
HE SAYS, "I CAN'T SAY YET"...
......
EXCEPT FOR ONE THING THAT HE ASKED ME TO RELAY TO ALL OF THE THIRD-I TEAM TAKAGI MEMBERS, INCLUDING MYSELF.
WHICH IS WHAT!?
THAT A SPY...
!!
HAS INFILTRATED THEIR WAY INTO THIRD-I...

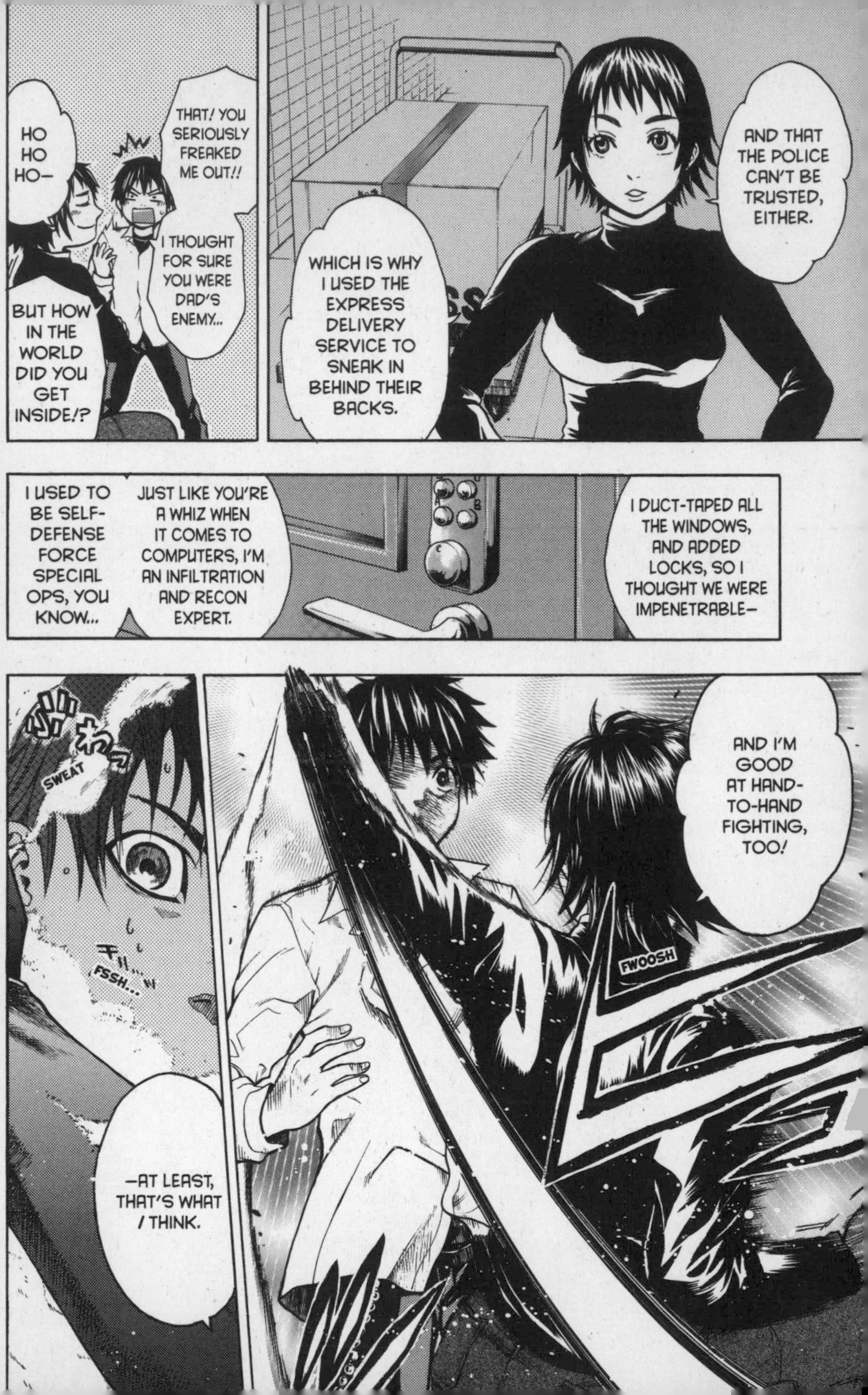
AND THAT THE POLICE CAN'T BE TRUSTED, EITHER.
WHICH IS WHY I USED THE EXPRESS DELIVERY SERVICE TO SNEAK IN BEHIND THEIR BACKS.
THAT! YOU SERIOUSLY FREAKED ME OUT!!
HO HO HO—
I THOUGHT FOR SURE YOU WERE DAD'S ENEMY...
BUT HOW IN THE WORLD DID YOU GET INSIDE!?
I DUCT-TAPED ALL THE WINDOWS, AND ADDED LOCKS, SO I THOUGHT WE WERE IMPENETRABLE—
JUST LIKE YOU'RE A WHIZ WHEN IT COMES TO COMPUTERS, I'M AN INFILTRATION AND RECON EXPERT.
I USED TO BE SELF-DEFENSE FORCE SPECIAL OPS, YOU KNOW...
AND I'M GOOD AT HAND-TO-HAND FIGHTING, TOO!
FWOOSH
SWEAT
FSSH...
—AT LEAST, THAT'S WHAT I THINK.

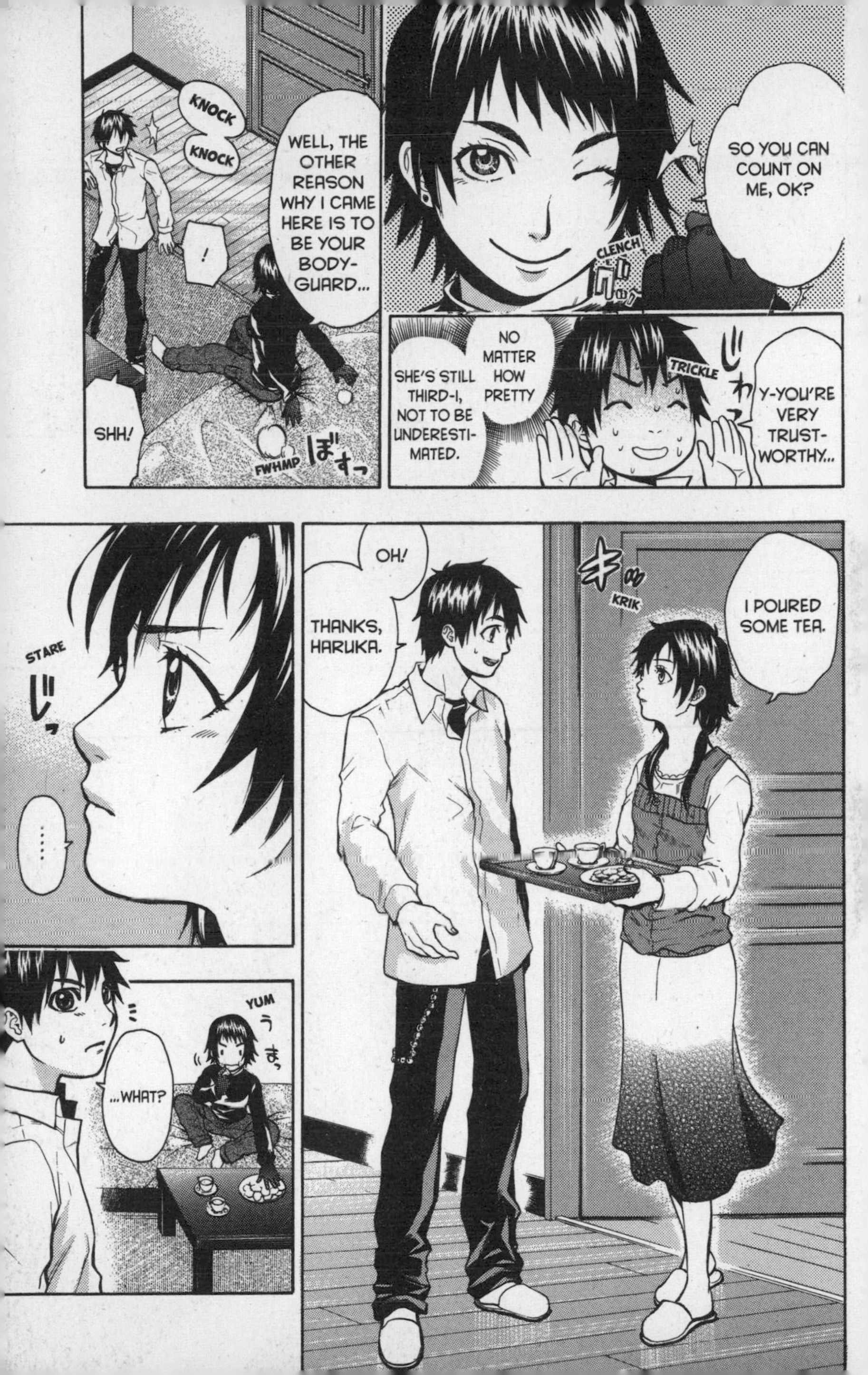
SO YOU CAN COUNT ON ME, OK?
CLENCH
Y-YOU'RE VERY TRUST-WORTHY...
TRICKLE
NO MATTER HOW PRETTY
SHE'S STILL THIRD-I, NOT TO BE UNDERESTI-MATED.
WELL, THE OTHER REASON WHY I CAME HERE IS TO BE YOUR BODY-GUARD...
KNOCK
KNOCK
!
SHH!
FWHMP
KRIK
I POURED SOME TEA.
OH!
THANKS, HARUKA.
STARE
......
YUM
...WHAT?

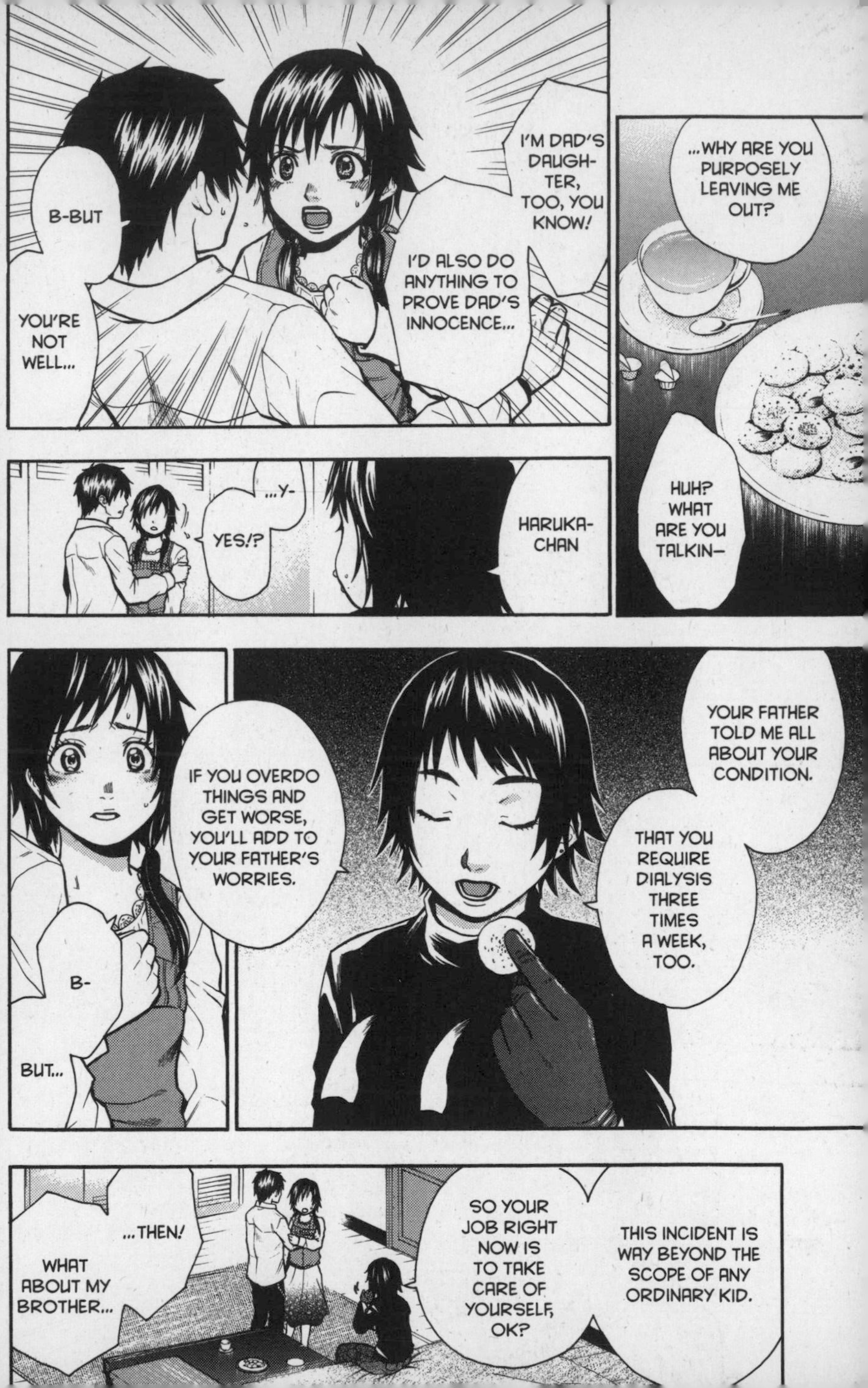
...WHY ARE YOU PURPOSELY LEAVING ME OUT?
HUH? WHAT ARE YOU TALKIN—
I'M DAD'S DAUGHTER, TOO, YOU KNOW!
I'D ALSO DO ANYTHING TO PROVE DAD'S INNOCENCE...
B-BUT
YOU'RE NOT WELL...
HARUKA-CHAN
...Y- YES!?
YOUR FATHER TOLD ME ALL ABOUT YOUR CONDITION.
THAT YOU REQUIRE DIALYSIS THREE TIMES A WEEK, TOO.
IF YOU OVERDO THINGS AND GET WORSE, YOU'LL ADD TO YOUR FATHER'S WORRIES.
B- BUT...
THIS INCIDENT IS WAY BEYOND THE SCOPE OF ANY ORDINARY KID.
SO YOUR JOB RIGHT NOW IS TO TAKE CARE OF YOURSELF, OK?
...THEN!
WHAT ABOUT MY BROTHER...

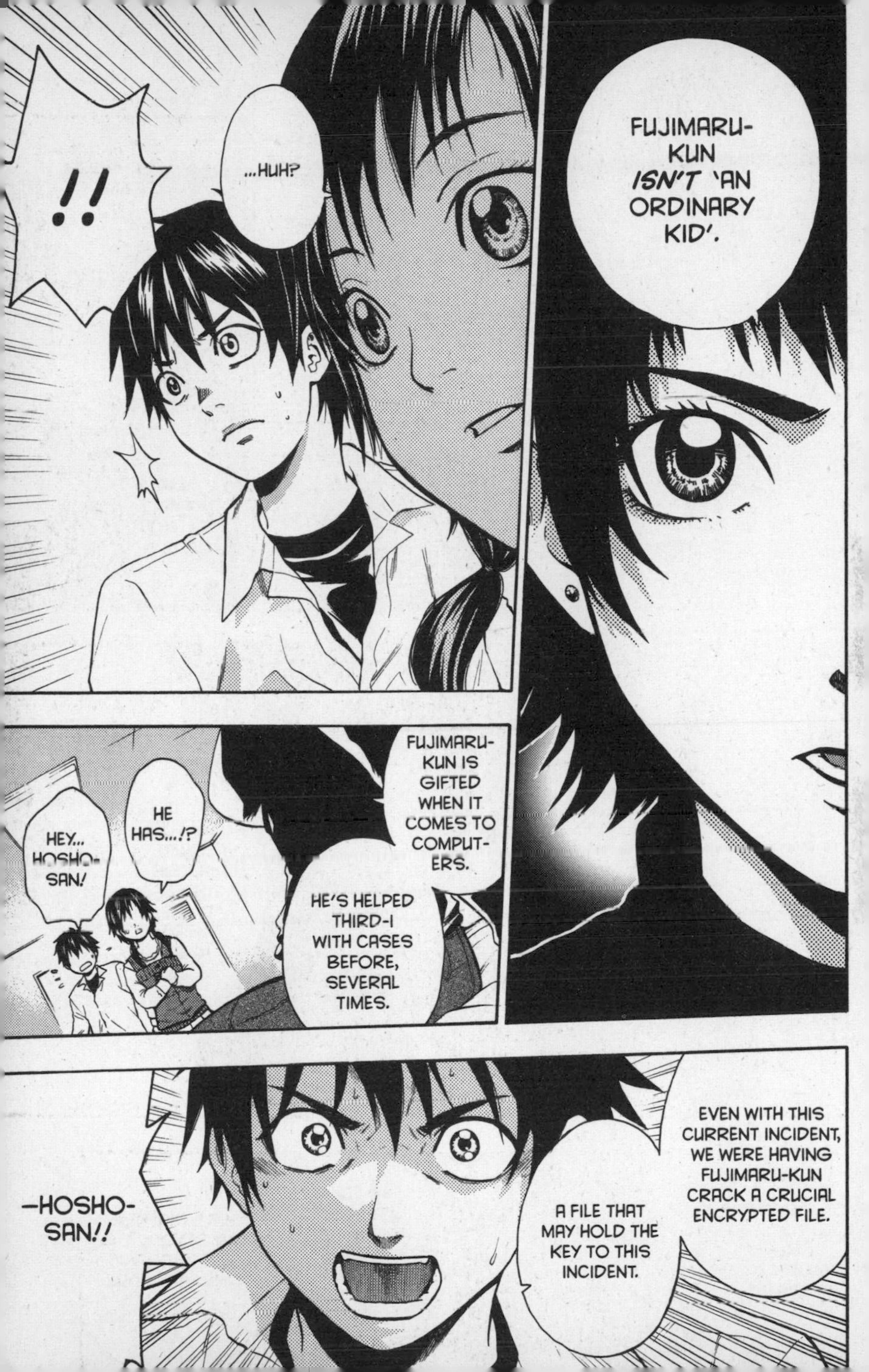
FUJIMARU-KUN *ISN'T* 'AN ORDINARY KID'.
...HUH?
!!
FUJIMARU-KUN IS GIFTED WHEN IT COMES TO COMPUTERS.
HE'S HELPED THIRD-I WITH CASES BEFORE, SEVERAL TIMES.
HE HAS...!?
HEY... HOSHO-SAN!
EVEN WITH THIS CURRENT INCIDENT, WE WERE HAVING FUJIMARU-KUN CRACK A CRUCIAL ENCRYPTED FILE.
A FILE THAT MAY HOLD THE KEY TO THIS INCIDENT.
—HOSHO-SAN!!

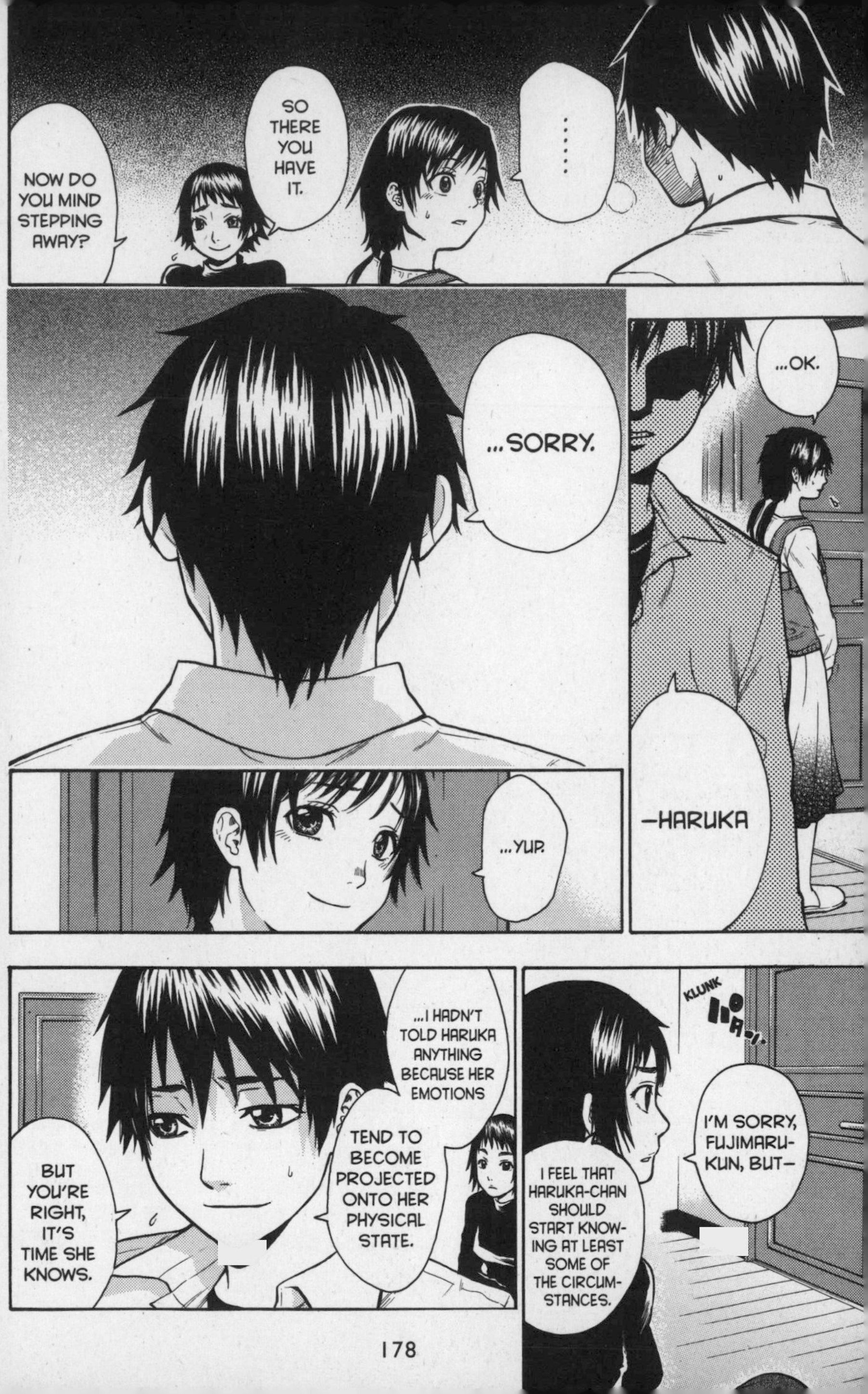
......
SO THERE YOU HAVE IT.
NOW DO YOU MIND STEPPING AWAY?
...OK.
—HARUKA
...SORRY.
...YUP.
KLUNK
I'M SORRY, FUJIMARU-KUN, BUT—
I FEEL THAT HARUKA-CHAN SHOULD START KNOWING AT LEAST SOME OF THE CIRCUMSTANCES.
...I HADN'T TOLD HARUKA ANYTHING BECAUSE HER EMOTIONS
TEND TO BECOME PROJECTED ONTO HER PHYSICAL STATE.
BUT YOU'RE RIGHT, IT'S TIME SHE KNOWS.

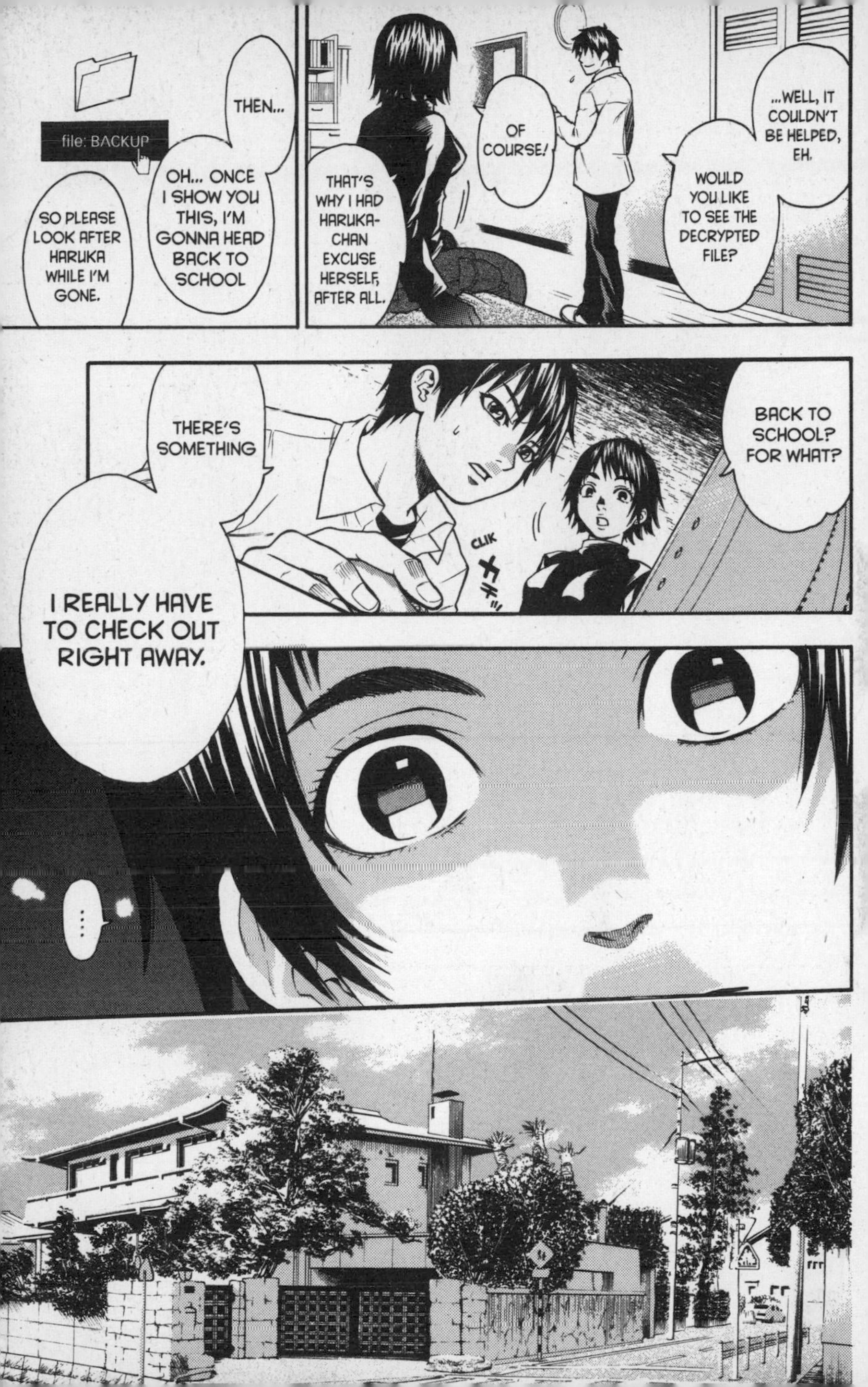
...WELL, IT COULDN'T BE HELPED, EH.
WOULD YOU LIKE TO SEE THE DECRYPTED FILE?
OF COURSE!
THAT'S WHY I HAD HARUKA-CHAN EXCUSE HERSELF, AFTER ALL.
THEN...
file: BACKUP
OH... ONCE I SHOW YOU THIS, I'M GONNA HEAD BACK TO SCHOOL
SO PLEASE LOOK AFTER HARUKA WHILE I'M GONE.
BACK TO SCHOOL? FOR WHAT?
CLIK
THERE'S SOMETHING
I REALLY HAVE TO CHECK OUT RIGHT AWAY.
.....

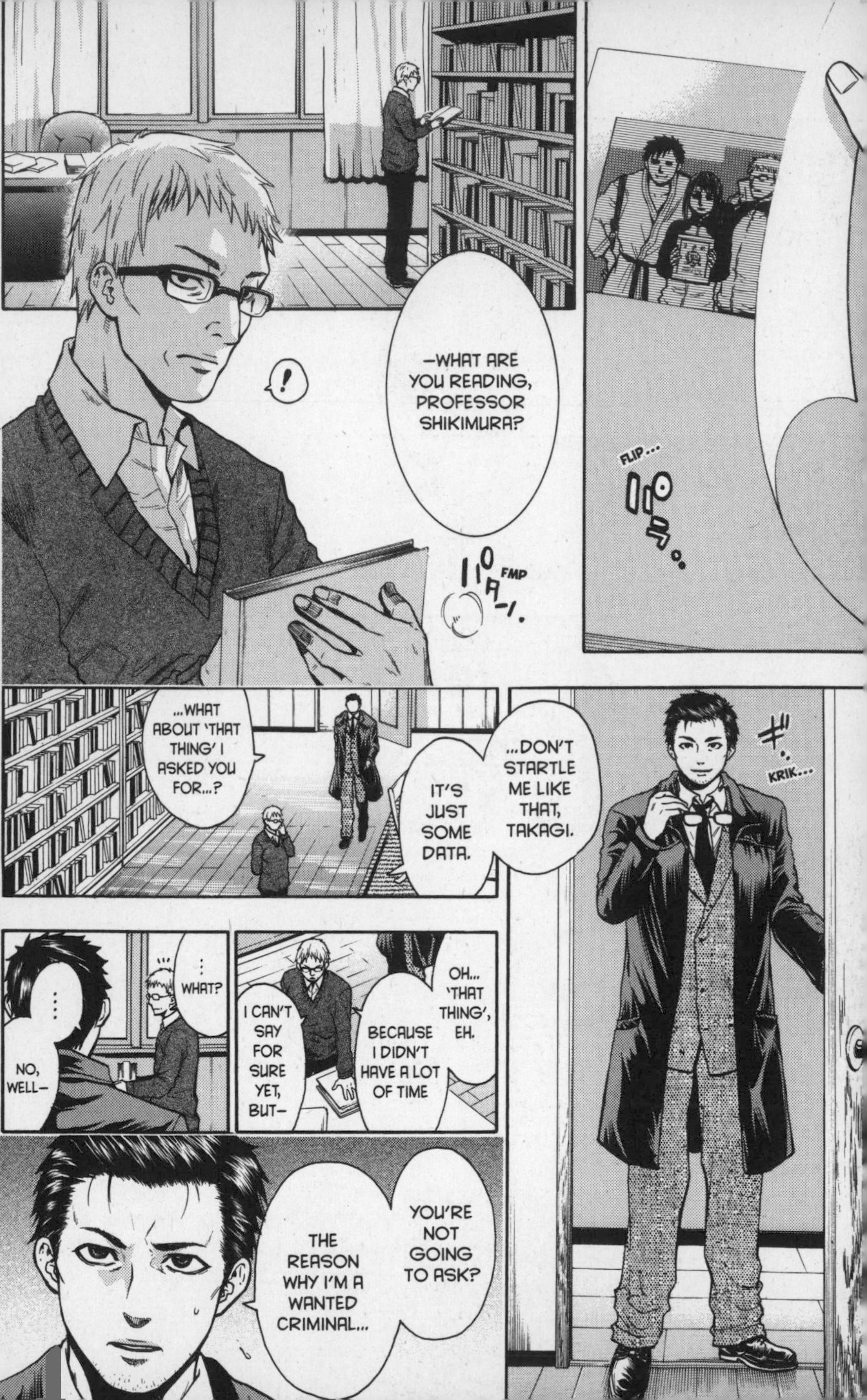
FLIP...
—WHAT ARE YOU READING, PROFESSOR SHIKIMURA?
!
FMP
KRIK...
...DON'T STARTLE ME LIKE THAT, TAKAGI.
IT'S JUST SOME DATA.
...WHAT ABOUT 'THAT THING' I ASKED YOU FOR...?
OH... 'THAT THING', EH.
BECAUSE I DIDN'T HAVE A LOT OF TIME
I CAN'T SAY FOR SURE YET, BUT—
...WHAT?
...
NO, WELL—
YOU'RE NOT GOING TO ASK?
THE REASON WHY I'M A WANTED CRIMINAL...

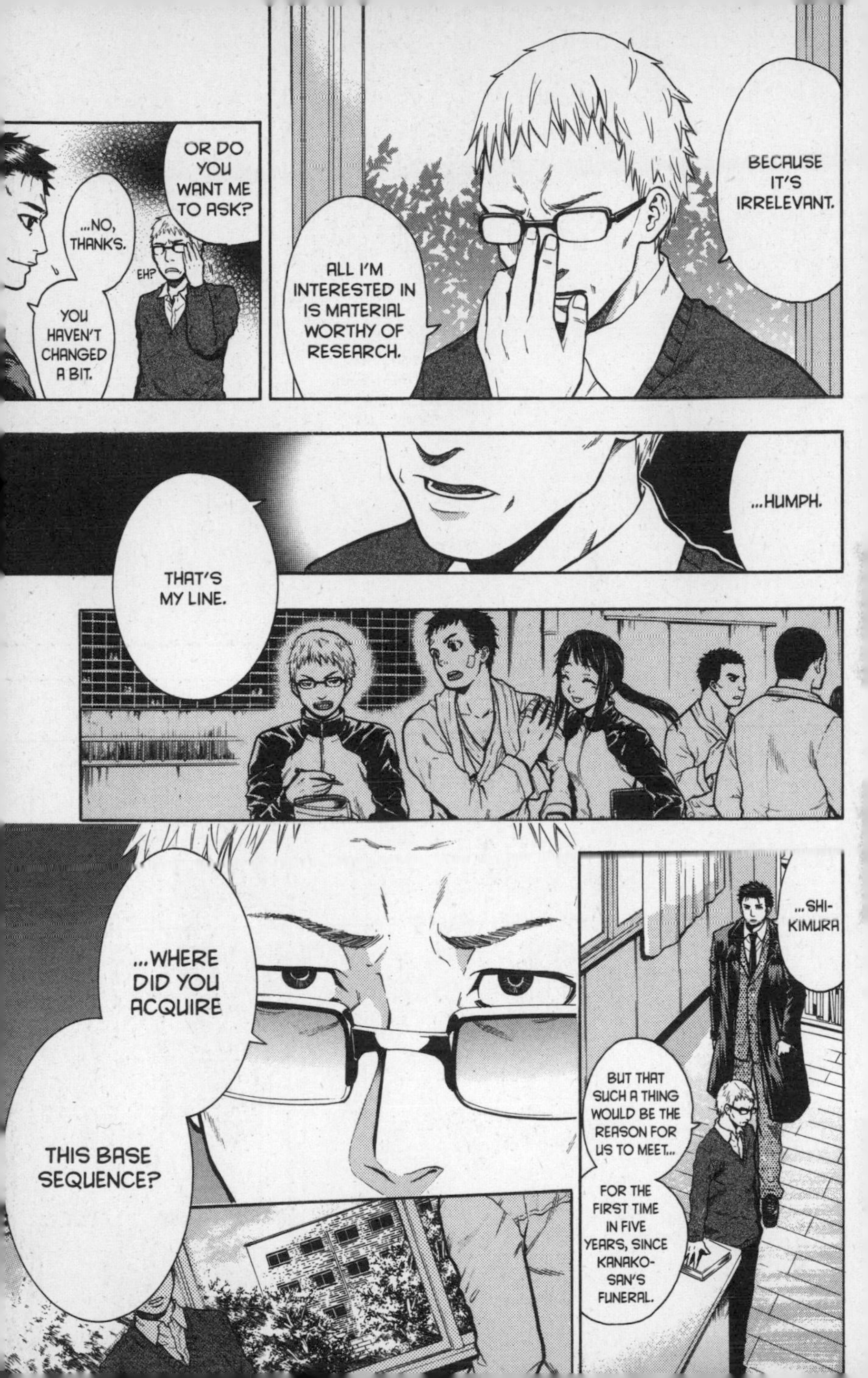
BECAUSE IT'S IRRELEVANT.
ALL I'M INTERESTED IN IS MATERIAL WORTHY OF RESEARCH.
OR DO YOU WANT ME TO ASK?
...NO, THANKS.
EH?
YOU HAVEN'T CHANGED A BIT.
...HUMPH.
THAT'S MY LINE.
...SHI-KIMURA
BUT THAT SUCH A THING WOULD BE THE REASON FOR US TO MEET...
FOR THE FIRST TIME IN FIVE YEARS, SINCE KANAKO-SAN'S FUNERAL.
...WHERE DID YOU ACQUIRE
THIS BASE SEQUENCE?

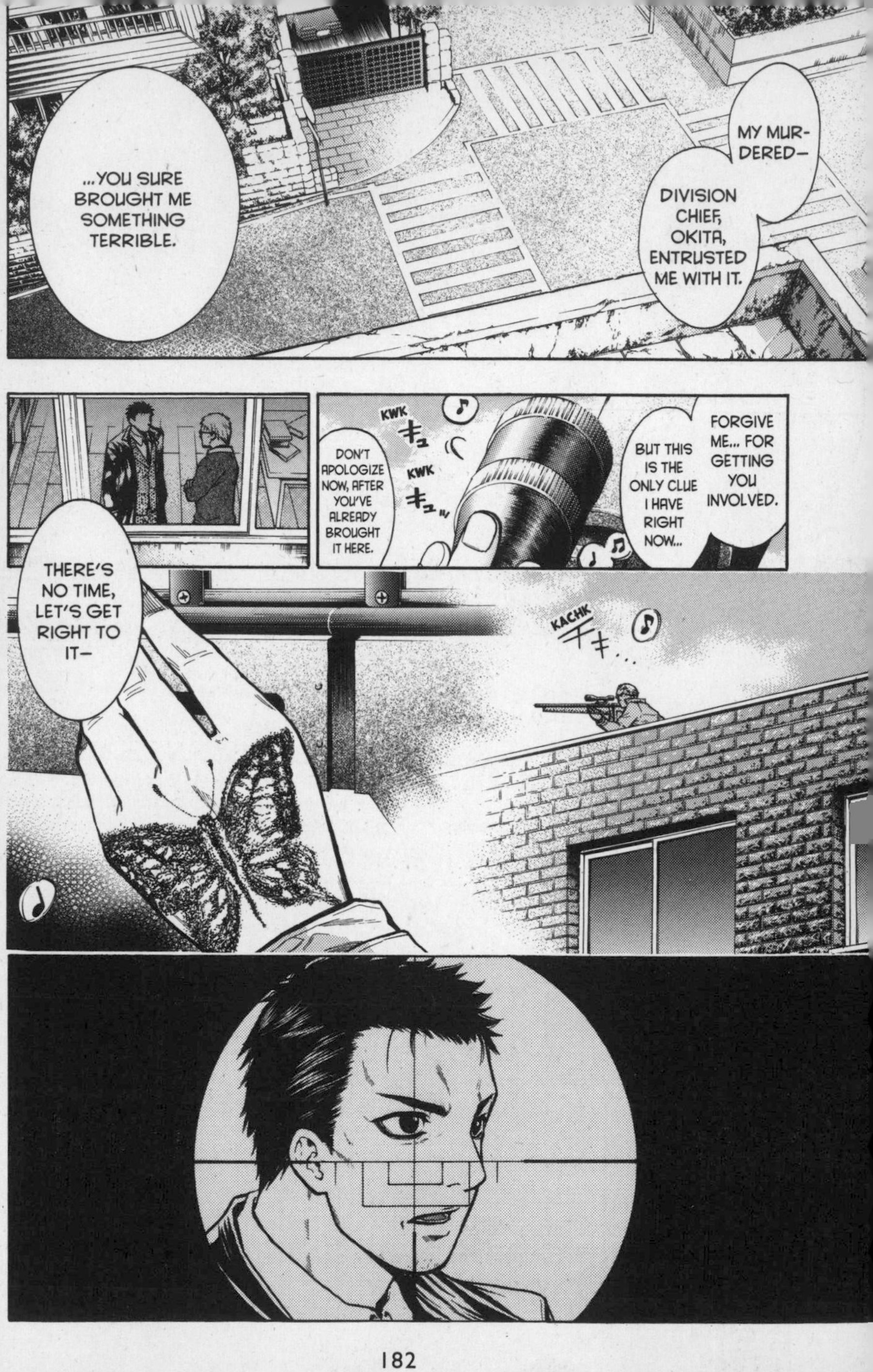
MY MURDERED—
DIVISION CHIEF, OKITA, ENTRUSTED ME WITH IT.
...YOU SURE BROUGHT ME SOMETHING TERRIBLE.
FORGIVE ME... FOR GETTING YOU INVOLVED.
BUT THIS IS THE ONLY CLUE I HAVE RIGHT NOW...
KWK
KWK
DON'T APOLOGIZE NOW, AFTER YOU'VE ALREADY BROUGHT IT HERE.
KACHK
THERE'S NO TIME, LET'S GET RIGHT TO IT—

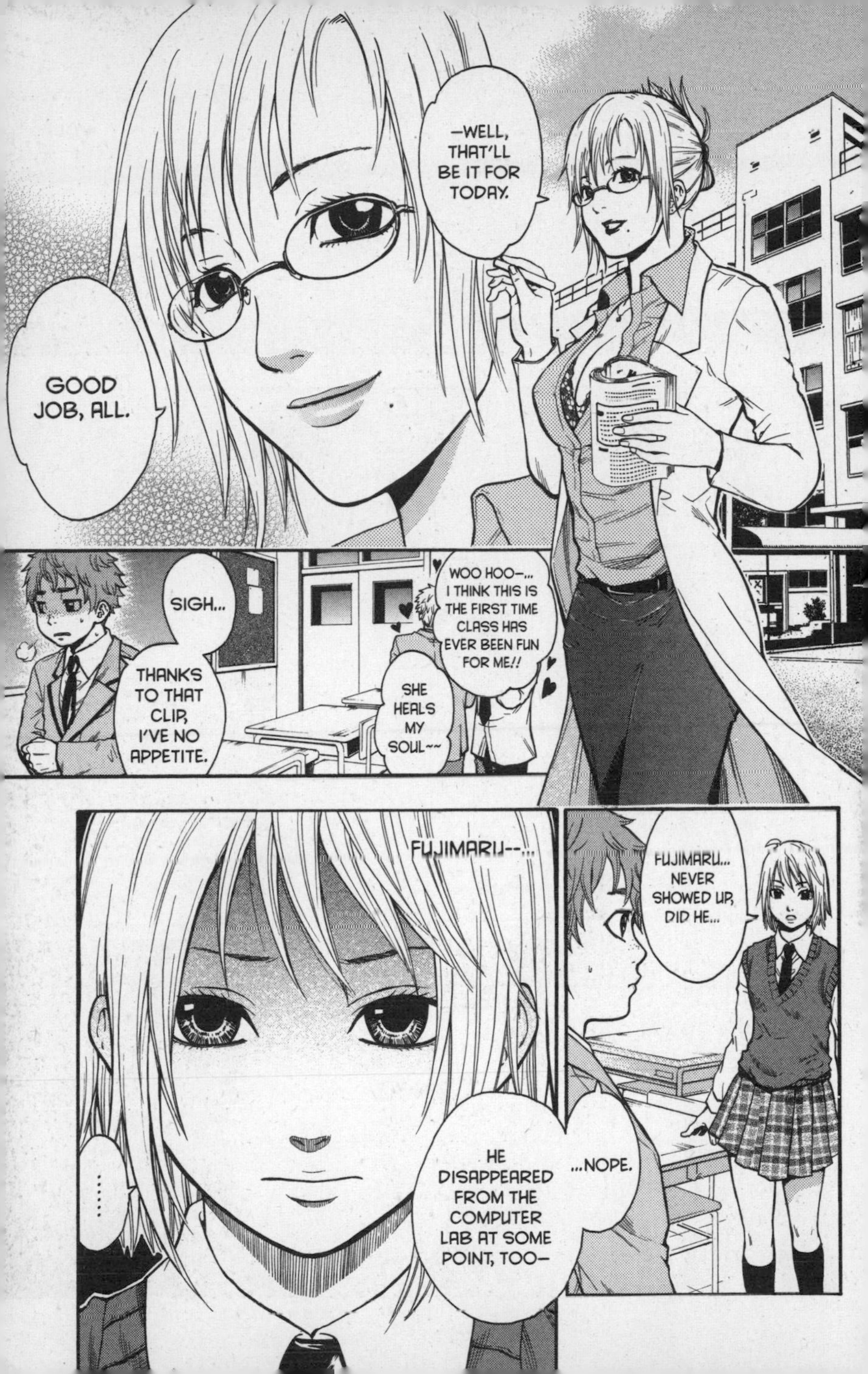
—WELL, THAT'LL BE IT FOR TODAY.
GOOD JOB, ALL.
WOO HOO—... I THINK THIS IS THE FIRST TIME CLASS HAS EVER BEEN FUN FOR ME!!
SHE HEALS MY SOUL~~
SIGH...
THANKS TO THAT CLIP, I'VE NO APPETITE.
FUJIMARU... NEVER SHOWED UP, DID HE...
...NOPE.
FUJIMARU--...
HE DISAPPEARED FROM THE COMPUTER LAB AT SOME POINT, TOO—
......

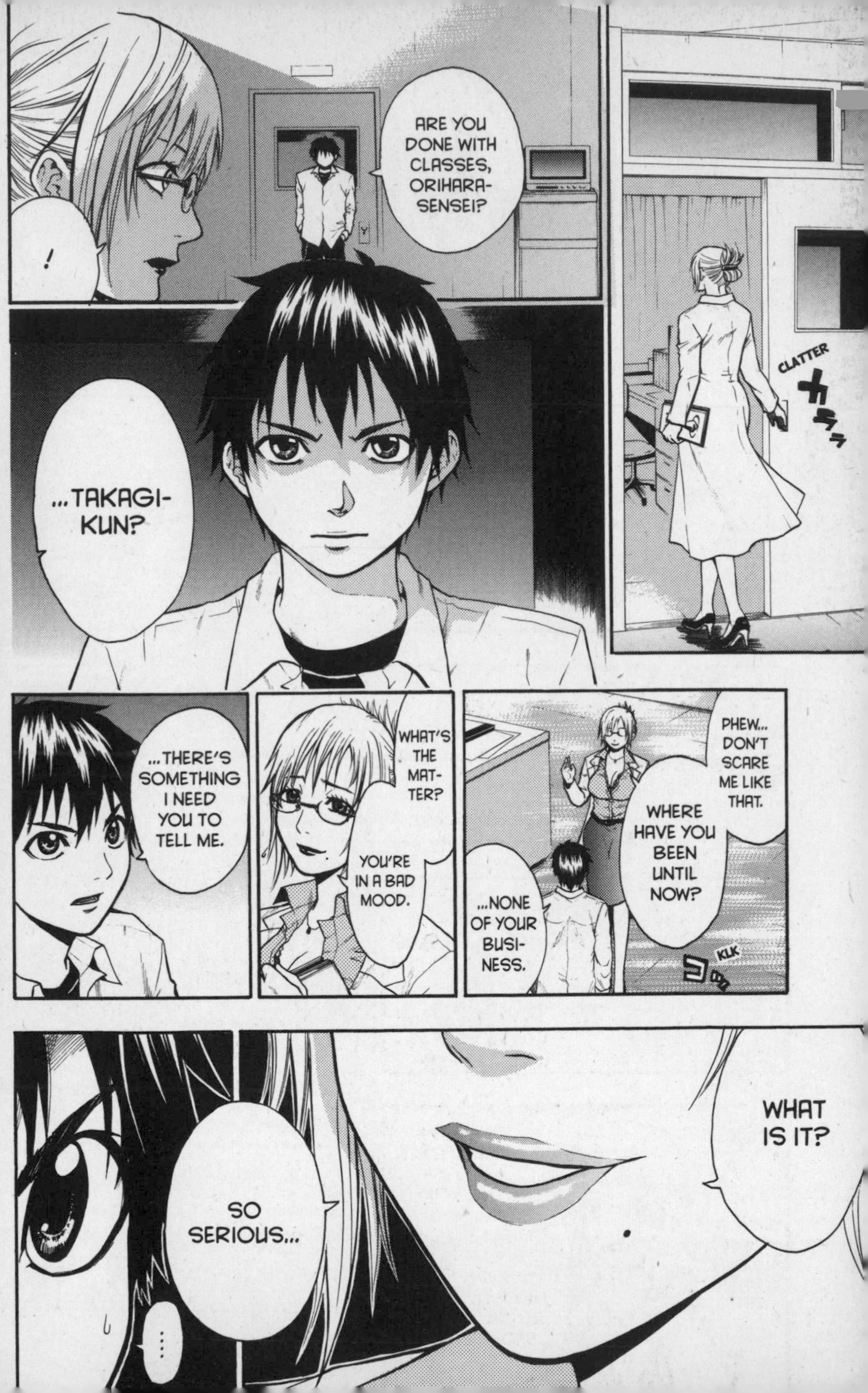
CLATTER
ARE YOU DONE WITH CLASSES, ORIHARA-SENSEI?
!
...TAKAGI-KUN?
PHEW... DON'T SCARE ME LIKE THAT.
WHERE HAVE YOU BEEN UNTIL NOW?
KLK
...NONE OF YOUR BUSI-NESS.
WHAT'S THE MAT-TER?
YOU'RE IN A BAD MOOD.
...THERE'S SOMETHING I NEED YOU TO TELL ME.
WHAT IS IT?
SO SERIOUS...
....

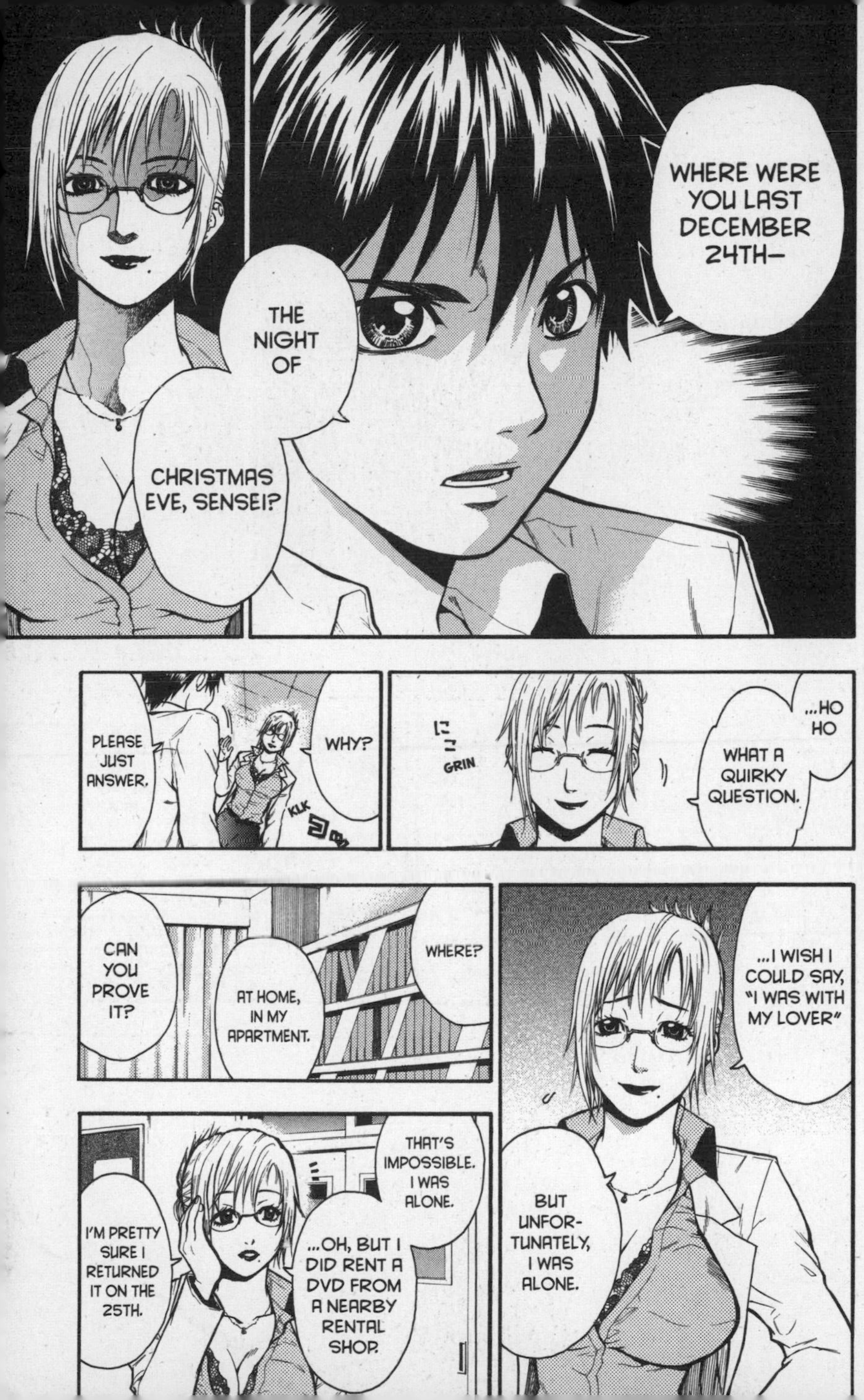
WHERE WERE YOU LAST DECEMBER 24TH—
THE NIGHT OF
CHRISTMAS EVE, SENSEI?
...HO HO
WHAT A QUIRKY QUESTION.
にこ GRIN
WHY?
PLEASE JUST ANSWER.
KLK
...I WISH I COULD SAY, "I WAS WITH MY LOVER"
BUT UNFORTUNATELY, I WAS ALONE.
WHERE?
AT HOME, IN MY APARTMENT.
CAN YOU PROVE IT?
THAT'S IMPOSSIBLE. I WAS ALONE.
...OH, BUT I DID RENT A DVD FROM A NEARBY RENTAL SHOP.
I'M PRETTY SURE I RETURNED IT ON THE 25TH.

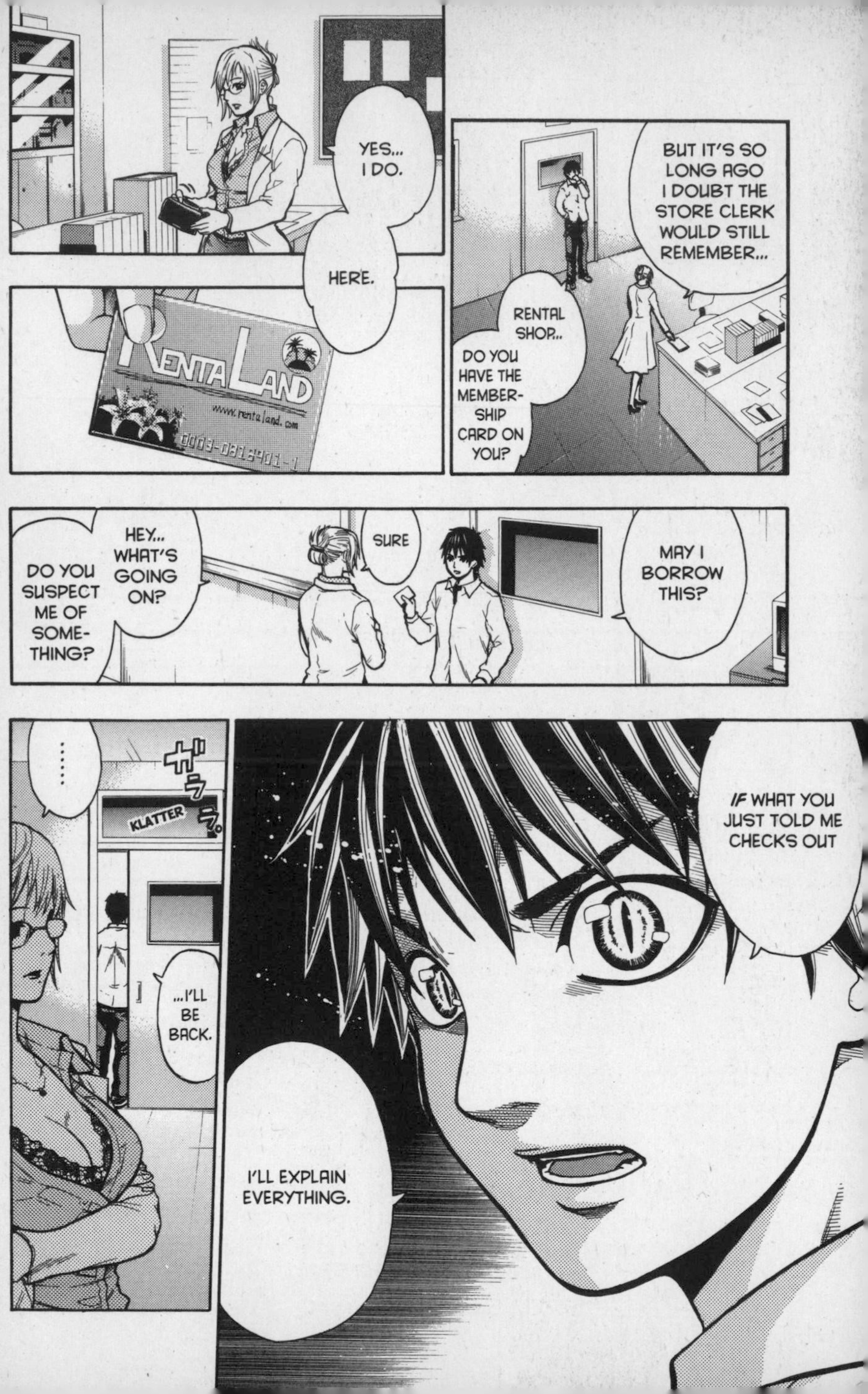
BUT IT'S SO LONG AGO I DOUBT THE STORE CLERK WOULD STILL REMEMBER...
RENTAL SHOP...
DO YOU HAVE THE MEMBER-SHIP CARD ON YOU?
YES... I DO.
HERE.
RENTALAND
MAY I BORROW THIS?
SURE
HEY... WHAT'S GOING ON?
DO YOU SUSPECT ME OF SOME-THING?
IF WHAT YOU JUST TOLD ME CHECKS OUT
I'LL EXPLAIN EVERYTHING.
KLATTER
......
...I'LL BE BACK.

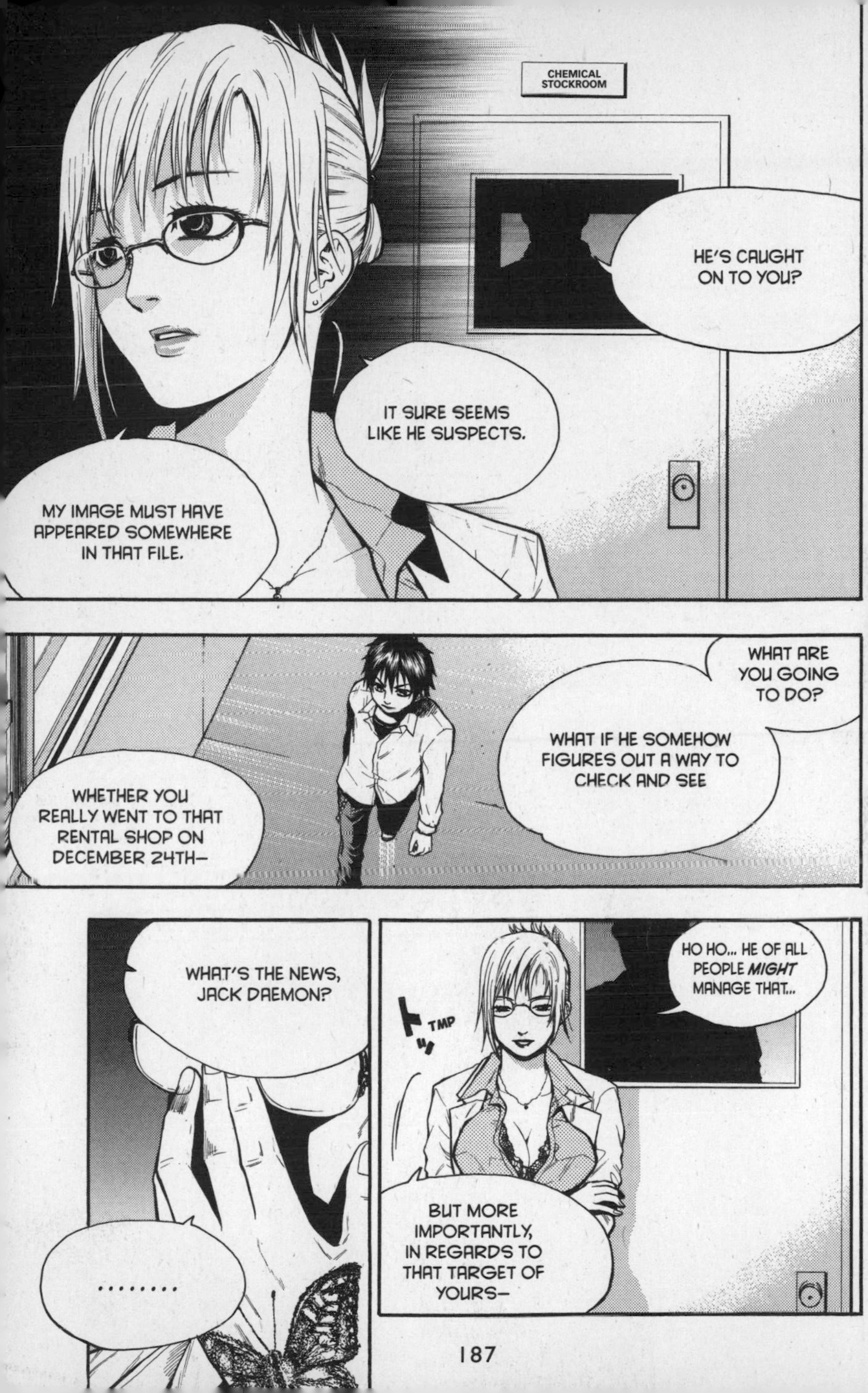
CHEMICAL STOCKROOM
HE'S CAUGHT ON TO YOU?
IT SURE SEEMS LIKE HE SUSPECTS.
MY IMAGE MUST HAVE APPEARED SOMEWHERE IN THAT FILE.
WHAT ARE YOU GOING TO DO?
WHAT IF HE SOMEHOW FIGURES OUT A WAY TO CHECK AND SEE
WHETHER YOU REALLY WENT TO THAT RENTAL SHOP ON DECEMBER 24TH—
HO HO... HE OF ALL PEOPLE *MIGHT* MANAGE THAT...
TMP
BUT MORE IMPORTANTLY, IN REGARDS TO THAT TARGET OF YOURS—
WHAT'S THE NEWS, JACK DAEMON?
....

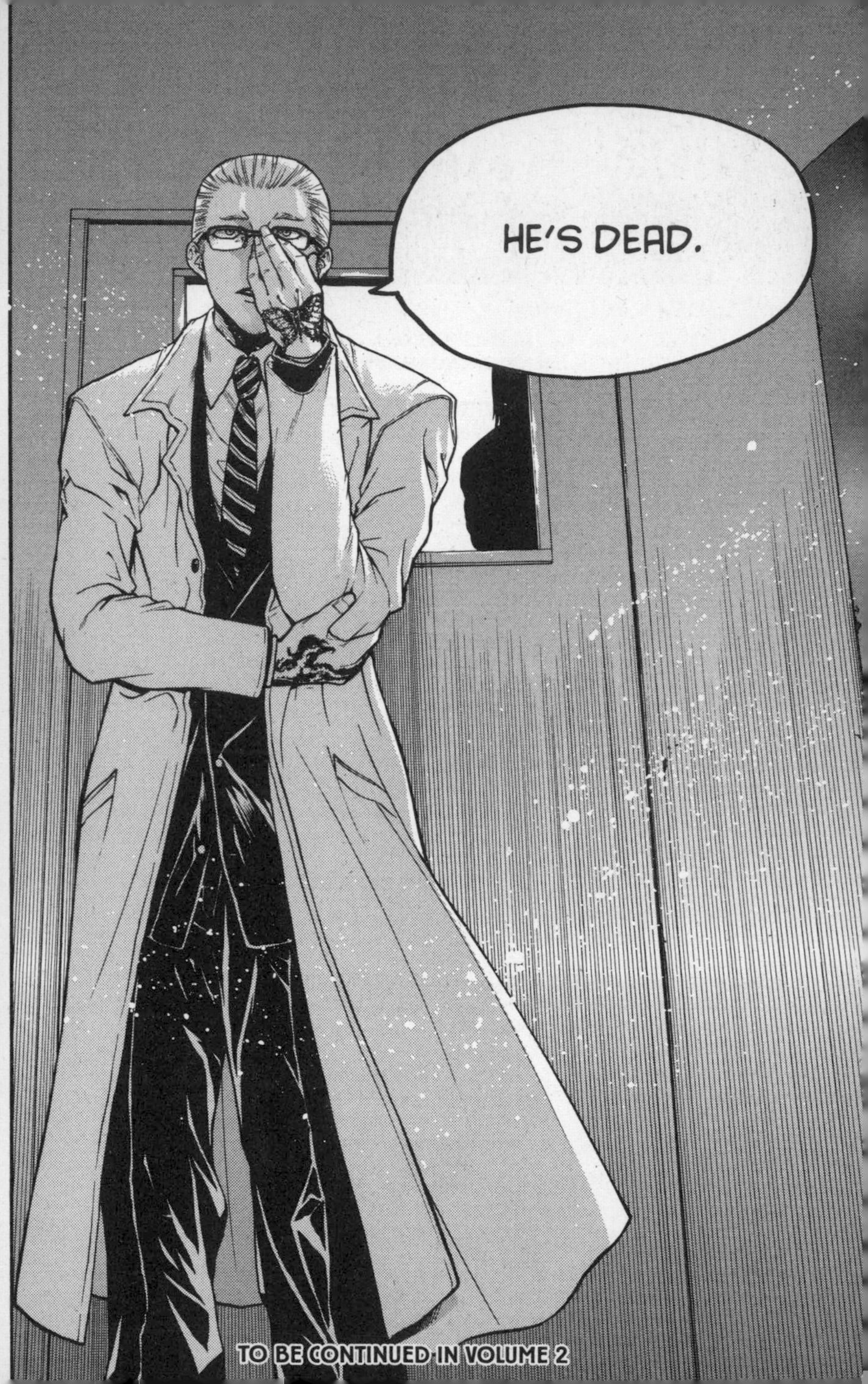
HE'S DEAD.
TO BE CONTINUED IN VOLUME 2

BLOODY MONDAY

~ GLOSSARY OF TERMS • LIST 2 ~

CYBERTERRORISM P60

LARGE-SCALE DESTRUCTIVE ACTIVITY THAT TAKES PLACE ON A COMPUTER NETWORK, SUCH AS THE INTERNET. DAMAGE IS CAUSED FROM DESTROYING OR LEAKING INFORMATION VIA THE REWRITING OF DATA OR DISTRIBUTION OF COMPUTER VIRUSES.

THERE HAVE ALSO BEEN INCIDENCES OF ALTERING, DEFACING, OR CREATING FAKE GOVERNMENT WEB PAGES, SUCH AS THAT OF AMERICA'S WHITE HOUSE AND JAPAN'S CENTRAL GOVERNMENT MINISTRIES AND AGENCIES.

CURRENTLY, THE NATIONAL POLICE AGENCY IS TAKING COUNTER-MEASURES SUCH AS THE CREATION OF A "CYBER FORCE".

KGB P61

THE ABBREVIATION FOR THE FORMER SOVIET UNION'S COMMITTEE OF STATE SECURITY (NATIONAL SECURITY AGENCY). STARTING WITH THE MONITORING AND SUPPRESSION OF ANTI-ESTABLISHMENT GROUPS, IT ALSO ENGAGED IN BORDER SECURITY AND BOTH NATIONAL AND INTERNATIONAL INTELLIGENCE ACTIVITY (ESPIONAGE), AMONG OTHER OPERATIONS. IT WAS DISSOLVED IN 1991, AND SUBSEQUENTLY DISAPPEARED FROM SIGHT.

RUSSIAN FEDERATION FEDERAL SECURITY SERVICE (FSB) P61

THE RUSSIAN FEDERATION'S DOMESTIC SECURITY AGENCY. ITS PRINCIPAL ACTIVITIES ARE COUNTER-INTELLIGENCE (THE PREVENTION OF INTELLIGENCE ACTIVITIES) AND CRIME PREVENTION. IT IS SAID THAT DEPENDING ON THE SITUATION, THE FSB HAS BEEN KNOWN TO DIRECTLY ENGAGE IN INTELLIGENCE ACTIVITY ITSELF. WITH THE KGB DISSOLVED, IT CAN ALSO BE SAID THAT THE FSB HAS TAKEN OVER KGB ROLES.

BACKUP P90

TO MAKE ONE OR MORE ADVANCE COPIES OF PROGRAMS OR DATA TO GUARD AGAINST THE POSSIBILITY OF ITS LOSS.

WIRELESS LAN P91

A LAN (LOCAL ACCESS NETWORK) THAT SENDS AND RECEIVES DATA VIA WIRELESS TRANSMISSION. TERMINALS REQUIRE A WIRELESS LAN CARD AND GO THROUGH A RELAY DEVICE CALLED A "BASE STATION" (OR "ACCESS POINT" —ED.) IN ORDER TO ACHIEVE TRANSMISSION.

* LAN
A NETWORK THAT ENGAGES IN DATA EXCHANGE BY CONNECTING COMPUTERS, PRINTERS, AND OTHER DEVICES WITHIN A LIMITED AREA, SUCH AS A SINGLE BUILDING, VIA FIBER-OPTIC OR OTHER SIMILAR CABLES.

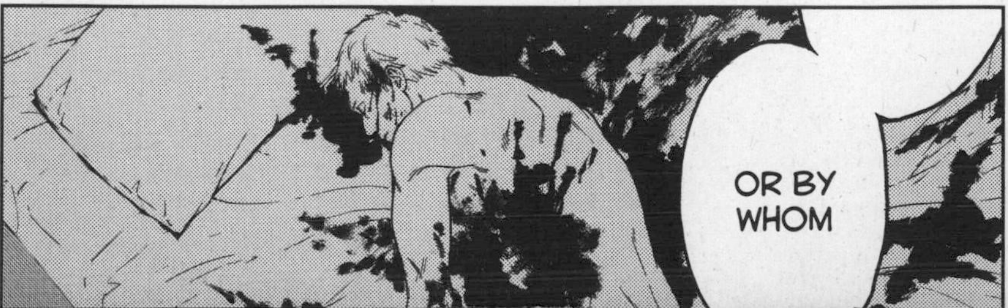
OR BY WHOM

BLOODY MONDAY

~ GLOSSARY OF TERMS • LIST 3 ~

WIDEBAND RECEIVER P111

A RECEIVER THAT CAN PICK UP AN EXCEEDINGLY VAST RANGE OF FREQUENCIES, THE WIDEST OF WHICH CAN RECEIVE FROM 0.1 1,300 MHZ (MEGAHERTZ). BECAUSE IT CAN PICK UP ANY SIGNAL OVER A VERY WIDE RANGE, IT IS POSSIBLE TO FERRET OUT WIRETAP BUGS.

SUPERCOMPUTER P116

AN ULTRA-HIGH SPEED COMPUTER UTILIZED FOR LARGE-SCALE SCIENTIFIC COMPUTING AND OTHER COMPLEX OPERATIONS. THEY ARE USED TO CREATE BLUEPRINTS AND SIMULATIONS IN FIELDS SUCH AS AVIATION, HIGH-RISE ARCHITECTURE, AND PHARMACEUTICALS.

EBOLA HEMORRHAGIC FEVER (EBOLA) P149

A POTENTIALLY LETHAL VIRAL HEMORRHAGIC FEVER, OUTBREAKS OF WHICH OCCUR IN AFRICA, AMONG OTHER PLACES. THE ROUTE OF TRANSMISSION AND RESERVOIR HOSTS IN NATURE ARE UNKNOWN, AND THE VIRUS IS SPREAD FROM PERSON TO PERSON THROUGH CONTACT WITH AN INFECTED INDIVIDUAL'S BLOOD AND BODILY FLUIDS, OR CONTAMINATED MEDICAL WASTE. INITIAL SIGNS OF ILLNESS ARE FLU-LIKE SYMPTOMS SUCH AS FEVER, HEADACHE, AND MUSCLE PAIN, WHICH MAY PROGRESS TO SEVERE HEMORRHAGE AND SHOCK BEFORE RESULTING IN DEATH.

SMALLPOX (VARIOLA) P149

A VIRULENT INFECTIOUS DISEASE CAUSED BY INFECTION WITH THE VARIOLA VIRUS. TRANSMISSION CAN OCCUR THROUGH EITHER AIRBORNE VECTORS OR DIRECT CONTACT. HIGH FEVER DEVELOPS AND BLISTERS FORM ALL OVER THE BODY, OFTEN RESULTING IN DEATH, AND EVEN IF ONE SURVIVES AND RECOVERS, POCKMARKS REMAIN. THANKS TO THE STRENUOUS INOCULATION (PREVENTATIVE VACCINATION TO CREATE IMMUNITY) EFFORTS OF THE WHO (WORLD HEALTH ORGANIZATION), IT IS SAID TO HAVE BEEN ERADICATED.

MOTION DETECTOR CAMERA P163

A CAMERA THAT SENSES MOVEMENT, SUCH AS THAT OF A PERSON, AND TAKES PHOTOGRAPHS AS A RESULT OF AN INFRARED SIGNAL.

BY SETTING UP A MOTION DETECTOR CAMERA IN ONE'S HOME AND CONNECTING IT TO ONE'S COMPUTER OR CELLULAR PHONE, IT IS POSSIBLE TO BE ALERTED TO ANY CHANGE INSIDE ONE'S HOME FROM A REMOTE LOCATION.

BASE SEQUENCE P181

THE ORDER OF GENETIC INFORMATION-CONTAINING NUCLEOTIDES, OF WHICH THERE ARE FOUR TYPES, IN A STRAND OF DNA, THE "BLUEPRINT OF LIFE". GENE EXPRESSION IS DETERMINED BY THIS SEQUENCE.

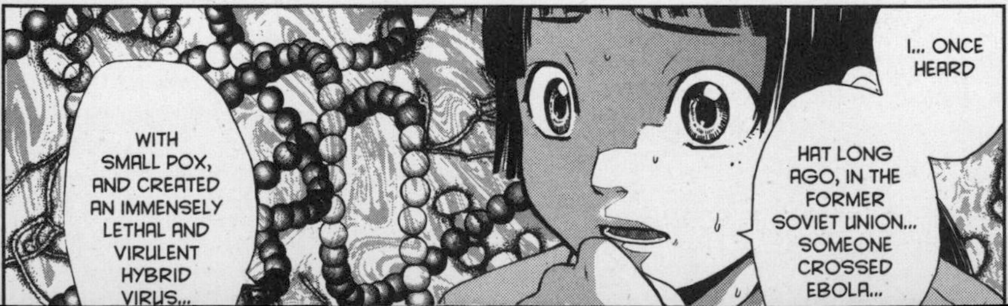
I... ONCE HEARD
HAT LONG AGO, IN THE FORMER SOVIET UNION... SOMEONE CROSSED EBOLA...
WITH SMALL POX, AND CREATED AN IMMENSELY LETHAL AND VIRULENT HYBRID VIRUS...

⚜ BLOODY MONDAY ⚜

- **Many thanks**
  Daiwa Mitsu   Kawabata Kunihiro   Takeda Manabu   Mattsun
  Uemura Kiyoshi   Terada Kôsuke   Kinoshita Satoshi

- **Editorial**
  Sugawara-san   Sato-san   Kawakubo-san   Nakata-san

- **Manga**
  Ryumon Ryou X Megumi Kouji

TRANSLATION NOTES

Japanese is a tricky language for most Westerners, and translation is often more art than science. For your edification and reading pleasure, here are notes on some of the places where we could have gone in a different direction with our translation of the work, or where a Japanese cultural reference is used.

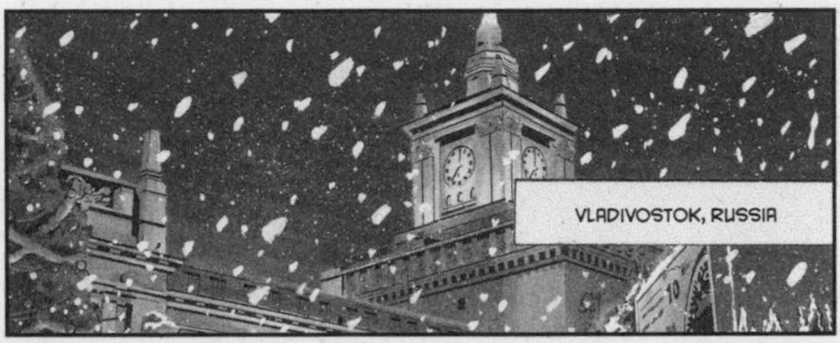
VLADIVOSTOK, RUSSIA

Vladivostok, page 3

Russia's largest port city on the Pacific, and one terminus of the Trans-Siberian Railway. It is located near Russia's border with both China and North Korea, and just across the Sea of Japan from northern Honshu.

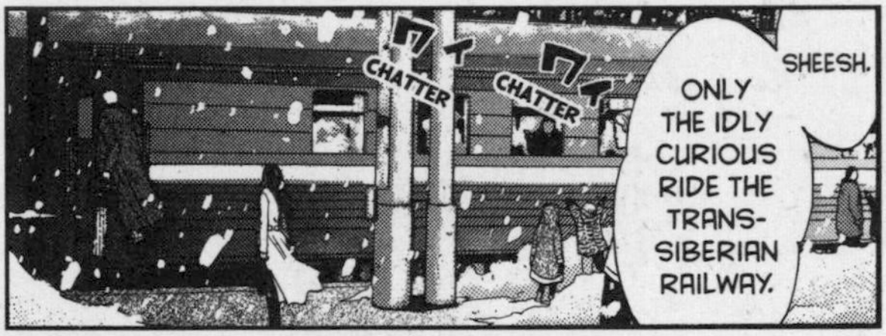
SHEESH.
ONLY THE IDLY CURIOUS RIDE THE TRANS-SIBERIAN RAILWAY.
CHATTER
CHATTER

Trans-Siberian Railway, page 11

The longest railway in the world, it was originally constructed to connect European Russia (St. Petersburg and Moscow) to the Russian Far East (Vladivostok). It travels through southern Siberia and part of Manchuria, China, on its way, and even now it takes 8 days to ride it from end to end.

Khabarovsk, page 11

The second largest city in the Russian Far East after Vladivostok. Also close to Russia's border with China.

School clothing code, page 19

Private schools such as Mishiro Academy may still have clothing codes even if there is no official school uniform. They dictate the cut and style of shirts, skirts, pants, shoes, and accessories such as socks, ties, and jewelry, plus may also rule on personal beauty care such as use of cosmetics or coloring of one's hair.

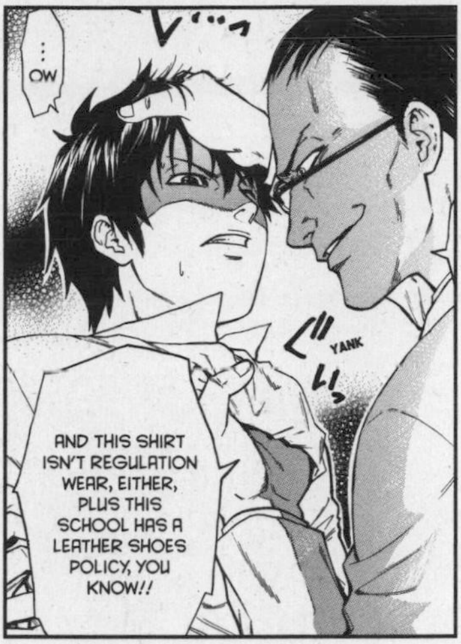
...OW
YANK
AND THIS SHIRT ISN'T REGULATION WEAR, EITHER, PLUS THIS SCHOOL HAS A LEATHER SHOES POLICY, YOU KNOW!!

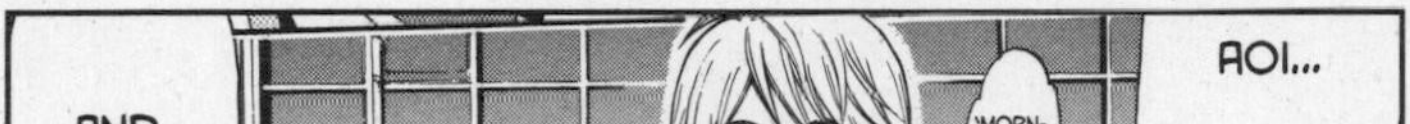
AOI...
'MORNING
AND ANKO!
PLEASE DON'T CALL ME 'ANKO'!!

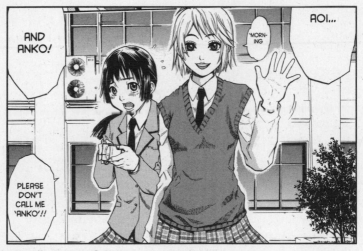

"Anko", page 21

Fujimaru's nickname for Mako. It is derived from the first syllable of her last name (*An*zai) and the last syllable of her first name (Ma*ko*), but Mako's objection is likely due to the fact that "anko" is also the Japanese word for "red bean paste".

"Shiny-Brow", page 48

"Pikage", or "Shiny-Brow", is the students' unflattering nickname for Hikage… it is a phonetic pun on "Hikage", as the hiragana character "pi" is a conjugation of "hi", and "pika" is the onomatopoeia for "blindingly shiny".

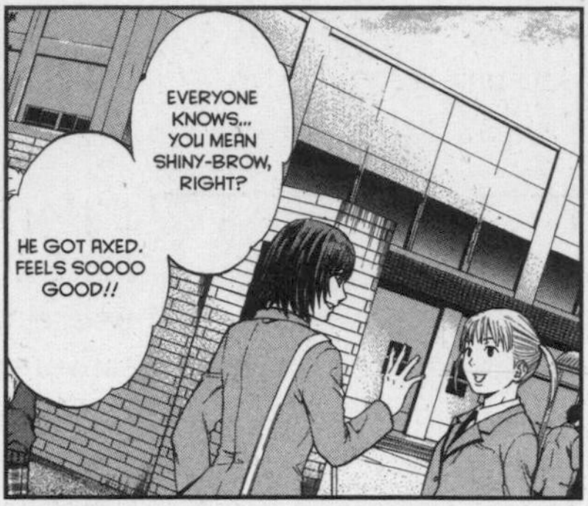
EVERYONE KNOWS... YOU MEAN SHINY-BROW, RIGHT?
HE GOT AXED. FEELS SOOOO GOOD!!

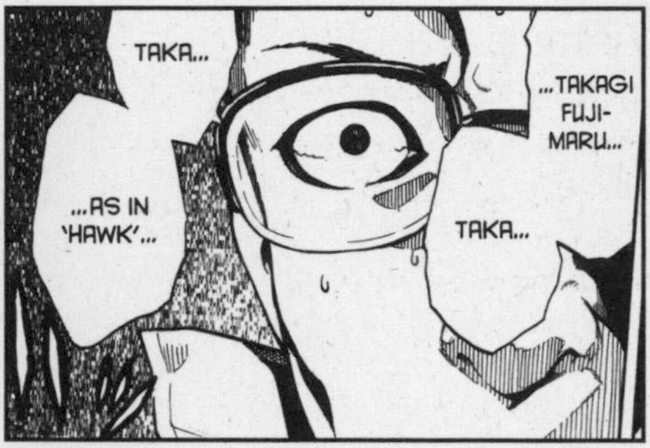
...TAKAGI FUJI-MARU...
TAKA...
TAKA...
...AS IN 'HAWK'...

"Falcon", page 52

Fujimaru's alter ego and hacker name. A phonetic pun, derived from the first syllable of his last name "Takagi"… it is only phonetic because his name uses a different kanji than that of the "taka" that means "hawk" or "falcon".

Hayaben, page 67

A custom practiced mostly by male junior and senior high school students, of eating their lunch during class or class breaks prior to lunch recess, ostensibly because their growth spurts make them so hungry that they cannot wait that long to eat.

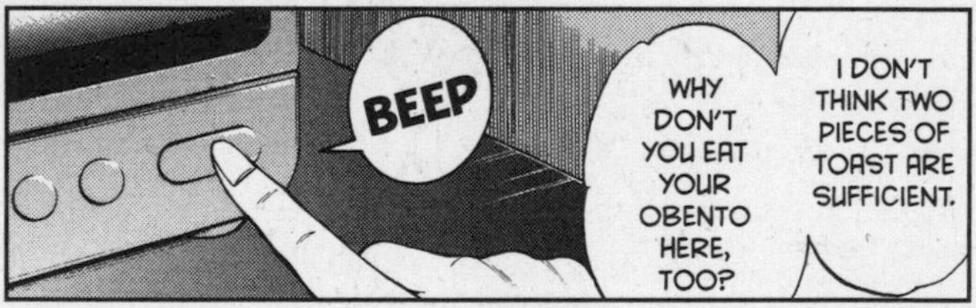
I DON'T THINK TWO PIECES OF TOAST ARE SUFFICIENT.
WHY DON'T YOU EAT YOUR OBENTO HERE, TOO?
BEEP

Obento, page 79

Boxed meals prepared for students or spouses by a family member (most commonly the mother/wife or sister/daughter). It can also refer to pre-prepared boxed meals available for purchase at train stations, supermarkets, and delis.

Dial 110, page 112

The emergency telephone number in Japan is 110 as opposed to 911.

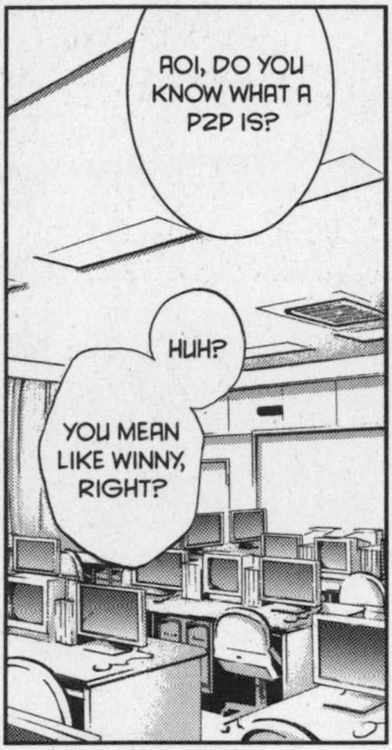
AOI, DO YOU KNOW WHAT A P2P IS?
HUH?
YOU MEAN LIKE WINNY, RIGHT?

P2P (Peer-to-Peer), page 131

P2P is a computing application structure where multiple computers logged onto the same network are linked together to share files and/or work loads (by making part of their processing power directly available to other participants).

Winny, page 131

Winny, or WinNY, is a Windows C++ based Japanese P2P file-sharing program that allows its users to be anonymous. Its name is a play on WinMX, a freeware P2P file-sharing program that runs on Microsoft Windows systems.

Pandora's Box, page 134

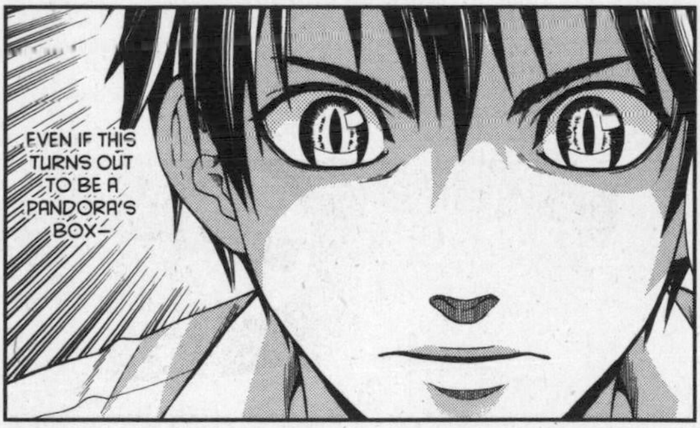
EVEN IF THIS TURNS OUT TO BE A PANDORA'S BOX—

Fujimaru is referring to the Greek myth used to explain why evil exists in the world. Pandora was the first woman on Earth, and had been given a large sealed jar (later mistranslated as "box") by Zeus, who also ordered her to never to look at its contents. When curiosity finally overcame her, various evils escaped forth from the jar before she could replace the lid, which ended up trapping Hope still inside. Current usage denotes an irreversible unleashing of evil.

Preview of

BLOODY MONDAY

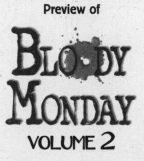

VOLUME 2

We're pleased to present you a preview from *Bloody Monday*, volume 2. Please check our website (www.kodanshacomics.com) to see when this volume will be available in English. For now you'll have to make do with Japanese!

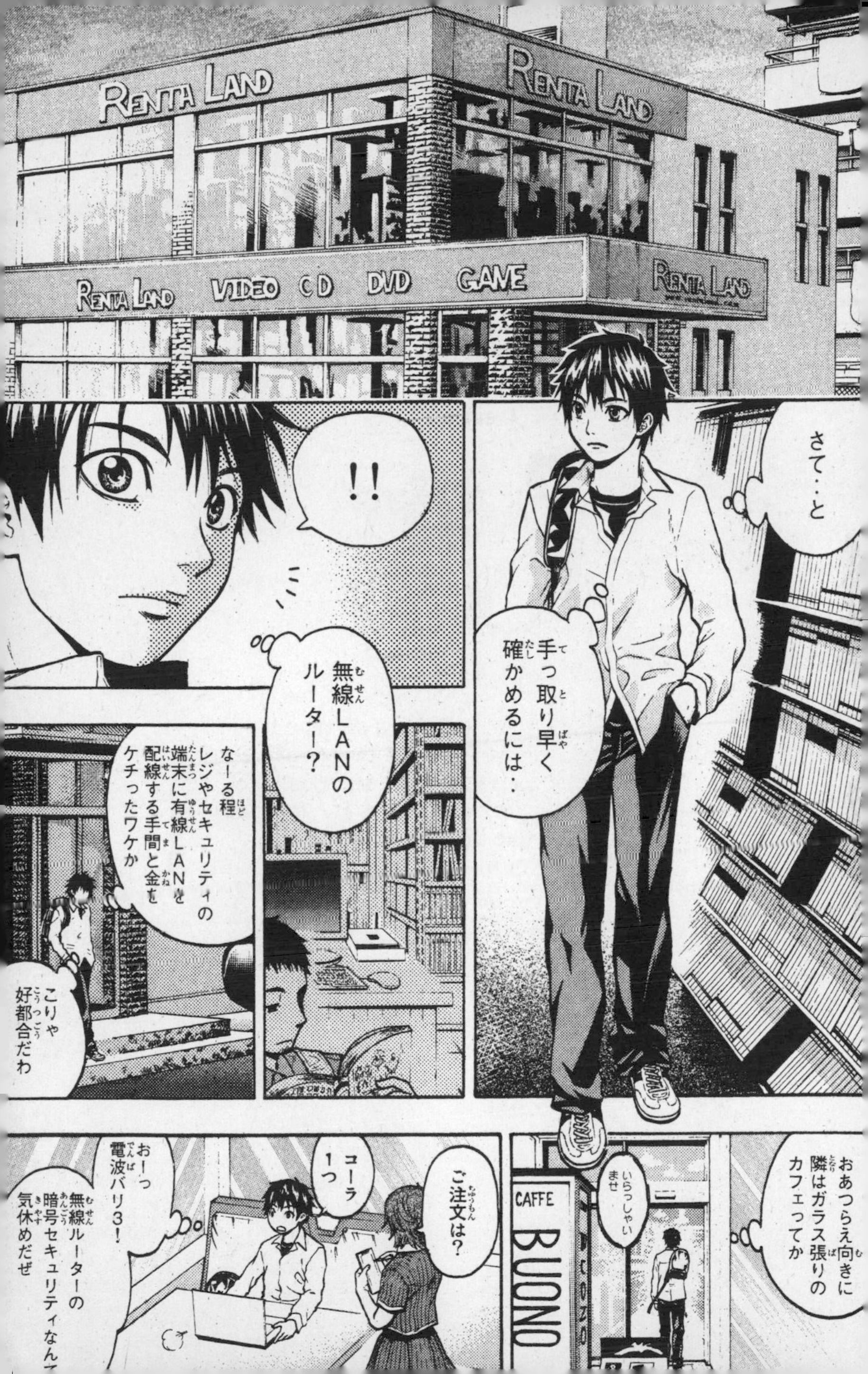
RENTA LAND
RENTA LAND
RENTA LAND VIDEO CD DVD GAME
RENTA LAND
さて‥と
手っ取り早く確かめるには‥
!!
無線LANのルーター?
なーる程 レジやセキュリティの端末に有線LANを配線する手間と金をケチったワケか
こりゃ好都合だわ
おあつらえ向きに隣はガラス張りのカフェってか
いらっしゃいませ
CAFFE BUONO
ご注文は?
コーラ1っ
おーっ電波バリ3!
無線ルーターの暗号セキュリティなんて気休めだぜ

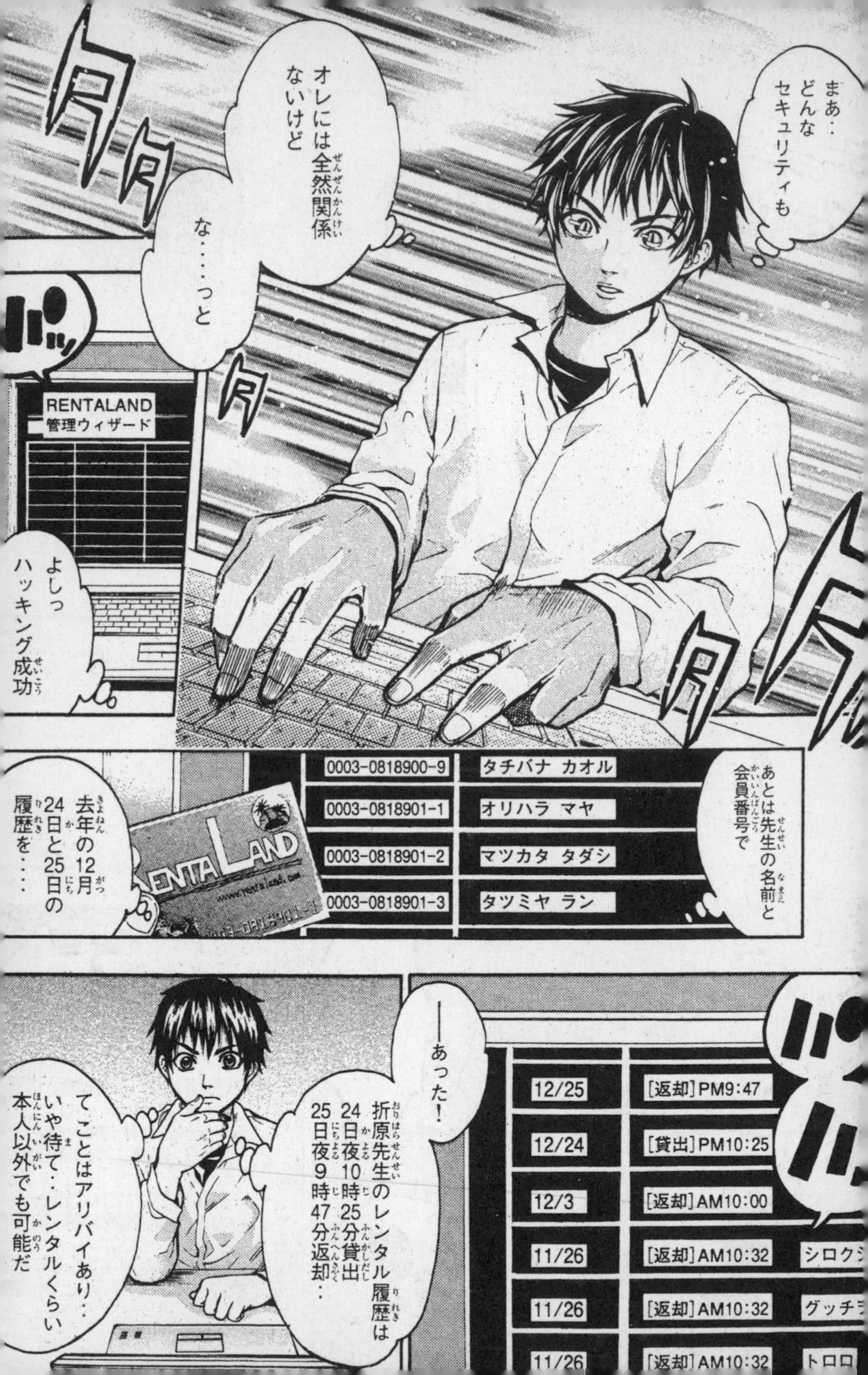
まあ…どんなセキュリティも
オレには全然関係ないけど
な…っと
RENTALAND
管理ウィザード
よしっ ハッキング成功
あとは先生の名前と会員番号で
0003-0818900-9 タチバナ カオル
0003-0818901-1 オリハラ マヤ
0003-0818901-2 マツカタ タダシ
0003-0818901-3 タツミヤ ラン
去年の12月24日と25日の履歴を…
12/25 [返却]PM9:47
12/24 [貸出]PM10:25
12/3 [返却]AM10:00
11/26 [返却]AM10:32 シロクシ
11/26 [返却]AM10:32 グッチ
11/26 [返却]AM10:32 トロロ
——あった！
折原先生のレンタル履歴は24日夜10時25分貸出 25日夜9時47分返却…
てことはアリバイあり…いや待て…レンタルくらい本人以外でも可能だ

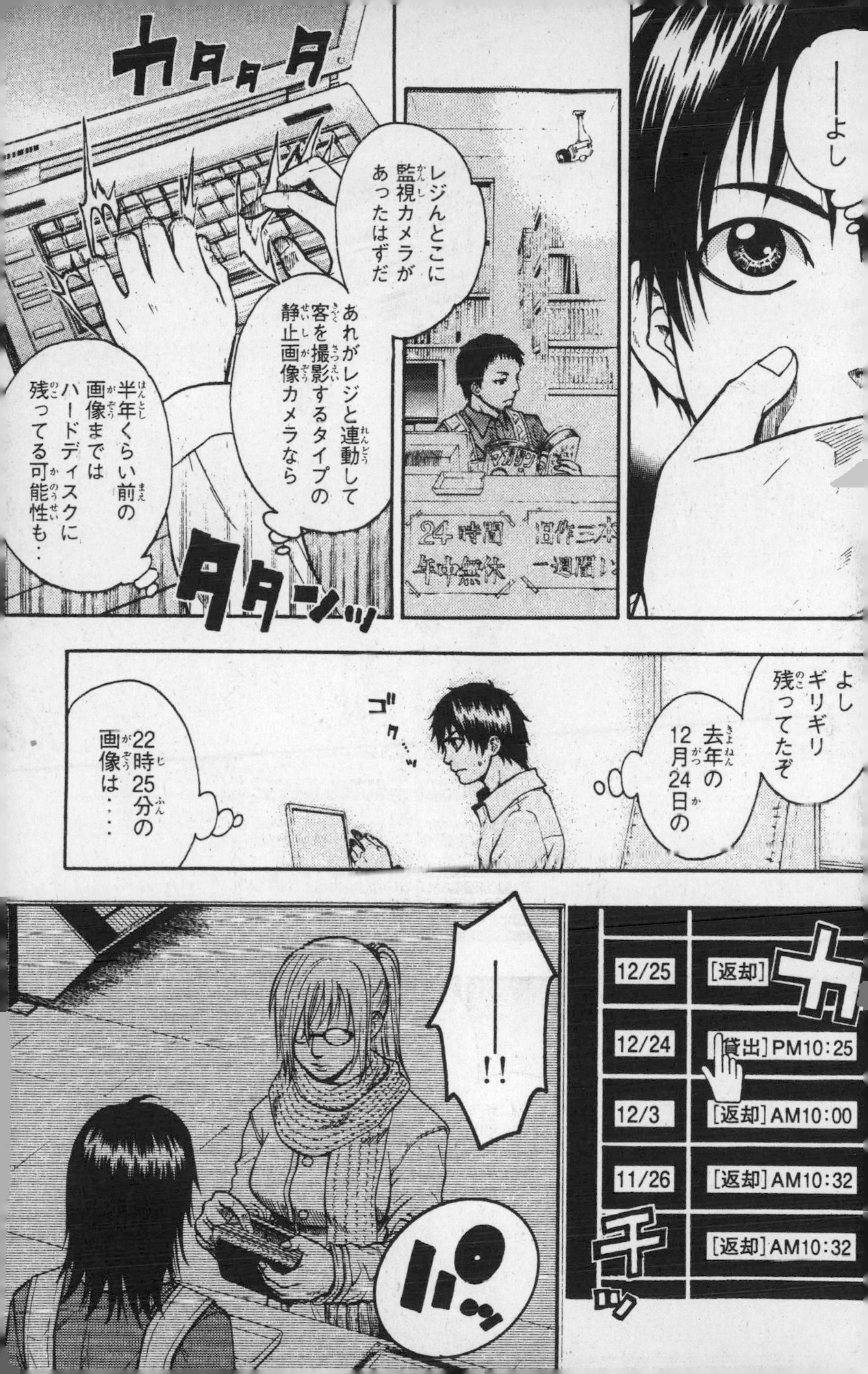
——よし
24時間
年中無休
カタタタ
レジんとこに監視カメラがあったはずだ
あれがレジと連動して客を撮影するタイプの静止画像カメラなら
半年くらい前の画像まではハードディスクに残ってる可能性も・・
タターンッ
よしギリギリ残ってたぞ去年の12月24日の
ゴク・・・
22時25分の画像は・・・
12/25
[返却]
カ
12/24
[貸出]PM10:25
12/3
[返却]AM10:00
11/26
[返却]AM10:32
[返却]AM10:32
チッ
——!!
ハッ

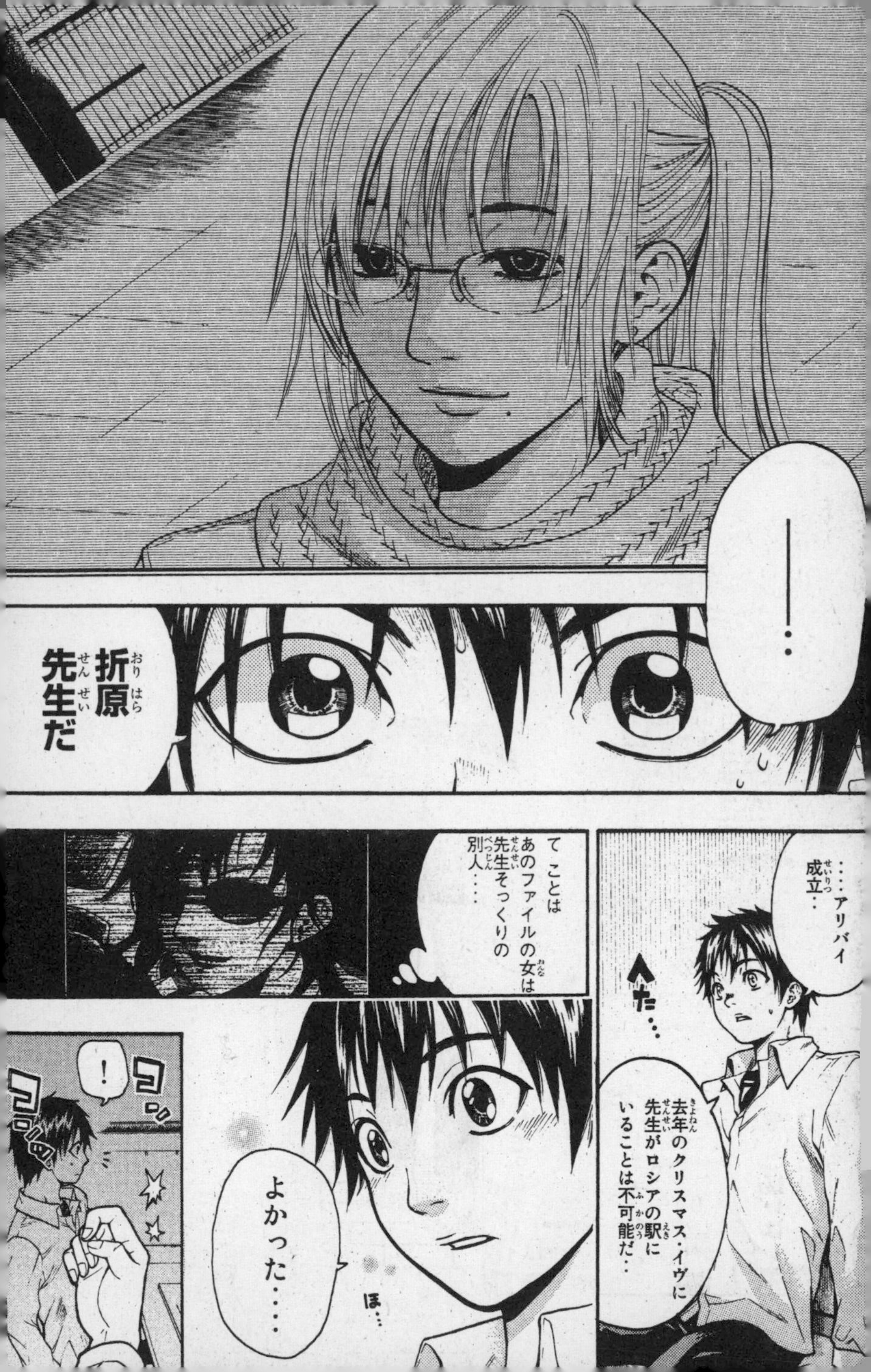
――!!
折原先生だ
……アリバイ成立……
た……
去年のクリスマス・イヴに先生がロシアの駅にいることは不可能だ……
てことはあのファイルの女は先生そっくりの別人……
よかった……
ほ…
!
コロ
コロ

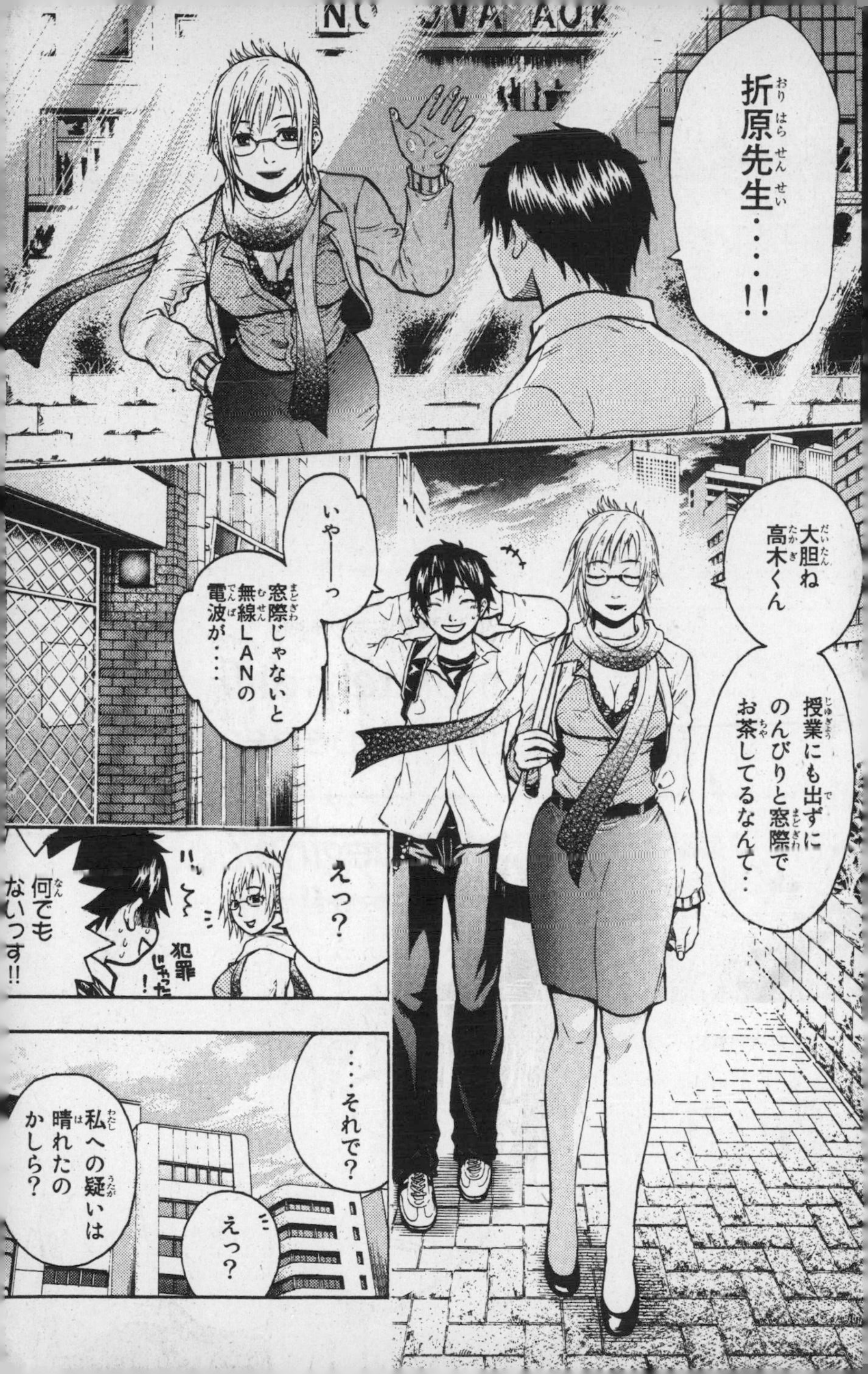
折原先生・・・・!!
大胆ね 高木くん
授業にも出ずにのんびりと窓際でお茶してるなんて・・・
いやーーっ 窓際じゃないと無線LANの電波が・・・・
えっ？
何でもないっす!!
・・・それで？
えっ？
私への疑いは晴れたのかしら？

TOMARE!

[STOP!]

You are going the wrong way!

Manga is a co_____ _____erent
type of read_____ __ce.

To start at ___ _____ng,
go to the end.

That's right! Authentic manga is read the traditional Japanese way—from right to left, exactly the opposite of how American books are read. It's easy to follow: Just go to the other end of the book, and read each page—and each panel—from the right side to the left side, starting at the top right. Now you're experiencing manga as it was meant to be.